D0111077

Eileen's Directory of Dog-Friendly Lodging & Outdoor Adventures in Arizona

Pet-Friendly Publications
P.O. Box 8459, Scottsdale, Az 85252
Tel: (800) 638-3637

Doin' Arizona With Your Pooch...
A Rewarding Experience

You and Your Dog Can:

- Hike trails to panoramic mountain peaks.
- Explore spectacular red-walled canyons.
- Witness incredible desert wildflower displays.
- Celebrate a Native American Pow Wow.

Don't leave your canine buddy at home or kenneled in a small cage when you vacation. Bring your best friend along. Double your pleasure and increase your safety. If your dog is a great companion at home, he can be an even better one on the road.

Copyright © 1996 Eileen Barish. All rights reserved.

No part of this book may be reproduced or transmitted in any form
or by any means now known or which will become known,without
written permission from the publisher.
Permission is granted for reviewers and others to quote brief
passages for use in newspapers, periodicals, or broadcasts provided
credit is given to:

DOIN' ARIZONA WITH YOUR POOCH!
by Eileen Barish

Pet-Friendly Publications
P.O. Box 8459, Scottsdale, AZ 85252
Tel: (800) 638-3637

ISBN #1-884465-03-X
Library of Congress Catalog Number: 95-073088

ATTENTION: Clubs, organizations, travel agencies, animal groups
and all interested parties; contact the publisher
for information on quantity discounts!
Every traveler who owns a pet should have this directory.

Printed and bound in the United States of America.

While due care has been exercised in the compilation of this directory,
we are not responsible for errors or omissions.
We are sorry for any inconvenience.

Inclusion in this guide does not constitute endorsement or
recommendation by the publisher. It is intended as a guide to assist
in providing information to the public and the listings are
offered as an aid to travelers.

CREDITS

Author & Managing Editor — Eileen Barish

Associate Editor — Harvey Barish

Lodging & Research Editor — Phyllis Holmes

Research/Writing Staff — Alison Dufner
Tiffany Geoghegan

Illustrator — Gregg Myers

Book Layout — Tawni Hensley

Photographer — Ken Friedman

Special Acknowledgements

For Harvey, doin' Arizona with my smooch
has been the best.

Special thanks to a doggone great staff.

And for Sam, the "best friend"
who is always with us.

TABLE OF CONTENTS

ARIZONA DIRECTORY OF LODGING AND OUTDOOR ADVENTURES

Arizona Directory of Lodging and Outdoor Adventures

HOW TO USE THIS DIRECTORY

Pooch comes along

If you're planning to travel in Arizona with your pooch or if you live in Arizona and would like to enjoy more of our state with your canine buddy, *Doin' Arizona With Your Pooch!* is the only reference source you'll need. Hundreds of dog-friendly accommodations, nearly a thousand outdoor adventures and chapters covering everything from travel training to travel etiquette are included.

Simplify vacation planning

The user-friendly format of *Doin' Arizona With Your Pooch!* combines lodging and recreation under individual city headings. Pick a city, decide on lodging and then reference the outdoor activities listed under that city. Or perhaps you've always wanted to hike a certain trail or visit a particular park. Just reverse the process. Using the index, locate the activity of choice, find the closest lodging and go from there. It's that easy to plan a vacation you and Rover will adore.

No more sneaking Snoopy

Choose lodging from hotels, B&Bs (aka Bed & Biscuits), motels, resorts, inns and ranches that welcome you and your dog - through the front door. From big cities to tiny hamlets, *Doin' Arizona With Your Pooch!* provides the names, addresses, phone numbers and room rates of hundreds of dog-friendly accommodations. Spend a pittance or a king's ransom. Arranged in an easy-to-use alphabetical format, this directory covers all of Arizona, from Ajo to Yuma and every place in between.

Just do it

Okay, now you've got your pooch packed and you're ready for the fun to begin. How will you make the most of your travel or vacation time? *Doin' Arizona With Your Pooch!* details nearly a 1,000 adventures you can share with your canine buddy. If you're into hiking, you'll find descriptions for hundreds of trails. These descriptions will tell you what to expect - from the trail rating (beginner, intermediate, expert) to the trail's terrain, restrictions, best times to hike, etc. If laid-back pastimes are more to your liking, you'll find green grassy areas perfect for picnics or plain chilling out. For parks, monuments and other attractions, expect anything from a quickie overview to a lengthy description. Written in a conversational tone, it'll be easy for you to visualize each area. Directions are also included.

No matter what your budget or outdoor preference, with this directory you'll be able to put together the perfect day, weekend or monthlong odyssey.

Increase your options

Many of the recreational opportunities listed in *Doin' Arizona With Your Pooch!* can be accessed from more than one city. See what activities are located in cities adjacent to your lodging choice and expand your options.

How to do it

Numerous chapters are devoted to making your travel times safer and more pleasurable. Training do's and don'ts, crate use and selection, carsickness, driving and packing tips, desert survival, doggie massage, pet etiquette, travel manners, what and how to pack for your pooch, first aid advice, hiking tips, emergency telephone numbers, a pet identification form and tons more are all discussed.

Not just for vacationers. A "must-have" reference for Arizona dog owners

Owning a copy of *Doin' Arizona With Your Pooch!* will mean you won't have to leave your trusted companion at home while you explore our beautiful state. So many places welcome Fido and Rover that there's rarely an occasion when your buddy can't come along. Exercise and outdoor stimulation are as good for his health as they are for yours. So include old brown eyes when you decide to take a walk, picnic in a forest glade, hike a mountain trail or rent a boat for the day. Armed with this guide, Arizonans who love their hounds can travel together, discovering all that Arizona has to offer.

No matter where you make your home in the state, you'll find dozens of places in your own backyard just perfect for a day's outing with your pooch. *Doin' Arizona With Your Pooch!* answers your travel dilemma of what to do with your pooch when you travel - take him along. Expand your travel horizons and give your devoted companion a new leash on life.

Do hotel & motel policies differ regarding pets?

Yes, but all the accommodations in *Doin' Arizona With Your Pooch!* allow dogs. Policies can vary on charges and sometimes on dog size. Some might require a damage deposit and some combine their deposit with a daily and/or one-time charge. Others may restrict pets to specific rooms, perhaps cabins or cottages. Residence-type inns which cater to long-term guests may charge a long-term fee. Some might require advance notice. But most accommodations do not charge fees or place restrictions in any manner.

BE AWARE THAT HOTEL POLICIES MAY CHANGE. AT THE TIME YOUR RESERVATIONS ARE MADE, DETERMINE THE POLICY OF YOUR LODGING CHOICE.

Go Take A Hike

Hundreds of the best day hikes in Arizona are detailed in ***Doin' Arizona With Your Pooch!*** Each hike indicates degree of difficulty, approximate time to complete the hike and round-trip distances. Unless otherwise indicated, trailhead access is free and parking is available, although it is sometimes limited. When additional information will prove helpful, phone numbers are included. In many areas, dogs may hike without being leashed.

When leashes are mandatory, notice is provided.
Please obey local ordinances so dogs
continue to be welcome.

Hike ratings

The majority of the hikes are rated beginner or intermediate. As a rule of thumb, beginner hikes are generally easy, flat trails suited to every member of the family. Intermediate hikes require more exertion and a little more preparation, but can usually be accomplished by anyone accustomed to some physical exercise, such as fast-paced walking, biking, skiing, swimming, etc. Some expert trails have also been included. Many times, their inclusion signals some outstanding feature. Expert hikes should only be considered if you feel certain of your own and your dog's abilities. But whatever your ability, remember you can always turn around and retrace your steps if the hike you've undertaken is too difficult. You're there to have a good time, not to prove anything.

Seasons change, so do conditions

Seasonal changes may effect ratings. If you're hiking during rainy season, you might encounter slippery going. Or if you've decided to take a trek during the winter and there's snow underfoot, that can up the difficulty rating. If it's springtime, small creeks can become rushing, perhaps impassable rivers. Whenever you're outdoors, particularly in wilderness areas, exercise caution. Know yourself and know your dog.

Hike time

Times are included for general reference. If you're short on time or energy, hike as long as you like. Never push yourself or your canine beyond either's endurance. Never begin a hike too late in the day, particularly in canyon areas where the sun can disappear quickly.

Directions

Directions are generally provided from the closest city with dog-friendly lodging. Odometer accuracy can vary so be alert to road signs. Unless specifically noted, roads and trailheads are accessible by all types of vehicles. In winter, access roads may be closed from November through May. Or you may experience heavy snow conditions where 4WD or snow chains are required. Remember too that National Forest roads can be narrow and twisting and are often used by huge logging trucks. Exercise caution. Slow down around blind corners.

Parking your vehicle

Lock valuables in your trunk. Lock all doors and close windows completely. If you're hiking in bear country, don't leave food *anywhere* in your car. Bears can smell the food and might think your vehicle is a closed restaurant. They've been known to rip windows off cars searching for food.

Permits/Fees

Wilderness permits are needed for most hikes in USFS wilderness areas. In addition most state parks and some national parks charge a nominal fee.

Common sense, don't hike without it

Consider potential hazards. Know your limitations. The overview descriptions included with hikes and other recreational activities are provided for general information. They are not meant to represent that a particular hike or excursion will be safe for you or your dog. Only you can make that determination.

Weather, terrain, wildlife and trail conditions should always be considered. It is up to you to assume responsibility for yourself and your canine. Apply common sense to your outings and they'll prove safe and enjoyable.

Leashes

Many hikes and other outdoor adventures do not require that dogs be leashed, but wildlife exists in all outdoor areas. Use caution and common sense. When a leash is mandatory, a notation will be made. When restrictions apply, they will also be noted. But in any case, keep a leash accessible. You never know when the need will suddenly arise.

Note: When leashes are required they must be six feet or less in length. Leashes should be carried at all times. They are prudent safety measures in wilderness areas.

BASIC DOG RULES:

THEY CAN'T BE AVOIDED AND THEY'RE REALLY
QUITE EASY TO LIVE WITH. BE A RESPONSIBLE
DOG OWNER AND OBEY THE RULES.

PREFACE

THE GRAND CANYON STATE

Home to one of the seven wonders of the world, Arizona is a land of diversity and diversions. From cowboys to city-slickers, gold prospectors to Golden Retrievers, mining towns to booming metropolitan areas, the state offers more than the mind can imagine. You and the pooch can explore deserts, picnic under ponderosa pines, play in snow on alpine peaks and perhaps catch a dinner of trout as you traverse the vastly different regions of America's sixth largest state. So, leash up the lad and get going, the wild west awaits.

From arid desert floors to frosty alpine peaks

Many people think of Arizona and only imagine a landscape of dry endless deserts. Rarely does the image of a sun dappled waterfall, or snowy mountain peak come to mind. But Arizona is a land of abundant and extraordinary natural phenomenons. From towers of rock that resemble people, battleships and legendary Indians, to meadows of wildflowers that soften the landscape with a cornucopia of color, Arizona offers a lifetime of eye pleasing, mind stimulating opportunities for people and their pooches.

The alluring architecture

Not all of Arizona's incredible scenery is nature made. Humans have lent a hand and added to the state's uncommon and varied terrain. Modern structure sniffers can marvel at two of Frank Lloyd Wright's masterpieces, while history hounds can relish the ruins of prehistoric dwellers. Ivory colored churches and weathered adobe ruins will remind travelers of Arizona's early Spanish settlers. Whatever your architectural pleasure, you and the pupster can gaze upon some of the nation's finest examples of architecture as you travel through the Grand Canyon State.

Arizona's seven wonders

Arizona can be divided into seven very distinct regions, all abounding with dog-friendly recreational opportunities. Lap dogs may prefer lapping up the soothing waters of Arizona's West Coast River Country, while spirited canines can have a howl of a time stalking through Indian Country. Visit Canyon Country and share an awestruck moment pondering the vastness of the Grand Canyon. This region will have you and the tail wagger exploring some of the country's most spectacular topography. History hounds can relive the past in the Central Territory, home to many of the west's oldest, most interesting mining and ghost towns.

Reckless Rovers will surely take a liking to the wilder side of Old West Country, especially Tucson and Tombstone, where old-time cowboys in faded denim add to the southwestern flavor that honeycombs this part of the state. If secluded mountaintops and crisp alpine surroundings hold special appeal, don't miss a journey to High Country. Visit in winter and be rewarded with a walk through untrammeled snowfields. In spring, laze the day away under a ponderosa pine, contentedly counting wildflowers. When fall arrives in High Country, it arrives in a kaleidoscopic burst - red, bronze, yellow and green autumnal colors create a vibrant contrast to the azure blue skies.

Fidos who love to see and be seen will fit right into the Valley of the Sun. Charming Old Town Scottsdale is laced with boutique lined streets where you can stroll for hours or simply shop till you drop. From western wear to haute couture, Stetson hats to pooch saddlebags, you'll find it all in downtown Scottsdale. For a great day's outing among the young and the restless, you can't beat Tempe for a taste of the college scene. This bustling campus town is loaded with eclectic shops and walk-away eateries catering to every taste. And there are plenty of green spaces just perfect for some Rexercise. Or spend an afternoon in downtown Phoenix where you can grab a sandwich to go, find a shaded bench in one of the grassy areas and people watch for hours.

However you add them up, the seven regions of Arizona can be counted on to provide fun times for you and the dawgus.

VALLEY OF THE SUN

Cities: Apache Junction, Avondale, Carefree, Casa Grande, Cave Creek, Chandler, Coolidge, Eloy, Florence, Fountain Hills, Gilbert, Glendale, Goodyear, Litchfield Park, Mesa, Paradise Valley, Peoria, Phoenix, Scottsdale, Sun City, Tempe.

The heartbeat of the desert

Whether you and Fido are popping into metro Phoenix for a few days, or are permanent residents of the growing population, the valley offers endless recreational activities. From remote mountain get-away hikes to citified strolls, you and the pooch will be dazzled by the days and starstruck by the nights in Arizona's liveliest region.

Go for the gold

Of course, shophounds can find incredible jewelry in Old Scottsdale - much with a Native American flare; but adventurous spirits might prefer to scour the trails of Lost Dutchman State Park. Legend holds that some lucky dog still has a chance to sniff out the infamous Lost Dutchman Mine whose walls hold riches beyond any pooch's imagination. Even if your search for gold doesn't pan out, you can strike a different kind of gold at day's end when the sun dips behind the jagged mountaintops and the golden colors of sunset paint the sky more beautifully than any artist's palette.

The Wright stuff

If you go dog wild for architecture, the Valley of the Sun has a few surprises in store for you. Not only can you savor the southwestern style, and be dazzled by unusual desert structures, you can view two of Frank Lloyd Wright's masterpieces. Visit Arizona State University in Tempe and repose with Rover outside Grady Gammage Auditorium. This dazzling feat of architecture was Wright's last major work, so be prepared to be left breathless. If you're stomping through north Scottsdale, hightail it to Taliesin West, a school and studio designed by Wright. Do a drive by and check out the architecture that blends so well with the skyline.

Take thee out to the ballgame

Yes, that's right - you and the pooch can watch the Giants warm up at the Indian School Park Ballfield. "Hot Dogs" aren't served, but "cool dogs" are permitted in the outdoor facilities. Spring is the time for training and many teams practice in Arizona. Catch the Cubs, A's, Angels, Brewers, Padres, and the Rockies warming up all over Arizona. Contact the Phoenix & Valley of the Sun Convention & Visitors Bureau for further information and specific practice locations and times.

Savor the old southwest

Several rustic western towns surround the Valley of the Sun. Roll into Rawhide with your leashed lad and check out the amenities, including Belle Starr's buffalo-horn table. If you're in the mood for even more authentic western flavor, take Fido to Cave Creek. This twofold town began in the 1880's when mining was at its peak, but took to ranching when miners got the shaft.

Bark parks

No matter where your travels take you in this burgeoning region, you'll never be far from a green oasis. Many of the larger recreation areas combine Rexercise with enlightenment along their interpretive trails. Whether you're looking for a quiet picnic spot or a tail wagging pathway, there's a park to meet your needs.

It's party time ... year round

Cultural fiestas, Parada del Sol, Native American Pow Wows, authentic rodeos, crooning cowboys, culinary festivals and "affairs of the arts," do their share to create an atmosphere of western sophistication and grace in a state already so blessed with natural beauty. Even when the town sizzles from the heat of summer (a dry heat claim the natives), nearby mountain (aka cool) communities can always be counted on to entertain and amuse with fairs, celebrations and good old-fashioned small town fun.

OLD WEST COUNTRY

Cities Ajo, Benson, Bisbee, Bowie, Clifton, Douglas, Duncan, Elgin, Gila Bend, Globe, Green Valley, Hayden, Miami, Morenci, Nogales, Oracle, Rio Rico, Safford, Sierra Vista, Sonoita, Thatcher, Tombstone, Tubac, Tucson, Willcox.

This area is A-OK

"A" Mountain receives a fresh coat of paint annually by freshmen at the University of Arizona and serves as an uplifting and colorful landmark for Tucson travelers. Popular as a filming location, the lush grasslands of San Rafael Valley was the setting for the film *OKLAHOMA*. And everyone has heard of the most famous shootout in our country's western history, the gunfight at the OK Corral. Reenactments of this event along with flavor of the old west can be found in Tombstone, the town "too tough to die."

For the more padded of paw, the area boasts some of the most magnificent mountain ranges in the state, and offers several bountiful fishing holes. Bird dogs will want to tote their binoculars - the varieties of hummingbirds alone number in the hundreds. Or just relax poolside in what is touted as the country's best all around climate.

What a lemmon!

Rising abruptly over Tucson's desert floor and beckoning scenery hounds to grab their cameras and head for the hills is magical Mt. Lemmon, the coolest place in all of Tucson. This popular recreation area is part of the Santa Catalinas, a vast mountain range with elevations over 9,000 feet.

Talk about polar opposites. It's entirely possible to catch a few rays and swim a few laps in the morning and then throw some snowballs in the afternoon. All it takes is an hour's drive from Tucson to the top of Mt. Lemmon.

This ski area is a favorite with Tucsonians looking to rack up some mileage on their snow skis. Don't forget to include a sweater and a picnic lunch. The mountain road to the top (the crest is at 9,157') is a scenic drive with several turnoffs perfect for leg stretching exploration or panoramic admiration. There's a ski lift and a lodge near the top (open seasonally) and plenty of wide open spaces for you and the pupster to roam.

At the top, you can spend the night in one of the cabins in Summerhaven. There is even a cafe for an evening's repast. Be prepared though for cool, almost cold nighttime temperatures. Your evening activity can be counting the stars. It's certain that you'll run out of steam before you run out of the twinkling gems. Or when day is done, head back into Tucson where dinner awaits at one of many fine eateries and the accoutrements of city life can end a very full, very invigorating outing.

A-hiking we can go

Old West Country offers some of the most interesting hiking in Arizona. With areas like Tucson Mountain Park and the Coronado National Forest, you and Fido can gad about many fascinating environments. Cactus are abundant and beautiful throughout most of Old West Country. If you've never seen a saguaro field at sunrise or sunset, you're in for a treat. The random scattering and unusual shapes of these cactus make for an enchanting sight at any time, but dawn and dusk add tones that will have camera snappers clicking with delight. FYI, the saguaro cactus is found only in the Sonoran Desert and within the U.S., only in Arizona.

Si si, Fi Fi

As you travel throughout the region, you will definitely notice that much of the architecture flaunts a Spanish flare. Spanish Missionaries settled here as early as the mid-1500s, making an historical mark long before other European settlers discovered the richness of the land. Festivals and fiestas commemorate the area's lustrous history, especially on Cinco de Mayo. Nogales offers authentic Mexican cuisine, international parades, and other celebrations of unbridled fun.

You and Rover won't want to miss some of the Native American happenings either. Visit the lively Crown Dances and Sunrise Ceremonies of the San Carlos Apaches. Enjoy the annual Tohono O'odham Tash celebration which includes a rodeo and fair. If you're looking for some good old western fun, don't miss Tombstone Territorial Days (March), or Wyatt Earp Days (May). Old West Country is so chock-full of fun in the sun that you and the pooch will run out of time before you run out of things to do.

HIGH COUNTRY

Cities: Alpine, Eagar, Fort Apache, Greer, Heber, Hon Dah, Overgaard, Payson, Pine, Pinetop/Lakeside, Show Low, Springerville, St. Johns, Strawberry, Whiteriver.

Take the high road to adventure

Able anglers, mountain toppers, hiking hounds, festival aficionados, arts and crafts devotees, snow skiers and snow bunnies can share an unforgettable experience traveling throughout Arizona's most colorful and mountainous region. Painted by hidden lakes and clear running streams, towering tree-draped mountains, striking wildflower displays and fall foliage to rival the "best of the east," this undiscovered wonderland has something for everyone and their canine cohort. And the "serenery" will leave an indelible impression in your memory bank.

Summertime is a special time

For a day you won't soon forget, plan a picnic atop the Mogollon Rim along Forest Road 300. Access FR 300 from Highway 260, just north of Payson or from Route 87, north of Strawberry. Four wheel drive is recommended, but there are plenty of station wagons and vans making their way around. The road runs on the edge of the Mogollon Rim, an escarpment more than 6,000 feet above sea level. Pick a rocky overlook point from among the half dozen you'll pass, spread out a blanket and nibble a picnic lunch while you drink in the unbelievable vistas of the desert and valley below. Vistas that stretch as long, as far and as wide as the eye can see. You won't want to leave this primo spot, it's that beautiful. And when you pack your picnic goodies, pack a sweater as well. No matter how hot it might be in the Phoenix area, it's always cool and often windy on the Rim. There isn't a more perfect place to chill out on a sizzling summer afternoon. "Point and Shoot" cameras had to be made to capture beauty like this.

Fall hard for Arizona

Okay, enough about escaping the summer heat on the escarpment. What about the other seasons? The Rim is great year round. A journey in late fall will make you think you've entered the twilight zone and somehow been transported to the heart of New England. That's right desert dwellers and eastern disbelievers, fall can be yours right here in Arizona. The high country is loaded with quaking aspens, oak, sycamore, cottonwood, big-tooth maple and Arizona ash. The farther north you travel, the later the fall season arrives but arrive it does with a colorful vengeance. And dogs just seem to have a special fondness for the sound of crisp, crackling leaves under paw. So give Rover a treat and spend at least one autumn day in the mountains of northern Arizona.

Not just for Huskies

Do you and the pupster long for a quiet, solitary walk in snow covered fields? Come north again where locals insist that most snowfall occurs at night and roads are often cleared by daylight. Of course, after really heavy storms, (blizzards are not unheard of) check with the local highway patrol to make sure the roads are passable. Yes, there's that much snow. If your vehicle is equipped with four-wheel drive (chains are a good idea in winter), head for any of the northern forests, find a pullout off the main road, bundle up and build a snowdog with your hounddog.

Flower power

Prefer the colors of the rainbow? The High Country comes alive in springtime, the surrounding mountains and fields vividly colored with yellow desert marigold, purple lupine, orange poppy, Indian paintbrush and purplish-pink owl clover. Forget trying to capture this wonder on film (unless you're the Ansel Adam type). Somehow, a 4" square just can't do justice to a field bursting with eye popping yellow. These wildflower scenes will have to be etched in your memory, not glued in your photo album. But good luck photo optimists.

INDIAN COUNTRY

Cities: Chinle, Holbrook, Kayenta, Second Mesa, Tuba City, Window Rock, Winslow.

Travel through timeless tradition

Ancient dinosaur footprints, preserved petrified wood, land carved by an earthbound meteor, and a culture that has remained true to its heritage make Indian Country one of the most mystical regions in the southwest.

Descendants of the remarkable Anasazi culture, the Hopi Indians inhabit a vast region of sandy plains and high plateaus. Their Reservation is totally surrounded by the Navajo Nation. The Hopi live on the land, in harmony with nature, their lives firmly rooted in centuries-old customs, their ancient villages still in place atop three high mesas.

Leave only footprints

The Hopi have opened some of their land and culture to visitors, but they request that cameras, recorders, sketch pads, and alcohol be left in the trunk if you and Rover choose to roam about their villages. Some cultural events are open to the public, but the Hopi prefer to remain a private culture. For keepsakes of your visit, visit the shops of Second Mesa.

The epitome of natural splendor, the Navajo Reservation is the largest in the United States. From plains to cool, pine scented mountains, from the Canyon de Chelly to the Canyon del Muerto, this is a land of spectacular form and color. The lives of the Navajos have remained relatively unchanged for hundreds of years. A solitary people - tending sheep and farming are at the center of their lifestyles.

Reminiscent of millenniums of erosion, windswept sands and towering mountains seem to guard the secrets of the past in buttes, spires and sandstone cliffs. The muted earth tones are guaranteed to soothe the senses of man and dog alike. Take your time and take Fido on an unforgettable journey through this pristine and primitive region. But remember that this is a sacred land deserving of your respect.

Maybe they saw Medusa

Towering trees that turned to stone over 225 million years ago are open for viewing in Indian Country's Petrified Forest. The actual cause of the transformation has been attributed to ancient swamps and waterborne minerals. Pick up a pamphlet and learn a little about the area before you and Rover marvel at its mysterious beginnings. Ancient fish, amphibians and reptiles are forever preserved in this fossilized forest. The largest petrified forest in the world will dazzle you with colors that change with the moving sunlight. Continue northbound to the Painted Desert where a staggering array of purple and red awaits you. Although the desert is stunning in any light, sunrise or sunset can prove unforgettable.

Paws in four states...at the same time

That's right, your pooch can say he plopped his paws in Arizona, Colorado, Utah and New Mexico...all at the same moment. Human companions will have to imitate their canine pals and get on all fours to share the experience. This is the only place in the United States where you can actually be in four states at once. Now that's something to bark home about.

A car trip to the moon?

About 50,000 years ago a meteor smashed into the Earth near what is now Winslow, Arizona, creating a crater one mile wide and 570 feet deep. This awesome display of force is responsible for the unearthly lunar-like terrain. In fact, NASA used Meteor Crater as a training ground for its Apollo astronauts. For an-out-of-this-world experience, take the 3.5 mile walk around the rim of this enormous depression.

Navajo Rodeo

Visit Window Rock in September and catch the world's largest Indian fair. The rodeo is part of a five-day festival in which visitors can enjoy some Native American cultural fun. Let Rover sniff his way to the Indian fry bread contest, or settle in and catch the Miss Navajo Nation competition. Listen to the songs, watch the dances, and admire the arts and crafts of a Nation rich in tradition and history. Don't miss Monument Valley while you're visiting this part of Arizona. You and the pooch can gear up for a 14-mile marked drive and take in the famous landmarks of the valley. Hollywood might have lent a hand in making the area famous and recognizable, but the Navajo have long appreciated the beauty and magic of their singular land.

CANYON COUNTRY

Cities: Ash Fork, Flagstaff, Page, Sedona, Williams.

Canyon Country sneak peek

Beautiful red rock canyons, trophy-winning trout fishing, postcardian snow-capped peaks, cool summertime hikes, breathtaking scenic drives...the list is endless. There's so much to see and do that you and the dawgus will have to make several return visits to get your fill of this enchanting, spiritual area of Arizona.

Canyons, canyons and more canyons

The Grand Canyon, Oak Creek Canyon, Sycamore Canyon, Verde River Canyon, Walnut Canyon, Havasu Canyon - it's no wonder this chunk of Arizona has been dubbed Canyon Country. Billions of years have been invested in making each canyon an unparalleled work of art affording visitors an endless choice of Minolta moments. So what are you waiting for? Grab your camera and Rover's leash and do some canyon hopping.

The Grand Canyon, the granddaddy of them all

Imagine an opening in the earth 277 miles long, 10 miles wide and a mile deep. Unimaginable? You're in good company. Until you've personally seen the almost indescribable grandeur of one of the seven wonders of the world, words are just words. Two billion years of persistent water and wind are responsible for carving this masterpiece of nature. After your first g-a-s-p, spend a few hours driving from one scenic point to the next, oohing and aahing as you go. Or try your paw at one of the dog-friendly trails listed in the directory section of this book. Come on, it's time for you and your canine to experience the best of the best.

Oak Creek Canyon - a kaleidoscope of color

On the scenery scale, this canyon gets two paws up. The views of the stunning red rock cliffs and monoliths are to die for, not to mention the variety of hiking trails that crisscross this unforgettable chunk of Arizona. If you're overwhelmed by feelings of deja vu, don't be surprised. Beginning with John Ford, hundreds of directors have chosen this location for western movies. Years after the first movie was filmed here, it remains a favorite among the nation's entertainment, media and art communities. And good news for "east coasters" who long for a taste of autumn, fall is an annual visitor to this lush canyon region. The brilliant red, orange and gold of the canyon will undoubtedly remind you of home.

If you're into scenic drives, one of the most beautiful in the United States (rated one of the nation's top eight scenic highways) is along US 89A as it snakes its way from the quaint town of Sedona to the heights of Flagstaff. Switchbacks mark your ascent, with staggering views in front, alongside and behind you. You won't know which way to look first. And the return trip from Flagstaff to Sedona will give you an entirely different perspective of this magnificent canyon drive.

Sycamore Canyon - the unsung hero

Calling all nature lovers, this is one canyon you won't want to miss. Sycamore Canyon may live in the shadows of its cousins, but it has plenty to offer, especially if you and the pooch crave peace and solitude. This roadless canyon assures that its beauty remains undisturbed by vehicles. Only two legged and four legged nature lovers can be found within its boundaries.

Sedona - a town for all seasons

Sedona, a mecca for spiritualists, nature lovers and art enthusiasts, offers solitary moments or small town western-style hubbub. The choice is yours. And the pooch's, of course. There's breathtaking scenery at every turn, combined with pleasant year-round weather. First rate hiking trails, exciting back road adventures, refreshing swimming and fishing holes and activity-filled state parks are all part of the scene. Summertime calls for shorts with temperatures in the 90's, while layers are a good idea in the winter months when temperatures may drop into the 40's. The little bit of snow Sedona occasionally receives is more like icing on a cinnamon bun than a weather problem. Regardless of the time of year, Sedona is sure to vie for the #1 spot on your top ten list of "Hot Spots For Spot."

Flagstaff - a town high on life

12,643-foot Mount Humphreys, Arizona's highest point and 5,000-acre Mormon Lake, Arizona's largest natural lake are just two reasons why you and the pupster should take some time to explore the charming college and ski resort town of Flagstaff. Snow-capped mountains, shimmering lakes, historic landmarks, dormant volcanoes, fascinating cinder cones, lush national forests and ancient Indian ruins are guaranteed to "peak" your interest. The vast National Forests and San Francisco Peaks contain hundreds of miles of hiking opportunities.

A visit in the summer is a sure cure for the hot dog days in the lower elevations. From the Phoenix area, it's only two hours from the desert to cool refreshment. Come winter, the beautiful landscape is covered with a thick white blanket of snow attracting both skiers and winter sports enthusiasts.

Fairs and festivals spell fun

Celebrations of culture and heritage are a popular, year-round pastime for the residents of Canyon Country. On any given weekend, you and Rover will find yourselves in the middle of some sort of celebration.

For a complete listing of fairs and festivals for individual cities, contact the Chamber of Commerce or Convention & Visitors Bureaus listed in the back of this book.

CENTRAL TERRITORY

Cities: Camp Verde, Chino Valley, Clarkdale, Cottonwood, Crown King, Jerome, Mayer, Prescott, Prescott Valley, Wickenburg.

Get territorial

The history, legends and ghost towns of this chunk of Arizona will provide insight into the past, while the scenery will captivate in the present. Stroll along the Verde River and admire the purple tinted mountains that dwarf the lush rows of colorful cottonwood. Prehistoric settlers recognized the serenity and beauty of the area while intuitive miners discovered the riches beneath the surface. Each left scattered testaments of their presence. The cliff dwellings and country-style historic homes within the Central Territory afford a glimpse of yet another aspect of Arizona's diversity.

Mining little daisy

Jerome State Historical Park is home to the mansion of pioneer mining magnate "Rawhide Jimmy" Douglas. As you amble along the quaint topsy turvy streets of this former ghost town consider that over 100 miles of mining tunnels and shafts lie beneath your feet and that nearly a billion dollars of ore was unearthed from this area. And you thought Fido could dig.

A ghost town no more. Jerome has been revitalized by an active art community. Boutiques and galleries dot this hillside town, the wares representing the work of many local artists. An aura of small town friendliness puts everyone at ease, including Fido.

Canoeing, cowboys, and castles in the land

Canoe with your canine down the tranquil waters of the Verde River. Try your hand at fishing. Catch sight of some genuine cowboys riding the high plains. Ponder the past at the Tuzigoot National Monument or the Montezuma Castle National Monument. Or get your Rexercise along the tail wagging trails of Central Territory's Prescott National Forest.

Crown King, Kool King of the Bradshaws

Cool off on a sweltering day with a visit to the hidden (aka rustic) oasis of Crown King. Even when it's over 100° in Phoenix, there's a good chance you'll need a sweater by the time you reach the crest. An undiscovered gem (if you have a four-wheel drive vehicle and a tushie cushion), plan a visit when you're not in any big hurry. The ride is slow going and bumpy.

Heading north from Phoenix on Interstate 17, take the exit to Crown King. In minutes, you'll be saying goodbye to smooth going. The rocky road climbs from the desert floor and rises through low and then high chaparral before reaching the greenery of the Prescott National Forest. Take your time, the twisting, turning mountain road offers plenty of visual appeal. Once you arrive at Crown King, the itsy bitsy town at the top, you'll find a small cafe and general store and a passel of friendly mutts to greet your own. Don't be surprised to see snow on the ground, even in June. During the day, the temperatures are probably thirty degrees cooler in this mountaintop region.

If you'd like to plan an overnight stay, begin your drive to Crown King early in the day. That'll give you enough daylight hours to take the Senator Highway, another scenic albeit jarring jaunt, through the picturesque Bradshaw Mountains to Prescott, a quaint, town - the movie *BACK TO THE FUTURE* could have been filmed here. Once you arrive in Prescott, wet your whistle in one of the historic saloons on Whiskey Row and partake of dinner in one of the town's eateries. There are lots of dog-friendly accommodations and even a casino in nearby Prescott Valley where you can try your luck at the slots while Fido recovers from the day's excitement. Before you head back to Phoenix, enjoy a stroll through the "fifties" feel of the downtown Prescott area.

WEST COAST RIVER COUNTRY

Cities: Bullhead City, Dateland, Kingman, Lake Havasu City, Parker, Quartzsite, Salome, San Luis, Somerton, Wenden, Yuma.

Well, I'll be dammed

The West Coast of Arizona is a land of water in the midst of desert country. The Bill Williams River is a tributary to the Colorado which is quelled by Parker and Hoover Dams. Both of these man-made plugs have created incredible, calm fishing areas for fly hounds. A memorable sojourn will transport you from the roaring banks of the Colorado to the soothing serenity of Lake Mead. Water is everywhere and the contrast of the scenery will surprise you. From tales of trappers in the old southwest, to a taste of England's finest, River Country offers travelers a bountiful experience that river Rovers will not soon forget.

Perfect for Lady, Duke and Duchess

Teacup Poodles and English Bulldogs will feel right at home in Lake Havasu, home to the London Bridge. Piece by piece, the world famous bridge was disassembled in London and rebuilt in Lake Havasu City. It now spans a section of the Colorado River. So leash up the old bloke and get a snoutful of fresh air. Break for biscuits and tea and partake of an authentic taste of English tradition.

Float your boat

Fishermen, pack your gear and pick your watering hole. Lake Mead is the largest man-made lake in the United States, its calm waters a blessing for tranquil trawlers. Lakes Mohave and Havasu also have dinner with your name on it swimming in the depths. You won't be disappointed as you row, row, row your boat through miles of placid water. Tow the line and savor the surroundings of blue waterways smack dab in the middle of desert country.

Who's hogging all the sun?

Yuma is one of the sunniest spots in Arizona. Farming and filming coexist side by side in this desert community. The vast sand dunes were used to create a perfect backdrop for the movie, LAWRENCE OF ARABIA. But there weren't any movie moguls in sight when Yuma Territorial Prison was in full swing. No longer a jail, it's now part of a state park. The prison unlocks tales of sin, snake pits, and western-style punishment. Your hound's hair may stand on end as the two of you peruse the iron walls that held violent men and women of the old Southwest. There are some grassy areas where pleasure and not punishment can end your day.

CLIMATE & MEAN TEMPERATURES

Few areas of the world can boast a climate as varied as Arizona's.

Arizona has five main climatic zones, classified by elevation, ranging from almost sea level to more than 12,000 feet above sea level. The lower-lying areas of Arizona have warm, pleasant winters and hot, dry summers. The highest elevations have cold, snowy winters and cool, pleasant summers. Elevation can be used as a general key to seasonal temperatures.

0 to 2,000 feet: The LOW DESERT areas, from near sea level to around 2,000 feet above sea level (Phoenix, Yuma, Gila Bend, Lake Havasu City). Phoenix, at 1,117 feet, is typical.

2,000 to 4,000 feet: The DESERT FOOTHILLS include Tucson, Tombstone and Wickenburg. This elevation is typified by Wickenburg at 3,000 feet.

4,000 to 6,000 feet: The HIGHLANDS include Payson, Prescott, Sedona and most of the Apache Reservation. Much of the HIGH PLATEAU area of the Navajo and Hopi Reservations in northeastern Arizona also falls into this category. Prescott, at 5,347 feet, is typical.

Above 6,000 feet: MOUNTAIN COUNTRY includes Flagstaff, the Mogollon Rim communities, Williams and several mountain ranges. Flagstaff, at 7,000 feet, is typical.

MEAN TEMPERATURES*

	Flagstaff		Phoenix		Tucson	
	High	Low	High	Low	High	Low
January	41.4	14.4	64.8	37.8	63.9	38.2
February	44.0	17.0	69.3	40.8	67.4	39.9
March	47.9	20.4	74.5	44.8	72.0	43.7
April	56.9	27.3	83.6	51.8	81.0	50.5
May	66.6	33.5	82.9	59.6	89.8	57.9
June	76.0	40.4	101.5	67.7	98.3	66.8
July	80.8	50.4	104.8	77.5	98.7	74.2
August	77.9	49.3	102.2	76.0	95.9	72.4
September	73.7	41.2	98.4	69.1	93.8	67.6
October	62.9	31.1	87.6	56.8	84.4	56.8
November	50.9	21.8	74.7	44.8	72.8	45.1
December	43.2	16.3	66.4	38.5	65.2	39.1

*Official National Weather Service Statistics

ARIZONA STATE FACTS

The name is derived from "Alehzon," an Indian phrase for "Little Spring." It was called Arizona by the Spaniards in the early 1700's.

Humans lived in this area 20,000 years ago. Traces of early civilizations are found throughout the state. Written history began when Marcos de Niza, a Franciscan priest entered the territory in 1539.

The land north of the Gila River became a territory of the United States after the Mexican-American War in 1848. The land south of the Gila was added by the Gadsden Purchase in 1853. Arizona was granted separate territorial status from New Mexico in 1863.

During these years, the early pioneers came to the Arizona Territory seeking gold, silver and copper. Farmers were attracted by the fertile soil and long growing season in Arizona's many river valleys. Some of the largest cattle holdings in the world were built on Arizona's rich grazing lands.

With the last of the Indian uprisings in 1886, settlement of the state surged forward and, in 1912, Arizona became the nation's 48th state.

Capitol
Phoenix

Highest Point
Humphrey's Peak, near Flagstaff, reaches almost 13,000 feet above sea level.

Lowest Point
The Colorado River dips to less than 100 feet above sea level near Yuma.

State Flower
The saguaro blossom is the state flower of Arizona. The giant saguaro cactus blooms with these beautiful white blossoms every spring. Saguaros attain heights of up to 50 feet and live for over 200 years. They are the largest cactus in the United States.

State Gem
Turquoise, the blue-green stone used for centuries in Indian jewelry, is the state gem.

State Seal
Arizona's original key enterprises are symbolized on the state seal: reclamation, farming, cattle ranching and mining.

State Neckwear
The bola tie, which originated in Arizona, is the official state neckwear. Silver with turquoise is the official style.

State Tree

Arizona's state tree, the paloverde, is found in the low desert. A green, bushy tree most of the year, in spring it blooms in a blaze of shimmering gold.

State Bird

The state bird is the cactus wren, a woody brown bird that often makes its home in the giant saguaro.

State Seal

Motto: Ditat Deus (God enriches).

State Flag

A copper star rising from a blue field of honor in a face of a setting sun. (Symbolic of the copper industry and growth.)

ARIZONA TRIVIA

- The ingenuity of Robert P. McCulloch led him to purchase the ailing London Bridge and relocate the historical landmark to Lake Havasu City. A skilled team of engineers took the bridge apart, block by block, and transported it to Arizona. The bridge was pieced back together and now stands in Lake Havasu City.

- The first known inhabitants of Arizona were the Paleo-Indians. These tribespeople hunted bison, camel, horse, antelope, and mammoth 20,000 years ago.

- Arizona has more national monuments than any other state.

- Happy Valentine's Day. President William H. Taft signed the proclamation which made Arizona the 48th State in the union on February 14, 1912.

- The year round ground temperature inside Colossal Cave (near Tucson) is 72 degrees.

- Lake Powell covers 1,900 miles of shoreline and spans two states.

- Monument Valley is home to the pair of well known rock spires called "The Mittens".

- Baker Butte, at 8074 feet, marks the highest point of the Mogollon Rim.

- The intermittent waterfall known as Grand Falls, located on the Little Colorado, is taller than Niagara Falls.

- Prescott was Arizona's first capital in 1864.

- Phillip Wrigley, the chewing gum magnate, built a hilltop mansion on the grounds of the Arizona Biltmore. It is now a private club.

- The Hopi Reservation is home to the oldest Spanish ruins in the State. These structures date back to 1628.

- The Navajo tribe is the largest in the state and is the tribe of the famous WWII "code talkers," the only code the Japanese couldn't break.

- Cliff paintings in Canyon de Chelly describe the travels of early Spanish settlers.

- The Navajo's traditional dwelling is called a hogan.

- The Pueblo people call their ceremonial chambers kivas.

- Arizona's San Francisco Peaks are sacred to both the Navajo and the Hopi.

- The long-gone Anasazi people built most of the ruins in the Canyon de Chelly and the Canyon del Muerto.

- Window Rock is the arch which gives its name to the Navajo Nation's capitol.

- The town of Show Low was aptly named by the outcome of a card game.

- The town of Jerome is named for the cousin of Winston Churchill's mother.

- In 1939, famed movie director John Ford used Monument Valley for the setting of the film *STAGECOACH*.

- Steven Spielberg grew up in Scottsdale.

- Andy Devine was a native of Kingman.

- Barry Goldwater took the photograph which graced the cover of the December, 1946 issue of Arizona Highways.

- Syndicated humor columnist, Erma Bombeck, resides in Paradise Valley.

- The remains of "Gertie," a 225 million year old dinosaur, were found in Petrified Forest National Park.

- The highest temperature ever recorded in Arizona was 127 degrees.

- Hawley Lake has recorded the greatest snowfall in Arizona during a season, a reported 400.9 inches. Phoenix's greatest accumulation to date is one inch.

- The night blooming Cereus blooms only in the desert's dark summer nights.

- The agave, aptly called the century plant, blooms every 25 years.

- Palm Canyon, located on the west side of the Kofa Mountains, is home to a few of the rare palm trees native to Arizona.

- The spadefoot toad lies dormant in the desert soil emerging only after torrential summer rains.

- The bristlecone pine is Arizona's oldest tree, estimated at 1400 years of age.

- The Supreme Court has seated two native Arizonans: Justice William H. Rehnquist, and Justice Sandra Day O'Connor.

Saguaro Cactus Tidbits

- Except for a scattered handful in California, saguaros are found only in the Sonoran Desert of Arizona and Mexico.

- Without a permit, it's illegal to remove saguaros from their natural habitat, or damage/vandalize in any way.

- Saguaros can live for 150-200 years and weigh up to 10 tons.

- Water accounts for more than 80% of their weight.

- On average, arm growth occurs around age 75.

- Pack rats, woodpeckers, hawks and owls depend upon saguaros for nesting purposes. Javelinas, bats, rabbits and birds feast on the saguaro's flowers and fruit.

The Rare Crestate Cactus

- Crestate cactus are rare saguaros, organ pipes and barrels with a fan-type crest.

- Crestate cactus are sterile: they neither bloom nor produce fruit.

- It is illegal to damage or remove any specimen from federal, state or private lands.

- If you're fortunate enough to happen upon a crestate cactus, the state of Arizona encourages you to photograph the cactus, write a detailed description of its location and then mail the information to: Jim McGinnis, Native Plant Section, Arizona Department of Agriculture, 1688 W. Adams St., Phoenix, AZ 85007. Your cooperation can help protect these unusual specimens.

SUMMER SAFETY TIPS

- **IN ARIZONA, IT'S ILLEGAL TO LEAVE AN ANIMAL IN A PARKED CAR FROM APRIL THROUGH OCTOBER - EVEN IF ALL THE WINDOWS ARE DOWN.**

- Cool water, rather than cold, will help reduce and regulate your dog's body temperature.

- Limit physical activity with your pooch to a brief jaunt in early morning or evening.

- In the summer, garages and outdoor doghouses are heat traps which can prove fatal.

- A pavement that is too hot for your bare feet is definitely too hot for your pooch's paws.

- High summertime temperatures are known to bring about a loss of energy and appetite in your pooch. DO NOT force exercise or food on your pooch.

- Early morning and late evening are the best times to feed your dog.

- Young, old, overweight and short-nosed dogs are easy prey for the blistering heat.

- Beds of pickup trucks provide no protection from the scorching sun, heightening a dog's chances of heatstroke. The beds also trap heat and can severely burn a dog's foot pads.

- Pickup trucks are extremely dangerous and even fatal. Over 100,000 dogs are killed each year due to falls from pickup trucks.

INTRODUCTION

Doing Arizona with Your Pooch!

Let me begin by saying very clearly that doing Arizona with your pooch can be easy. Don't be intimidated. Don't think it takes special training or expertise. It doesn't. All it takes is a little planning and a little patience. Believe me, the rewards are worth the effort. This directory is filled with information to make traveling with your dog more pleasurable. From training tips to what to take along, to the do's and don'ts of travel, almost all of your questions will be addressed.

Vacationing with dogs?

Not something I thought I'd ever do. But as the adage goes, necessity is the mother of invention. What began as my necessity turned into a new lifestyle. A lifestyle that has improved every aspect of my vacation and travel time.

Although my family had dogs on and off during my childhood, it wasn't until my early thirties that I decided it was time to bring another dog into my life. And the lives of my young children. I wanted them to grow up with a dog; to know what it was like to have a canine companion, a playmate, a friend who would always be there. To love you, no questions asked. A four-legged pal who would be the first to lick your teary face or your bloody knee. Enter Samson, our family's first Golden Retriever.

Samson

For nearly fifteen years, Sammy was everything a family could want from their dog. Loyal, forgiving, sweet, funny, neurotic, playful, sensitive, smart, too smart, puddle loving, fearless, strong and cuddly. He could melt your heart with a woebegone expression or make your hair stand on end with one of his pranks. Like the time he methodically opened the seam on a bean bag chair and then cheerfully spread the beans everywhere. Or when he followed a jogger and ended up in a shelter more than 20 miles from home.

As the years passed, Sam's face turned white and one by one our kids headed off to college. Preparing for the inevitable, my husband Harvey and I decided that when Sam died, no other dog would take his place. We wanted our freedom, not the responsibility of another dog.

Sammy left us one sunny June morning with so little fanfare that we couldn't believe he was actually gone. Little did we realize the void that would remain when our white-faced Golden Boy was no longer with us.

Rosie and Maxwell...life goes on

After planning a two-week vacation through California, with an ultimate destination of Lake Tahoe, Harvey and I had our hearts stolen by two Golden Retriever puppies...Rosie and Maxwell. Two little balls of fur that would help to fill the emptiness Sam's death had created. The puppies were ready to come home only weeks before our scheduled departure date. What to do? Kennel them? Hire a caretaker at our home? Neither solution felt right.

Sooo...we took them along

Oh, the fun we had. And the friends we made. Both the two-legged and four-legged variety. Having dogs on our trip made us more a part of the places we visited. We learned that dogs are natural conversation starters. Rosie and Maxwell were the prime movers in some lasting friendships we made during that first trip together. Now when we revisit Lake Tahoe, we have old friends to see as well as new ones to make. The locals we met made us feel at home, offering insider information on little known hikes, wonderful restaurants and quiet neighborhood parks. This knowledge enhanced our trips and made every day a grand adventure.

Since that first trip, our travels have taken us to many places. We've visited national forests, mountain resorts, seaside villages, island retreats, big cities and tiny hamlets. We've shared everything from luxury hotel rooms to rustic cabin getaways. I can't imagine going anywhere without our dogs.

Only one regret remained. Why hadn't it occurred to me to take Sammy along on our travels? He would have loved the adventures. That regret led to the writing of this book. I wanted others to know how easy it could be to vacation with their dogs.

When I watch Rosie and Maxwell frolic in a lake or when they accompany us on a hike, I think of Sammy and remember the legacy of love and friendship he left behind. So for those of you who regularly take your dog along and those who would if you knew how, come share my travel knowledge. And happy trails to you and yours.

Is my pooch vacation-friendly?

Most dogs can be excellent traveling companions. Naturally, the younger they are when you accustom them to traveling, the more quickly they will adapt. But that doesn't mean that an older dog won't love vacationing with you. And it doesn't mean that the transition has to be a difficult one.

Even if your dog hasn't traveled with you in the past, chances are he'll make a wonderful companion. You'll find yourself enjoying pensive moments watching him in new surroundings, laughing with others at his antics. But most of all, you'll find that spending quality time with your dog enhances every day of your travels. So get ready for a unique and rewarding adventure - filled with memories to last a lifetime.

A socialized pooch is a sophisticated traveler

Of course, every pooch is different. And you know yours better than anyone. To be sure that he will travel like a pro, accustom him to different environments. Take him for long walks around your neighborhood. Let him accompany you while you do errands. If your chores include stair climbing or taking an elevator, take him along. The more exposure to people, places and things, the better. Make your pet worldly. The sophistication will pay off in a better behaved, less frightened pet. It won't be long until he will happily share travel and vacation times with you.

Just ordinary dogs

Rosie and Maxwell, my traveling companions, are not exceptional dogs to anyone other than me. Their training was neither intensive nor professionally rendered. They were trained with kindness, praise, consistency and love. And not all of their training came about when they were puppies. I too had a lot to learn. And as I learned what I wanted of them, their training continued. It was a sharing and growing experience. Old dogs (and humans too) can learn new tricks. Rosie and Maxwell never fail to surprise me. Their ability to adapt to new situations has never stopped. So don't think you have to start with a puppy. Every dog, young and old, can be taught to be travel-friendly.

Rosie and Maxwell know when I begin putting their things together that another holiday is about to begin. Their excitement mounts with every phase of preparation. They stick like glue - remaining at my side as I organize their belongings. By the time I've finished, they can barely contain their joy. Rosie runs to grab her leash and prances about the kitchen holding it in her mouth while Max sits on his haunches and begins to howl. If they could talk, they'd tell you how much they enjoy traveling. But since they can't, trust this directory to lead you to a different kind of experience. One that's filled with lots of love and an opportunity for shared adventure with your dogs.

During my travels with Rosie and Maxwell, I've encountered a myriad of people, each having their own thoughts on traveling with dogs. While some can't conceive of the idea and others believe their dogs would be unmanageable, most simply never even realized it was a viable option. Not only is it an option, vacationing with your pooch has become the travel trend of the decade.

Now that you've made the decision to take your pooch along, keep in mind that every new way of life takes some adjustment. New experiences need a degree of patience and a willingness to succeed. So with an open mind and an open heart, pack your bags and pack your pooch. Slip this handy book into your suitcase or the glove compartment of your car and let the adventure begin.

ARIZONA DIRECTORY
OF DOG-FRIENDLY
LODGING
& OUTDOOR ACTIVITIES

Dogs May Be Unleashed Unless Otherwise Indicated

BE AWARE THAT HOTEL POLICIES MAY CHANGE. AT THE TIME YOUR RESERVATIONS ARE MADE, DETERMINE THE POLICY OF YOUR LODGING CHOICE.

A J O

<u>LODGING</u>

A SIESTA MOTEL
2561 N Ajo-Gila Bend Hwy (85321) Rates: $26-$38;
Tel: (520) 387-6569

MARINE MOTEL
1966 N 2nd Ave (85321) Rates: $30-$69;
Tel: (520) 387-7626

A L P I N E

<u>LODGING</u>

CORONADO TRAILS CABINS & RV PARK
25302 Hwy 191(85920) Rates: $45+;
Tel: (520) 339-4772

TAL-WI-WI LODGE
40 County Road 2220 (85920) Rates: $49-$89;
Tel: (520) 339-4319

<u>RECREATION</u>

BEAR WALLOW TRAIL HIKE - Leashes

Intermediate/15.2 miles/7.5 hours

Info: Lush with vegetation, this forest setting offers cool seclusion. Perfect for you and the pooch to enjoy some quality outdoor time. Anglers will want to include their gear. The streamside trail is stocked with delicious Apache trout. For more information: (520) 393-4384.

Directions: From Alpine, head south on Highway 191 to FR 25. Go west on FR 25 for 2.8 miles to the trailhead.

BONANZA BILL TRAIL HIKE - Leashes

Intermediate/1.0-24.2 miles/0.5-12.0 hours

Info: Hike a mile or plan a full day's excursion along this meandering, bi-state scenic trail through a canyon divide. You and Rover will cross into New Mexico for a couple of miles without so much as an "Adios Amigos". If you hike as far as Bonanza Bill Point, you'll be rewarded with views of the Steeple Watershed, the San Francisco Valley and Devil's Monument. For more information: (520) 339-4384.

Directions: Take Highway 180 east out of Alpine to FR 281. Travel south on FR 281 for 20.7 miles to FR 232. Go east on FR 232 for 4.7 miles until you reach the trailhead.

Note: This area is remote. Inform someone of your plans and carry a map.

ESCUDILLA MOUNTAIN TRAIL HIKE

Intermediate/6.6 miles/3.5 hours

Info: Delight your senses during fall when the yellow leaves of quaking aspen present a sunny contrast to the trees' white bark. Summer hikers, you'll enjoy meadows of wildflowers as you gradually ascend 1,300-feet into a bowl-shaped mountain that travels through an aspen forest before crossing Profanity Ridge. From the ridge, take the trail branching north to the lookout and vistas of Mount Baldy and the San Francisco Peaks. At an elevation of 11,000 feet, you'll feel as if you're on top of the world. For more information: (520) 339-4384.

Directions: From Alpine, take Highway 191 north to the Forest Service Road 56 turnoff (Terry Flats) and go right. Follow for 3.6 miles to Terry Flats. Turn left at the fork and travel .5 miles to the parking area near the bottom of Toolbox Draw. Trail begins just before FR 56 turns south. Pick up a map at the trailhead.

GOBBLER POINT TRAIL HIKE

Expert/5.4 miles/3.5 hours

Info: You'll need some power munchies for yourself and some power biscuits for the pooch if you tackle this strenuous hike. Beginning immediately with a steep descent into a side drainage of Bear Wallow Creek, the trail bottoms out at the canyon floor. But not before you've enjoyed some spectacular vistas of the Black River, Mount Graham and the San Carlos Indian Reservation. This trail is the shortest route to the creek. If you're a rod packing hiker, you might get lucky and catch a dinner of Apache trout - the creek's brimming with them. For more information: (520) 339-4384.

Directions: Take Highway 191 south approximately 3.5 miles past Hannagan Meadow to Forest Road 25. Go west on FR 25 to where FR 25C forks off. Follow FR 25C to the end and the trailhead.

HINKLE SPRING TRAIL HIKE

Intermediate/9.0 miles/4.5 hours

Info: You and the pupster will want to set aside an entire afternoon to fully appreciate this picturesque canyon hike. The trail follows the Blue River before snaking up Cow Canyon. The ascent is steep at times, but ridgetop views are worth the trek. Eventually this trail joins the Bonanza Bill Trail where you can turn around and retrace your steps. For more information: (520) 339-4384.

Directions: Take Highway 180 east out of Alpine 3.5 miles to the FR 281 turnoff. Head south on FR 281 approximately 21 miles. You've gone too far if you reach Blue Campground. The trailhead is just south of the junction of Blue River Road (FR 232) and FR 281.

Dogs May Be Unleashed Unless Otherwise Indicated

HORSE RIDGE TRAIL HIKE - Leashes

Intermediate/10.0 miles/5.0 hours

Info: Pack plenty of film for this hike. Castle Rock, Bell Rock, red rock canyons, the Mogollon Rim, Bear Mountain and Whiterocks Mountain - you won't know where to point and shoot first. The trail descends into Foote Creek Canyon, joining Foote Creek Trail at the canyon floor. And then it's up the way you came down - only tougher. For more information: (520) 339-4384.

Directions: Take Highway 191 south 14 miles from Alpine to the Beaverhead Lodge. Another .5 miles further south is the Horse Ridge Trailhead on the east (left) side of the highway.

Note: This area is remote. Inform someone of your plans and carry a map.

KP TRAIL HIKE TO WATERFALL - Leashes

Intermediate/6.0 miles/3.0 hours

Info: Experience a diversity of landscape along this streamside, meadow-filled trail. When the trail drops off, you'll be at your turnaround point, where the South and North Forks of KP Creek come together and create a beautiful waterfall. If you want to go another couple of miles, there's some good fishing further downstream. When you and the pooch have had your fun quotient for the day, turn around and head back the way you came. For more information: (520) 339-4384.

Directions: From Alpine, head south on Highway 191 for 28 miles to the KP Cienega Campground turnoff on the left. Another 1.3 miles leads to the trailhead.

LANPHIER TRAIL HIKE - Leashes

Intermediate/11.2 miles/5.5 hours

Info: Take the high road and the low one on this up and down trail. Ascend for views of Bear Mountain, Lanphier Peak and scenic overlooks of Lanphier Canyon. When you snake your way into the canyon you'll be surrounded by a lush landscape and running water - an ideal rest area for your aquatic pooch to do a little paw dipping. When playtime is over, continue to Cow Flat Trail #55, your turnaround point. For more information: (520) 339-4384.

Directions: From Alpine, head east on Highway 180 for 3 miles to FR 281. Go south on FR 281 for 23 miles to the Blue Administration Site.

Note: This area is remote. Inform someone of your plans and carry a map.

RASPBERRY TRAIL HIKE - Leashes

Expert/1.0-18.8 miles/0.5-11.0 hours

Info: A delight for all the senses, this hike is chock-full of canyons, mountain peaks and verdant forests of Douglas and white fir, alder and ash. Wind your way through Rattlesnake Ranch to Raspberry Canyon. Continue further to the ridgetop and then to the river where some doggie paddling awaits. When you reach Blue River Road, make an about-face and hightail it home. For more information: (520) 339-4384.

Directions: Take Highway 191 south from Alpine for 32 miles to the Strayhorse Campground. The trailhead is located at the back of the campground.

RENO TRAIL HIKE - Leashes

Intermediate/3.8 miles/2.0 hours

Info: Look no further for a secluded hike. A series of switchbacks drops you into the canyon where the trail then follows a drainage. A true wilderness adventure awaits you and the pupster on this trek into the Bear Wallow Wilderness. For more information: (520) 339-4384.

Directions: Take Highway 191 south through Hannagan Meadow. 3.5 miles south of Hannagan Meadow, Forest Road 25 cuts off to the west (right). Take FR 25 to the Reno Lookout and the trailhead.

Note: This area is remote. Inform someone of your plans and carry a map.

ROSE SPRING TRAIL HIKE - Leashes

Intermediate/10.8 miles/5.4 hours

Info: The Mogollon Rim creates a magnificent backdrop along much of this trail, making it one of the most scenic in the Alpine District. Whether you hike only as far as the Schell Trail intersection, at about 3 miles in or you and fur face do it all, you'll experience amazing views of Red Mountain, Rose Peak, Maple Mountain and Mount Graham. For more information: (520) 339-4384.

Directions: Head south on Highway 191 from Alpine to FR 54. Go west on FR 54 for 6 miles to the fork in the road. Veer right through the gate to the trailhead.

S CANYON TRAIL HIKE - Leashes

Intermediate/11.6 miles/6.0 hours

Info: This trail offers you and the pooch a chance to experience a pristine, seldom traveled wilderness. With overlooks of stunning steep-walled canyons and majestic mountain ranges, this hike is challenging but certainly worth the price of admission. For more information: (520) 339-4384.

Directions: From Alpine go east to FR 281 (Blue River Road). Go south on FR 281 for 23 miles to the parking area at the Blue Administration Site. Take the trailhead to the east, following the Blue River upstream. After about three river crossings, you'll come to the trailhead at the mouth of S Canyon on the east side of the river.

TUTT CREEK TRAIL HIKE - Leashes

Expert/8.4 miles/6.0 hours

Info: Get ready for some serious Rexercise if you plan to tackle this trail. Your climb starts in the desert and takes you to a lofty ridge with far reaching panoramas of the Blue Mountain Range. You might get lucky and catch sight of a Rocky Mountain Bighorn. For more information: (520) 339-4384.

Directions: From Alpine, take Highway 191 south and turn east on FR 567. Travel 11 miles to a jeep road. Four-wheel drive is necessary from this point on, or you can hike the remaining .8 miles.

APACHE JUNCTION

LODGING

APACHE JUNCTION MOTEL
1680 W Apache Tr (85220) Rates: $27-$63;
Tel: (602) 982-7702

RECREATION

APACHE LAKE

Info: Quieter breeds will appreciate the solitude this lake offers. Wrapped in a dramatic Sonoran Desert landscape, Apache Lake is a scenic oasis for water lovers and their pooches. For more information: Tonto National Forest Service (520) 467-2236.

Directions: Head north out of Apache Junction on Highway 88 until it becomes the Apache Trail and follow the signs for Apache Lake.

CANYON LAKE

Info: You and your canine crony can cruise through narrow canyon walls that tower toward the sky as you whisk along the waters of Canyon Lake. Aptly named, this area provides enough startling contrasts and abrupt canyons to fill a dozen albums. Pack a biscuit basket and have a floating lunch as you and your best buddy feast your eyes on the scenery. For more information: Tonto National Forest Service (520) 467-2236.

Directions: Head north out of Apache Junction on Highway 88 until it becomes the Apache Trail and follow the signs for Canyon Lake.

FISH CREEK CANYON HIKE

Intermediate/6.0 miles/3.0 hours

Info: Don't let the saguaros at the beginning of the trail fool you. This is anything but arid desert hiking. Fish Creek Canyon Trail is a boulder-hopping adventure, so be prepared for wet tootsies. Your paw wetting journey will take you across, up, over and between volcanic rocks that are strewn throughout the canyon. The rocks can be particularly slippery after a rainstorm so use caution. And you'll need some navigational skills as well, the trail sometimes vanishes into thin air. For more information: (602) 640-5504.

Directions: Head north out of Apache Junction on Highway 88 until it becomes the Apache Trail. Follow the Apache Trail east to the trailhead at the one-lane Fish Creek Bridge.

JACOB'S CROSSCUT TRAIL HIKE - Leashes

Beginner/13.0 miles/6.5 hours

Info: The Superstition Mountains and Four Peaks form the backdrop to the Sonoran Desert on this picturesque trail. A sense of the old west contrasts sharply with present day views of Metro Phoenix making this outing a pleasurable one. And you never know - perhaps Fido will sniff out the lost gold of the Superstitions and really make your day. For more information: (602) 379-6446 or (602) 982-4485.

Directions: From the junction of Highway 88 and Highway 60, go east on Highway 60 for 0.9 miles. Exit north at Royal Palm Drive, then take a right on Broadway Road. Follow Broadway for 3.4 miles to the Broadway trailhead.

Note: Fee may be required if entering through Lost Dutchman State Park.

Dogs May Be Unleashed Unless Otherwise Indicated

LAKE ROOSEVELT

Info: From fishy stories of giant catfish to Swiss-like countrysides, from arid desert scenes to ice blue water and sandy shorelines, Lake Roosevelt is a heavenly haven for desert dwellers and a puppy paradise for their canine cohorts. Take Fido and plenty of Fuji on your excursion to the windswept waters of a lake surrounded by so much beauty and so many mountains, you won't know where to look first. Sunlight and clear skies bring warmth to daytime pleasure seekers, while sunset and nighttime bring unparalleled tranquility and splendor to serenity-seeking city escapees. For more information: Tonto National Forest Service (520) 467-2236.

Directions: Head north out of Apache Junction on Highway 88 (The Apache Trail). Roosevelt Lake and the dam are 46 miles northeast on the partially paved (hazardous) road.

LOST DUTCHMAN STATE PARK - Leashes

Info: The location of the Lost Dutchman's Mine has never been discovered, but this 300-acre park at the foot of the Superstition Mountains offers riches of its own. The park serves as a picnic area, a campground and a starting point for five different hikes into the mountains. For more information: (602) 982-4485.

Directions: Take Highway 88 north for five miles to the park entrance.

Note: $3.00 per vehicle entrance fee.

1) DISCOVERY TRAIL HIKE - Leashes

Beginner/0.7 miles/0.5 hours

Info: If your pup is a couch potato, he'll love this park trail. It's short, simple and scenic. The interpretive signs provide a quickie education on the area's geology, flora and fauna. For more information: (602) 982-4485.

Directions: From Apache Junction, take Highway 88 north to the Lost Dutchman State Park. Access the trail from either the day use area or the campground. Pick up a trail map at the park entrance.

2) NATIVE PLANT TRAIL HIKE - Leashes

Beginner/0.25 miles/0.3 hours

Info: Broaden your knowledge of indigenous plants on this short, paved trail. For detailed descriptions, pick up a trail guidebook at the Ranger Station. Don't forget to admire the pretty views of the Superstitions as you and the dawgus stroll the pathway. For more information: (602) 982-4485.

Directions: Take Highway 88 north to the trailhead at the Ranger Station located just before you enter Lost Dutchman State Park. Park in the lot next to the trailhead. There is no fee charged to hike this trail, but there is a $3.00 entrance fee if you decide to enter the park.

3) PROSPECTOR'S VIEW TRAIL HIKE - Leashes

Intermediate/3.4 miles/1.5 hours

Info: A connector trail to three other trails in the park- Treasure Loop, Jacob's Crosscut and Siphon Draw - you and the dawgus can wander an afternoon away in this pretty part of the Sonoran Desert. Just remember to bring plenty of Perrier. And bring your Kodak too, the Superstitions form a scenic backdrop. For more information: (602) 982-4485.

Directions: From Apache Junction, take Highway 88 north to the Lost Dutchman State Park. This trail can only be accessed via other trails in the park, such as the Treasure Loop Trail which leads east from the trailhead. Access to this trailhead is between the day use area and the group camp area. Hike about one mile on the Treasure Loop Trail to the Prospector's View Trail. Park maps are available at the entrance.

4) SIPHON DRAW TRAIL HIKE - Leashes

Expert/3.2 miles/2.0 hours

Info: Steep best describes this challenging trail into the Siphon Draw Canyon. The surrounding desert landscape is beautiful and bountiful. You'll follow a wash before reaching the clifftops and some unforgettable views. For more information: (602) 982-4485.

Directions: From Apache Junction, take Highway 88 north to the Lost Dutchman State Park. Turn right into the park and follow the loop to the trailhead.

5) TREASURE LOOP TRAIL HIKE - Leashes

Intermediate/4.8 miles/2.5 hours

Info: This trail may not be all that short, but it's definitely sweet. From Green Boulder, an incredible area of rocky steeples and spires, to unrivaled views of downtown Phoenix and Camelback Mountain, you and your canine buddy will be delighted by this easy hike. For more information: (602) 982-4485.

Directions: Take Highway 88 north to the Lost Dutchman State Park. Turn right into the park and follow the loop to the trailhead.

PERALTA TRAIL HIKE - Leashes

Intermediate/4.6 miles/3.0 hours

Info: If you're seeking a calorie burning workout, you and Rover have come to the right place. Your trek will traverse the boulder strewn terrain of the Superstitions, crisscrossing a rocky wash and continuing up the canyon to Fremont Saddle. Most of the year, you'll find pools of water where you and the pooch can cool your heels and take a refreshing break. For more information: (602) 225-5200.

Directions: Take Highway 60 east out of Apache Junction to Milepost 204 and Peralta Road (Forest Road 77). Take Peralta Road north for eight miles (veering first left, then right to stay on FR 77). The road ends at the trailheads. Peralta Trail is to the right.

WEST BOULDER CANYON TRAVELWAY to SOUTH SUMMIT HIKE

Expert/7.0 miles/4.0 hours

Info: Only experienced hikers and their physically fit Fidos should attempt this intense and rigorous butt-kicker into the Superstitions which climbs over 2,600 feet in just 3.5 miles. Beginning at Carney Springs, the trail ascends to an unnamed pass at 3,600 feet and then heads west/southwest to Peak 4391. The last stretch clambers to 5,057-foot South Summit where memorable bird's-eye views of Phoenix and the Superstition Wilderness await you and the pooped pupster. For more information: (602) 255-5200.

Directions: Take Highway 60 east out of Apache Junction to Milepost 204 and Peralta Road (Forest Road 77). Take Peralta Road north for about eight miles (veering first left, then right to stay on FR 77) to the Carney Springs junction. Turn left and follow another mile to the Carney Springs Trailhead.

APACHE LAKE

LODGING
APACHE LAKE MARINA & RESORT
Hwy 88 (85290) Rates: $39-$64;
Tel: (520) 467-2511

RECREATION
APACHE LAKE

Info: Quieter breeds will appreciate the solitude this lake offers. Wrapped in a dramatic Sonoran Desert landscape, Apache Lake is a scenic oasis for water lovers and their pooches. For more information: Tonto National Forest Service (520) 467-2236.

Directions: Head north out of Apache Junction on Highway 88 until it becomes the Apache Trail and follow the signs for Apache Lake.

ASH FORK

LODGING
STAGECOACH MOTEL
823 Park Ave (86320) Rates: $20-$30;
Tel: (520) 637-2278

RECREATION

CEDAR CREEK TRAIL HIKE

Beginner/8.4 miles/4.5 hours

Info: Enrich your memory banks with an afternoon jaunt on this flat, easy trail through the scenic Sycamore Canyon Wilderness. The surrounding red rock cliffs make for great photographs. Tote enough water for you and the pupster. Avoid this trail during the summer- it's too hot. For more information: (520) 636-2302.

Directions: Take Highway 89 south from Interstate 40 (just east of Ash Fork) for about 15 miles. Take the Drake turnoff (Forest Road 680) southeast. From Drake take FR 492 for 11 miles to its end at FR 354. Take FR 354 south about 2 miles to FR 181. Turn left (east) and continue 6 miles to Henderson Flats and the trailhead.

LONESOME POCKET TRAIL HIKE

Expert/3.5 miles/2.0 hours

Info: You and your furry sidekick will get a genuine workout on this steep hike into the upper reaches of the Sycamore Canyon Wilderness. The breathtaking vistas from atop the rim overlooking Sycamore Canyon are your reward. A great spring or fall outing. For more information: (520) 636-2302.

Directions: From Interstate 40 (just east of Ash Fork) take Highway 89 south about 15 miles. Take the Drake turnoff (Forest Road 680) southeast to FR 492. Continue 11 miles to its end at FR 354. Take FR 354 south about 2 miles to FR 181. Turn left (east) and travel 6 miles to Henderson Flats and the trailhead.

BENSON

LODGING

BEST WESTERN QUAIL HOLLOW INN
699 N Ocotillo St (85602) Rates: $38-$48;
Tel: (520) 586-3646; (800) 528-1234

RECREATION

SWEETWATER CANYON TRAIL HIKE

Intermediate/6.0 miles/4.0 hours

Info: The prettiest time to take this lovely canyon hike to Wasson Peak is in the spring when the desert is in full bloom. You'll be dazzled by hyacinth, marigold, Mexican poppies, fairy duster, chia and filaree. Bring your binoculars, Gila woodpeckers, cardinals and fly-catchers are abundant. You might even be serenaded by canyon and cactus wrens as you and fur-face make your way through the towering walls of Sweetwater Canyon. Two miles into the hike, you'll reach a low saddle where the trail meets Kings Canyon and your ascent will begin. If you've planned a picnic lunch, this area contains some grassy, shaded spots.

The views over the next mile are spectacular-from the Sonoran Desert to the vast Avra and Altar Valleys. Those white-domed telescopes in the distance are on Kitt Peak. When the trail intersects the Hugh Norris Trail, you're just .3 miles from 4,687-foot Wasson Peak. If you're hiking on a blue sky day, you'll be able to count more than fifteen mountain ranges, stretching from the Superstitions east of Phoenix to Boboquivari Peak, close to the Mexican border. For more information: (520) 586-2842.

Directions: Head east on Interstate 10, exiting at Ruthrauff-Camino del Cerro west. Follow El Camino del Cerro until the pavement ends, turning left after .6 miles. Unless you have 4-wheel drive, park and walk the next mile to the trailhead.

BISBEE

<u>LODGING</u>

THE BISBEE INN BED & BREAKFAST
45 0K St (85603) Rates: $29-$45;
Tel: (520) 432-5131

MAIN STREET INN
26 Main St (85603) Rates: $40-$95;
Tel: (520) 432-5237; (800) 467-5237

MILE HIGH COURT TRAVEL LODGE
901 Tombstone Canyon (85603) Rates: $35-$50;
Tel: (520) 432-4636

PARK PLACE BED & BREAKFAST
200 E Vista in Warren (85603) Rates: $40-$60;
Tel: (602) 990-0682; (800) 456-0682

SAN JOSE LODGE & RV PARK
1002 Naco Hwy (85603) Rates: $35+;
Tel: (520) 432-5761

BOWIE

RECREATION

FORT BOWIE - APACHE PASS HISTORIC TRAIL - Leashes

Intermediate/6.5 miles/3.25 hours

Info: History buffs won't want to miss this trail, once a battleground between the cavalry and the Apache Indians. There's a trail guide available which will make your jaunt more interesting and educational. For more information: (520) 247-2500.

Directions: From Bowie, take Apache Pass Road south for approximately 15 miles to the parking area.

FORT BOWIE NATIONAL HISTORIC SITE - Leashes

Info: This site is a must-see for history hounds. Pick up a pamphlet for a little background information and prepare yourself for a strenuous 1.5 mile hike, amongst manzanita, mountain mahogany, willows, walnuts and cottonwoods. Visit in spring and treat yourself to a colorful wildflower display of baileyes, alionia and mallow. Bring binoculars - you just might spot a grey fox, coyote or bobcat. A visit in the summer can be hot so bring plenty of water.

Directions: Trailhead to the park is located on Apache Pass Road 13 miles south of Bowie off Interstate 10.

BULLHEAD CITY

LODGING

ARIZONA BLUFFS
2220 Karis Dr (86442) Rates: $192/week ;
Tel: (520) 763-3839

COLORADO RIVER RESORT
434 Riverglen Dr (86440) Rates: $25-$65;
Tel: (520) 754-4101

DAYS INN
2200 Karis Dr (86442) Rates: $38-$125;
Tel: (520) 758-1711; (800) 225-6903 (AZ)

DESERT RANCHO MOTEL
1041 Hwy 95 (86430) Rates: $30-$45;
Tel: (520) 754-2578

LA PLAZA INN
1978 Hwy 95 (86442) Rates: $26-$35;
Tel: (520) 763-8080

LAKE MOHAVE RESORT & MARINA
At Katherine Landing (86430) Rates: $60-$83;
Tel: (520) 754-3245; (800) 752-9669

MOTEL 6
1616 Hwy 95 (86442) Rates: $26-$36;
Tel: (520) 763-1002; (800) 440-6000

RIVER QUEEN RESORT MOTEL
125 Long Ave (86430) Rates: $35-$53;
Tel: (520) 754-3214

SUNRIDGE HOTEL & CONFERENCE ROOMS
839 Landon Dr (86429) Rates: $59+;
Tel: (520) 754-4700

TRAVELODGE
2360 4th St (86429) Rates: $40-$45;
Tel: (520) 754-3000; (800) 578-7878

RECREATION
COLORADO RIVERFRONT-SHORELINE TRAIL HIKE - Leashes
Beginner/6.0 miles/3.0 hours

Info: Walk along the banks of the Colorado with your pooch. Pack a picnic, kick back and enjoy the scenery as you listen to the rushing river. This is definitely a tailwagging way for mellow fellows to spend a Sunday afternoon. For more information: (520) 763-9400.

Directions: From Highway 95 go west on Riverview Drive to the trailhead.

CAMERON

LODGING
CAMERON TRADING POST MOTEL
Hwy 89, P. O. Box 83 (86020) Rates: $49-$79;
Tel: (520) 679-2231

CAMP VERDE

LODGING
BEST WESTERN CLIFF CASTLE LODGE
Middle Verde Rd, P. O. Box 3430 (86322)
Rates: $42-$150; Tel: (520) 567-6611; (800) 528-1234
FORT VERDE MOTEL
628 S Main St (86322) Rates: $35+;
Tel: (520) 567-3486

RECREATION
APACHE MAID TRAIL HIKE

Intermediate/1.0 to 19.0 miles/0.5 to 10.0 hours

Info: Collect incredible views of Wet Beaver Creek Canyon along this switchbacking trail through an area distinguished by ancient volcanic action. Casner Butte, the San Francisco Peaks and Sedona are other views afforded by this trail. But the best part of this panoramic hike is that you and your pooch are the judges of your day's hiking destiny. Hike a few miles or take the 9.5 mile (one way) trek to the lookout tower on the Apache Maid Mountain. Since there is parking at either end, a shuttle system is a great idea if you're hiking the entire trail one way. For more information: (520) 567-4501.

Directions: Head north on Interstate 17 to the Highway 179 exit. Drive east on Forest Road 618 for 1.5 miles to the Beaver Creek Ranger Station turnoff. Turn left (north) and drive for .25 miles to the trailhead and parking lot.

BELL TRAIL to BELL CROSSING HIKE

Intermediate/7.0 miles/3.5 hours

Info: This riparian oasis has a little something for everyone. You can lace up your boots and hike the day away in Wet Beaver Creek Canyon. Or detour down a side trail and spend the afternoon doggie paddling with your pooch in one of the canyon's delightful swimming holes. Most hikers and their water loving pups never even make it to Bell Crossing - the gurgling creek and deep pools are just too alluring. Don't forget your fishing pole, dinner beckons.

Dogs May Be Unleashed Unless Otherwise Indicated

Bell Crossing is the 3.5 mile mark to turn around and head back. If you want to continue further, your payback will be beautiful vistas of Sedona and the San Francisco Peaks. Park your fanny and your Fido on a lofty, grassy plateau and fill your eyes with some of nature's best. For more information: (520) 567-4501.

Directions: Head north on Interstate 17 to the Highway 179 exit. Drive east on Forest Road 618 for 1.5 miles to the Beaver Creek Ranger Station turnoff. Turn left (north) and drive for .25 miles to the trailhead and parking lot.

BLODGETT BASIN TRAIL HIKE

Intermediate/5.0 miles/2.5 hours

Info: Spend a delightful afternoon with the pupster at this canyon wonderland. Options include hiking, swimming, fishing, and picnicking.

The trail starts on a pinyon juniper flat where you'll descend 1,700-feet via switchbacks to the canyon floor and the cooling waters of West Clear Creek. This trail provides glimpses of one of the rarest habitats in the world - the creek is home to a desert riparian zone on which nearly 80% of Arizona's wildlife species are dependent. Chill out at the bottom, the return trip is all uphill. For more information: (520) 567-4501.

Directions: From Camp Verde, drive east on Highway 260 to FR 618. Go left and continue 4 miles to FR 214. Then turn right to the trailhead.

COLD WATER TRAIL HIKE - Leashes

Expert/11.4 miles/6.0 hours

Info: Not for the padded of paw, this challenging hike definitely tests your endurance. Bring plenty of water and munchies for refueling. Expect serenity and beauty. The silence will be broken only by the serenade of songbirds and the wind rustling the pinyon and juniper pines. You will have traveled four miles when you cross Cold Water Creek and begin a brief descent. If you've had your fill, this is the perfect place for a 180° because the trail climbs very steeply to Tule Mesa at the end.

If you continue further to Cold Water Spring, keep a snout out for a stunning stand of Arizona cypress trees. All along the trail, the rough and rocky terrain and the ubiquitous Verde River enhance the scenery. For more information call (520) 567-4121.

Directions: Take Salt Mine Road. (FR 574) south 14.5 miles south to Gap Creek. Park at the locked gate and walk .3 miles to the Cedar Bench Wilderness boundary where the trail begins.

FORT VERDE STATE HISTORIC PARK - Leashes

Info: Military mutts will love this historic park. The park sits on 12 acres of land, so a picnic lunch might be a fun idea. Fido is prohibited from entering the museum, but can visit the homes of the three officers who lived on the site long ago. These interesting, restored buildings contain period furnishings allowing visitors a peek into the past. What's that tail wagging for? A reenactment? Lucky dogs visiting in mid-October or near Armed Forces Day can get a sense of early army life by observing costumed volunteers who actually live on-site for the weekend.

Directions: From Camp Verde, head east on Highway 260 to the park entrance.

Note: $2 per vehicle entrance fee. Call for reenactment information and requests: (520) 567-3275.

HOT LOOP TRAIL to HORSE MESA HIKE

Intermediate/Expert/8.0 miles/4.5 hours

Info: You and your faithful sidekick are in for a workout on this demanding canyon hike. The trail begins along an old jeep road which is actually the start of the Woods Canyon Trail. Watch for the metal sign indicating the Hot Loop Trail. The trail begins its canyon climb to the top of Horse Mesa, leveling out as it crosses a flat plain to an overlook with panoramas of Red Rock Country. Expert hikers can lengthen the hike by continuing another 2 miles to Woods Canyon. Caution: during spring snowmelt and after summer thunderstorms, this area can experience flash floods. For more information: (520) 282-4119.

Directions: Take Interstate 17 north to Highway 179 and head northwest toward Sedona. Approximately 2 miles past the Jacks Canyon Road turnoff, you'll come to a dirt road on the left side of Highway 179. Proceed through the closed gate to the parking area. Hike along the Woods Canyon Trail to the marked signage for Hot Loop Trail.

JACKS CANYON TRAIL HIKE

Intermediate/Expert/11.4 miles/6.0 hours

Info: For an aerial view of glorious Red Rock Country, Jacks Canyon Trail is the next best thing to flying. The trail follows an old jeep road to Jacks Canyon Tank before dropping into the drainage bottom. You'll then begin to climb by crisscrossing a dry streambed. When you reach the upper canyon, the trail snakes up to a high saddle which connects the Mogollon Rim and Munds Mountain. If the pup isn't pooped, continue further. The views from atop Munds Mountain are worth the workout. For more information: (520) 282-4119.

Directions: Take Interstate 17 north to Highway 179 and head northwest toward Sedona. About 7.3 miles south of Sedona is Jacks Canyon Road. Turn right (east) and go 3 miles to the trailhead.

MAIL TRAIL HIKE

Intermediate/6.2 miles/3.0 hours

Info: A riparian oasis awaits exploration on this trail beginning atop the Mogollon Rim and bottoming out in the Fossil Springs Wilderness. The trail passes through a luxuriant and varied riparian area created by the permanent water from the springs. The springs pour out over a million gallons of water an hour, creating an incredibly diverse oasis which provides a habitat for over 30 species of trees and shrubs and 100 species of birds.

As you and the dawgus delve deeper into the wilderness, the trail becomes harder to follow. When you reach a grassland, follow the rock cairns to stay on track as follows: the trail turns north, traverses a small drainage, runs next to Fossil Creek, crosses Mud Tank Draw, heads east, crosses Fossil Creek, meets up with Fossil Springs Trail and ends after one final creek crossing. For more information: (520) 567-4501.

Directions: Take Highway 260 east for 13 miles (past West Clear Creek Bridge) to FR 9247B, turn right. Follow FR 9247B (as it parallels the powerlines) to the road just past the cattle guard and turn left. This road leads to the parking area near the stock tank. On the east side of the parking area, follow the rock cairns to the beginning of the trail. FR 9247B is recommended for high-clearance vehicles only.

Note: High clearance vehicles only.

MONTEZUMA CASTLE NATIONAL MONUMENT - Leashes

Info: These impressive 5-story, 20-room cliff dwelling ruins were abandoned by the Sinagua Indians in the early 1400's. The .5 mile self-guided tour is an interesting, history-laden walk. For more information: (520) 567-3322.

Directions: From Camp Verde, take Interstate 17 north to Exit 289. Follow the signs for three miles to the monument.

Note: $2.00 per person entrance fee.

TOWEL CREEK TRAIL HIKE

Intermediate/7.0 miles/4.0 hours

Info: Spend a pleasant afternoon with your tail wagger hiking this trail (popular with local ranchers moving cattle between seasonal ranges). Depending on the distance covered, you'll experience vegetation ranging from manzanita, scrub oak, sycamore, willow and cottonwood on the lower sections to juniper and pinyon on higher ground. Don't miss the short side hike to Towel Spring...the scenery is a definite two paws up. Towel Creek is the turnaround spot. For more information: (520) 567-4501.

Locate Other Dog-Friendly Activities...Check Nearby Cities

Directions: From Camp Verde, head east on Highway 260 approximately 6 miles to FR 708. Turn right (southeast) and go about 9 miles to the trailhead near Needle Rock.

WEIR TRAIL HIKE

Beginner/6.0 miles/3.0 hours

Info: As you and your pup make your way to Wet Beaver Creek, note the striking change in the vegetation. Juniper, agave, catclaw and prickly pear give way to riparian vegetation such as willow, cottonwood, sycamore, ash and oops poison ivy. Remember, leaves of three, let it be. Good news for fishing Fidos, the creek is home to bass, trout and round-tail chub. For more information: (520) 567-4501.

Directions: Take Interstate 17 north to Exit 298 (Sedona). Head east on 618 to FR 618A. Take 618A for 2 miles and make a left into the parking lot. From the parking lot, it's a 2.25 mile hike to the junction of Bell Trail #13 and Weir Trail. The Weir Trailhead begins at the information board on Bell Trail.

WEST CLEAR CREEK TRAIL HIKE - Leashes

Intermediate/1.0-15.5 miles/0.5-8.0 hours

Info: Cover the distance on this one and your pooch will earn his kibble. The streamside trail requires several crossings, so be prepared for wet paws. You can make this a loop trail by hiking to FR 214 and walking 1.3 miles to Blodgett Basin Trail #31. Follow a side canyon down the rim back to the West Clear Creek Trail. Pristine and seldom traveled, you can really become one with nature on this outing. For more information: (520) 567-4501.

Directions: From Camp Verde, take Highway 260 east to FR 618. Go left and follow for 2 miles to FR 215. Take a right into the park.

CAREFREE

LODGING

THE BOULDERS
34631 N Tom Darlington Rd (85377)
Rates: $240-$525; Tel: (602) 488-9009; (800) 553-1717

RECREATION

SEVEN SPRINGS RECREATION AREA/
CAVE CREEK TRAIL HIKE

Intermediate/10.0 miles/5.0 hours

Info: In just five hours, you'll experience an unbelievably diverse display of nature on this scenic trail in the Seven Springs Recreation Area of the Tonto National Forest. From open desert terrain and desert plantlife to sycamore woodlands, juniper forests and invigorating swimming holes, this trail has it all. In autumn, thick rustly leaf beds make perfect playtime spots for Spot. There are a number of interconnecting trails to vary your hiking experience.

You and the pooch can begin your hike on Cave Creek Trail before heading left on Cottonwood Trail. To stay en route, turn right on Skunk Creek Trail and link up with Cave Creek Trail. Go right for the return leg of the hike. A bit of boulder hopping is required to cross Cave Creek, the icing on an already spectacular day trip. For more information: (602) 488-3441.

Directions: Take Cave Creek Road east for 17 miles. After 9 miles, the paved road gives way to the gravel of Forest Service Road 24. Take FR 24 north to the Seven Springs Campground. The trailhead is a half mile beyond the campground.

CASA GRANDE

LODGING

BEST WESTERN CASA GRANDE SUITES
665 Via Del Cielo (85222) Rates: $59-$99;
Tel: (520) 836-1600; (800) 528-1234

FRANCISCO GRANDE RESORT & GOLF CLUB
26000 Gila Bend Hwy (85222) Rates: $56-$196;
Tel: (520) 836-6444; (800) 237-4238

HOLIDAY INN CASA GRANDE
777 N Pinal Ave (85222) Rates: $58-$72;
Tel: (520) 426-3500;
(800) 858-4499 (AZ); (800) 465-4329 (US)

MOTEL 6
4965 N Sunland Gin Rd (85222) Rates: $32-$38;
Tel: (520) 836-3323; (800) 440-6000

SE-TAY MOTEL
901 N Pinal Ave (85222) Rates: $29-$40;
Tel: (520) 836-7489

SUNLAND INN
7190 S Sunland Gin Rd (85222) Rates: $32-$38;
Tel: (520) 836-5000

RECREATION
CALLOWAY TRAIL HIKE
Beginner/1.0 miles/0.5 hours

Info: When you and pooch-face are short on time, but long for exercise and fresh air, this easy-does-it leg stretcher is a perfect hike. Massive, volcanic Picacho Peak towers above as you traverse its base. Come springtime, the peak puts on an impressive wildflower show. For more information: (520) 466-3183.

Directions: From Interstate 10 south of Casa Grande take Picacho Peak Road (exit 219) west into the park. Follow the road to the trailhead.

Note: $3.00 per vehicle entrance fee.

CATALINA

RECREATION
CATALINA STATE PARK/
50-YEAR TRAIL HIKE - Leashes
Intermediate/1.0-15.6 miles/0.5-8.0 hours

Info: This is one of many trails within the 5,500-acre Catalina State Park. No matter how far in you hike, you'll be awestruck by the scenery. Whether you saunter a mile or travel for ten, the Sonoran Desert will move you with its quiet beauty. The Pusch Ridge Wilderness and the Santa Catalina Mountains create a stunning backdrop for all photographers. Leash up the pup and set out for an amazing desert adventure. For more information: (520) 628-5798.

Directions: Take Highway 77 to Catalina State Park. Trailhead is located beyond the campground.

Note: $3.00 per vehicle entrance fee.

Locate Other Dog-Friendly Activities...Check Nearby Cities

CHAMBERS

LODGING

BEST WESTERN CHIEFTAIN INN
P. O. Box 39 (86502) Rates: $54-$69;
Tel: (520) 688-2754; (800) 528-1234

CHANDLER

LODGING

ALOHA MOTEL
445 N Arizona Ave (85224) Rates: $79-$200;
Tel: (602) 963-3403

SUPER 8 MOTEL
7171 W Chandler Blvd (85226) Rates: $41-$66;
Tel: (602) 961-3888; (800) 800-8000

WYNDHAM GARDEN HOTEL
7475 W Chandler Blvd (85226) Rates: $73-$115;
Tel: (602) 961-4444; (800) 822-4200

RECREATION

CASA GRANDE RUINS NATIONAL MONUMENT - Leashes

Info: The four-story, free-standing structure built by the ancient Hohokam people became the first Federal Archeological Preserve in 1892. Take the self-guided tour through the monument grounds. For more information: (520) 723-3172.

Directions: Take Country Club Drive (Highway 87) south. Follow Highway 87 to the town of Coolidge. The monument is located at the north end of town. Follow the signs.

Note: $2.00 per vehicle entrance fee.

Dogs May Be Unleashed Unless Otherwise Indicated

SUNRAY PARK - Leashes

Info: Hidden behind the southern mountains, this 15-acre sports-minded park is one of Chandler's secrets. Open ball fields create plenty of fetching space for Fido.

Directions: Located at 40th Street and Ray Road.

CHINLE

LODGING
HOLIDAY INN-CANYON DE CHELLEY/CHINLE
BIA Rt 7, P. O. Box 1889 (86503) Rates: $59-$109;
Tel: (520) 674-5000; (800) 465-4329

CLARKDALE

LODGING
BIRD'S EYE VIEW BED & BREAKFAST/GUEST COTTAGES
Hwy 89A (86324) Rates: $55-$75; Monthly: $600;
Tel: (602) 990-0682; (800) 456-0682

CLIFTON

RECREATION
HAGAN CORRAL TRAIL HIKE
Expert/6.2 miles/3.0 hours

Info: A 1,500-foot change in elevation through rugged terrain accounts for the difficulty rating of this trail. Beginning at 7,200 feet, you'll connect with the Strayhorse Trail at 5,700 feet. For more information: (520) 359-9026.

Directions: Take Highway 191 north for 47 miles to the trailhead on the east side of the highway.

Note: This area is remote. Inform someone of your plans and carry a map.

LENGTHY TRAIL HIKE

Expert/6.6 miles/3.5 hours

Info: You and Bowser can boogie on this one. Starting at 7,200 feet, you'll quickly and steeply drop to the canyon bottom at 6,000 feet. The trail zigzags through a pretty forest of oak and pine. If you've packed a biscuit basket, now's the time to chow down. You'll need some energy for the uphill return. For more information: (520) 359-9026.

Directions: Take Highway 191 north for 50 miles to the signed trailhead on the east side of the highway. If you reach the Strayhorse Campground, you've gone 5 miles too far.

Note: This area is remote. Inform someone of your plans and carry a map.

SPUR CROSS TRAIL HIKE

Intermediate/12.0 miles/6.0 hours

Info: Get a healthy dose of exercise on this somewhat difficult trail. Enjoy great vistas of the Painted Bluff Mountains, Grey's Peak and the San Carlos Apache Indian Reservation. The trail ascends to 6,900 feet before dropping down into Dark Canyon. This is an isolated, wilderness hike, so be prepared and head home once you and Rover have roved enough. For more information: (520) 687-1301.

Directions: Take Highway 191 north through Morenci to the Granville Campground. The trailhead is at the upper end of the campground.

Note: This area is remote. Inform someone of your plans and carry a map.

Dogs May Be Unleashed Unless Otherwise Indicated

COTTONWOOD

LODGING

BEST WESTERN COTTONWOOD INN
993 S Main St (86326) Rates: $50-$99;
Tel: (520) 634-5576;
(800) 528-1234 (US); (800) 350-0025 (AZ)

LITTLE DAISY MOTEL
34 S Main St (86326) Rates: $36-$40;
Tel: (520) 634-7865

THE VIEW MOTEL
818 S Main St (86326) Rates: $34-$48;
Tel: (520) 634-7581

RECREATION

BLACK CANYON TRAIL HIKE

Intermediate/9.0 miles/4.5 hours

Info: You'll definitely break out in a sweat and Fido will surely be panting at the top of this one. The trail climbs steeply from 4,100 feet to 6,000 feet and ends with extraordinary bird's-eye views of Red Rock Country, the San Francisco Peaks and the Verde Valley. The trail continues 2.1 miles further up Gaddes Canyon to FR 413 ascending another 500 feet. For more information: (520) 567-4121.

Directions: From Cottonwood, take Highway 260 south for 4.5 miles to Forest Road 335 which becomes Forest Road 359. Turn west (right) and drive 4.5 miles to Quail Springs and the trailhead.

COLEMAN TRAIL HIKE

Beginner/Expert/3.6 miles/2.0 hours

Info: After the first mile or so of this trail, you'll probably wonder why the expert rating. Wonder no more. The last 1/2 mile of trail involves a steep switchbacking descent to the junction of FR 413. Use caution, this section of trail may be severely eroded making it difficult to maintain your footing. It's a good idea to leash your buddy for this section. The trail affords terrific views of the Verde Valley and the Red Rock Country in a woodsy setting of ponderosa, alligator juniper, turbinella oak and deerbrush. For more information: (520) 567-4121.

Directions: Take Highway 89A west 10 miles to Forest Road 104. Take FR 104 south (left) for 2.6 miles to the Mingus Mountain Campground. At the campground take the right fork and go .5 miles to the trailhead.

DEAD HORSE RANCH STATE PARK - Leashes

Info: Spend an idyllic day hiking, fishing or picnicking in this tranquil 325-acre park. Quetta pines and cottonwoods offer plenty of shade for you and the pupster to laze the day away beside the Verde River.

Dead Horse Ranch State Park and the adjoining Verde River Greenway, provide a spectacular setting for outdoor recreational and educational opportunities in the heart of the Verde Valley. The park offers camping and day-use facilities, and the lagoon and Verde River are popular for fishing. The elevation makes this parkland an ideal setting year-round. Information is available at the Ranger Station as you enter the park. For more information: (520) 634-5283.

Directions: From Cottonwood, take Main Street to 10th Street and turn north. Cross the river via the bridge to the park entrance.

Note: $5 per vehicle entrance fee.

1) HICKEY DITCH TRAIL HIKE - Leashes

Beginner/2.5 miles/1.0 hours

Info: Are you and your furry friend in the mood for a hike, but not a workout? Then head for this no-sweat trail in Dead Horse Ranch State Park. Don't forget your binoculars, this place is heavensent for birdwatchers. For more information: (520) 634-5283.

Directions: Take Main Street to 10th Street and turn north. Cross the river via the bridge and continue on to any of the day use areas. The trail is accessible from various locations in the park.

2) VERDE RIVER GREENWAY TRAIL HIKE - Leashes

Beginner/1.5 miles/1.0 hours

Info: This easy trail skirts riverside and loops around the lagoon in Dead Horse State Park where picnicking and fishing opportunities abound. For more information: (520) 634-5283.

Directions: Take Main Street to 10th Street, turning north. Cross the river via the bridge and continue on to the River Day Use Area.

GADDES CANYON TRAIL HIKE

Intermediate/4.6 miles/2.5 hours

Info: For an aerial view of Gaddes Canyon, simply follow this ponderosa-clad trail. The trail makes an initial descent to Gaddes Spring where your aquatic pup can do a little paw dipping before continuing to the ridgetop overlook for the canyon. Delight in the scenery before tackling the last leg of your trip - a steep drop to the junction of FR 413. Don't be surprised if you happen upon a deer or two during your journey. For more information: (520) 567-4121.

Directions: Take Highway 89A west about 10 miles to Forest Road 104. Take FR 104 south (left) for 2.25 miles to the Mingus Mountain Recreation Area. From there take Lookout Road (FR 104B) south. The trailhead is .1 mile past the lookout trailhead on the left side of the road.

LITTLE YEAGER TRAIL HIKE

Intermediate/3.8 miles/2.0 hours

Info: Easy may describe the first half mile of this trail which traverses a ridge, but the going gets tough with a vertical, switchbacking descent into Yeager Canyon ending at Highway 89A. If you and puppy-face still want more, there's a trail connecting the Yeager Canyon Trail with the Yeager Cabin Trail, a 5.7 mile loop. For more information: (520) 567-4121.

Directions: Take Highway 89A west about 10 miles to Forest Road 104. Take FR 104 south for 1.3 miles to FR 413. Take FR 413 west for .8 miles, then south for 1.4 miles to FR 132. Follow FR 132 southwest to where it intersects FR 105. Go west on FR 105 for .4 miles to the trailhead, just past the trailhead for Yeager Cabin Trail (#111).

LOY CANYON TRAIL HIKE

Beginner/6.0 miles/3.0 hours

Info: Looking for a simple, yet extremely panoramic hike? The Loy Canyon Trail fits the bill. A gradual climb takes you through the chaparral-clad canyon. Backdropped by beautiful reddish colored bluffs and cliffs, you'll encounter fascinating rock formations carved by years of water runoff. If you visit shortly after a rainstorm, you might happen upon rejuvenating pools, perfect spots to escape the summer heat. For a more aerobic workout, continue another two miles to the summit of Secret Mountain and some "see forever" views. For more information: (520) 282-4119.

Directions: From Highway 89A north, take Forest Road 525 north for 9.3 miles to the trailhead.

NORTH MINGUS TRAIL HIKE

Intermediate/7.4 miles/3.5 hours

Info: Autumn is the best time to hike the northern slope of Mingus Mountain. The rich, fall colors of aspens, maples and oaks paint the landscape. The cushy leaves underfoot and the distant horizon of the Verde Valley, Cottonwood and Jerome will make this day a memorable one.

The trail heads north for .75 miles before descending steeply for a half-mile to the junction of TR #105A. In order to reach the north side of the mountain, stay on the main trail which heads northwest. Once you reach the intersection of FR 338, it's time to turn around and retrace your steps. For more information: (520) 567-4121.

Directions: Take Highway 89A west about 10 miles to Forest Road 104. Take FR 104 south (left) for 2.6 miles to the Mingus Mountain Campground. At the campground take the left hand fork to the hang-glider site and the trailhead.

PARSONS TRAIL HIKE

Beginner/8.0 miles/4.0 hours

Info: This delightfully shaded trail through Sycamore Canyon is effortless and beautiful. Stunning multi-colored cliffs and bluffs surround you as you stroll amid a lush, riparian oasis. You and the wonderdog won't be the only ones admiring the landscape, this is one of the region's most popular trails. Parson Springs marks an end to the trail, but the views on the return trip will restock your memory bank. For more information: (520) 282-4119.

Directions: From Highway 89A south, take the Tuzigoot National Monument turnoff. Turn right, and go over the Verde River, then immediately turn left onto Forest Road 131. Follow FR 131 for 11 miles through twists and turns to the sign directing you to the trailhead.

RAILROAD DRAW TRAIL HIKE - Leashes

Intermediate/Beginner/6.0 miles/3.0 hours

Info: After the initial short but steep ascent from Sycamore Creek, the trail levels off for an easy-does-it hike through the Sycamore Canyon Wilderness. When you reach the junction of FR 639, turn around and go back. For more information: (520) 636-2302.

Directions: From Highway 89A south, take the Tuzigoot National Monument turnoff. After crossing the bridge immediately turn left onto the road paralleling the river (Forest Road 131). Stay on FR 131 for 10 miles to Sycamore Canyon overlook, Packard Ranch and Sycamore Creek. Past the Packard Ranch, the road gets rougher. After 1.5 miles you'll come to a gate which may or may not be locked. The trailhead is 1.3 miles past the gate.

TUZIGOOT NATIONAL MONUMENT - Leashes

Info: Built between 1100 and 1450 A.D., the Tuzigoot ruins are among the largest pueblos of the ancient Sinagua people. The two-story main building contains over 100 rooms. There's a quarter-mile, self-guided loop trail which includes informative displays. For more information: (520) 634-5564.

Directions: From Highway 89A south, take the Tuzigoot National Monument turnoff. Follow the signs to the monument's entrance.

VIEW POINT TRAIL HIKE

Intermediate/3.8 miles/2.0 hours

Info: For an autumnal outing you and the dawgus won't soon forget, hike Mingus Mountain and see how the greens of summer give way to the reds and yellows of fall. And treat your pup to some frolicking fun in a pile of newly fallen leaves.

This well-maintained trail begins with a steep .75 mile descent, continues on to the junction of TR #105A, then terminates in a half mile at FR 413. Along the way you'll find yourself oohing and aahing at the loveliness of your surroundings. For more information: (520) 567-4121.

Directions: Take Highway 89A west about 10 miles to Forest Road 104. Take FR 104 south for 2.6 miles to the Mingus Mountain Campground. The trailhead is in the campground.

YEAGER CABIN TRAIL HIKE

Beginner/3.6 miles/1.5 hours

Info: This feel good trail is perfect for those lazy, spring days when you and your couch slouch don't feel like doing much but still long for the great outdoors. This hike beside the drainage of Little Yeager Canyon requires little time and even less effort. The trail is part of a 5.7 mile loop, along with the Yeager Canyon Trail and the Little Yeager Trail #111. For more information: (520) 567-4121.

Directions: Take Highway 89A west about 10 miles to Forest Road 104. Take FR 104 south for 1.3 miles to FR 413. Take FR 413 west for .8 miles to the #28 trailhead. Follow this trail for .1 miles to where it intersects the Yeager Cabin Trail.

YEAGER CANYON TRAIL HIKE

Intermediate/4.0 miles/2.0 hours

Info: Deciduous describes the first section of trail along the bottom of Yeager Canyon. Difficult describes the switchbacking climb out of the canyon to the ponderosa pine-clad western slope of Mingus Mountain.

At this point, you have two options - either retrace your steps or take advantage of the inter-connecting trail system. Yeager Canyon Trail is the initial trail which connects with the 1.8 mile Yeager Cabin Trail, and the 1.9 mile Little Yeager Trail completes the 5.7 mile loop. For more information: (520) 567-4121.

Directions: Take Highway 89A west for approximately 12 miles. The trailhead is on the east (right) side of the highway. If you see the twin powerlines, you've gone 1.5 miles too far west.

CROWN KING

Cool off on a sweltering day with a visit to the hidden (aka rustic) oasis of Crown King. Even when it's over 100° in Phoenix, there's a good chance you'll need a sweater by the time you reach Crown King. An undiscovered gem (if you have a four-wheel drive vehicle and a tushie cushion), plan a visit when you're not in a big hurry. The ride is slow going and b-b-b-bumpy.

Heading north from Phoenix on Interstate 17, take the exit to Crown King. In minutes, you'll be saying goodbye to smooth going. The rocky road climbs from the desert floor and rises through low and then high chaparral before reaching the green-ery of the Prescott National Forest. Take your time, the twisting, turning mountain road offers plenty of visual appeal. Once you arrive at Crown King, the itsy bitsy town at the top, you'll find a small cafe and general store and a passel of friendly mutts to greet your own. Don't be surprised to see snow on the ground, even in June. During the day, the tem-peratures are probably thirty degrees cooler in this mountaintop region.

RECREATION
EAST FORT TRAIL HIKE

Beginner/1.6 miles/0.75 hours

Info: If only all things in life could be as simple and pleasant as this wilderness hike. The trail traverses the Bradshaw Mountains, passing granite boulders that are nearly 2 billion years old - talk about ancient. Before you and the pupster know it, you're at your destination - East Fort Ruin. This old Indian fortress is a protected archaeological site, so paws off. Leave only footprints, take only memories. For more information: (520) 445-7253.

Directions: From Crown King take FR 259A south for .5 miles to FR 52. Then take FR 52 southeast approximately eight miles. Past the Kentuck Campground take the right fork (staying on FR 52) for another mile to the trailhead.

HORSETHIEF CANYON TRAIL HIKE

Intermediate/Expert/3.7 miles/2.0 hours

Info: As the name implies, this trail was once used by outlaws to transport stolen horses to their headquarters - the Horsethief Ranch. The days of horse thievery may be over, but the trail lives on. It's now a popular hiking route into the scenic Castle Creek Wilderness affording hikers an up-close look at granite and metamorphic boulders as old as 1.8 billion years.

The trail begins on the southern slope of Bradshaw Mountain with an immediate 1,000-foot descent into Horsethief Canyon. This rather steep drop takes you through forests of ponderosa pine and pinyon-juniper. The junction for Trail #225 is your signal to turn around and retrace your steps. For more information: (520) 445-7253.

Directions: From Crown King take FR 259A south for .5 miles to FR 52F. Then take FR 52F southeast for 7.5 miles to the Turney Gulch Campground. If you're in a sedan, park at the campground and hike up to the trailhead. FR 52F becomes a 4 wheel drive road for the remaining .5 miles to the trailhead.

KENTUCK TRAIL HIKE

Intermediate/2.2 miles/1.5 hours

Info: For wonderful vistas of Black Canyon, the Bradshaw and New River Mountains follow this relatively short trail to the Horsethief Lookout Tower. It's a steady climb to the tower, but the views are worth the effort. If there's a lookout on duty, the tower will be open to the public. If you and your sidekick aren't ready to call it quits, the trail continues past the tower another mile to the junction of FR 9236B. For more information: (520) 445-7253.

Directions: From Crown King take FR 259A south for .5 miles to FR 52. Then take FR 52 east for five miles to Kentuck Spring Campground. The trailhead is located on the inner circle of the campground between sites #14 and #15.

LANE TRAIL HIKE

Expert/6.4 miles/3.5 hours

Info: Definitely not for the fair of paw or out of shape. Only experienced hikers and their hounddogs need apply (their skills) for this one. Located in the most demanding section of the southern Bradshaws, the trail starts at 7,000 feet and slithers to Lion Springs, a sometimes watering hole for thirsty mountain lions, (hence the name.) Continuing downhill, the trail leads to Lane Mine and then follows a switchback descent into Copper Basin at 4,400 feet. The junction of FR 9268K signals the halfway point - time to turn around and climb back to the trailhead. The fact that the trail is not well maintained adds to the difficulty level. For more information: (520) 445-7253.

Directions: From Crown King take FR 259A south for .5 miles to FR 52. Then take FR 52 southeast 4 miles to FR 100. Follow FR 100, (a high clearance vehicle road), a short distance southeast to the trailhead at road's end.

Note: High clearance vehicles only. Or park at FR 100 and walk to the trailhead.

DOUGLAS

LODGING

MOTEL 6
111 16th St (85607) Rates: $26-$32;
Tel: (520) 364-2457; (800) 440-6000

PRICE CANYON GUEST RANCH
P. O. Box 1065 (85607) Rates: $85-$170;
Tel: (520) 558-2383

THRIFTLODGE
1030 19th St (85607) Rates: $32-$45;
Tel: (520) 364-8434;
(800) 578-7878 (US); (800) 525-9055 (AZ)

DRAGOON

LODGING

KELLY'S WHISTLESTOP BED & BREAKFAST
I-10 & Hwy 191 (85609) Rates: $50-$60;
Tel: (602) 990-0682; (800) 456-0682

DUGAS

BEEHOUSE TRAIL HIKE

Intermediate/Expert/8.0 miles/4.0 hours

Info: Beehouse Canyon lends itself to a hiking excursion you won't soon forget. But use caution when you traverse the steep, rocky terrain of the canyon - certain sections of the trail are eroded. The ruggedness of the hike diminishes once you climb out of the canyon. The trail continues south another 2 miles to its end at the junction of Trail #159. Retrace your steps for your return. For more information: (520) 567-4121.

Directions: Take FR 68 (Dugas Road) southeast for 18 miles to the Pine Flat Trailhead (#159) which is 1.25 miles east of Double-T Ranch on Sycamore Creek. Park at the Salt Flats Campground and hike along Nelson Trail #159 for .8 miles to the junction with Beehouse Trail.

Note: High clearance vehicles only.

NELSON TRAIL HIKE

Intermediate/6.5 miles/3.0 hours

Info: This is more than a trail, it's the link connecting the outside world to the labyrinth of trails within the Pine Mountain Wilderness. Hike along this pathway and enter a world of infinite outdoor adventures. You and your hiking hound won't want the day to end. Turn around at the junction of Willow Springs Trail (#12). For more information: (520) 567-4121.

Directions: Take Forest Road 68 (Dugas Road) east approximately 18 miles to the trailhead. Be sure to stay right when FR 68 forks with FR 68G.

Note: High clearance vehicles only.

NELSON TRAIL to PINE MOUNTAIN TRAIL HIKE

Intermediate/8.9 miles/4.5 hours

Info: If you're looking for the trail less traveled, this is it. A quasi-extension of the Nelson Trail, Pine Mountain is often overlooked by other hikers. Once you reach the junction of Pine Mountain Trail, the initial quarter-mile is a steep climb. Then it's smooth sailing to the Verde Rim. The trail crosses a region damaged by the wildfire of 1989. Take a few minutes to examine the regeneration process of the forest - it's humbling. For more information: (520) 567-4121.

Directions: Take Forest Road 68 (Dugas Road) east approximately 18 miles to the trailhead. Be sure to stay right where FR 68 forks with FR 68G. Follow the Nelson Trailhead for 3.25 miles to its intersection with Pine Mountain Trail.

Note: High clearance vehicles only.

NELSON TRAIL to WILLOW SPRINGS TRAIL HIKE

Intermediate/9.7 miles/5.0 hours

Info: Branching off the Nelson Trail, Willow Springs begins a steady 750-foot ascent through a riparian bottom. Evergreens, maples, deciduous oaks and aspens line the trail, while javelina, mule deer, elk and white-tailed deer roam the terrain. From atop the Verde Rim, you'll have the opportunity to gaze upon Four Peaks, the Superstitions and Red Rock Country. For more information: (520) 567-4121.

Directions: Take Forest Road 68 (Dugas Road) east approximately 18 miles to the trailhead. Be sure to stay right where FR 68 forks with FR 68G. Follow the Nelson Trailhead for 2.75 miles to where it intersects the Willow Springs Trail.

Note: High clearance vehicles only.

PINE FLAT TRAIL HIKE

Intermediate/6.4 miles/3.0 hours

Info: This trail traverses rocky terrain in Beehouse Canyon. It begins with a quick jaunt on the Nelson Trail before branching off to Pine Flat Trail. Once the trail climbs out of the rugged canyon, it's downhill for 2 miles before hooking up once again with the Nelson Trail. For more information: (520) 567-4121.

Directions: Take Forest Road 68 (Dugas Road) east approximately 18 miles to the trailhead. Stay right at the fork on FR 68 and FR 68G. Follow the Nelson Trailhead for .8 miles to where it intersects the Pine Flat Trail. This .8 mile jaunt adds 1.6 miles to the total length of the hike.

Note: High clearance vehicles only.

VERDE RIM TRAIL HIKE - Leashes

Intermediate/1.0-15.2 miles/0.5-8.0 hours

Info: When you and the pupster are seeking peace, solitude and pristine wilderness, this is the trail for you. Even in summer, you'll find shade beneath the pine-scented ponderosas. A challenging hike, the rugged, get-away-from-it-all feeling of the place will make you wish the day would never end. For more information: (520) 567-4121.

Directions: From Dugas, go east on Dugas Road (FR 68 east) to Tule Mesa and the trailhead.

Note: This area is remote. Inform someone of your plans and carry a map.

EAGAR

LODGING

BEST WESTERN SUNRISE INN
128 N Main St (85925) Rates: $42-$99;
Tel: (520) 333-2540; (800) 528-1234

RECREATION

PHELPS TRAIL HIKE (formerly East Baldy Trail)

Intermediate/6.0 miles/3.0 hours

Info: Visit Colorado in Arizona. Get a taste of the Rocky Mountains on this alpine-like hike through the Mount Baldy Wilderness. About 3 miles into the hike when you encounter very mature Douglas firs and ponderosa pines, retrace your path. For more information: (520) 333-4372.

Directions: Take Highway 260 west to Highway 273 south on the Fort Apache Reservation. Highway 273 crosses into the Apache-Sitgreaves National Forest. Turn on FR 113G to the trailhead at Phelps/Horse Corrals, north of the Phelps Ranger Station.

SHEEP CROSSING TRAIL HIKE

Intermediate/12.0 miles/6.5 hours

Info: Summer heat got you down? Then pack your gear and head for the cool confines of the White Mountains. Make tracks along the west fork of the Little Colorado River and listen as warblers and gray jays sing a song from their lofty perches.

You'll begin your trek at 9,300 feet and climb through alpine meadows to 11,200 feet, just 1 mile short of the top of Mt. Baldy, an extinct volcano. Since Mt. Baldy is sacred to the Apaches, hiking is prohibited. For more information: (520) 333-4372.

Directions: Take Highway 260 west to Highway 273 on the Fort Apache Reservation. Take 273 south and into Apache-Sitgreaves National Forest to FR 113. Look for the trailhead on the west side, approximately 8 miles in from Highway 260.

SOUTH FORK TRAIL HIKE

Beginner/Intermediate/12.0 miles/6.0 hours

Info: A do-your-own-thing hike, you and Fido can make this a leg stretcher or a full-day excursion. The trail zigzags through South Fork Canyon, a dense forestland with lots of shade, piney scents and memorable views of Mount Baldy and Mount Thomas. You'll ascend through a stand of ponderosa pine before reaching Mexican Hay Lake, a fine place for a picnic lunch. For more information: (520) 333-4372.

Directions: Take Highway 260 west approximately five miles to Forest Road 560. Take FR 560 south for two miles to the trailhead at South Fork Campground.

EHRENBERG

<u>LODGING</u>

BEST WESTERN FLYING J MOTEL
P. O. Box 801 (85334) Rates: $40-$60;
Tel: (520) 923-9711;
(800) 528-1234 (US); (800) 292-9711 (AZ)

FLAGSTAFF

<u>LODGING</u>

ARIZONA MOUNTAIN INN
685 Lake Mary Rd (86001) Rates: $65-$100;
Tel: (520) 774-8959; (800) 239-5236

BEST WESTERN KINGS HOUSE MOTEL
1560 Santa Fe (86001) Rates: $42-$85;
Tel: (520) 774-7186; (800) 528-1234

COMFORT INN
914 S Milton Rd (86001) Rates: $38-$88;
Tel: (520) 774-7326; (800) 221-2222

DAYS INN HWY 66
1000 W Route 66 (86001) Rates: $48-$85;
Tel: (520) 774-5221; (800) 329-7466

DAYS INN I-40
2735 S Woodlands Village Blvd (86001)
Rates: $60-$90; Tel: (520) 779-1575; (800) 329-7466

FLAGSTAFF INN
2285 E Butler (86001) Rates: $30-$75;
Tel: (520) 774-1821; (800) 533-8992

FRONTIER MOTEL
1700 E Route 66 (86001) Rates: $18-$80;
Tel: (520) 774-8993

Dogs May Be Unleashed Unless Otherwise Indicated

HALEY'S HIDEAWAY BED & BREAKFAST
5705 Townsend-Winona Rd (86004) Rates: $85;
Tel: (800) 526-1780

HIGHLAND COUNTRY INN
223 S Milton Rd (86001) Rates: $46-$93;
Tel: (520) 774-5041; (800) 642-4186

HOLIDAY INN-FLAGSTAFF/GRAND CANYON
2320 E Lucky Ln (86004) Rates: $79-$109;
Tel: (520) 526-1150; (800) 465-4329

HOWARD JOHNSON HOTEL
2200 E Butler Ave (86004) Rates: $60-$119;
Tel: (520) 779-6944; (800) 446-4656

INNSUITES OF FLAGSTAFF
1008 E Route 66 (86001) Rates: $29-$69;
Tel: (520) 774-7356; (800) 842-4242

KNIGHTS INN SUITES-FLAGSTAFF/GRAND CANYON
602 W Route 66 (86001) Rates: $33-$110;
Tel: (520) 774-4581; (800) 654-4667

MASTER HOSTS INNS/FIVE FLAGS INN
2610 E Route 66 (86004) Rates: $42-$65;
Tel: (520) 526-1399; (800) 251-1962

MOTEL 6
2010 E Butler Ave (86004) Rates: $29-$43;
Tel: (520) 774-1801; (800) 440-6000

MOTEL 6
2440 E Lucky Ln (86001) Rates: $29-$40;
Tel: (520) 774-8756; (800) 440-6000

MOTEL 6
2745 S Woodlands Village Blvd (86001)
Rates: $32-$43; Tel: (520) 779-3757; (800) 440-6000

MOTEL 6
2500 E Lucky Ln (86004) Rates: $34-$40;
Tel: (520) 779-6164; (800) 440-6000

Locate Other Dog-Friendly Activities...Check Nearby Cities

PINECREST MOTEL
2818 E Route 66 (86001) Rates: $24-$54;
Tel: (520) 526-1950

QUALITY INN
2000 S Milton Rd (86001) Rates: $59-$105;
Tel: (520) 774-8771; (800) 228-5151

RAMADA LIMITED SUITES
2755 S Woodlands Village Blvd (86001)
Rates: $59-$135; Tel: (520) 773-1111;
(800) 272-6232 (US); (800) 255-3050 (AZ)

RELAX INN MOTEL
1416 E Santa Fe (86001) Rates: $35-$44;
Tel: (520) 774-5123

RESIDENCE INN BY MARRIOTT
3440 N Country Club Dr (86004) Rates: $99-$189;
Tel: (520) 526-5555; (800) 331-3131

RODEWAY INN EAST
2350 E Lucky Ln (86004) Rates: $30-$98;
Tel: (520) 779-3614; (800) 424-4777

ROYAL INN
2140 E Route 66 (86001) Rates: $52-$120;
Tel: (520) 774-7308

SKI LIFT LODGE
6355 Hwy 180 (86001) Rates: $20-$65;
Tel: (520) 774-0729; (800) 472-3599

SUPER 8 MOTEL
3725 Kasper Ave (86004) Rates: $48-$68;
Tel: (520) 526-0818; (800) 800-8000

TOWN HOUSE MOTEL
122 W Route 66 (86001) Rates: $24-$49;
Tel: (520) 774-5081

Dogs May Be Unleashed Unless Otherwise Indicated

TRAVELODGE-FLAGSTAFF I-40/GRAND CANYON
2520 E Lucky Ln (86004) Rates: $69-$75;
Tel: (520) 779-5121; (800) 578-7878

TRAVELODGE-UNIVERSITY/GRAND CANYON
801 W Hwy 66 (86001) Rates: $28-$85;
Tel: (520) 774-3381; (800) 578-7878

WESTERN HILLS MOTEL
1580 E Route 66 (86001) Rates: $20-$65;
Tel: (520) 774-6633

RECREATION

ABINEAU TRAIL HIKE

Intermediate/4.6 miles/2.5 hours

Info: Have you ever asked yourself why you're always admiring the towering San Francisco Peaks from afar? Well, now's your chance to change that by hiking this trail through the spectacular Peaks. You'll be ushered through forests of spruce and fir on the northern slopes affording magnificent panoramas of the Grand Canyon. After this sojourn, you and the pupster will no longer settle for distant glimpses. For more information: (520) 526-0866.

Directions: From Flagstaff, take Highway 89 north 14 miles to FR 418. Head west on FR 418 for 7 miles to FR 9123J, turn south. Follow this road for 1.2 miles to the trailhead and parking area.

ARIZONA TRAIL/MARSHALL LAKE to FISHER POINT HIKE - Leashes

Intermediate/10.0 miles/5.0 hours

Info: This section of the 750 mile, cross-state Arizona Trail is perfect for wildlife lovers. The majority of the hike extends across the verdant and spacious Anderson Mesa, home to abundant wildlife. Odds are you'll catch sight of a whitetail deer, coyote, pronghorn antelope, elk, mule deer, wild turkey or Abert's squirrel. Don't forget your binoculars - Marshall Lake is a wetland habitat for bald eagles, hawks and osprey. A leash might be prudent considering the temptations.

As you near Fisher Point, you'll begin a descent into Walnut Canyon. If you've got a camera, now's the time to capture some terrific shots of the San Francisco Peaks. For more information: (520) 556-7474 or (520) 774-1147.

Directions: From Flagstaff take Lake Mary Road (FH3) southeast for 9.2 miles to Forest Road 128 and turn left (east). Drive 2.2 miles on FR 128 to Marshall Lake. The trailhead is on the west side of the lake.

ARIZONA TRAIL/ MORMON LAKE SEGMENT HIKE - Leashes

Intermediate/1.0-12.0 miles/0.5-6.0 hours

Info: Ah, splendor in the grass. Most of this trail stretches across the Anderson Mesa, an expansive grassy region. Great for scenery and wildlife viewing, this trail will satisfy your longing for a slice of nature. The pathway traverses lovely uplands on the way to Walnut Canyon, the perfect place for a scenery/biscuit break. While Fido's munching out, look around. Notice how the stunning canyon walls look aglow as if they'd been painted red. Hey, don't overlook the glorious backdrop of the Peaks either. Breathe deeply, the pure mountain air is hard to replicate. For more information: (520) 556-7474 or (520) 774-1147.

Directions: This trail can be accessed from two points, Sandy's Canyon and Marshall Lake. To Sandy's Canyon TH: From Flagstaff, take Lake Mary Road (FH3) southeast for 6 miles, turning left past the second cattle guard. To Marshall Lake TH: Take Lake Mary Road (FH3) southeast past the Sandy's Canyon turnoff to FR 128. Turn left and continue 2.2 miles to the trailhead.

ARIZONA TRAIL/ PEAKS SEGMENT-EQUESTRIAN BYPASS HIKE - Leashes

Intermediate/1.0-18.0 miles/0.5-9.0 hours

Info: A pick-your-pleasure hike, this trail offers miles of "serenery." Inspiring views of the San Francisco Peaks will provide photo opportunities galore. Walnut Canyon and Mount Elson are part of this picturesque setting as well. Enjoy some quiet moments as you and the mutt walk within one of Arizona's most glorious regions. For more information: (520) 526-0866.

Directions: From Interstate 40 take the Country Club Road exit and continue south to FR 303, and the trailhead. You can go right or left from trailhead.

BEAR JAW TRAIL HIKE

Intermediate/4.5 miles/2.5 hours

Info: Beat the summer heat on this high elevation trail in the Kachina Peaks Wilderness. Winding through the woodsy San Francisco Peaks, you and your furry friend can chill out in a cool retreat. In early summer, don't be surprised if you happen upon some lingering snowfields. For more information: (520) 526-0866.

Directions: Take Highway 89 north to FR 418. Head west on FR 418 to FR 9123J, turn south. Follow this road to the trailhead and parking area. You'll travel a short distance on the Abineau Trail before reaching the Bear Jaw Trail.

Note: Due to the high elevation, the weather is unpredictable.

BOW AND ARROW PARK - Leashes

Info: Sniff your way around the open space in this small urban park.

Directions: Located at the intersection of Lake Mary Road and Cochise Drive.

BROOKBANK TRAIL HIKE

Intermediate/5.0 miles/2.5 hours

Info: Tranquility and excellent views go hand in hand on this trail which moseys through lush forests and verdant meadows. Follow the trail upward along a forested wash for uncluttered views of Flagstaff and Oak Creek Canyon. As you climb, views of Flagstaff give way to the towering San Francisco Peaks. Although a popular weekend escape for many recreational uses, the peacefulness of the area remains undisturbed. Sightings of mule deer, elk, goshawks and blue grouse are not uncommon. When you reach Sunset Trail, turn around and retrace your steps. For more information: (520) 526-0866.

Directions: Take Highway 180 north from Flagstaff to Schultz Pass Road (FR 420). Turn right (east) and drive one mile until FR 420 takes a sharp left turn. Continue on FR 557 for 3 miles to the trailhead.

BUFFALO PARK - Leashes

Info: If you're a nature lover, you'll feel right at home as you enjoy this undeveloped park. Restless roamers will enjoy the two mile walking course that laces through this lovely, scenic area.

Directions: Located on Cedar east of Turquoise.

BULL BASIN TRAIL HIKE

Intermediate/9.0 miles/5.0 hours

Info: For a close-up look at the remains of an old logging area, spend an afternoon with Fido hiking this somewhat demanding trail. You'll zigzag up the north slope of Kendrick Mountain to a vast mountain meadow, just the spot for lunch or a game of fetch with Fido. The trail then heads south along a rocky ridge to a seasonal spring. If your timing is right, Fido's tail will be wagging away as he savors this icy water hole. Past the spring is historic Kendrick Lookout Cabin. This old logging cabin was built in 1912. Its elevated location provides great views of the surrounding area. For more information: (520) 635-2676 or (520) 635-2633.

Directions: From Flagstaff, take Interstate 40 west to the Parks exit. Turn left across the overpass, take a left at the "T" intersection and turn right at the Parks Country Store onto FR 141. Continue north on FR 141 for about 11 miles to FR 144. Follow FR 144 about 6 miles and turn right on FR 90. Go about 5 miles to FR 90A, turn and follow to the trailhead.

BUSHMASTER PARK - Leashes

Info: Bustling with activity, this park offers something for everyone. Social sports sorts can enjoy the picnic ramada, sand volleyball, basketball courts, and tennis matches. Quieter breeds will appreciate the grassy knolls.

Directions: Located at the intersection of Alta Vista and Lockett Road.

CHESHIRE PARK - Leashes

Info: You'll have an ear to ear grin as you frolic through the grassy areas and enjoy the day with your canine companion.

Directions: Located at the intersection of Fremont Boulevard and Fort Valley Road.

DAIRY SPRINGS TRAIL HIKE

Beginner/1.0 miles/0.5 hours

Info: Even sofa loafers will appreciate this leg stretcher. Forests of white fir, ponderosa pine and juniper canopy this easy self-guided nature trail on the lower slopes of Mormon Mountain. Depending upon the season, trail guides are available from the campground host. For more information: (520) 556-7474.

Directions: From Flagstaff, take Lake Mary Road (FH3) southeast for 20 miles to its intersection with Forest Road 90. Take FR 90 west (right) and drive 3.5 miles to the Montezuma Lodge turnoff. Turn right (west) and drive .6 miles to the trailhead past the campground.

DONEY TRAIL HIKE

Intermediate/1.0 miles/0.5 hours

Info: For its size, this hike packs a big punch. This short jaunt offers a unique experience - a climb up the side of a volcanic cinder cone. The trail is dotted with interpretive signs which highlight the historic and ecologic aspects of the land. You'll also pass two, well-signed ancient ruins which once played an important role in farming. At the top of the trail, signs provide the Hopi as well as the Americanized names of all discernible landmarks. Take a few moments to relish in the beautiful vistas. For more information: (520) 526-0866.

Directions: Take Highway 89 north from Flagstaff for 22 miles to the northern entrance of the Wupatki Loop Road. Turn east for 9.5 miles to the Doney Picnic Area. The trailhead is in the picnic area.

Note: Remain on the Doney Trail - surrounding areas are not dog-friendly.

ELDEN LOOKOUT TRAIL HIKE

Expert/6.0 miles/3.0 hours

Info: Make sure you and fur-face are up to this challenge. Stretch out the kinks and get ready for a strenuous 2,300 foot climb to the top of Mt. Elden. Don't be fooled by the relative ease of the first section of the trail (also called Fatman's Loop Trail). Once Lookout Trail branches off on its own, it's steep going from there.

As you ascend this mountainside of petrified lava, take in the landscape from numerous lookouts. Near the summit, stop and ponder the devastating effects of forest fires. Once a lush pine forest, the area is currently in a state of rebirth beginning with the sprouting of aspens, temporary plantings, the first step in the healing process. Eventually, another pine forest will flourish and begin the cycle anew. When it's time to call it a day, turn around and do the descent thing. For more information: (520) 526-0866.

Directions: Follow Santa Fe Avenue (Highway 89) northeast past the Flagstaff Mall and the Peaks Ranger Station. Trailhead parking is on the north side of the road.

FATMAN'S LOOP TRAIL HIKE

Beginner/2.0 miles/1.0 hours

Info: This pleasant, scenic trail escorts you through a display of flora including ponderosa pine, white fir, alligator juniper, broadleaf yucca and cliffrose. But it's the volcanic rock formations that make the trail extraordinary. Don't miss the Mt. Elden rock formation - it's the one you have to squeeze through...hence the trail name. For more information: (520) 526-0866.

Directions: Follow Santa Fe Avenue (Highway 89) northeast past the Flagstaff Mall and the Peaks Ranger Station. Trailhead parking is on the north side of the road.

FOXGLENN PARK - Leashes

Info: If sports enthusiasts aren't at play, the grassy fields provide a spacious area to exercise your pooch.

Directions: Located at the intersection of Foxglenn Street and Butler Avenue.

HEART TRAIL HIKE

Expert/4.0 miles/2.0 hours

Info: Portions of this hike are bonafido calorie burners, especially the rigorous, switchbacking ascent along the east side of Mt. Elden. As you climb, you'll witness the regeneration process of the forest as it fights to recover from a devastating fire. For more information: (520) 526-0866.

Directions: Take Highway 89 north past the Peaks Ranger District Station. Continue another 1.5 miles to the Sandy Seep Trailhead. Heart Trail branches off from the Sandy Seep Trail.

INNER BASIN TRAIL HIKE

Beginner/4.0 miles/2.0 hours

Info: If your pooch has a little Husky in his heritage, try a late spring hike when snow still covers the San Francisco Peaks but sunny skies and warmer weather prevail. Snow or not, this is a lovely hike through mountainous terrain.

The trail begins in Lockett Meadow, particularly beautiful in the fall when the aspen groves put on a vivid show of golden autumn. The trail leads through the heart of a land once prone to explosive volcanic action but now blanketed with trees. Dried mounds of lava are still discernible, evidence of the region's volcanic past. For more information: (520) 526-0866.

Directions: Take Highway 89 north approximately 12.5 miles to Forest Road 552 (just .75 miles past the Sunset Crater National Monument turnoff). Turn west (left) for 1 mile. Bear right at the Lockett Meadow sign and continue a few more miles. The Inner Basin Trailhead is near Lockett Meadow.

KACHINA TRAIL HIKE - Leashes

Intermediate/10.0 miles/5.0 hours

Info: You and the pooch can share a diverse wilderness experience along this trail. Well defined with a gently rolling course, the path moseys among stands of ivory-barked Aspen and forests of mixed conifers. In spring, the meadows which separate the different areas boast beautiful, brilliant flowers. In autumn, listen closely for the mating calls of elk that roam the region. For more information: (520) 526-0866.

Directions: Take Highway 180 north to the Snow Bowl turnoff. Follow to the trailhead located in the lower south parking lot.

KIWANIS SOUTHSIDE PARK - Leashes

Info: If you and Spot happen to be socializing on the Northern Arizona University campus, take a break at this park. Located next to the Sky Dome, Kiwanis Park offers several picnic tables for weary walkers.

Directions: Located next to the N.A.U. Sky Dome on McConnell Circle.

LAKE VIEW TRAIL HIKE

Beginner/4.0 miles/2.0 hours

Info: Canine connoisseurs give this walk the high five. The views along the trail start at impressive, end at stupendous. Whether you're lolling your way through a pine forest or gawking at an overlook, you'll be oohing and aahing in every direction. The vistas of Mormon Lake and the surrounding landscape are postcard-perfect. This place eats film so bring plenty.

When you can pull yourself away from this vista wonderland, continue strolling through forestlands of quaking aspen and meadows of rolling greenery (where the deer and the antelope often play) until you reach Winsor Tank where the trail begins the return trip. For more information: (520) 774-1147.

Directions: From Flagstaff, take Lake Mary Road (FH3) southeast for 20 miles to Forest Road 90. Head west on FR 90 for 4.6 miles to Double Springs Campground. The trailhead is located at the south end of the campground.

LEDGES TRAIL HIKE

Beginner/2.0 miles/1.0 hours

Info: Even telly bellies won't complain on this easy trail through groves of pine, juniper and gambel oak. Your destination is an overlook with memorable views of Mormon Lake and the adjacent volcanic hills. Wildlife seekers, watch for elk and mule deer grazing in the meadows edging the trail. Birdwatchers - pack those trusty binoculars - this is a primo location for spotting bald eagles and hawks. In springtime, the meadows are covered with sunshine yellow wildflowers. For more information: (520) 774-1147.

Directions: Take Lake Mary Road southeast for 20 miles to the Forest Road 90 intersection. Take FR 90 west (right) and drive 3.5 miles to the Montezuma Lodge turnoff. Turn right (west) and follow to the trailhead, just past the campground.

McPHERSON PARK - Leashes

Info: Roam with Rover along one of several hiking trails that lead to Buffalo Park. Mellow parkgoers might prefer the scenery and sun while doing lunch at one of the picnic areas.

Directions: Located at the intersection of Foxglenn Street and Butler Avenue.

MORMON MOUNTAIN TRAIL HIKE

Intermediate/6.0 miles/3.0 hours

Info: You and the dawgus can get your daily dose of Rexercise on this scenic mountain hike through a patchwork forest of mixed conifer, aspen and ponderosa pine. The trail begins along the self-guided nature path before branching off towards its own destination - the peak of 8,449-foot Mormon Mountain. A 1,500-foot gradual ascent deposits you atop the mountain with its far reaching views of Mormon Lake and the San Francisco Peaks. For more information: (520) 774-1147.

Directions: Take Lake Mary Road (FH3) southeast for 20 miles to Forest Road 90, turn west (right). Drive 3.5 miles to the Montezuma Lodge turnoff. Turn right (west) and drive .6 miles to the trailhead.

OLD TOWN SPRINGS PARK - Leashes

Info: If you're dog-tired of driving, take a break and stretch your legs at this petite park.

Directions: Go north on Santa Fe to Coconino Avenue and turn left.

OLDHAM TRAIL HIKE

Intermediate/11.0 miles/6.0 hours

Info: For "top of the world" views of Flagstaff, the Painted Desert, Oak Creek Canyon and Sunset Crater, head for Oldham Trail. This interesting section of the Arizona Trail begins in Buffalo Park before depositing you and your hiking hound in a land of boulders and strange rock configurations as it climbs the south slope of Mt. Elden, an extinct volcano. The 2,000-foot ascent is treemarkable, the woodlands changing from ponderosa pine to aspen, spruce and fir.

Explore Oldham Park, the trail's namesake, close to the mountain's summit. See nature's inspirational healing process firsthand. This area was ravaged by a 1977 wildfire. You can't help but admire nature's handiwork. For more information: (520) 526-0866.

Directions: The Oldham Trailhead is at the northern end of Buffalo Park on Cedar Street in northern Flagstaff. Take 4th Street north to Cedar and turn left (west). The park entrance is on the right (north).

PIPELINE TRAIL HIKE

Beginner/5.6 miles/3.0 hours

Info: Rocky canyons, ancient lava flows, groves of gambel oak and ponderosa pine, fields of sunflowers, wildlife sightings...all this and more await you on this relatively simple trail. Just follow the gas pipeline, hence the name of the trail, along the base of Mt. Elden.

The majority of the trail leads you on an exploration of the Mt. Elden Environmental Study Area (ESA), designated by the Forest Service as an outdoor study resource for students and environmental groups. Raccoons, coyotes and gray foxes inhabit the land, while hawks, steller's jays and juncos soar overhead. Come springtime, the air is filled with the sweet aroma of cliffrose; summertime heralds an explosion of sunflowers and harmonic songs of meadowlarks. Leashing the pup might be a wise move. For more information: (520) 526-0866.

Directions: Access the Pipeline Trail via the Oldham Trail at the northern end of the park. Take 4th Street north to Cedar and turn left (west). The park entrance is on the right (north).

PONDEROSA PARK - Leashes

Info: From horseshoes to volleyball, this park is bustling with a variety of activity. A lawn area offers sniffing ground for four-legged visitors.

Directions: Located at the intersection of First Street and Sixth Avenue.

PUMPKIN TRAIL HIKE

Intermediate/11.0 miles/6.0 hours

Info: Spend some quality time with your pooch in the great outdoors on this trail in the Kendrick Mountain Wilderness. Stands of juniper and pine mark the beginning of your hike, while woodlands of mixed conifers, fir and aspen signal your approach to Kendrick Peak. Pack your Kodak, the mountain's summit provides spectacular vistas.

The trail follows an old logging road, climbs a steep canyon, leads through a pole gate, ascends a ridgetop, passes an old helispot and continues to Kendrick Peak, crossing mountain meadows and forestlands along the way. Enjoy the views from atop the peak and then retrace your steps. For more information: (520) 635-2676 or (520) 635-2633.

Directions: From Flagstaff, take Interstate 40 west to the Parks exit. Turn left across the overpass and continue north on FR 141 for about 11 miles. Continue onto FR 144 and go about 2.5 miles to FR 171. Turn right onto FR 171 for 2.8 miles to the right-angle curve in the road. Turn right onto FR 149 just south of the curve, and travel for about one mile to the parking area at the trailhead.

ROCKY RIDGE TRAIL HIKE

Beginner/4.5 miles/2.0 hours

Info: Thickets of gambel oak, ponderosa pine and alligator juniper make for a pleasant forest hike along this trail on the lower slopes of Dry Lake Hills. Prickly pear cactus, cliffrose and broadleaf yucca are reminders that desert country is just a stone's throw away. If your hound is a flower sniffer, plan your outing in spring or early summer when the landscape explodes in a riot of color. In summer, listen for the melodic song of hermit thrush. Year round, look for the tracks of coyote and elk. For more information: (520) 526-0866.

Directions: Take Highway 180 north to Schultz Pass Road (FR 420). Turn right (east) and drive one mile to a gate and cattle guard. Turn right (east), heading towards Schultz Creek and the park. The trailhead is near the creek, marked by a rock cairn.

SANDY SEEP TRAIL HIKE

Intermediate/3.0 miles/1.5 hours

Info: The trail traverses an area which was severely damaged during the wildfire of 1977, offering insight into nature's indomitable spirit. Aside from some great views, you might just sight a mule deer or two; this mountainside area is a major habitat for this unusual looking species. To protect their environment, the trail is off limits to motor vehicles and closed when muddy. For more information: (520) 526-0866.

Directions: Take Highway 89A east for a half mile beyond the Townsend-Winona Road intersection, turn west onto FR 9139. Follow FR 9139 to the trailhead.

SANDY'S CANYON TRAIL HIKE

Beginner/2.0 miles/1.0 hours

Info: Rated beginner for effort, it's expert at rewards. This cinchy trail begins with a fabulous view of the San Francisco Peaks before skirting the rim of Walnut Canyon (a mini Grand Canyon) and dropping into Sandy's Canyon. The path continues on an old jeep road and intersects with the Arizona Trail. Begin ogling - the Permian Age sand dunes will take your breath away. Turn back here or extend your hike along the Arizona Trail. For more information: (520) 774-1147.

Directions: Take Lake Mary Road (FH3) southeast for six miles. Immediately past the second cattleguard, turn left (north) to the trailhead.

SCHULTZ CREEK TRAIL HIKE

Beginner/7.0 miles/3.5 hours

Info: The gentle terrain of this trail follows seasonal Schultz Creek. Visit at the right time and your water-loving pup may be able to dip a paw or two in the fast flowing creek while you enjoy a serenade of hermit thrush. There's only one drawback - sometimes the peace and quiet is marred by off-road cyclists and mountain bikers. For more information: (520) 526-0866.

Directions: Take Highway 180 north for 2 miles to FR 420 (Schultz Pass Road). Head east on FR 420 for 1 mile to a gate and cattle guard. Turn right towards Schultz Creek and the park. The trailhead is by the creek and is marked by a rock cairn.

SLATE MOUNTAIN TRAIL HIKE

Intermediate/4.8 miles/2.5 hours

Info: The Grand Canyon, San Francisco Peaks, Painted Desert and Kendrick Mountain are all visible from atop Slate Mountain, your final destination. The lure of the scenery should provide the impetus to lace up your hiking boots and tackle the 2.4 mile gradual albeit steady climb to the summit. The trail follows an old jeep road which is posted with interpretive signs highlighting the various trees and shrubs. For more information: (520) 526-0866.

Directions: Take Highway 180 northwest for 35 miles to Forest Road 191 and turn left (west). Follow for 2 miles to the trailhead on the right.

SMOKERISE PARK - Leashes

Info: Benches and picnic tables are provided for those who just wish to sit and soak up some sunshine.

Directions: Located at the intersection of Smokerise and Squaw Drives.

SUNSET TRAIL HIKE

Beginner/8.0 miles/4.0 hours

Info: When you and your furry sidekick crave an afternoon of outdoor fun and spectacular vistas, strap on a backpack, fill the water bottles, load the Minolta and head for the high country of Mt. Elden. This relatively easy trail will guide you through groves of virgin fir and pine while providing breath-taking views of Flagstaff, Sunset Crater, the Peaks and the Painted Desert. Glimpse too how nature has managed to overcome the destruction of the wildfire of 1977. Sightings of elk and mule deer are not unusual. For more information: (520) 526-0866.

Directions: Take Highway 180 north to FR 420 (Schultz Pass Road) and head northeast for 6 miles to the trailhead. The trailhead is at the parking area on the south side of the road.

TAYLOR CABIN TRAIL HIKE

Expert/4.6 miles/2.5 hours

Info: Strenuous and rugged, this trail is intended for expert hikers only, both human and canine sorts. But if you and Bowser have the right stuff you'll capture some beautiful moments. Descend to the canyon floor and allow yourself an awestruck moment. Sycamore Canyon is a natural wonder, replete with beautiful cliffs and buttes. Regal

Douglas firs and towering pines form a fragrant canopy over the precipitous trail on your way down. There's a chance your timing might be perfect and the seasonal river will be flowing. Enough said! For more information: (520) 282-4119.

Directions: Take Woody Mountain Road (FR 231) south from Flagstaff for 21 miles to FR 231A and turn right past the Turkey Butte Lookout Tower. Follow FR 231A about 3.3 miles to FR 538 and head south 3 miles past FR 538H to the parking area at milepost 2.9. This 3 mile section can be confusing because many unmarked forest roads branch off from FR 538. Follow the powerline and you won't get lost. From the parking area, hike the last few hundred yards to the trailhead - the one to the right. Do not drive beyond the parking lot at mile 2.9.

Note: High clearance vehicles only for last mile before trailhead.

THORPE PARK - Leashes

Info: Be social at the picnic ramada, or laze alone with your best Lassie on the grassie.

Directions: Located at the intersection of Sante Fe and Toltec Streets.

UNIVERSITY HEIGHTS PARK

Info: This small park will do for a quick leg stretcher.

Directions: Located at the intersection of Jewell and Melissa Streets.

WEATHERFORD TRAIL HIKE - Leashes

Expert/17.4 miles/10.0 hours

Info: If you've got the stamina, hike the entire trail or just go far enough to delight in some peace and quiet with your favorite four-legged friend. A semi-historic trail, the beginning covers an old toll road that was completed in the 1920s. Along the way, you'll earn some magnificent panoramic views of Oak Creek Canyon and the Verde (boy is it green) Valley. The trail crosses a diverse forestland of ponderosa pine which paves the way to limber pine, corkbark fir and bristlecone pine. Make it to the 9,000-foot summit, catch your breath and listen for the loud cackling of Clark's Nutcracker. A fitting end to the hike. For more information: (520) 526-0866.

Directions: Take Highway 180 north to Snow Bowl Road. Turn right and follow for 2 miles. Turn east on FR522 to the trailhead.

WHEELER PARK - Leashes

Info: Cloudgaze from the grassy knoll or chill out under a mature shade tree.

Directions: Located at the intersection of Aspen Avenue and Humphreys Street.

FLORENCE

LODGING

BLUE MIST MOTEL
40 S Pinal Pkwy (85232) Rates: $28-$45;
Tel: (520) 868-5875

<u>RECREATION</u>

J.F. TRAIL 106 HIKE

Intermediate/6.0 miles/3.0 hours

Info: Spend an afternoon exploring the Superstition Wilderness with your pooch and you just may have this trail all to yourselves. Leave your worries behind and allow the peacefulness of this beautiful rustic area to soothe your senses. The oddly twisted alligator juniper marks the 4,000-foot Tortilla Pass and the trail's end. Head back by retracing your steps. For more information: (520) 225-5200.

Directions: From Florence, take Highway 89 north 16 miles to Florence Junction. Go right on Highway 60 east for two miles past Florence Junction to Queen Valley Road. Take Queen Valley Road north for 1.5 miles to Hewitt Station Road (FR 357). Turn right and follow Hewitt Station Road for 3.0 miles to FR 172. Turn left (north) onto FR 172 and continue 11 miles to the Woodbury Trailhead.

Note: High clearance vehicles only.

FOUNTAIN HILLS

<u>RECREATION</u>

McDOWELL MOUNTAIN REGIONAL PARK - Leashes

Info: Geographically located between the Fort McDowell Indian Reservation on the east, Fountain Hills on the south, and Scottsdale on the west, this regional park is easily accessible from Scottsdale and Fountain Hills. It harbors some of the most picturesque country within the county park system. If a road trip appeals to you, the drive to and through the park is beautiful. The slight rise in elevation on the drive from Scottsdale to Fountain Hills gives you some pretty desertscapes, as well as a feel for the vastness of the Valley which stretches across citified desert land to distant mountain ranges.

If your intentions lean more to enjoying the outdoors on foot, over 50 miles of hiking trails lace this lush, desert landscape. Pick a trail and pick your pleasure. Some trails to consider are: the Gordon Wagner Memorial, Lousley Hill, Pemberton, Scout Trails and Stoneman Historic. Check Fountain Hills for listings and always pack enough water, this is desert terrain.

Directions: Access to the park is from McDowell Mountain Road, 4 miles north of Fountain Hills. The park is 15 miles northeast of Scottsdale.

Note: $2 per vehicle weekend entrance fee. Picnic area closes at sunset. Campgrounds closed Memorial Day-Labor Day. Call (602) 471-0173.

1) GORDON WAGNER MEMORIAL HIKE - Leashes

Beginner/1.0 miles/0.5 hours

Info: Learn a little about the Sonoran Desert on this short stroll within the McDowell Mountain Regional Park. A self-guided trail provides a condensed overview of the region. For more information: (602) 506-2930.

Directions: Take McDowell Mountain Road north towards McDowell Mountain Regional Park. Turn left on McDowell Mountain Park Drive to Palisades Drive. Follow the signs to the trailhead at the group campground and park.

2) LOUSELY HILL TRAIL HIKE - Leashes

Intermediate/2.5 miles/1.25 hours

Info: You'll want a camera for this excursion. This trail is one of the most scenic within the McDowell Mountain Range. Not only is the area home to some of the finest specimens of saguaros and paloverde trees, but when you reach the crest you can see the blue waters of Bartlett Lake and the green oasis of the Verde River Valley. In the distance, Four Peaks and the Superstitions loom over the splendid desert landscape. Pack plenty of water - especially in summer. Dry heat or not you'll need it. For more information: (602) 506-2930.

Directions: Take McDowell Mountain Road north towards McDowell Mountain Regional Park. Turn left on McDowell Mountain Park Drive to Lousely Drive South. The trailhead is well marked.

3) PEMBERTON TRAIL LOOP HIKE - Leashes

Intermediate/15.0 miles/7.5 hours

Info: This long loop trail leads you among thick, saguaro-dotted Sonoran vegetation and several points of interest, like the ruins of Pemberton Ranch and Bartlett Dam which are visible by looking north. Load up your fanny pack, fill the water bottles and hike away the day. For more information: (602) 506-2930.

Directions: Take McDowell Mountain Road north towards McDowell Mountain Regional Park. Turn left on McDowell Mountain Park Drive to Shallmo Drive. Follow the signs to the trailhead at the horse staging area.

4) SCOUT TRAIL HIKE - Leashes

Beginner/0.6 miles/0.5 hours

Info: Nature lovers rejoice. Even when you're short on time, this leisurely self-guided tour lets you and Fido observe a variety of flora and fauna. It's definitely worth a look-see. For more information: (602) 506-2930.

Directions: Take McDowell Mountain Road north towards McDowell Mountain Regional Park. Turn left on McDowell Mountain Park Drive to Scout Camp Drive. The trailhead is past the gate in the Youth Group Area.

5) STONEMAN HISTORIC TRAIL HIKE - Leashes

Intermediate/1.0-7.0 miles/0.5-3.0 hours

Info: History hounds will find traveling this once well-trodden road rather interesting. Named after the road's founder, Stoneman Trail offers many sightseeing opportunities as well as a sneak peek into the past. The route was established in 1870 as a wagon road from the Aqua Fria River to Fort McDowell. The ending of the Indian Wars in 1890 meant the end of Fort McDowell and the abandonment of Stoneman Road. For more information: (602) 506-2930.

Directions: Take McDowell Mountain Road north to the McDowell Mountain Regional Park. The trailhead is located in the trailhead group area.

SUNFLOWER TRAIL HIKE - Leashes

Intermediate/10.0 miles/5.0 hours

Info: Beautiful sycamores mark the start of this trail. Walk towards the dry streambed and look north to locate a large concrete water structure. Cross Sycamore Creek at that point and continue on the trail to the large culvert under Highway 87. Once through the culvert, you'll come to an open meadow where you'll continue heading west. The trail traverses a variety of settings including chaparral, pinyon and juniper forests. You and the pooch can commune with nature as you make your way amid the lovely landscape. This trail is part of the 750-mile, cross-state Arizona Trail from Mexico to Utah. For more information: (602) 379-6446.

Directions: Head north on Highway 87 to FR 22 (Bushnell Tanks), a half mile east of Sunflower. Keep your eyes peeled for a right turn at .5 miles in, just before a cattle guard and a major creek crossing. Take the turn, drive into a large area covered with mature sycamore trees and park.

FREDONIA

LODGING
CRAZY JUG MOTEL
465 S Main (86022) Rates: $38-$49;
Tel: (520) 643-7752

RECREATION
KAIBAB-PAIUTE EDUCATIONAL HIKING TRAIL-
Leashes
Beginner/1.0 miles/0.5 hours

Info: Before you begin, pick up a trail booklet. It will make finding your way that much easier. And the brief descriptions of the area correspond with the trail's lettered marking system.

Short and picturesque, you and the pooch-face will enjoy your walk in Muuputs Canyon where a cornucopia of nature awaits. Past the "I" marker, the trail forks. Take the Muuputs Trail to the right. It follows a wash, leading to a petroglyph-filled canyon. At trail's end, petroglyphs can be found at the "L" marker. Look around - you're in a natural amphitheatre, compliments of the canyon walls.

Other petroglyphs can be found at the "K" marker. To reach the "K", bear right off the main trail past the "J" marker. Hey, this trail should be called Alphabet Soup. It may sound a little confusing but it's not and it's quite interesting. For more information: (520) 643-7245.

Directions: Head west on Hwy 389 to the Kaibab-Paiute Indian Reservation. The trailhead is on the Reservation. Stop by the tribal office for information.

SWAPP TRAIL HIKE

Intermediate/4.0 miles/2.0 hours

Info: Escape from everyday life on this remote wilderness trail, but be prepared to pay your hiking dues. Sections of the trail are steep and rugged.

Directions: Take Highway 89A west to FR 422 south. Follow FR 422 for 12 miles to Gunsight Road. Drive west on Gunsight Road for approximately 10 miles, following the signs for the trail.

Note: This area is remote. Inform someone of your plans and carry a map.

Notes

_____

_____

_____

_____

_____

_____

_____

_____

_____

_____

_____

_____

Notes

GILA BEND

LODGING

BEST WESTERN SPACE AGE LODGE
401 E Pima St (85337) Rates: $46-$76;
Tel: (520) 683-2273; (800) 528-1234

YUCCA MOTEL
836 E Pima St (85337) Rates: $20-$33;
Tel: (520) 683-2211

GLENDALE

LODGING

BEST WESTERN SAGE INN
5940 NW Grand Ave (85301) Rates: $40-$77;
Tel: (602) 939-9431; (800) 528-1234

RECREATION

BICENTENNIAL PARK - Leashes

Info: 5 acres of verdant lawn await you and the pupster. Picnic tables dot the park, some with grills if you and your buddy feel like having a kibble cookout.

Directions: Located at Missouri and 71st Avenues.

BONSALL PARK - Leashes

Info: This 17-acre oasis is divided into two parts by Bethany Home Road. Choose from a wide variety of activities to satisfy your athletic inclinations.

Directions: Located at Bethany Home Road and 59th Avenue.

Dogs May Be Unleashed Unless Otherwise Indicated

BUTLER PARK - Leashes

Info: 5 acres of lawn, benches, a playground and occasionally, front row seats at a soccer game make this a pleasant way to spend an hour or so with your pooch.

Directions: Take Olive Avenue (Dunlap Avenue in Phoenix) to 57th Avenue and turn south to the park.

CARMEL PARK - Leashes

Info: This small neighborhood park offers 5 acres of lawn for you and Fido. Find a bench under a tree and spend an hour or so watching the hoopsters.

Directions: From Union Hills Drive take 51st Avenue north to Oraibi and turn west (left) to the park.

CHOLLA PARK - Leashes

Info: Nearly 6 acres of soft grass, sport fields galore, picnic tables, shaded benches and a playground comprise this park providing a pleasant way to spend the day.

Directions: From Cactus Avenue take 53rd Avenue south to the park.

CLAVELITO PARK - Leashes

Info: You and the pupster will enjoy 5 acres of greenery in this small, uncrowded neighborhood park. There are picnic tables, grills and shaded benches.

Directions: From Bethany Home Road take 51st Avenue north to Ocotillo Road. Turn west (left) to the park.

COUNTRY GABLES PARK - Leashes

Info: A leisurely outing is yours at this 4-acre park. Picnic tables, grills, benches, a soccer field and a playground round out the offerings.

Directions: From Thunderbird take 51st Avenue north to Acoma. Take Acoma west one block to 52nd Avenue, turn right (north) and go for two blocks.

DELICIAS PARK - Leashes

Info: Let your pooch stretch his legs in this 5-acre lawned park. Picnic tables offer a place to sit and enjoy some quiet time.

Directions: From Glendale Avenue take 51st Street north to Orangewood Avenue. Turn east (left) and drive to 48th Street and the park.

DESERT ROSE PARK - Leashes

Info: When it's time to frolic, this is the place to do it with your four-footed friend. 7 acres of lawn can be yours along with benches, picnic tables and BBQ grills in this small neighborhood park.

Directions: From Bell Avenue take 63rd Avenue south a few blocks to the park.

DESERT VIEW PARK - Leashes

Info: 6 acres of spacious greenery beckon at this local park. Soccer and baseball fields provide lots of room for your retriever to bag a wild frisbee.

Directions: From Cactus Avenue take 61st Avenue north to Sweetwater and the park road.

FOOTHILLS PARK - Leashes

Info: Although mostly a sports area, there are 42 acres here for you and your pooch. Practice your batting while Fido practices fetching.

Directions: From Union Hills Drive take 57th Avenue north over the Skunk Creek Wash. The park is just on the other side of the wash.

HILLCREST PARK - Leashes

Info: Nestled in the northernmost corner of Glendale, this 8-acre neighborhood park is off the beaten path, making it much less crowded than other area parks. You and your canine crony can spend a leisurely afternoon picnicking, BBQing and plain old relaxing.

Directions: Take 67th Avenue north to Deer Valley Road. Turn west (left) onto Deer Valley Road and go to 71st Avenue. Turn north (right) and drive to the park.

HORIZON PARK - Leashes

Info: 5 open acres of greenery make this small park an ideal way for you and your dog to spend some time together. Picnic tables and benches dot the park.

Directions: From either Olive to the north, or Northern to the south, take 47th Avenue to Diana Avenue and the park.

LIONS PARK - Leashes

Info: Plan to spend the day outdoors with your canine accomplice in this 10-acre turf.

Directions: From Northern Avenue take 63rd Avenue south to Frier Drive.

Locate Other Dog-Friendly Activities...Check Nearby Cities

MARY SILVA PARK - Leashes

Info: Looking for a pleasant stroll? This 5-acre park can be a nice break from your day. Picnic tables, benches and a playground are a part of this small park.

Directions: From Grand Avenue, between Camelback and Bethany Home Roads, take Missouri east to 45th Avenue. Turn north (left) onto 45th and drive one block to the park.

MARYLAND LAKES PARK - Leashes

Info: 6 acres of grass offer the pupster a perfect opportunity to run and prance.

Directions: Located at 47th Avenue and Maryland, between Bethany Home and Glendale.

MONDO PARK - Leashes

Info: Play fetch with Fido at this 5-acre parkland. He'll have a tailwagging good time chasing that elusive tennis ball.

Directions: From Olive Avenue take 57th Avenue north for two blocks.

MONTARA PARK - Leashes

Info: Laze a few hours away with your doggie buddy in this small 5.5-acre park. Basketball, tennis and racquetball courts are available for the athletically inclined. Soft grass, a good book and dappled shade will appeal to leisure seekers.

Directions: Located at Peoria and 64th Avenue.

NEW WORLD PARK - Leashes

Info: This 8-acre park is tucked right in the middle of a development circle and is therefore less likely to be crowded than other more accessible parks. There are soccer and baseball fields and basketball and tennis courts for sporting types. Or just pull up a bench and enjoy the sunshine with the dawgus.

Directions: From Olive Avenue take 51st Street south to Barbara Avenue, turn east (left) and drive to the park.

O'NEIL PARK - Leashes

Info: Spend the afternoon with your canine companion on 11 acres of lush lawn. Picnic tables with grills and shaded benches round out the offerings.

Directions: From Bethany Home Road take either 64th or 65th Avenue south to the park.

ROSE LANE PARK - Leashes

Info: Your canine buddy will love this 19-acre lawned park. Romp together along the exercise course and then take a biscuit break at one of the picnic areas.

Directions: From the intersection of Bethany Home Road, Grand Avenue and 51st Avenue take 51st Avenue north two blocks to the park.

SAHUARO RANCH PARK - Leashes

Info: One of the biggest of Glendale's lawned parks, Sahuaro Park offers 80 acres of fun for you and your Fido. Stroll the grounds, toss the frisbee or find a shaded spot and chill out together.

Locate Other Dog-Friendly Activities...Check Nearby Cities

Directions: Located at 59th Avenue between Olive and Peoria Avenues, just north of Glendale Community College.

SANDS PARK - Leashes

Info: 5.5 acres of turf should satisfy Bowser's daily constitutional.

Directions: Located on 55th Avenue midway between Glendale and Northern Avenues.

SUNNYSIDE PARK - Leashes

Info: Bring a ball along for your sidekick - 8 acres of open lawn await your visit. Or plan an aerobic outing and do the exercise course.

Directions: Located on 63rd Avenue between Cactus and Peoria Avenues.

SUNSET PALMS PARK - Leashes

Info: This small neighborhood park is nestled away from the crowds. Grassy expanses, sports facilities and numerous picnic spots comprise this 8-acre area.

Directions: From Thunderbird take 55th Avenue south around the bend and to the park.

TIERRA BUENA PARK - Leashes

Info: Along with sports areas and picnic grill spots, you'll find 5 acres of cool grass for your cool canine.

Directions: From Greenway take 57th Avenue north into the park.

THUNDERBIRD PARK - Leashes

Info: If the quietude of desert hiking appeals to you and your pooch, this park has your name on it. Located at the northernmost end of Glendale, the park encompasses 1,000 acres. Hike the flat terrain or challenge yourself to a mountainous climb. Go mid-afternoon and plan a BBQ at sundown.

Directions: Take 59th Avenue north past Beardsley into the park.

THUNDERBIRD PASEO

Info: Running alongside the Arizona Canal, this pretty green park offers 55 acres of fun for you and the pupster.

Directions: Starting at Thunderbird and 52nd Avenue stretching across 67th Avenue, this park runs northwest with the canal until it reaches 72nd Avenue and Paradise.

Other Neighborhood Parks in Glendale:

ACOMA PARK - Leashes

From Thunderbird take 51st Avenue north to Acoma. Take Acoma west two blocks to the park.

HERITAGE PARK - Leashes

Located at 55th Avenue at Mountain View Road, between Olive and Peoria Avenues.

KINGS PARK - Leashes

From Bell Avenue take 51st Avenue south to Kings Avenue. Turn west (right) it's two blocks to the park.

Locate Other Dog-Friendly Activities...Check Nearby Cities

MEMMINGEN PARK - Leashes

From Cactus take 51st Avenue south to Cholla. Turn east (left), drive to 49th Avenue and the park.

MISSION PARK - Leashes

From Peoria Avenue take 45th Avenue south for seven blocks to the park.

MYRTLE PARK - Leashes

Located on 55th Avenue midway between Glendale and Northern Avenues.

PASADENA PARK - Leashes

From Camelback Road take 87th Avenue north one block to the park.

PASEO RACQUET CENTER - Leashes

Located at Thunderbird Road and 63rd Avenue.

SUNSET PARK - Leashes

From Peoria Ave. take 45th Ave. south to the park.

UTOPIA PARK - Leashes

From Union Hills Drive take 75th Avenue north to Utopia. Turn east (right) to 72nd Avenue.

WINDSOR PARK - Leashes

From Camelback Road turn north onto 63rd Avenue and drive one block to the park.

GLOBE

LODGING

CLOUD NINE MOTEL
1649 E Ash St (85501) Rates: $47-$69;
Tel: (520) 425-5741

EL REY MOTEL
1201 E Ash St (85501) Rates: $20-$36;
Tel: (520) 425-4427

RECREATION

SIXSHOOTER CANYON TRAIL HIKE - Leashes

Intermediate/11.0 miles/5.5 hours

Info: In use since 1901, this trail offers hikers close-up scrutiny of the vegetation common to the area. If Fido is a looker, not a barker, you might get a chance to see whitetail deer, mule deer, foxes or hawks. Mountain wildflowers bloom at intervals throughout the year. Wild berries (not all are edible) can often be found trailside. Other trails within this area create opportunities for loop trips. For more information: (520) 425-7189.

Directions: Take FR 112S from Globe to Icehouse CCC Camp. The trail begins adjacent to the parking lot and ends near the Upper Pinal Recreation Area.

GOODYEAR

LODGING

BEST WESTERN-PHOENIX/GOODYEAR INN
1100 N Litchfield Rd (85338) Rates: $39-$89;
Tel: (602) 932-3210; (800) 528-1234

SUPER 8 MOTEL
1710 N Dysart Rd (85338) Rates: $37-$53;
Tel: (602) 932-9622; (800) 800-8000

RECREATION
PACK SADDLE HISTORIC TRAIL HIKE - Leashes
Beginner/4.8 miles/2.5 hours

Info: History buffs can retrace the path of early pioneers on their way from Phoenix to Rainbow Valley along this fascinating trail. If you dare to visit in summer, you'll marvel at the determination of the hearty homesteaders who settled the west. For more information: (602) 506-2930.

Directions: Take SR 85 to Bullard Avenue south. Turn right on Vineyard to the Estrella Mountain Regional Park entrance.

RAINBOW VALLEY TRAIL HIKE - Leashes
Expert/6.0 miles/3.0 hours

Info: Three's a charm, or a loop in this case. Grab Fido's leash and get your daily dose of exercise on this inter-connecting trail. Follow the Rainbow Valley Trail (#147) from the Horse/Rodeo Arena to the Pack Saddle Historic Trail (#143), heading west to the Rock Knob Buggy Trail (#148) which loops back to the starting point. For more information: (602) 506-2930.

Directions: Take SR 85 to Bullard Avenue south. Turn right on Vineyard to the Estrella Mountain Regional Park entrance. Follow signs to the trailhead at the Horse/Rodeo Arena.

ROCK KNOB BUGGY TRAIL HIKE - Leashes

Beginner/5.8 miles/3.0 hours

Info: Originally designed for horse drawn vehicles, this trail is very easy to traverse. Enjoy the majestic mountain views and diversity of vegetation on this relaxing getaway hike. For more information: (602) 506-2930.

Directions: Take SR 85 to Bullard Avenue south. Turn right on Vineyard to the Estrella Mountain Regional Park entrance. Follow signs to the trailhead at the Horse/Rodeo Arena.

GRAND CANYON NATIONAL PARK-SOUTH RIM

(For North Rim recreation see Jacob Lake and Marble Canyon)

Hotels listed below do not allow dogs in rooms, however, overnight accommodations are available for canines. Leashed dogs are permitted in the park. For more information: (520) 638-7888.

LODGING

BRIGHT ANGEL LODGE & CABINS
P. O. Box 699 (86023) Rates: $55-$95;
Tel: (520) 638-2401

EL TOVAR HOTEL
P. O. Box 699 (86023) Rates: $115-$175;
Tel: (520) 638-2631

KACHINA LODGE
P. O. Box 699 (86023) Rates: $99-$109;
Tel: (520) 638-2631

MASWIK LODGE
P. O. Box 699 (86023) Rates: $75-$104;
Tel: (520) 638-2631

QUALITY INN GRAND CANYON-SOUTH RIM
Hwy 64, P. O. Box 520 (86023) Rates: $68-$138;
Tel: (520) 638-2673; (800) 221-2222

RED FEATHER LODGE
Hwy 64, P. O. Box 1460 (86023) Rates: $49-$150;
Tel: (520) 638-2414; (800) 538-2345

THUNDERBIRD LODGE
P. O. Box 699 (86023) Rates: $99-$109;
Tel: (520) 638-2631

YAVAPAI LODGE
P. O. Box 699 (86023) Rates: $82-$92;
Tel: (520) 638-2631

RECREATION

RED BUTTE TRAIL HIKE - Leashes

Intermediate/2.4 miles/1.5 hours

Info: Share an awestruck moment with your pooch ogling the Grand Canyon and the distant San Francisco Peaks from your lofty perch at 7,326-foot Red Butte. Geology buffs - this hike's for you. From Moenkopi formation and Shinarum conglomerate to the cap of basalt, to the Kaibab limestone composition of the Coconino Plateau, Red Butte is a geologic prize.

The first .75 miles of this well-marked trail is an easy, gradual ascent. The next .50 mile of switchbacks to the Red Butte Crest is a lot more strenuous but the dramatic views are definitely worth the effort. For more information: (520) 638-2443.

Directions: Take Highway 180/64 south about 10 miles past the Grand Canyon Airport to Forest Road 305. Take 305 east (left) for 2 miles to the junction with FR 305A. Turn right (south) staying on FR 305. After .5 miles veer right onto FR 340. Take it 1.5 miles further south to the spur road from the east. Take that .25 miles to the trailhead.

Note: Keep your dog leashed at all times, this land is sacred to the Havasupai Indians.

THE RIM TRAIL HIKE - Leashes

Beginner/8.0 miles/4.0 hours

Info: When you see the Grand Canyon, you'll understand all the adjectives you've ever heard. The beauty of this natural wonder can be easily accessed with a hike along the Rim Trail. Although most visitors drive from viewpoint to viewpoint, it's a lot more interesting to amble along this peaceful, unbelievably scenic trail.

Shaded and cool, this paved trail is one of the canyon's best kept secrets. At an elevation of 7,000 feet, groves of pinyon and ponderosa pine line the trail. Sweeping, endless vistas await your perusal at Trail Views I and II. That sliver of blue at the very bottom of the canyon is the Colorado River. From this elevation, it's hard to appreciate the fierceness of that powerful body of water. The Rim Trail is divided into two sections. The East Rim Trail begins at Powell Point, west of the Visitor's Center. The West Rim Trail begins at Yavapai Point, east of the Visitor's Center. For more information: (520) 638-7888.

Directions: From the park's entrance, follow Rim Road to the trailhead at either Yavapai Point and Museum or Powell Point.

GREEN VALLEY

LODGING

QUALITY INN
111 S La Canada Dr (85614) Rates: $69-$115;
Tel: (520) 625-2250; (800) 221-2222

GREER

LODGING

MOLLY BUTLER LODGE & THE ASPENS CABINS
P. O. Box 70 (85927) Rates: $30-$80;
Tel: (520) 735-7232

HOLBROOK

LODGING

BEST WESTERN ADOBE INN
615 W Hopi Dr (86025) Rates: $40-$58;
Tel: (520) 524-3948; (800) 528 1234

BEST WESTERN ARIZONIAN INN
2508 E Navajo Blvd (86025) Rates: $40-$62;
Tel: (520) 524-2611; (800) 528-1234

BUDGET HOST INN
235 W Hopi Dr (86025) Rates: $18-$28;
Tel: (520) 524-3809; (800) 283-4678

COMFORT INN
2602 E Navajo Blvd (86025) Rates: $44-$72;
Tel: (520) 524-6131; (800) 221-2222

ECONO LODGE
2596 E Navajo Blvd (86025) Rates: $32-$58;
Tel: (520) 524-1448; (800) 424-4777

HOLIDAY INN EXPRESS
1308 E Navajo Blvd (86025) Rates: $45-$59;
Tel: (520) 524-1466; (800) 465-4329

MOTEL 6
2514 E Navajo Blvd (86025) Rates: $30-$36;
Tel: (520) 524-6101; (800) 440-6000

RAINBOW INN
2211 E Navajo Blvd (86025) Rates: $30-$47;
Tel: (520) 524-2654; (800) 551-1923

RAMADA INN
2608 E Navajo Blvd (86025) Rates: $40-$65;
Tel: (520) 524-2566; (800) 272-6232

TRAVELODGE
2418 E Navajo Blvd (86025) Rates: $30-$46;
Tel: (520) 524-6815; (800) 578-7878

RECREATION

PETRIFIED FOREST NATIONAL PARK TRAILS - Leashes

Info: The Petrified Forest definitely falls into the category of a must-see, must-do excursion. Take advantage of the opportunity to examine rocks and chunks of wood which have been around for millions of years. You also have the option of hiking three unique trails, each offering fascinating insight into this prehistoric wonderland. Pack up and get set for an out-of-this world experience. The Giant Logs Trail is not dog-friendly so leashed or not, it's a no-no for Fido.

Directions: There are two ways into the park, one from the north, the other from the south. Heading east, take Highway 180 southeast from Holbrook to the north park entrance. This route will bring you to the exit on the north end of the park, directly onto Interstate 40 where you can continue traveling east. On a westward approach, take the main park entrance (south entrance) off Interstate 40. This will deposit you on Highway 180 and you'll have a pleasant drive into Holbrook on your return to Interstate 40. For more information: (520) 524-6228.

1) AGATE HOUSE TRAIL HIKE - Leashes

Beginner/1.0 miles/0.5 hours

Info: Short and sweet, even telly bellies will enjoy the outing. This historic trail traces the ruins of archaic Indian dwellings built from petrified wood. For more information: (520) 524-6228.

Directions: Located about 1.5 miles in from the Southern Entrance Station. Turn southwest onto the clearly marked side road to the parking area.

2) BLUE MESA TRAIL HIKE - Leashes

Beginner/1.0 miles/0.5 hours

Info: Journey to prehistoric times along this pleasant, simple trail. Traverse terrain that was once swamp covered and dominated by dinosaurs. Today, millions of years later, the marshes and dinosaurs are gone but beautiful multi-colored rocks, cliffs and petrified wood remain. The siliconized wood chunks are remnants of ancient trees, some as tall as 200 feet.

Dogs May Be Unleashed Unless Otherwise Indicated

The trail descends 200 feet into the fascinating betonite badlands, The Blue Forest - an area of blue volcanic clay. Lace up those moon boots - this is the closest you and Dino will come to a Neil Armstrong-like experience. Although it's called The Blue Forest, depending on the weather and time of the day, you might not see a speck of blue - grays and purples often reign supreme. And remember to leave only footprints, take only memories. For more information: (520) 524-6228.

Directions: Located midway through the park between the Puerco Indian Ruins to the north and Agate Bridge to the south, the access road to Blue Mesa runs east. The trailhead is at the northern end of the loop.

3) CRYSTAL FOREST TRAIL HIKE - Leashes

Beginner/0.5 miles/0.5 hours

Info: Running short on time? Leash up your canine buddy and take a quick jaunt around this looping trail, a teaser of what the park has to offer. When you have more time, return and hike one of the longer trails. For more information: (520) 524-6228.

Directions: Located in the southern third of the park, the Crystal Forest Trailhead is on the east side of the main highway about two miles south of Agate Bridge.

RECREATION CENTER COUNTY PARK - Leashes

Info: Let your pup work off some of those biscuits with a game of catch or fetch in the wide open spaces of this 80-acre park.

Directions: Take Highway 77 south for two miles to the Recreation Area Entrance.

Locate Other Dog-Friendly Activities...Check Nearby Cities

JACOB LAKE/GRAND CANYON NATIONAL PARK-NORTH RIM

<u>RECREATION</u>

NANKOWEAP TRAIL HIKE

Expert/8.0 miles/4.0 hours

Info: Strenuous and scenic best describe this wilderness hike. Take plenty of H2O and high energy snacks along before tackling this one. You'll want a camera too, the vistas of Navajo Mountain, Marble Canyon and the red and white cliffed canyons are definitely filmworthy.

Ponderosa pine, aspen, locust and mixed conifer line the steep, often narrow pathways. Spring and fall are the most popular times for this trail which meets up with the Grand Canyon National Park's Nankoweap Trail. Avoid in summer - too hot. For more information: (520) 643-7395.

Directions: From Jacob Lake, take Highway 67 south for 26.5 miles to Forest Road 611 (just past DeMotte Campground). Head east on FR 611 after 1.4 miles turn south on FR 610 to the trailhead at road's end.

Note: This area is remote. Inform someone of your plans and carry a map.

NORTH CANYON TRAIL HIKE

Expert/14.0 miles/7.0 hours

Info: Your canine companion will certainly be your best friend on this hike into the remote confines of the Saddle Mountain Wilderness. Blissful solitude makes this wilderness trek an ideal hike for those seeking to escape from the hustle/bustle of everyday life. If Fido's a water lover, he'll have a tail wagging good time at the stream crossings.

The initial descent into North Canyon is comprised of oak groves and mixed conifer woodlands. This wilderness area contains many rock outcroppings, narrow passages and numerous stream crossings. The perennial stream is home to protected native trout. The flowers, plants and birds you'll encounter are unique to the area. For more information: (520) 643-7395.

Directions: From Jacob Lake take Highway 67 south for 26.5 miles to Forest Road 611 (just past DeMotte Campground). Take FR 611 (east) for approximately 3 miles to the trailhead.

Note: This area is remote. Inform someone of your plans and carry a map.

SADDLE MOUNTAIN TRAIL HIKE
Intermediate/12.0 miles/6.0 hours

Info: One of the easiest ways to experience the Saddle Mountain Wilderness is along this trail where you'll be able to appreciate some fine views of House Rock Valley, Kaibab Plateau, the Vermillion Cliffs and Marble Canyon. Trail #31 (Saddle Mountain) leaves Trail #57 about a mile from the trailhead at FR 445. Your course will lead you along the pinyon and juniper bench ending about a mile from the edge of Marble Canyon where the trail ends. The mile-long side trip to the edge is easily accessed and definitely worth the extra effort, especially for the views you'll collect of the Colorado River. When you're finished taking in the scenery, retrace your steps for the return journey. For more information: (520) 643-7395.

Directions: From the North Kaibab Visitor Center, go east on Highway 89A for about 20 miles and turn south on FR 445. Go 27 miles to the wilderness boundary and Trail #57 trailhead. (Stay on right-hand fork of FR 445).

Note: This area is remote. Inform someone of your plans and carry a map. Hot in summer, tote plenty of water. Last 27 miles are over a dirt road, suitable for all vehicles in dry weather.

SOUTH CANYON TRAIL HIKE

Expert/3.0 miles/2.0 hours

Info: Talk about aerobic. This rigorous hike into South Canyon will definitely separate the dogs from the pups. As long as you're up to the physical challenge, you won't be disappointed, the views of Marble Canyon are impressive.

The hike into South Canyon begins with a steep descent through mixed conifers, aspens and ferns. Rock outcroppings and narrow paths account for the expert rating. And remember, what's steep going downhill can be a genuine buttkicker going uphill. Avoid in summer, the temperatures are extreme. For more information: (520) 643-7395.

Directions: Take Highway 67 south for 26.5 miles to Forest Road 611 (just past DeMotte Campground). Head east on FR 611 to FR 610 and turn right (south). Follow for 7.5 miles to the trailhead.

JEROME

LODGING

THE SURGEON'S HOUSE BED & BREAKFAST
101 Hill St (86331) Rates: $75-$110;
Tel: (602) 990-0682; (800) 456-0682

RECREATION

JEROME STATE HISTORIC PARK - Leashes

Info: This park offers a glimpse into Arizona history. The landscape and architecture are yours to admire but the building interiors are off limits to Snoopy. Plaques are posted for outdoor-only sightseers to learn about the rich history of Jerome. For more information: (520) 634-6381.

Directions: Located in Jerome off Highway 89A.

Note: $2.00 per vehicle entrance fee.

KAYENTA

LODGING

GOULDING'S TRADING POST & LODGE
(Monument Valley, UT (84536)
P. O. Box 360001; Rates: $72-$102;
Tel: (801) 727-3231

KEARNY

LODGING
GENERAL KEARNY INN
P. O. Box 188 (85237) Rates: $40;
Tel: (520) 363-5505

KINGMAN

LODGING
BEST WESTERN A WAYFARER'S INN
2815 E Andy Devine (86401) Rates: $43-$61;
Tel: (520) 753-6271; (800) 528-1234

BEST WESTERN KING'S INN
2930 E Andy Devine (86401) Rates: $43-$64;
Tel: (520) 753-6101; (800) 528-1234

DAYS INN EAST
3381 E Andy Devine (86401) Rates: $60+;
Tel: (520) 757-7337; (800) 329-7466

DAYS INN WEST
3023 E Andy Devine (86401) Rates: $45-$65;
Tel: (520) 753-7500; (800) 329-7466

HIGH DESERT INN
2803 E Andy Devine (86401) Rates: $19-$29;
Tel: (520) 753-2935

HILL TOP MOTEL
1901 E Andy Devine (86401) Rates: $22-$36;
Tel: (520) 753-2198

HOLIDAY INN
3100 E Andy Devine (86401) Rates: $39-$54;
Tel: (520) 753-6262; (800) 465-4329

MOTEL 6
424 W Beale St (86401) Rates: $29-$38;
Tel: (520) 753-9222; (800) 440-6000

MOTEL 6
3351 E Andy Devine (86401) Rates: $30-$36;
Tel: (520) 757-7151; (800) 440-6000

MOTEL 6
3270 E Andy Devine (86401) Rates: $27-$34;
Tel: (520) 757-7121; (800) 440-6000

QUALITY INN
1400 E Andy Devine (86401) Rates: $40-$69;
Tel: (520) 753-4747; (800) 424-6423

RODEWAY INN
411 W Beale St (86401) Rates: $26-$45;
Tel: (520) 753-5521; (800) 424-4777

SILVER QUEEN MOTEL
3285 E Andy Devine (86401) Rates: $24-$34;
Tel: (520) 757-4315

SUPER 8 MOTEL
3401 E Andy Devine (86401) Rates: $32-$49;
Tel: (520) 757-4808; (800) 800-8000

RECREATION

CHERUM PEAK TRAIL HIKE

Intermediate/4.0 miles/2.0 hours

Info: The scenic surroundings make this trail outstanding. On the north side of Cherum Peak, you'll experience gorgeous vistas of the Music Mountains, Hualapai Valley, Red Lake Playa, Mount Charleston, Detrital Valley and the Black Mountains. Coming or going, you'll walk in splendor. For more information: (520) 757-3161.

Directions: From Kingman, take Highway 93 north for 35 miles to Chloride-Big Wash Road. Head east to the trailhead at road's end.

HUALAPAI MOUNTAIN PARK

Info: 2,300 acres of pure natural beauty are yours for the taking at this parkland. Whether you hike the day away on the inter-connecting trail system or chill-out under a shade tree, you're in for some great outdoor fun. Summertime at this cool, mountainous park gets two paws up from desert dwelling dogs. Take a deep breath... aah, nothing compares to fresh, pine-scented air. If hiking is your game plan, don't forget lunch. You and the pupster are sure to work up an appetite on one of the following five trails. For more information: (520) 757-0915.

Directions: From Kingman, take Interstate 40 south to Exit #51. Continue south on Stockton Hill Road (which turns into Hualapai Mountain Road) for 14 miles to the park.

1) ASPEN SPRINGS TRAIL HIKE - Leashes

Beginner/1.7 miles/1.0 hours

Info: Even couch potato people and their pooches will like this short and easy hike. Interpretive signs are a bonus of flora and fauna knowledge. And if you decide to extend your visit, this trail links to four other trails, equally easy to take. For more information: (520) 757-3859.

Directions: Take Hualapai Mountain Road southeast for 14 miles to Hualapai Mountain Park. Enter the park at the rental cabin entrance. Stay right, following the road to the parking area just before the Camp Levi Levi Boy Scout Camp entrance. The trailhead is on the other side of the road.

2) ASPEN SPRINGS TRAIL to ASPEN PEAK TRAIL HIKE - Leashes

Beginner/3.25 miles/1.5 hours

Info: Follow Aspen Springs Trail to the first right fork of the Potato Patch Loop Trail and take it to where the Aspen Peak Trail branches off to the left. You'll cross a wooden bridge and hike through forests of aspen and ponderosa pine as the trail loops to 8,239-foot Aspen Peak. For more information: (520) 757-3859.

Directions: See Aspen Springs Trail Hike.

3) ASPEN SPRINGS TRAIL to HAYDEN PEAK SOUTH TRAIL HIKE - Leashes

Beginner/5.0 miles/2.5 hours

Info: Follow the Aspen Springs Trail to the Potato Patch Loop and take the right fork of the loop trail. Follow to where the Hayden Peak South Trail branches off to the left. Enjoy a pleasant hike with your four-pawed friend through a grab bag forest of aspen, white fir, ponderosa and Douglas fir. Once you reach Hayden Peak, admire the pretty vistas from the park bench. The intermediate rating reflects the partial uphill return. For more information: (520) 757-3859.

Directions: See Aspen Springs Trail Hike.

4) ASPEN SPRINGS TRAIL to HAYDEN PEAK WEST TRAIL HIKE - Leashes

Beginner/4.0 miles/2.0 hours

Info: Follow the same path as the preceding hike but where Hayden Peak South branches left, you want to go right. This is the shortest and least demanding of the five interconnecting trails within Hualapai Mountain Park. Mosey about forests of ponderosa, white fir, Douglas fir, gambel oak and aspen. When you reach trail's end, share a moment with your pooch enjoying the views. For more information: (520) 757-3859.

Directions: See Aspen Springs Trail Hike.

5) ASPEN SPRINGS TRAIL to POTATO PATCH LOOP TRAIL HIKE - Leashes

Beginner/6.9 miles/3.5 hours

Info: The Aspen Springs Trail leads to this simple connecting loop trail. You'll walk among pine and fir, oak and juniper before reaching the Potato Patch Lookout. Just before the lookout, the trail to the left is the loop back to Aspen Springs Trail. For more information: (520) 757-3859.

Directions: See Aspen Springs Trail Hike.

LAKE MEAD

Info: Created by the Hoover Dam, a masterpiece of modern engineering, Lake Mead spans 105 miles and is recognized as the largest artificial lake in the United States. Rent a boat or bring your own and take the dawgus on an unforgettable journey through emerald waters, white sand beaches, jagged rocky shorelines and distinct desert terrain.

Tote a camera and capture memorable moments. Sunset brings haunting hues of red, gold and grey to the remarkable geologic formations lining the shore. Nighttime shines with the brilliance of countless stars while sunrise offers a picturesque beginning to another unforgettable day of fun in the sun. For more information: Lake Mead National Recreation Area, 601 Nevada Highway, Boulder City, NV 89005, (702) 293-8906.

Directions: Take Route 93 north to the Hoover Dam exit. Follow signs for Lake Mead.

LAKE HAVASU CITY

LODGING

BEST WESTERN-LAKE PLACE INN
31 Wing's Loop (86403) Rates: $45-$89;
Tel: (520) 855-2146;
(800) 528-1234 (US); (800) 258-8558 (AZ)

BRIDGEVIEW MOTEL
101 London Bridge Rd (86403) Rates: $35-$110;
Tel: (520) 855-5559

EZ-8 MOTEL
41 S Acoma Blvd (86403) Rates: $25-$40;
Tel: (520) 855-4023; (800) 326-6835

HAVASU MOTEL ALL-SUITE INN
2035 Acoma Blvd (86403) Rates: $20-$45;
Tel: (520) 855-2311

HOLIDAY INN
245 London Bridge Rd (86403) Rates: $45-$70;
Tel: (520) 855-4071; (800) 465-4329

ISLAND INN HOTEL
1300 W McCulloch Blvd (86403) Rates: $65-$85;
Tel: (520) 680-0606; (800) 243-9955

LAKEVIEW MOTEL
440 London Bridge Rd (86403) Rates: $25-$45;
Tel: (520) 855-3605

LONDON BRIDGE RESORT
1477 Queens Bay Rd (86403) Rates: $75-$150;
Tel: (520) 855-0888; (800) 624-7939

PECOS II CONDOMINIUMS
451 B Lake Havasu Ave (86403) Rates: $385 weekly;
Tel: (520) 855-7444

PIONEER HOTEL LAKE HAVASU CITY
271 Lake Havasu Ave (86403) Rates: $54-$64;
Tel: (520) 855-1111; (800) 528-5169

SANDMAN INN
1700 N McCulloch Blvd (86403) Rates: $30-$90;
Tel: (520) 855-7841; (800) 835-2410 (US)

SUPER 8 MOTEL
305 London Bridge Rd (86403) Rates: $36-$63;
Tel: (520) 855-8844; (800) 800-8000

WINDSOR INN
451 London Bridge Rd (86403) Rates: $26-$49;
Tel: (520) 855-4135; (800) 245-4135

RECREATION

THE ISLAND BIKE/JOGGING PATH - Leashes

Info: Get your daily dose at this dog-friendly park which provides clean-up bags along the walking path - talk about hospitality. The trail provides Sunday strollers with fine lake, mountain and city views.

Directions: Take Highway 95 to Mesquite Avenue. Take Mesquite Avenue to McCulloch Boulevard. Follow McCulloch to London Bridge. Cross the bridge and you are on the island.

JACK HARDIE PARK - Leashes

Info: A neighborhood park, you can take a stroll, watch a game of horseshoes or plan a picnic lunch.

Directions: On Dayton Avenue between Bunker and Baron Drives.

LAKE HAVASU

Info: You and your aquatic pup can float, troll, skim or sail along the surface of this popular water wonderland. With the wind in your hair and blue waters all around, escape the pressure of city life and enter a wet and wild world of recreation. In just a few hours you can pass under the London Bridge, sip on British tea, sup with your pup on a houseboat, take in some serious desert scenery and catch a morsel or two to grill on a good old-fashioned American BBQ. For more information: Lake Havasu Chamber of Commerce, 1930 Mesquite Avenue, Suite 3, Lake Havasu City, AZ 86403, (800) 242-8278 or (520) 855-4115.

Directions: The lake is accessible from many locations in Lake Havasu City.

WHYTES LOOP TRAIL HIKE - Leashes

Beginner/3.0 miles/1.5 hours

Info: Stroll along the shoreline of Lake Havasu to Whytes Retreat or venture from the shoreline on the looping trail through low desert hills and a shallow gorge framed with bluffs. Either way, you and the pupster can't go wrong. For more information: (520) 855-1223.

Directions: Take Highway 95 south to Cattail Cove State Park. The trailhead is located in the park at the boat launch ramp.

Note: $5.00 per vehicle entrance fee.

LAKE MONTEZUMA

Lodging
BEAVER CREEK INN
462 S Montezuma Ave (86342) Rates: $39-$48;
Tel: (520) 567-4475

LAKESIDE

Lodging
BARTRAM'S WHITE MOUNTAIN BED & BREAKFAST
Rt 1, Box 1014 (85929) Rates: $60-$75;
Tel: (520) 367-1408; (800) 257-0211

LAKE OF THE WOODS
2244 W White Mtn Blvd (85929) Rates: $43-$83;
Tel: (520) 368-5353

LAZY OAKS RESORT COTTAGES
Rt 2, Box 1215 (85929) Rates: $50-$65;
Tel: (520) 368-6203

MOONRIDGE LODGE & CABINS
P. O. Box 1058 (85929) Rates: $35-$135;
Tel: (520) 367-1906

THE PLACE RESORT CABINS
Rt 3, Box 2675 (85929) Rates: $66-$74;
Tel: (520) 368-6777

RECREATION
BIG SPRINGS TRAIL HIKE
Beginner/1.0 miles/0.5 hours

Info: Set aside half an hour for a leisurely stroll on this ponderosa-shaded trail. Your journey includes a verdant meadow and the gushing Big Spring. For more information: (520) 368-5111.

Directions: Take Woodland Road south to the trailhead.

TIMBER MESA TRAIL HIKE
Intermediate/6.0 miles/3.0 hours

Info: As you hike along Timber Mesa, you'll be treated to views of Frost Canyon on your way to the historic chimneys of the Jacques Family Ranch. A picture-perfect mountain scene forms the backdrop for your walk. Don't miss the wonderful views of Jacques Marsh and Pinetop-Lakeside as the trail loops back. This is definitely a doggone good day excursion. For more information: (520) 368-5111.

Directions: From Lakeside Ranger Station drive south on Highway 260. Turn left on Porter Mountain Road. Drive approximately 2.2 miles, turn left at the cattleguard. Drive about 50 feet to the cindered trailhead on the right.

LITCHFIELD PARK

LODGING

THE WIGWAM RESORT
Indian School & N Litchfield Rds (85340)
Rates: $90-$420; Tel: (602) 935-3811; (800) 327-0396

MARBLE CANYON

LODGING

LEES FERRY LODGE
HC67, Box 1 (Vermilion Cliffs 86036) Rates: $47+;
Tel: (520) 355-2231

MARBLE CANYON LODGE
Box 1, Hwy 89A (86036) Rates: $40-$50;
Tel: (520) 355-2225; (800) 726-1789

RECREATION

ONE MILE RIVER TRAIL HIKE - Leashes

Beginner/2.0 miles/1.0 hours

Info: Take a pleasurable, riverside stroll with your pooch through this richly historic area set against the prehistoric Vermilion Cliffs. Beginning at Lees Ferry Historic Fort and continuing along an old wagon road to the main ferry crossing site, you'll pass the remnants of Lonely Dell (the farm of John Doyle Lee) and the wreck of the steamboat Charles H. Spencer. Best times to visit are spring and fall. Summer is too hot, winter is too cold. For more information: (520) 645-8200.

Directions: From Highway 89A take the Lees Ferry junction, just 300 yards west of the Navajo Bridge. Follow to the trailhead at Lees Ferry Historic Fort. Parking is at the boat launching ramp.

MESA

LODGING

ARIZONA GOLF RESORT & CONFERENCE CENTER
425 S Power Rd (85206) Rates: $85-$165;
Tel: (602) 832-3202; (800) 528-8282 (US & CAN)

BEST WESTERN MESA INN
1625 E Main St (85203) Rates: $34-$80;
Tel: (520) 964-8000; (800) 528-1234

BEST WESTERN SUPERSTITION SPRINGS INN & SUITES
1342 S Power Rd (85206) Rates: $49-$150;
Tel: (602) 641-1164; (800) 528-1234

DAYS INN
333 W Juanita (85210) Rates: $40-$175;
Tel: (602) 844-8900; (800) 329-7466

HAMPTON INN
1563 S Gilbert Rd (85204) Rates: $53-$83;
Tel: (602) 926-3600; (800) 426-7866

HOLIDAY INN
1600 S Country Club Dr (85210) Rates: $49-$99;
Tel: (602) 964-7000; (800) 465-4329

MARICOPA INN MOTOR HOTEL
3 E Main St (85201) Rates: $28-$49;
Tel: (602) 834-6060; (800) 627-2144

MOTEL 6
336 W Hampton Ave (85202) Rates: $30-$36;
Tel: (602) 844-8899; (800) 440-6000

MOTEL 6
1511 S Country Club Dr (85201) Rates: $29-$35;
Tel: (602) 834-0066; (800) 440-6000

MOTEL 6
630 W Main St (85201) Rates: $30-$36;
Tel: (602) 969-8111; (800) 440-6000

QUALITY INN ROYAL MESA
951 W Main St (85201) Rates: $42-$99;
Tel: (602) 833-1231;
(800) 228-5151 (US); (800) 333-5501 (AZ)

RAMADA INNSUITES
1410 S Country Club Dr (85201) Rates: $35-$99;
Tel: (602) 964-2897; (800) 272-6232

RAMADA LIMITED EAST VALLEY
1750 E Main St (85203) Rates: $39-$76;
Tel: (602) 969-3600; (800) 272-6232

RODEWAY INN
5700 E Main St (85205) Rates: $36-$99;
Tel: (602) 985-3600;
(800) 424-4777 (US); (800) 888-3561 (AZ)

SAN DEE MOTEL
6649 E Apache Tr (85205) Rates: $45-$58;
Tel: (602) 985-1912

SUPER 8 MOTEL
1550 S Gilbert Rd (85204) Rates: $37-$58;
Tel: (602) 545-0888; (800) 800-8000

TRAVELODGE MESA
22 S Country Club Dr (85202) Rates: $20-$69;
Tel: (602) 964-5694; (800) 255-3050

RECREATION

BALLANTINE TRAIL HIKE to BOULDER FLAT

Intermediate/8.0 miles/4.5 hours

Info: Flowers, flowers everywhere. Come springtime, this trail explodes in a kaleidoscope of color. Poppies, lupine, owl clover, ocotillo and brittlebush are just a sampling of the blooms that make this a popular wildflower watching hike.

Beginning with an easy half-mile streamside stroll along the northern portion of Pine Creek Loop Trail, cottonwoods and mesquite line the way as you hook up with the Ballantine Trail and enter the heart of wildflower country. You and your pooch will get your Rexercise over the next 3.5-mile climb which ends at Boulder Flat. If you've packed picnic goodies, this is the perfect place for lunch. Whenever you're ready, retrace your steps on the return trip. For more information: (602) 379-6446.

Directions: Take Route 87 (the Beeline Highway) northeast from Mesa for approximately thirty miles. At Milepost 210.0 start looking for the trailhead and parking area on the right (east).

SAGUARO LAKE

Info: Fido doesn't have to fight for snout space in the car window anymore. He can let his ears flap in the breeze and turn his snout skyward as you slice through the clear blue of this beautiful lake in your open-air watercraft. Pull up the outboard and venture onto shore for some desert exploring and leg stretching. After you and Fido have had your fill of terra firma, rev up the engines for some serious water-filled fun. For more information: Mesa Convention & Visitors Bureau, 120 N. Center, P. O.

Locate Other Dog-Friendly Activities...Check Nearby Cities

Box 5529 (85211), Mesa, AZ 85201, (800) 283-MESA or (602) 827-4700.

Directions: Take Highway 87 (Beeline Highway) north about 10 miles past the Shea Boulevard intersection. Take a right and follow signs for the lake.

USERY MOUNTAIN RECREATION AREA - Leashes

Info: The park was named after King Usery, a late 19th century horse thief and desperado. Thief or not, King Usery couldn't steal the inherent beauty of the area so it remains for you and your pooch to enjoy. Several hiking trails are scattered throughout the Sonoran Desert landscape, some leading to incredible views of the Salt River Basin and the Superstition Mountains. Take your time and a camera, you'll find plenty of photo opportunities. For more information: (602) 506-2930 or (602) 984-0032.

Directions: Take Usery Pass Road two miles north of McKellips Road to the park entrance.

Note: Hours 6AM-7:30PM. $2 per vehicle entrance fee charged November-April. This area is remote. Inform someone of your plans and carry a map.

1) BLEVINS TRAIL HIKE
Beginner/2.9 miles/1.5 hours

Info: Whoa Nellie! Enter at either the west or the east side of the Horse Staging Area to find the trailhead. This loop trail (popular with the equestrian set) gallops through lush Sonoran Desert terrain and offers something for everyone, from bird serenades to excellent views of the Superstition and Goldfield Mountains. For more information: (602) 506-2930 or (602) 984-0032.

Dogs May Be Unleashed Unless Otherwise Indicated

Directions: Take Usery Pass Road/Ellsworth Road 2 miles north of McKellips Road to Usery Mountain Recreation Area.

2) MERKL MEMORIAL SPUR TRAIL HIKE

Intermediate/0.8 miles/0.5 hours

Info: You and your hiking hound are in for a short, scenic hike. Take your time and enjoy the spectacular desert views. For more information: (602) 506-2930 or (602) 984-0032.

Directions: Take Usery Pass Road/Ellsworth Road 2 miles north of McKellips Road to Usery Mountain Recreation Area. Follow Usery Park Road to the trailhead at the picnic area.

3) MERKL MEMORIAL TRAIL HIKE - Leashes

Beginner/0.9 miles/0.5 hours

Info: This loop trail provides panoramic desert vistas while providing an education on the flora with plant identification signs. For more information: (602) 506-2930 or (602) 984-0032.

Directions: Take Usery Pass Road/Ellsworth Road 2 miles north of McKellips Road to Usery Mountain Recreation Area. Follow Usery Park Road to the picnic area. The trail is marked.

4) PASS MOUNTAIN TRAIL HIKE - Leashes

Expert/7.1 miles/3.5 hours

Info: You and fur-face will want to stretch out before beginning your journey. Rough and tough, you'll earn the amazing views along this arduous loop trail which circles Pass Mountain. Six distinct mountain ranges can be seen from the trail, each more spectacular than the one before. For more information: (602) 506-2930 or (602) 984-0032.

Directions: Follow Usery Park Road past the park's entrance to Blevin's Drive. Turn right and follow signs for the Horse Staging Area.

5) WIND CAVE TRAIL HIKE

Intermediate/3.2 miles/2.0 hours

Info: Wind Cave Trail is located among the volcanic-formed cliffs of Pass Mountain. Only 2.6 miles in length, this trail is no Sunday stroll. It rises 1,000 feet in elevation before reaching its namesake, erosion-carved Wind Cave. You and the canine will want to catch your breath, and enjoy a look-see in this shaded area before beginning your downward journey. For more information: (602) 506-2930.

Directions: Take Usery Pass Road/Ellsworth Road 2 miles north of McKellips Road to Usery Mountain Recreation Area. Once through the gatehouse, the parking area is on Wind Cave Drive.

MIAMI

LODGING

BEST WESTERN COPPER HILLS INN
Rt 1, Box 506 (85539) Rates: $54-$74;
Tel: (520) 425-7151; (800) 528-1234

RECREATION

JUG TRAIL HIKE
Intermediate/4.0 miles/2.0 hours

Info: You and the pupster are in for a real wilderness experience on this secluded hike through the Salome Creek Wilderness. For more information: (520) 467-3200.

Directions: Take Highway 60 east to Highway 88 northwest. At the town of Roosevelt, Highway 88 becomes Highway 188. Continue north on Highway 188 to the north end of Roosevelt Lake, turning onto FR 60 for 10 miles to the trailhead. Parking is available for only a few cars.

Note: This area is remote. Inform someone of your plans and carry a map.

PARKER CREEK TRAIL HIKE
Intermediate/8.0 miles/4.0 hours

Info: Far reaching vistas of Roosevelt Lake and the Four Peaks Wilderness make this long, somewhat demanding trek worth the effort. As you and your canine companion hike alongside Parker Creek, you'll climb 2,000 feet in elevation- from 5,080 feet to 7,080 feet. Watch the change in flora during your ascent. For more information: (520) 462-3311.

Directions: Take Highway 60 east to Highway 88 northwest. From Highway 88, head north on Highway 288 to Sierra Ancha Experimental Forest Headquarters and the trailhead.

Note: This area is remote. Inform someone of your plans and carry a map.

REAVIS GAP TRAIL HIKE

Expert/5.0 miles/2.5 hours

Info: For experienced hikers and physically fit pooches only. This demanding trail climbs through the remote eastern portion of the Superstition Wilderness. After the steep ascent to Reavis Gap, you'll encounter a trail intersection. Continue on the trail branching left. The trail levels out and involves a couple creek crossings before ending at Reavis Ranch. For more information: (520) 467-3200.

Directions: Take Highway 88 west to FR 449. Head south on FR 449 to FR 449A. The trailhead is located at the end of FR 449A.

Note: This area is remote. Inform someone of your plans and carry a map.

REYNOLDS CREEK TRAIL HIKE

Intermediate/7.4 miles/3.5 hours

Info: You and your hiking hound are in for a scenic, switchbacking adventure on this wilderness trail. Reynolds Creek Falls and the Sierra Ancha Mountains are just two of the beautiful sights along the way. For more information: (520) 462-3311.

Directions: Take Highway 60 east to Highway 88 northwest. From Highway 88, head north on Highway 288 to FR 410. Head southeast on FR 410 for 4 miles to the north trailhead.

Note: This area is remote. Inform someone of your plans and carry a map.

Dogs May Be Unleashed Unless Otherwise Indicated

THOMPSON TRAIL HIKE

Intermediate/2.8 miles/1.5 hours

Info: Great views of sun splashed Roosevelt Lake await you and your four-pawed sidekick on this steep, rugged trail. For more information: (520) 467-3200.

Directions: Take Highway 60 east to Highway 88 northwest to the Tonto Basin Ranger Station. Directly across from the Ranger Station is a road leading to the Lakeview Trailer Park. Follow this road into the park, making your first right. The parking area and the Cemetery Trailhead are straight ahead. Access the Thompson Trail from the .2 mile Cemetery Trail.

TONTO NATIONAL MONUMENT - Leashes

Info: This is one of a handful of prehistoric ruins which welcomes both you and your leashed pooch. After a beautiful drive on Route 88, you can spend the afternoon wandering amidst the remains of what was once home to an entire civilization - the Salado Indians. Ancient artifacts and interpretive signs furnish an historic glimpse into the life of the fascinating Salado. Leave only footprints, take only memories. Avoid in the summer - too hot.

Directions: Take Highway 60 east to Highway 88 northwest. Go 30 miles to the monument's entrance.

Note: $4.00 per vehicle entrance fee; hours are 8:00 AM - 4:00 PM.

1) CACTUS PATCH TRAIL HIKE - Leashes

Beginner/0.25 miles/0.25 minutes

Info: Short and sweet describes this Sonoran Desert trail.

Directions: Take Highway 60 east to Highway 88 northwest. Go 30 miles to the monument's entrance.

2) LOWER RUIN TRAIL HIKE - Leashes

Intermediate/1.0 miles/0.5 hours

Info: You and your furry sidekick will get a bit of an aerobic workout on the 350-foot vertical climb to the hike's main attraction - a 19-room ancient cliff ruin. There are interpretive trail signs which offer insight into the lives of the Salado Indians. Stay on the designated trail. Leave only footprints, take only memories. Avoid in summer - too hot.

Directions: Take Highway 60 east to Highway 88 northwest. Go 30 miles to the monument's entrance.

MOUNT LEMMON

(See Summerhaven and Tucson listings for lodging & recreation.)

THE MOUNT LEMMON DRIVE

Info: Escape the desert heat and chill out with Bowser along the way to the top of Mount Lemmon. Thirty miles north and a couple of weather zones from Tucson, Mount Lemmon offers cool temperatures and a tempting array of activities.

As you ascend the south side of the mountain, you'll climb from the desert floor to an elevation of

8,200 feet. A granite outcropping situated at 6,600 feet, make Windy Point Vista your first stop. From this lofty perch, you'll have some staggering views of the Tucson Valley and numerous mountain ranges. If you're in a fishing mode, Rose Canyon Lake should be your next stop. Just past Milepost 17, eleven acres of trout-filled water await your bait.

Directions: From Tucson, take Tanque Verde Road north to Catalina Highway and head east. Catalina Highway runs into General Hitchcock Forest Highway - the road to the mountaintop.

MUNDS PARK

LODGING
MOTEL IN THE PINES
P. O. Box 18171 (86017) Rates: $35-$65;
Tel: (520) 286-9699

NOGALES

LODGING
AMERICANA MOTOR HOTEL
639 N Grand Ave (85621) Rates: $44-$67;
Tel: (520) 287-7211; (800) 874-8079

BEST WESTERN SIESTA MOTEL
673 N Grand Ave (85621) Rates: $36-$60;
Tel: (520) 287-4671; (800) 528-1234

BEST WESTERN TIME MOTEL
921 N Grand Ave (85621) Rates: $34-$50;
Tel: (520) 287-4627; (800) 528-1234

MOTEL 6
141 W Mariposa Rd (85621) Rates: $32-$38;
Tel: (520) 281-2951; (800) 440-6000

RECREATION

ATASCOSA TRAIL HIKE
Intermediate/5.0 miles/2.5 hours

Info: As you zigzag up this trail, get an eyeful of the seemingly endless views of Montana Peak, Castle Rock, Baboquivari Peak, Sycamore Canyon, the Huachuca Mountains and the Santa Rita Mountains. For more information: (520) 281-2296.

Directions: Take Interstate 19 north to Highway 289 west. Follow Highway 289 for 9 miles to FR 39. Take FR 39 for 6 miles to the trailhead.

CHINAMAN TRAIL HIKE
Beginner/5.2 miles/2.5 hours

Info: From Tunnel Spring to Bear Spring, this level trail traces an old water ditch as it guides you through Casa Blanca Canyon. Once you reach Bear Spring retrace your steps. For more information: (520) 281-2296.

Directions: Take Highway 82 north to Highway 83 north. Approximately 4 miles north of Sonoita, head west on FR 92. After .75 miles, bear left at the fork and continue for 4 miles to another fork, bearing right for 2.5 miles to FR 785. Head southwest on FR 785 for three miles to the trailhead at Tunnel Spring.

GARDNER CANYON TRAIL HIKE

Intermediate/6.0 miles/3.0 hours

Info: Hiking endurance and directional skills are the key to completing this demanding hike. The trail begins by following a jeep trail which gives way to a foot trail. After a quarter mile, turn right on Gardner Canyon Road and hike another mile to road's end where another foot trail begins. This foot trail takes you out of Gardner Canyon and meets up with the Super Trail #134. Head right on TR #134 to 8,780-foot Baldy Saddle. You and your trooper poocher will have climbed over 2,000 feet in elevation. Take time for a biscuit break before turning around and heading back the way you came. For more information: (520) 281-2296.

Directions: Take Highway 82 north to Highway 83 north. Approximately 4 miles north of Sonoita, head west on FR 92. After .75 miles, bear left at the fork and continue for 4 miles to another fork, bearing right for 2.5 miles to FR 785. Turn left on FR 785 and follow for 5 miles to the trailhead.

SYCAMORE CANYON TRAIL HIKE

Expert/8.0 miles/5.0 hours

Info: From a gurgling stream and miniature waterfall to massive sandstone monoliths and 80-foot sycamore trees, this hike within the Pajarita Wilderness has it all. The flying antics of wrens, jays, red-tailed hawks and hummingbirds fill the sky, while blue morning glory and other wildflowers including the rare Arizona poppy dot the terrain.

Regardless of the season, you'll want to break out your waterproof boots for this one. The trail involves a bit of stream hopping and Sycamore

Creek is perennial - perfect for all aquatic pups. Once past the waterfall, it's only another mile to a bonafido reward - enormous Arizona sycamores. For more information: (520) 281-2296.

Directions: On Highway 19 about 12 miles north of Nogales is the Highway 289 intersection. Take 289 west to Pena Blanca Lake. Then continue west on Forest Service Road 39 for 10 miles to the trailhead.

Note: Gnats and mosquitoes inhabit the streamside areas. Use insect repellent before hiking. Spray the pooch too.

ORACLE

LODGING

VILLA CARDINALE BED & BREAKFAST

1315 W Oracle Ranch Rd (85623) Rates: $45-$60; Tel: (520) 896-2516

RECREATION

CODY TRAIL HIKE

Intermediate/7.4 miles/3.5 hours

Info: As you hike this section of the Arizona Trail, look around and enjoy vistas of the San Pedro River Valley and the Galiuro Mountains. A popular trail through the Santa Catalina Mountains, it hooks up with the Oracle Ridge Trail, your turnaround point. For more information: (520) 749-8700.

Directions: Take FR 38 (Mt. Lemmon Road) south to the American Flag Trailhead, which is also the Cody Trailhead.

Dogs May Be Unleashed Unless Otherwise Indicated

OVERGAARD

RECREATION

TALL TIMBER PARK

Info: Hot dogs love the cool shade of towering ponderosa pines along the hiking trails in this 42-acre park. Day use activities also include picnicking, racquetball, basketball and shuffleboard. For more information: (520) 535-4406.

Directions: Head east on Highway 260 to the park's entrance.

PAGE

LODGING

BEST WESTERN WESTON INN
207 N Lake Powell Blvd (86040) Rates: $34-$91;
Tel: (520) 645-2451;(800) 528-1234 (US);
(800) 637-9183 (AZ)

ECONO LODGE
121 S Lake Powell Blvd (86040) Rates: $35-$90;
Tel: (520) 645-2488; (800) 424-4777

EMPIRE HOUSE MOTEL
100 S Lake Powell Blvd (86040) Rates: $50-$62;
Tel: (520) 645-2406

HOLIDAY INN-PAGE/LAKE POWELL
287 N Lake Powell Blvd (86040) Rates: $52-$106;
Tel: (520) 645-8851;
(800) 465-4329 (US); (800) 232-0011 (AZ)

INN AT LAKE POWELL
716 Rim View Dr (86040) Rates: $35-$92;
Tel: (520) 645-2466; (800) 826-2718

LAKE POWELL MOTEL
Highway 89 N (86040) Rates: $54-$65;
Tel: (520) 645-2477

WAHWEAP LODGE & MARINA RESORT
100 Lake Shore Dr (86040) Rates: $65-$127;
Tel: (520) 645-2433; (800) 528-6154

RECREATION

LAKE POWELL NATIONAL RECREATION AREA

Info: As the second largest artificial lake in the United States, Lake Powell spans a length of 186 miles and offers a 2,000-mile shoreline (800 miles longer than California's coastline). Your water loving pooch can accompany you on a houseboat rental and you can float, fish, swim, ski or sightsee your way through time-carved cliffs atop glacier blue and sometimes emerald green water. Pack a camera, your camping gear and plenty of water toys before you and Fido embark on this view-filled adventure of waterfalls, beaches, red-walled canyons, glowing sunsets and star studded skies. Reservations are required for spring and summer rentals. For more information: ARA Leisure Services, P. O. Box 56909, Phoenix, AZ 85079, (800) 528-6154.

Directions: Access the southernmost entry to Lake Powell by heading north on U.S. Route 89 to Wahweap Marina.

PARKER

LODGING

BUDGET INN MOTEL
912 Agency Rd (85344) Rates: $35-$45;
Tel: (520) 669-2566

EL RANCHO MOTEL
709 California Ave (85344) Rates: $35+;
Tel: (520) 669-2231

HAVASU SPRINGS RESORT
Rt 2, Box 624 (85344) Rates: $75-$85;
Tel: (520) 667-3361

HOLIDAY KASBAH
604 California Ave (85344) Rates: $39-$63;
Tel: (520) 669-2133

STARDUST MOTEL
700 California Ave (85344) Rates: $30-$75;
Tel: (520) 669-2278

RECREATION

BUCKSKIN MOUNTAIN STATE PARK - Leashes

Info: This park caters to a wide variety of interests. Avoid the beach areas - dogs aren't permitted there. Instead, sniff your way through a cornucopia of flora, fauna and fascinating rock formations as you explore one of the numerous hiking trails. Perhaps an in-the-water-experience is more to your liking. Rent a boat and just float - the scenery is dreamery. If you'd rather stay on terra firma, enjoy some puppy playtime in the large grassy picnic area. Whatever your pleasure, a doggone good time awaits you and the pooch at this 1,676-acre park.

Directions: From Parker, take Highway 95 north for 11 miles to the park.

Note: $5.00 per vehicle entrance fee.

1) BUCKSKIN-LIGHTNING BOLT TRAILS HIKE - Leashes

Intermediate/6.2 miles/3.0 hours

Info: Escape the confining indoors into the great outdoors on this scenic trail through the Buckskin Mountains. Feast your eyes on beautiful desert flora and spectacular views of the Colorado River. Your hiking excursion brings you to a point where the trail splits: head left to a historic mining area or branch right to a scenic overlook. Indecisive types, a coin flip may help you and your pooch decide which way to go first. For more information: (520) 667-3386 or 667-3231.

Directions: Take Highway 95 north for 11 miles to Buckskin Mountain State Park. The trailhead is in the park.

LA PAZ COUNTY PARK - Leashes

Info: Frolic with Fido on the beach at this dog-friendly park. For more information: (520) 667-2069.

Directions: Located 8 miles north of Parker off Highway 95.

Note: $2 day use fee for non-county residents

PATAGONIA

LODGING

STAGE STOP INN
Box 777 (85624) Rates: $49-$95;
Tel: (520) 394-2211

RECREATION

CAVE CANYON TRAIL HIKE
Intermediate/4.0 miles/2.0 hours

Info: A little pain for a lot of gain - in elevation. Ascend the Santa Ritas to Florida Saddle, the trail's destination and gaze upon mountain and valley views, including 9,446-foot Miller Peak - Bow-Wow! For more information: (520) 281-2296.

Directions: Take Highway 82 north to Highway 83 north. Approximately 4 miles north of Sonoita, head west on FR 92. After .75 miles, bear left at the fork and continue for 4 miles to another fork, bearing right for 10.3 miles to the trailhead.

Note: High clearance vehicles only.

JOSEPHINE CANYON TRAIL HIKE
Intermediate/5.6 miles/3.0 hours

Info: A steep ascent marks your passage through the lush Josephine Canyon where some great views of Josephine Peak and Mt. Wrightson are yours for the looking. Depending on the season, Spot might spot a cascading waterfall or two. Once you reach Josephine Saddle, do the descent thing. For more information: (520) 281-2296.

Directions: From Patagonia, take Highway 82 north to FR 143, turn right. Follow FR 143 to FR 4082 and make a right. Continue 2 miles to the trailhead.

PATAGONIA LAKE STATE PARK - Leashes

Info: On your way to some south-of-the-border shopping, detour into Patagonia Lake State Park and expend some energy before you spend some pesos. Rent a boat and try your hand at fishing. The lake is stocked with tasty trout during the winter months. It's also home to bass, bluegill, catfish and crappie. Pooches are allowed everywhere on a leash except inside buildings and the beach.

If you'd rather hike, there are several trails scattered throughout the 640-acre state park. At an elevation of 3,750 feet, the park's weather is pleasant year round.

Directions: West of Highway 82, south of Patagonia.

Note: $5.00 per vehicle entrance fee.

WALKER BASIN TRAIL HIKE

Intermediate/5.2 miles/2.5 hours

Info: Solitude and gentle terrain combine to make for a great mountain hike. Delight in the whisper quiet atmosphere of the Santa Ritas while your eyes feast on the postcardian vistas of Mt. Josephine and Mt. Wrightson. For more information: (520) 281-2296.

Directions: From Patagonia, head north on 1st Avenue to the Coronado National Forest Boundary where the road becomes FR 72. Follow FR 72 for approximately 4 miles to the FR 72/FR 72A junction. Continue on FR 72 to the trailhead at road's end.

Note: High clearance vehicles only.

PAYSON

LODGING

CHRISTOPHER CREEK LODGE/MOTEL
Star Rt Box 119 (85541) Rates: $40-$75;
Tel: (520) 478-4300

GREY HACKLE LODGE
Star Rt Box 145 (85541) Rates: $40-$95;
Tel: (520) 478-4392

KOHL'S GUEST RANCH RESORT
E Hwy 260 (85541) Rates: $49-$79;
Tel: (520) 478-4211; (800) 331-5645

MAJESTIC MOUNTAIN INN
602 E Hwy 260 (85541) Rates: $36-$140;
Tel: (520) 474-0185; (800) 408-2442

PAYSON PUEBLO INN
809 E Hwy 260 (85541) Rates: $34-$135;
Tel: (520) 474-5241; (800) 888-9828

SWISS VILLAGE LODGE
801 N Beeline Hwy (85541) Rates: $59-$109;
Tel: (520) 474-3241; (800) 247-9477

TRAVELODGE
101 W Phoenix St (85541) Rates: $50-$85;
Tel: (520) 474-4526; (800) 578-7878

RECREATION

ABERT NATURE TRAIL HIKE

Beginner/2.0 miles/1.0 hours

Info: Running short on time? This interpretive trail lets you learn and squeeze in a bit of exercise while you're at it. The trail pamphlet provides a quickie education on the area's flora and fauna. And the woodsy locale makes for a pleasant excursion.

Locate Other Dog-Friendly Activities...Check Nearby Cities

Directions: From Payson, take Highway 260 northeast for 13 miles to the trailhead at Ponderosa Campground.

BABE HAUGHT TRAIL HIKE

Intermediate/3.8 miles/2.0 hours

Info: This historic trail was established to transport produce from Pleasant Valley to the small towns above the Mogollon Rim. An area of quiet beauty, of forest and meadows, the Rim is an escarpment at 6,000 feet above the Valley floor. The trail begins in the drainage of Tonto Creek and climbs 1,200 feet to the Rim's crest. The views are outstanding and a definite highlight of the trip. For more information: (520) 474-7900.

Directions: Take Highway 260 east, turning north on FR 289. The trailhead is located near the entrance road of the Tonto Creek Fish Hatchery.

CALLOWAY TRAIL HIKE

Intermediate/1.0 miles/0.5 hours

Info: As long as you and your pooch have some hiking experience under your belt/leash, you'll be able to handle the steepness of this short trail. The only maintained trail leading into the upper reaches of the area from the south side, this pathway offers a unique view of West Clear Creek. The rapid descent to the creek and canyon bottom slithers along limestone and sandstone cliffs. Cool off by wading in the icy cold waters before heading out of the canyon. If your pooch is a water hound, good luck getting him to leave. For more information: (520) 354-2216.

Directions: From Payson, take Highway 260 north for 2.5 miles until you reach Forest Road 144, turn right (east). Go for about a mile to FR 149. Turn left (north) and drive to FR 142. Turn left (west) and go about 4 miles to FR 142B. Turn right (north) and go to the trailhead at road's end.

Note: High clearance vehicles only.

COLONEL DEVIN TRAIL HIKE

Expert/4.0 miles/2.5 hours

Info: Tough and tougher best describes this trail which gains 1,400 feet in just 2 miles. Make sure you and the pupster are in good shape before attempting this one. Two paws up for scenery, the trail climbs the Mogollon Rim from top to bottom. Part of the Arizona Trail, it links the Highline and Fred Haught Trails. For more information: (520) 474-7900.

Directions: Take Highway 87 north to FR 199. Head east on FR 199 for 10 miles to FR 64 west. Follow FR 64 for .75 miles to FR 32 and turn north. Continue 3.3 miles to FR 32A and go north for .5 miles to the trailhead. The trailhead is approximately 100 feet past the kiosk.

DEER CREEK TRAIL HIKE - Leashes

Intermediate/1.0-17.6 miles/0.5-8.5 hours

Info: No matter how much of this trail you decide to tackle, your excursion will be filled with delightful sights, pleasant senses, and hours of peaceful solitude. Beginning in an upper desert landscape, you and Bowser will descend into Deer Creek Canyon. Be prepared for wet tootsies. You'll crisscross the creek many times during this outing before climbing out of the canyon to a forest of ponderosa. FR 201 is your turnaround point, time to retrace your steps for the trip back. For more information: (520) 467-2236.

Directions: Take Highway 87 south for 17 miles to the Highway 188 junction. Trailhead is located on the west side of Highway 87, 100 yards from the road. Pay close attention to the signs, three trails head out from this spot. Deer Creek Trail will be the first one you reach.

DREW CANYON TRAIL HIKE

Expert/2.0 miles/1.5 hours

Info: The motto of this trail should be. "No pain, no elevation gain". This demanding hike covers a 1,000-foot change in one mile, but the payback views are breathtaking. The trail starts at the General Crook Trail in a forest of firs, ponderosa pines and bracken ferns, crosses the Hole-in-Ground gravel pit road and then drops off the rim. To keep you on track, certain sections of the trail are flagged and blazed. As you hike, watch for the old lag tree. Back in the days before towers, lag trees were used as fire lookouts. For more information: (520) 289-2471.

Directions: Take Highway 260 east for 30 miles, turning left on FR 300. Follow FR 300 to FR 195. The trailhead is off to the left of FR 300.

HIGHLINE TRAIL HIKE - Leashes

Intermediate/1.0-29.2 miles/0.5-15.0 hours

Info: This path crosses six other trails as it winds through pine, juniper and oak brush, so keep track of the trail markers. The area is filled with wildlife so bring your binoculars - you might catch sight of a wild turkey or a sly fox. For more information: (520) 474-7900.

Directions: From Payson take Highway 87 north for 15 miles to FR 297. Follow FR 297 to the trailhead and parking.

HORTON CREEK TRAIL HIKE

Beginner/6.8 miles/4.0 hours

Info: The first half-mile of this trail is unimpressive. The next three miles escort you through beautiful Mogollon Rim country along a secluded picturesque creek. Delightful views of the Tonto Basin and numerous cascading waterfalls make this one of the prettiest hikes on the Rim.

This rather easy journey involves a moderate climb in elevation - just over 1,000 feet to Horton Creek Springs, your turnaround point. Even couch potato pooches will love this outing through forests of deciduous and coniferous trees. For more information: (520) 474-7900.

Directions: 16 miles east of Payson on Highway 260 just past Kohls Ranch Resort is Forest Service Route 289. Take it north for a mile to the trailhead at Upper Tonto Creek Campground.

HORTON SPRINGS TRAIL HIKE

Expert/2.7 miles/1.5 hours

Info: The Mogollon Rim is an area of unending beauty, laced with scenic overlooks and trails. Some are easy, others are not. This one falls in the tough category. The trail starts on level ground, but quickly takes a dramatic change in direction with a steep descent via a series of rocky switchbacks, ending at the junction with the Horton Creek Trail. The creek marks the end of your descent and the begining of your uphill return. For more information: (520) 474-7900.

Directions: Take Highway 260 east for 30 miles to FR 300. Head west on FR 300 approximately 17 miles to the signed trailhead.

LAKE ROOSEVELT

Info: From fishy stories of giant catfish to Swiss-like countrysides, from arid desert scenes to ice blue water and sandy shorelines, Lake Roosevelt is a heavenly haven for desert dwellers and their canine cohorts. Take the family, Fido and plenty of Fuji to the windswept waters of a lake surrounded by so much beauty and so many mountains, you won't know where to look first. Sunlight brings warmth to daytime pleasure seekers, while sunset brings unparalleled tranquility to serenity-seeking city escapees. For more information: Tonto National Forest Service (520) 467-2236.

Directions: From Payson, take Highway 87 south to the junction with Highway 188. Continue southeast on Highway 188 to Punkin Center and the lake.

MEADOW TRAIL HIKE

Beginner/3.0 miles/1.5 hours

Info: From beginning to end, this simple hike has a lot to offer. At the southern end you'll find a series of scenic vistas affording wonderful views, while at the northern end, Woods Canyon Lake awaits. Interpretive signs describe the wildlife and ecology of the area and keep the hike interesting as you and the pupster journey from the vistas to the lake or vice versa. For more information: (520) 289-2471.

Directions: Take Highway 260 east for 30 miles to FR 300. Turn left for 3 miles to the trailhead at Woods Canyon Vista. This is just one of the six locations which provides access to the trail. The other five are: Crook Campground, Aspen Campground, Spillway Campground, the group area between Aspen and Spillway and the store parking lot at lakeside.

MILITARY SINKHOLE TRAIL HIKE

Intermediate/5.0 miles/2.5 hours

Info: Believe it or not, this overgrown trail provides one of the least challenging routes down the Mogollon Rim. As expected, the Rim lives up to its reputation by affording absolutely breathtaking vistas. For more information: (520) 289-2471.

Directions: Take Highway 260 east for 30 miles to FR 300. Turn left for 2 miles to the parking lot and unmarked trailhead at the second Vista View Point.

PROMONTORY BUTTE TRAIL HIKE

Expert/1.5 miles/1.0 hours

Info: Climbing 1,000 feet in only .75 miles, this formidable trail is also a bit difficult to follow in certain sections. It's definitely for experienced hikers and hounds only. If you're up to it, the rewards will be gorgeous views from both below and above the Rim. For more information: (520) 289-2471.

Directions: Take Highway 260 east for 30 miles to FR 300. Turn left, following FR 300 to FR 76 and make a left. Take FR 76 to FR 76B, and make a right. Follow FR 76B to the trailhead at road's end. Be advised that FR 76B is not signed and the trailhead is difficult to find.

RIM LAKES VISTA TRAIL HIKE

Beginner/5.5 miles/3.0 hours

Info: This easy trail ranks at the top of its class for scenery. But would you expect anything less from the Mogollon Rim? The trail wanders through a forest of ponderosa pine, white and Douglas fir and treats you and Fido to stunning panoramas from three overlooks - Woods Canyon Vista, Rim Vista and Military Sinkhole Vista. Check out the interpretive signs and educate yourself on the Rim's history and the area's geology. For more information: (520) 289-2471.

Directions: Take Highway 260 east for 30 miles to FR 300 and turn left. Follow FR 300 to the trailhead at the Rim Campground.

SEE CANYON TRAIL HIKE

Expert/6.9 miles/3.5 hours

Info: Endurance is the key to completing this difficult hike to the top of the Mogollon Rim. You and your tenacious pooch won't be disappointed when you reach your final destination. The escarpment commands long reaching views and makes the trek worth the effort. The trail follows Christopher Creek as it climbs over 1,700 feet in elevation through ponderosa, ferns, grasses and mint. Wildlife is abundant - don't be surprised if you encounter an animal or two. For more information: (520) 474-7900.

Directions: Take Highway 260 east for 21 miles to Christopher Creek and turn left on FR 284. Follow FR 284 for 1.5 miles to the parking area. Follow the Highline Trail for .25 miles to the junction with See Canyon Trail.

Dogs May Be Unleashed Unless Otherwise Indicated

PEORIA

RECREATION

APACHE PARK - Leashes

Info: 10 acres of sniffing space for you and Fido to explore, Apache Park is a convenient place to stretch your paws.

Directions: Located at 8633 W. John Cabot Road.

BRAEWOOD PARK - Leashes

Info: Spend some quality time with your pooch strolling through this four-acre neighborhood park.

Directions: Located at 8742 W. Mercer.

CENTRAL SCHOOL - Leashes

Info: Pack a picnic and spend the lunch hour enjoying the outdoors with your faithful friend in this five-acre park.

Directions: Located at 10350 N. 83rd Avenue.

CLARENCE B. HAYES MEMORIAL PARK - Leashes

Info: Happy tails to you as you enjoy the open space and pleasant walking path in this 15-acre park.

Directions: Located at 9845 N. 75th Avenue.

KIWANIS PARK - Leashes

Info: Exercise lagging limbs on the course or meander over one of the multi-purpose fields in this 5-acre park.

Directions: Located at 12687 N. 78th Drive.

LAKE PLEASANT

Info: A newly completed Waddell Dam increased the size of Lake Pleasant threefold - creating three times more fun for you and Bowser. You can row, paddle or power over 10,000 acres of surface water as you eagerly search for that perfect photo opportunity. Surrounded by the Sonoran Desert and picture-postcard mountain peaks, this lake offers waterdogs a chance to chill their paws in a desert oasis. For more information: Maricopa County Parks and Recreation Department, (602) 506-2930.

Directions: Located on the Carefree Highway, fifteen miles west of Interstate 17.

MURPHY PARK - Leashes

Info: Tails will be wagging as you pass some time with your pooch in the open play area of this 5-acre park.

Directions: Located at 7230 W. Cheryl Drive.

OLIVE PARK - Leashes

Info: Looking for a peaceful way to spend the day? Leash up your lad and head out to Olive Park where you can enjoy 23 acres of parkland. If you prefer designated trails, there's a walking path for your roaming pleasure. This park deserves two paws up.

Directions: Located at 9180 N. 71st Avenue.

SWEETWATER PARK - Leashes

Info: Hotdog! Burn off some lunchtime calories on the walking path of this 10-acre park.

Directions: Located at 75th and Sweetwater Avenues.

VARNEY PARK - Leashes

Info: Satisfy those pleading eyes by taking Rover for a frolic in this 8-acre park.

Directions: Located at 11730 N. 81st Avenue.

Other Neighborhood Parks in Peoria:

MONROE PARK - Leashes
Located at 8820 W. Monroe.

WASHINGTON PARK - Leashes
Located at 8306 W. Washington Street.

WESTGREEN PARK - Leashes
Located at 8555 N. 87th Avenue.

WINDROSE PARK - Leashes
Located at 8350 W. Windrose.

Notes

_____

_____

_____

_____

_____

_____

_____

_____

_____

_____

_____

_____

Notes

_____

_____

_____

_____

_____

_____

_____

_____

_____

_____

_____

PHOENIX (and vicinity)

LODGING

BEST WESTERN AIRPORT INN
2425 S 24th St (85034) Rates: $55-$105;
Tel: (602) 273-7251; (800) 528-1234

BEST WESTERN BELL MOTEL
17211 N Black Canyon Hwy (85023) Rates: $39-$75;
Tel: (602) 993-8300; (800) 528-1234

COMFORT INN-AIRPORT
4120 E Van Buren Pkwy (85008) Rates: $28-$58;
Tel: (602) 275-5746; (800) 221-2222

COMFORT INN-TURF PARADISE
1711 W Bell Rd (85023) Rates: $42-$89;
Tel: (602) 866-2089; (800) 221-2222

DAYS INN-COLISEUM
2420 W Thomas Rd (85015) Rates: $39-$69;
Tel: (602) 257-0801; (800) 329-7466

DAYS INN-PHOENIX AIRPORT
3333 E Van Buren St (85008) Rates: $45-$79;
Tel: (602) 244-8244; (800) 329-7466

ECONO LODGE
1520 N 84th Dr (Tolleson 85353) Rates: $42-$64;
Tel: (602) 936-4667; (800) 424-4777

EMBASSY SUITES-PHOENIX WEST
3210 NW Grand Ave (85017) Rates: $64-$134;
Tel: (602) 279-3211; (800) 362-2779

EMBASSY SUITES-THOMAS RD/AIRPORT WEST
2333 E Thomas Rd (85016) Rates: $59-$109;
Tel: (602) 957-1910; (800) 362-2779

E-Z 8 MOTEL
1820 S 7th St (85034) Rates: $26-$33;
Tel: (602) 254-9787

Dogs May Be Unleashed Unless Otherwise Indicated

FOUNTAINS SUITE HOTEL
2577 W Greenway Rd (85023) Rates: $69-$129;
Tel: (602) 375-1777; (800) 338-1338

HAMPTON INN I-17
8101 N Black Canyon Hwy (85021) Rates: $47-$79;
Tel: (602) 864-6233; (800) 426-7866

HOLIDAY INN-AIRPORT EAST
4300 E Washington St (85034) Rates: $49-$119;
Tel: (602) 273-7778; (800) 465-4329

HOLIDAY INN CROWN PLAZA/OMNI ADAMS HOTEL
P. O. Box 1000 (85001-1000) Rates: $59-$164;
Tel: (602) 257-1525; (800) 227-6963

HOLIDAY INN & HOLIDOME- PHOENIX CORP CENTER
2532 W Peoria Ave (85029) Rates: $59-$149;
Tel: (602) 943-2341; (800) 465-4329

HOLIDAY INN NORTH CENTRAL
4321 N Central Ave (85012) Rates: $39-$109;
Tel: (602) 277-6671; (800) 465-4329

HOWARD JOHNSON
3400 Grand Ave (85017) Rates: $41-$73;
Tel: (602) 264-9164; (800) 446-4656

HOWARD JOHNSON LODGE
124 S 24th St (85034) Rates: $49-$89;
Tel: (602) 244-8221; (800) 446-4656

KNIGHTS COURT
5050 N Black Canyon Hwy (85017) Rates: $45-$80;
Tel: (602) 242-8011; (800) 843-5644

KNIGHTS INN-AIRPORT
2201 S 24th St (85034) Rates: $45-$50;
Tel: (602) 267-0611; (800) 843-5644

LA QUINTA INN-COLISEUM
2725 N Black Canyon Hwy (85009) Rates: $45-$72;
Tel: (602) 258-6271; (800) 221-4731

LA QUINTA PHOENIX NORTH
2510 W Greenway Rd (85023) Rates: $54-$91;
Tel: (602) 993-0800; (800) 221-4731

LEXINGTON HOTEL & CITY SQUARE SPORTS CLUB
100 W Clarendon (85013) Rates: $69-$149;
Tel: (602) 279-9811; (800) 537-8483

LOS OLIVOS EXECUTIVE HOTEL
202 E McDowell Rd (85004) Rates: $59-$99;
Tel: (602) 258-6911; (800) 776-5560

MOTEL 6
214 S 24th St (85034) Rates: $26-$32;
Tel: (602) 244-1155; (800) 440-6000

MOTEL 6
2323 E Van Buren St (85006) Rates: $26-$32;
Tel: (602) 267-7511; (800) 440-6000

MOTEL 6
5315 E Van Buren St (85008) Rates: $27-$33;
Tel: (602) 267-8555; (800) 440-6000

MOTEL 6
1530 N 52nd Dr (85043) Rates: $35-$41;
Tel: (602) 272-0220; (800) 440-6000

MOTEL 6
2548 W Indian School Rd (85017) Rates: $33-$39;
Tel: (602) 248-8881; (800) 440-6000

MOTEL 6
8152 N Black Canyon Hwy (85051) Rates: $30-$36;
Tel: (602) 995-7592; (800) 440-6000

MOTEL 6
4130 N Black Canyon Hwy (85017) Rates: $30-$36;
Tel: (602) 277-5501; (800) 440-6000

MOTEL 6
2330 W Bell Rd (85023) Rates: $33-$39;
Tel: (602) 993-2353; (800) 440-6000

MOTEL 6
2735 W Sweetwater Ave (85029) Rates: $30-$36;
Tel: (602) 942-5030; (800) 440-6000

PHOENIX SUNRISE MOTEL
3644 E Van Buren St (85008) Rates: $33+;
Tel: (602) 275-7661; (800) 432-6483

PREMIER INN
10402 N Black Canyon Hwy (85051) Rates: $49-$99;
Tel: (602) 943-2371; (800) 786-6835

QUALITY HOTEL CENTRAL PHOENIX
3600 N 2nd Ave (85013) Rates: $59-$99;
Tel: (602) 248-0222; (800) 424-6423

QUALITY INN-AIRPORT
3541 E Van Buren St (85008) Rates: $29-$69;
Tel: (602) 273-7121; (800) 228-5151

QUALITY INN-SOUTH MOUNTAIN
5121 E La Puente Ave (85044) Rates: $49-$99;
Tel: (602) 893-3900;
(800) 228-5151 (US); (800) 562-3332 (AZ)

RADISSON PHOENIX AIRPORT HOTEL/SOUTHBANK
3333 E University Dr (85034) Rates: $169-$189;
Tel: (602) 437-8400; (800) 333-3333

RAMADA INN-METRO CENTER
12027 N 28th Dr (85029) Rates: $42-$110;
Tel: (602) 866-7000; (800) 272-6232

RESIDENCE INN BY MARRIOTT
8242 N Black Canyon Hwy (85051) Rates: $119-$199;
Tel: (602) 864-1900; (800) 331-3131

RITZ CARLTON-PHOENIX
2401 E Camelback Rd (85016) Rates: $95-$225;
Tel: (602) 468-0700; (800) 241-3333

Locate Other Dog-Friendly Activities...Check Nearby Cities

ROYAL PALMS INN
5200 E Camelback Rd (85018) Rates: $60-$210;
Tel: (602) 840-3610;
(800) 672-6011 (US); (800) 548-1202 (CAN)

SHERATON CRESCENT HOTEL
2620 W Dunlap Ave (85021) Rates: $109-$185;
Tel: (602) 943-8200; (800) 423-4126

SUPER 8 MOTEL PHOENIX CENTRAL
4021 N 27th Ave (85017) Rates: $32-$54;
Tel: (602) 248-8880; (800) 800-8000

TRAVELODGE METROCENTER
8617 N Black Canyon Hwy (85021) Rates: $38-$90;
Tel: (602) 995-9500; (800) 578-7878

TRAVELODGE SUITES
3101 N 32nd St (85018) Rates: $58-$150;
Tel: (602) 956-4900; (800) 578-7878

UPTOWN BED & BREAKFAST
7th Ave & Thomas Rd (85007) Rates: $60-$75;
Tel: (602) 990-0682; (800) 456-0682

WYNDHAM GARDEN HOTEL
2641 W Union Hills Dr (85027) Rates: $65-$105;
Tel: (602) 978-2222; (800) 996-3426

WYNDHAM WESTCOURT/METROCENTER
10220 N Metro Pkwy E (85051) Rates: $59-$109;
Tel: (602) 997-5900; (800) 996-3426

RECREATION

ACACIA PARK - Leashes

Info: This small park offers over five acres where you and the pupster can stretch your legs.

Directions: From Thunderbird take 30th Avenue north to the park.

Dogs May Be Unleashed Unless Otherwise Indicated

ACOMA PARK - Leashes

Info: Get your Rexercise along the park's exercise course. The spacious soccer field is also a good place for romping.

Directions: From 35th Avenue, between Thunderbird and Greenway Roads, take Acoma Drive west to 39th Avenue and the park.

ALICIA PARK - Leashes

Info: Over eight acres of open fields await you and your pooch in this park.

Directions: From Dunlap take 19th Avenue south to Alicia Avenue. Turn west (right) and drive past the school to the park.

ALKIRE PARK - Leashes

Info: Take a break from city life and treat Fido to a picnic in this snazzy urban park.

Directions: Located at 17th Avenue and Papago Street.

ALTADENA PARK - Leashes

Info: Spray pads will cool your paws as you chill out with your pal in this 79-acre urban setting.

Directions: Located at 37th Street and Altadena Avenue.

ARCADIA PARK - Leashes

Info: You can make your trip to this park last all afternoon. Nearly ten acres of lawn await you and your pooch. An exercise course and playfield offer opportunities for the athletically inclined.

Directions: While the park is at the southwest corner of Indian School Avenue and 56th Street, the best way in is from Osborn Road one block south.

BARRIOS UNIDOS PARK - Leashes

Info: This 14-acre park offers many a pleasant diversion for you and your pooch. Picnic tables with grills dot the park, while softball and soccer fields provide a front row seat to amateur sports events. There's a spray pad where you and your canine can cool your toes.

Directions: From Buckeye Road take 15th Street south a few blocks to the park.

BLACK CANYON CAMPGROUND HIKE - Leashes

Beginner/4.0 miles/2.0 hours

Info: Take a break from the bustle of the city and spend a relaxing few hours strolling along this scenic nature trail. Use the information posts scattered throughout the trail to take a self-guided tour and learn about various desert plant species. If you have a hunting hound, keep that leash taut. Birds, reptiles and mammals often frolic in the area. The not so gung ho may choose to take the Spur Trail shortcut - same lovely surroundings but half the hiking distance. For more information: (602) 506-2930.

Directions: Take Interstate 17 north to Carefree Highway. Go west on Carefree Highway to the Black Canyon Shooting Range. Enter the park on Black Canyon Boulevard, and turn left on Sportsman Way to find the trailhead.

CACTUS PARK - Leashes

Info: This spacious 33-acre park can be an afternoon's adventure for you and your pupster. Picnic tables dot the park. Basketball and volleyball courts offer ongoing games, while the soccer and softball fields provide wide open grassy areas for your pooch to chase a fast moving ball.

Directions: Located at 38th Avenue and Cactus Road.

CAVE CREEK PARK RECREATION AREA - Leashes

Info: This large, pleasant park is split by the Cave Creek Wash for its entire length as it stretches from Cactus to Thunderbird Road. Basically an expanse of land running alongside a wash, small parks are found throughout the area. Picnic tables with grills offer places for you and the dawgus to sit and enjoy a quiet lunch. Playfields and sport courts pepper the park. For more information: (602) 262-6575.

Directions: Located at Cactus and 25th Avenues for the southern end, or Thunderbird and 24th for the northern end. Access to the entire length of the park is available along 23rd Avenue.

CAVE CREEK RECREATION AREA - Leashes

Info: Spend the afternoon frolicking with Fido at this extraordinary 2,900-acre park. Burn some calories on one of the hiking trails as you collect Kodak-worthy vistas of the unique geologic formations. For more information: (602) 465-0431.

Directions: Located at N. 32nd Street, 3 miles west of Cave Creek Road.

CESAR CHAVEZ PARK - Leashes

Info: This park offers one of the few lakes in the metropolitan Phoenix area. Boat launches are available and fishing is an option. Numerous ramada and open picnic areas provide a nice way for you and your canine to spend some time.

Directions: Located at 35th Avenue and Baseline Road.

CHARLES M. CHRISTIANSEN
MEMORIAL TRAIL HIKE - Leashes

Intermediate/1.0-21.4 miles/0.5-11.0 hours

Info: City dwellers - would you believe that a true desert experience lies practically in your backyard? That's right, no more hour-long car trips. Simply grab Fido's leash and head for this trail through the scenic Phoenix Mountain Preserve. Whether you hike 2 or 22 miles, you and the hound will not be disappointed. For more information: (602) 262-7901.

Directions: The trail begins at 7th Avenue but there are many access points along the way: 7th Street, Cave Creek Road, Dreamy Draw Park, 40th Street and Tatum Boulevard.

CHOLLA COVE PARK - Leashes

Info: Over 4 acres of lawn await you and your doggie pal. An exercise course is the perfect place for your daily constitutional.

Directions: Between Shea Boulevard and Cactus Road, take 40th Street to Cholla. Turn east to 41st Street and the park.

CHRISTY COVE PARK - Leashes

Info: This small secluded neighborhood park at the foot of the Phoenix Mountain Preserve offers over three acres of green lawn for frolicking. There are picnic tables and benches ideal for a quiet lunch with your furry sidekick.

Directions: Located between Cactus Road and Shea Boulevard on 24th Street at Desert Cove.

CIELITO PARK - Leashes

Info: If you're looking for lots of roaming room, this 44-acre park with grassy areas is the one for you and your best pal. Basketball and tennis courts, baseball, softball and soccer fields, an exercise course, picnic tables, playground and restrooms, this park has it all.

Directions: Located at 35th Avenue between Camelback and Indian School Roads at Campbell.

CIRCLE K PARK - Leashes

Info: We're talking over 12 acres of fun for you and your pooch at this park. The soccer and ballfields offer wide open spaces for a game of fetch. Picnic tables provide a place to sit and enjoy a quiet lunch afterwards. The Highline Canal runs the length of the park's northern border.

Directions: From Baseline Road take 7th Street south over the canal to South Mountain Avenue. Turn east (left) and drive a few blocks to the park.

CONOCIDO PARK - Leashes

Info: This uniquely shaped park covers nearly thirty acres, although you'd never know it looking at the small extension that touches 35th Avenue. The large open area is set back among the winding neighborhood roads. A spacious soccer field offers your pooch a grand opportunity for some quality playtime.

Directions: Although the park can be accessed from 35th Avenue and Paradise Lane (between Greenway Road and Bell Road), you can reach the park's main area by taking 30th Avenue south from Bell to the park.

CORONADO PARK - Leashes

Info: This small 5-acre park offers a quick chance for you and your hound to stretch your legs. Baseball and softball fields offer wide open lawn areas ideal for your canine to romp, while picnic tables furnish a place for you to share a brown-bag lunch.

Directions: From McDowell Road take 12th Street north one block to the park.

CORTEZ PARK - Leashes

Info: When you think of Phoenix, you don't normally think lagoons, but that's what makes this park special. Nearly twenty acres of green lawn surrounding a lake can be yours at this unusual oasis.

Directions: Located at 35th Avenue and Dunlap Avenue.

Dogs May Be Unleashed Unless Otherwise Indicated

COUNTRY GABLES PARK - Leashes

Info: Overshadowed by the much larger Conocido Park just a few blocks north, this small neighborhood park is one of those little known secrets off the beaten path. Take your best friend out for a pleasant stroll on the lush green lawn.

Directions: From Greenway Road take 35th Avenue south to Banff Lane. Turn east (left) and drive a few blocks to the park.

CROSSED ARROWS PARK - Leashes

Info: This medium sized park offers loads of wide open spaces where Fido can run, romp and frisk. Tucked into a quiet neighborhood, if you've got the ball, the pupster's got the time.

Directions: Located on Acoma Drive, between Thunderbird and Greenway Roads, at 61st Street.

DEER VALLEY PARK - Leashes

Info: Over thirty acres of green grass await you and the Bowser at this large park. Wide open fields offer excellent opportunities for your pooch to bag a frisbee in midflight. And an exercise course gives you the chance to work up a sweat as well. Afterwards, picnic tables and benches provide chill-out spaces.

Directions: Located at 19th Avenue, just south of Beardsley Road.

DESERT FOOTHILLS PARK - Leashes

Info: Not many people know that Phoenix extends well beyond the south mountains, but it does. This large desert park is squirreled away in the seldom visited southern corner of Phoenix. A leisurely stroll through the Sonoran Desert landscape is the main appeal of the park.

Directions: From Interstate 10 take Chandler Road west. Chandler Road hiccups where it meets Ray Road, but continues on westward. After a few more miles you'll reach Desert Foothills Parkway and the park.

DESERT HORIZON PARK - Leashes

Info: A delightful afternoon beckons you and your cohort at this park. Over 20-acres of spacious lawn in the form of baseball, softball and soccer fields provide the perfect place for your bird-loving dog to encounter that rare, low flying, frisbee bird.

Directions: Located at 56th Street and Paradise, between Greenway and Bell Roads.

DESERT WEST PARK - Leashes

Info: Over 40-acres of greenery invite you and your pup to spend some time in the outdoors. A fast moving ball is sure to keep your pooch occupied.

Directions: Located on 67th Avenue between McDowell and Thomas Roads.

DESERT WILLOW PARK - Leashes

Info: Nestled in the far northeast corner of Phoenix, this 14-acre lush green park is the perfect antidote for the indoor blahs. Take along a frisbee or tennis ball, there's an open soccer field just perfect for some playtime.

Directions: Take Cave Creek Road northwest to where it intersects with Tatum. Turn west (left) onto Tatum and continue until it bends and becomes northbound 40th Street. The park is a few blocks further.

DREAMY DRAW RECREATION AREA - Leashes

Info: This area lives up to its name. Pick a paloverde or a mesquite tree, unbuckle your back pack and daydream the hours away while feasting your eyes on a natural setting of desert and granite rock formations. A man-made pond attracts many songbirds, so bring binoculars and chalk up some bird sightings or stroll down an interpretive nature trail and gain insight into the flora and fauna of the area. Most walking paths within Dreamy Draw are paved. If you prefer a more rustic setting, hop on the trail out to the Preserve. Rated intermediate to expert, you can walk twenty minutes or twenty miles. In any case, don't forget to take water - enough for you and your hiking hound. For more information: (602) 495-0222.

Directions: Located at 2421 East Northern Avenue.

ECHO CANYON RECREATION AREA - Leashes

Info: Towering red cliffs and postcardian panoramas surround you and the pupster as you climb through the 75+ acres of this recreation area...and climb you will. Echo Canyon may only have two miles of designated hiking trails, but they are the toughest two miles you'll encounter in any Phoenix park. Both the Camelback Mountain and the Echo Canyon Trails are steep, calorie burning treks which unquestionably separate the pups from the dogs. Bring plenty of water, especially in the warmer months. For more information: (602) 256-3220.

Directions: Located south of McDonald Drive just east of Tatum Boulevard.

EDISON PARK - Leashes

Info: Light up your pup's life by strolling through the playing fields in Edison Park.

Directions: Located at 19th Street and Roosevelt.

EL OSO PARK - Leashes

Info: Nearly 30 acres of grounds await you and your canine companion. Spend the afternoon and plan a kibble cookout for early evening. Occasional concerts in the amphitheater can provide a lovely ending to a lovely day. Of course your pooch might appreciate romping on the wide open soccer field more than tapping his paws to Mozart, but every dog can use a little culture.

Directions: Located on 75th Avenue, between Indian School and Thomas Roads, at Osborn Road.

EL PRADO PARK - Leashes

Info: This park has a 30-acre green scene for you and fur-face to peruse.

Directions: Located on 19th Avenue, a few blocks south of Southern Avenue.

EL REPOSO PARK - Leashes

Info: Over 30 acres of grassy areas and pleasant picnic spots await you and your canine sidekick at this medium sized park.

Directions: Located on 7th Street, one block south of Southern Avenue.

ENCANTO PARK - Leashes

Info: Covering well over 80 acres, this park not only has a lake, but an island as well. Popular and often crowded on weekends, in addition to the usual sports amenities, you'll find an exercise course and picnic tables - ideal for a brown-bag lunch break.

Directions: Located on 15th Avenue at Encanto Boulevard, between McDowell and Thomas Roads.

ESTEBAN PARK - Leashes

Info: With more than 60 acres of grounds, this park is a perfect place to take your pooch for a romp. Ramada covered picnic areas speckle the park so you and Rover can do lunch or simply chill-out.

Directions: Take Interstate 10 to the University Drive exit. Turn south off the freeway and follow University to where it becomes 32nd Street at Broadway. Continue on to the park at Roeser Road.

ESTRELLA MOUNTAIN REGIONAL PARK - Leashes

Info: Padded paws will be in heaven as they leisurely stroll through 56 acres of grass. Hiking trails provide a more rugged terrain for the heartier hounds who wish to explore the Sonoran Desert. This area boasts a variety of vegetation and spectacular mountain views. Altogether, the park encompasses 19,200 acres of developed and natural landscape. So pack a snack for you and the pupster and set out to explore one of the county's largest parks.

Beep! Beep! Watch out for roadrunners and other species of desert life. Mule deer, kit foxes, coyotes, cottontails, jackrabbits and kangaroo rats inhabit the area. The sky is speckled with colorful birds such as cardinals, red-tailed hawks, mockingbirds, and cactus wrens. You might choose to rest under a paloverde, mesquite, or desert ironwood. Stay until sundown and chances are you'll experience an orange streaked or pink washed sky. Whatever your pleasure, the diversity of this region makes it a worthwhile adventure for you and your canine companion. For more information: (602) 932-3811.

Directions: From Phoenix, take Interstate 10 west to Estrella Parkway (exit 126). Continue south on Estrella Parkway for six miles to the park entrance.

FALCON PARK - Leashes

Info: This small 10-acre park offers ramada-covered picnic areas where you and Willie can while away the day.

Directions: Located at 35th Avenue and Roosevelt Street.

G.R. HERBERGER PARK - Leashes

Info: Start your jog along the Arizona Canal from this small, but convenient park.

Directions: Located on the north side of Indian School Road, east of 56th Street.

GRANADA PARK - Leashes

Info: Wander among the art sculptures and around the two lagoons in this grassy park. Or take a biscuit break in one of the shaded picnic areas.

Directions: Located at 20th Street and Maryland.

GRANT PARK - Leashes

Info: Bring a rawhide and your best buddy and take in a ball game at Grant Park.

Directions: Located at 701 South 3rd Avenue north of Buckeye.

GREEN VALLEY PARK - Leashes

Info: Although this park is located in the shadow of the freeway, its five green acres still make for a leisurely stroll or a place where your pupster can chase his favorite ball.

Directions: From the eastbound Maricopa Freeway (60/17) take the 16th Street offramp. Go south on 16th Street for one block to Watkins Street. Turn west (right) for two blocks to the park.

HARMON PARK - Leashes

Info: Activity sniffing canines will wag their tails for this 10-acre, action-packed park. Watching all the sports might make you hungry, so be sure you pack a scrumptious picnic lunch for you and your pooch.

Directions: Located at 5th Avenue and Yavapai Street (south of Buckeye).

HAYDEN PARK - Leashes

Info: Romping Rovers will find over 10 acres of verdant lawn at this park.

Directions: From the southeast corner of 7th Avenue and Broadway Road, the park is accessible from mid-block on either 7th Avenue or Broadway.

HERBERGER PARK - Leashes

Info: Get your bike out or put your running shoes on as this small lawned park is an excellent staging area for a trip alongside the Arizona Canal. On the weekend Sunnyslope High School just to the north provides parking while you and dawgus do the distance.

Directions: Located at Central Avenue and the Arizona Canal, south of Dunlap Avenue.

HERMOSO PARK - Leashes

Info: Over 20 acres of grassy areas await the adventurous pooch and his person.

Directions: Located on Southern Avenue at 20th Street.

HOLIDAY PARK - Leashes

Info: This small lawned park is a good place for a daily dose of fast-paced walking.

Directions: Located on 67th Avenue at Minnezona, between Indian School and Camelback Roads.

HOSHONI PARK - Leashes

Info: Take a short, leisurely stroll around this pleasant 4-acre park.

Directions: Located on 39th Avenue at Butler Drive, between Northern Avenue and Dunlap Avenue. (Dunlap is called Olive Avenue in Glendale.)

JACKRABBIT PARK - Leashes

Info: This park isn't very wide, but it does run for two blocks. Your buddy will have the room to pick up serious running speed as he chases a fast moving frisbee.

Directions: Paradise Lane is between Greenway Road and Bell Road. Jackrabbit Park runs along Paradise from 58th to 60th Streets.

KACHINA PARK - Leashes

Info: A stretch of sod awaits you and your sidekick at this small neighborhood park.

Directions: Located along Campbell Avenue at 42nd Street, between Indian School and Camelback Roads.

LA PRADERA PARK - Leashes

Info: Besides offering nearly 10 acres of greenery for pooch shenanigans, this park's exercise course gives you a way to burn some calories and stay fit.

Directions: Located at 40th and Glendale Avenues.

LINDO PARK - Leashes

Info: At this little known park, you and your pup can enjoy anything from a short walk around its 5 acres to an afternoon picnicking under ramadas.

Directions: Take 19th Avenue south from Broadway Road to Roeser. Turn west (right) and go three blocks to the park.

LITTLE CANYON PARK - Leashes

Info: There's enough verdant lawn at this park to make for a nice little getaway and a bit of relaxation with your pooch.

Directions: Missouri Avenue runs between Camelback Road and Bethany Home Road. The park runs along Missouri between 30th and 33rd Avenues. Take Missouri from either 27th Avenue or 35th Avenue.

LOOKOUT MOUNTAIN PARK/ RECREATION AREA - Leashes

Info: Ensconced at the foot of Lookout Mountain, this 120-acre grassy park serves as a launching point for hikes into the Desert Lookout Mountain Preserve. If scrambling up the side of a mountain isn't enough of a workout, an exercise course and an open play-field should round off your calorie burning session. For more information: (602) 262-6696.

Directions: The same road is called Thunderbird from the west and Cactus from the east. Cactus and Thunderbird divide the park in two. No matter which way you're coming from, take 18th Street north to the end and the park.

LOS OLIVOS PARK - Leashes

Info: Your pooch can romp on more than eight acres of green grass. Or the two of you can do a round on the exercise course. If you plan your visit at lunchtime, tote a brown bagger and chill-out at one of the picnic tables scattered around the park.

Directions: Located on 28th Street at Glenrosa, between Indian School and Camelback Roads.

MA HA TAUK PARK - Leashes

Info: This small park serves as a green diving board into the much larger South Mountain Park. Spend the day hiking in the hills with your pupster and then picnic under shaded ramadas surrounded by plush green lawns.

Directions: Located at the southern end of 7th Avenue at the foot of the mountains.

MADISON PARK - Leashes

Info: Snuggled between a hospital and a school this medium sized park offers you and your pup wide open sports areas where your canine friend can stretch his legs while pursuing wild and furry tennis balls.

Directions: Located on 16th Street at Glenrosa, between Indian School and Camelback Roads.

MARGARET T. HANCE PARK - Leashes

Info: The sidewalk around the perimeter of this park makes for a pleasant stroll for you and your canine companion. There is plenty of shade to keep you cool if you want a laid back kind of outing.

Directions: From 3rd Street to 3rd Avenue, the park is located above the Interstate 10 tunnel.

NORTH MOUNTAIN RECREATION AREA - Leashes

Info: The padded-of-paws will have a ball lollygagging in this scenic recreation area. Try your paw at one of the hiking trails with city and desert views. No matter what, you're bound to enjoy your visit. For more information: (602) 262-7901.

Directions: Located at 10600 North 7th Street.

NORTH MOUNTAIN SUMMIT TRAIL HIKE

Intermediate/3.2 miles/1.5 hours

Info: Pack some snacks, a couple of canteens and head for the North Mountain Recreation Area and fill your fitness quotient on this visually stimulating hike. Enjoy the wilderness and count the cactus - more than 300 different species thrive in this arid landscape. Once you reach the ridge, take it all in - skyscrapers to pristine wilderness - what contrasts! For more information: (602) 262-7901.

Directions: Take 7th Street to Peoria Avenue. Head west until you reach the trailhead.

PAPAGO PARK - Leashes

Info: Leash up that lapdog and head on out to Papago Park. This area has something for everyone. Several lagoons and accompanying birdlife are scattered throughout the park for your viewing pleasure, but please - no dog paddling. For the more active parkgoer, hiking trails lead up from the hilly desert terrain into the buttes. Papago Park makes for a terrific day trip for active city slickers. For more information: (602) 256-3449.

Directions: Located at Van Buren Street and Galvin Parkway.

PATRIOTS SQUARE PARK - Leashes

Info: This park is an easily accessible city block of entertainment. Buy some lunch from one of the concessionaires and prepare for a tailwagging good time people watching. Visit between noon and one and you might be treated to a mini-cultural fiesta of live entertainment.

Directions: Located on Central Avenue and Washington Street between 1st and Central.

PENNY HOWE BARRIER FREE TRAIL HIKE - Leashes

Beginner/0.6 miles/0.5 hours

Info: This trail offers much more than serenity and stunning views. Take the opportunity to learn about your surroundings while sauntering on what was once the North Mountain Nature Trail. A wealth of information is provided on interpretive plaques along the pathway for those interested in the flora and fauna of the Sonoran Desert. Put your best paw forward, and get ready for an interesting day in this informative recreation area. For more information: (602) 262-7901.

Directions: Take 7th Street south to westbound Peoria. Take Peoria until you reach North Mountain Park. Trailhead is located in the northwest corner of the Havasupai Ramada.

PERL CHARLES MEMORIAL TRAIL HIKE - Leashes

Intermediate/9.6 miles/5.0 hours

Info: Challenging and scenic, this hike offers you and Fido the chance to escape the city and enjoy desert and mountain terrain. The pathway is geared toward solitude seekers and nature enthusiasts. Pack a snack, biscuits and water and prepare for a rustic experience. Don't forget your binoculars, birds are abundant. For more information: (602) 262-7901.

Directions: Take 16th Street north past Glendale Avenue and go east on Myrtle to the trailhead. You can also start at the trailhead just east of 16th Street on the north side of the Arizona Canal.

THE PHOENIX MOUNTAIN PRESERVE - Leashes

Info: Encompassing nearly 26,000 acres of parks and preserves and over 100 miles of designated hiking trails, the Phoenix Mountain Preserve is a popular, much loved gateway for hikers and their four-pawed sidekicks into the beautiful Sonoran Desert - the last of the Valley's pristine desert regions. From easy nature trails to challenging mountain climbs, shaded picnic ramadas to sun-splashed lagoons, ancient petroglyphs to unique geologic formations, desert cactus to vibrant colored wildflowers, the Preserve has something for everyone.

The Phoenix Mountain Preserve is bordered by Bell Road to the north, Lincoln Drive to the south, 19th Avenue to the west and Tatum Boulevard to the east. The following recreation areas are accessible from various points: Dreamy Draw, Lookout Mountain, North Mountain, Shadow Mountain*, Shaw Butte and Squaw Peak. For additional information and specific directions to the major recreation areas, refer to the individual descriptions (listed alphabetically under Phoenix) or contact the Phoenix Mountain Preserve at (602) 262-7901.

*Shadow Mountain Recreation Area is an undeveloped preserve. Designated hiking trails and other facilities are currently under construction.

PHOENIX MOUNTAIN PRESERVE THUMBNAIL DESCRIPTIONS OF HIKING TRAILS:

CHARLES M. CHRISTIANSEN MEMORIAL TRAIL HIKE (#100)
Location: Runs through the Shaw Butte, North Mountain, Dreamy Draw and Squaw Peak Recreation Areas.
Mileage: 21.4 miles
Elevation: 1,290 feet to 2,080 feet
Difficulty Rating: Beginner to Intermediate

DREAMY DRAW NATURE TRAIL HIKE (#220 and 220A)
Location: Dreamy Draw Recreation Area
Mileage: 3.0 miles
Elevation: 1,380 feet to 1,580 feet
Difficulty Rating: Beginner to Intermediate

LOOKOUT MOUNTAIN CIRCUMFERENCE TRAIL HIKE (#308)
Location: Lookout Mountain Recreation Area
Mileage: 5.2 miles
Elevation: 1,550 feet to 1,700 feet
Difficulty Rating: Beginner to Intermediate

LOOKOUT MOUNTAIN SUMMIT TRAIL HIKE (#150)
Location: Lookout Mountain Recreation Area
Mileage: 1.2 miles
Elevation: 1,580 feet to 2,054 feet
Difficulty Rating: Intermediate to Expert

MOUNTAIN VIEW NATURE TRAIL HIKE (#60)
Location: North Mountain Recreation Area
Mileage: 2.4 miles
Elevation: 1,290 feet to 1,480 feet
Difficulty Rating: Beginner to Intermediate

NORTH MOUNTAIN SUMMIT TRAIL HIKE (#40)
Location: North Mountain Recreation Area
Mileage: 3.2 miles
Elevation: 1,490 feet to 2,104 feet
Difficulty Rating: Intermediate to Expert

PENNY HOWE BARRIER FREE TRAIL HIKE (#44)
Location: North Mountain Recreation Area
Mileage: 0.6 miles
Elevation: 1,380 feet to 1,420 feet
Difficulty Rating: Beginner

PERL CHARLES MEMORIAL TRAIL HIKE (#1A)
Location: N.E. of the Squaw Peak Recreation Area
Mileage: 9.6 miles
Elevation: 1,340 feet to 2,200 feet
Difficulty Rating: Intermediate to Expert

Dogs May Be Unleashed Unless Otherwise Indicated

QUARTZ RIDGE TRAIL HIKE (#8)
Location: N.E. of the Squaw Peak Recreation Area
Mileage: 4.8 miles
Elevation: 1,640 feet to 1,860 feet
Difficulty Rating: Beginner to Intermediate

QUARTZ RIDGE TRAIL HIKE (#8A)
Location: Squaw Peak Recreation Area
Mileage: 3.4 miles
Elevation: 1,300 feet to 1,800 feet
Difficulty Rating: Beginner to Expert

SHAW BUTTE TRAIL HIKE (#306)
Location: Shaw Butte Recreation Area
Mileage: 8.0 miles
Elevation: 1,390 feet to 1,890 feet
Difficulty Rating: Intermediate to Expert

SQUAW PEAK CIRCUMFERENCE TRAIL HIKE (#302)
Location: Squaw Peak Recreation Area
Mileage: 3.7 miles
Elevation: 1,400 feet to 2,120 feet
Difficulty Rating: Intermediate to Expert

Note: Dogs are not permitted on the Squaw Peak Summit Trail.

SQUAW PEAK MOHAVE TRAIL HIKE (#200)
Location: Squaw Peak Recreation Area
Mileage: 0.8 miles
Elevation: 1,480 feet to 1,788 feet
Difficulty Rating: Beginner to Intermediate

SQUAW PEAK MOHAVE TRAIL HIKE (#200A)
Location: Squaw Peak Recreation Area
Mileage: 3.0 miles
Elevation: 1,300 feet to 1,500 feet
Difficulty Rating: Beginner to Intermediate

SQUAW PEAK NATURE TRAIL HIKE (#304)
Location: Squaw Peak Recreation Area
Mileage: 3.0 miles
Elevation: 1,610 feet to 1,790 feet
Difficulty Rating: Beginner to Intermediate

PLAYA MARGARITA PARK - Leashes

Info: Do lunch with Rover in the ramada or lead your lad along the perimeter of this sporty urban park.

Directions: Located at 36th Avenue and Roeser Road, between Southern and Broadway.

QUARTZ RIDGE TRAIL HIKE - Leashes

Intermediate/4.8 miles/2.5 hours

Info: Keep your herding hound in step and be ready to share this trail with horseback riders, mountain bikers and the abundant wildlife that inhabits this densely vegetated region. Large drainages along the route create amazing plant diversity for nature lovers to investigate. If solitude is more your style, there are several well-marked sidetrips you can take to add privacy to your journey. For more information: (602) 262-7901.

Directions: Take Shea Boulevard to 40th Street. Go south on 40th Street until it ends at the trailhead.

REACH 11 LOOP TRAIL HIKE - Leashes

Intermediate/1.0-16.5 miles/0.5-9.0 hours

Info: Big brown eyes begging to go outside? Reward Rover with a long walk which encompasses sections of Phoenix and Scottsdale. The trail is well-groomed and suited for all breeds. The natural surroundings on various portions along the hike will help city dwellers forget the hustle/bustle of urban life - at least for awhile. For more information: (602) 262-7901.

Directions: Trail can be accessed from Scottsdale Road north of Bell Road, or from Cave Creek Road and Tatum Boulevard.

REACH 11 RECREATION AREA - Leashes

Info: This area isn't measured in acres but rather in miles - miles of hiking trails just waiting for you and your pooch to explore. Running alongside the Central Arizona Project aqueduct, you'll journey amidst a desert environment and wildlife nature area as well as an equestrian center tucked in the middle of it all. For more information: (602) 262-7901.

Directions: Depending where you're coming from, there are three ways to reach this area The west entrance is from Cave Creek Road about a mile north of Beardsley Road. The middle entrance is from Tatum Boulevard north of where Union Hills intersects with Tatum. The east entrance is from Scottsdale Road north of Bell Road/Frank Lloyd Wright Blvd. on the north side of the Central Arizona Project Canal.

REACH 11 WILDLIFE AREA HIKE - Leashes

Intermediate/6.4 miles/3.2 hours

Info: Produce a tailwag in your buddy with a trek along the Central Arizona Project aqueduct, the waterway responsible for the lush vegetation. Animal and plant lovers will enjoy the diversity of the surroundings in this beautiful landscape. Take a zoom lens for your camera so you can focus on the cornucopia of desert dwelling flora and fauna that inhabit this picturesque environment. For more information: (602) 262-7901.

Directions: Take Scottsdale Road north past Bell Road/Frank Lloyd Wright Blvd. and the Central Arizona Project until you reach the trailhead on the left.

RIO SALADO INDUSTRIAL RECREATIONAL PARK - Leashes

Info: A visit can easily turn into an afternoon of playtime for you and the pupster. With well over fifteen acres of lawn overlooking the Salt River Wash, your pooch can really work the kinks out. Get your daily dose of Rexercise along the grassy areas and then chill-out with a brown bagger and biscuit combo at one of the shaded picnic tables.

Directions: Located on Elwood Street, which is north of Broadway. The park is between 7th and 16th Streets.

ROADRUNNER PARK - Leashes

Info: A small lake surrounded by acres of verdant lawn await you at this lovely park on the east side of town. Whether you stroll lakeside, toss a frisbee or spectate at a game of soccer, this park has many ways to spend some leisure time with your fur-face.

Directions: Located at Cactus Road and 35th Street.

ROESLEY PARK - Leashes

Info: This small lawned park offers your pup a chance to roll in the grass and chase the elusive yellow billed tennis ball.

Directions: Located at 15th Avenue at Romley Avenue, between Southern and Broadway.

ROYAL PALM PARK - Leashes

Info: With well over ten acres of frolic-proof grass, this park offers your pup a chance to romp and play to his heart's content. Picnic tables dot the area so you and the dawgus can relax when play time is over. Go ahead, break some bread and biscuits, and enjoy.

Directions: Located at 15th Avenue and Butler, between Northern and Dunlap Avenues.

SANDPIPER PARK - Leashes

Info: Tucked away on the eastern edge of Phoenix, this small park offers over five acres of fun in the sun for your canine sidekick. With lots of open space, this park is perfect if there's a frisbee in your dog's future (or in your backpack).

Directions: Located on Hearn Road, north of Thunderbird, between 64th Street and Scottsdale Road.

SERENO PARK - Leashes

Info: A bit of adventure awaits you and your canine at this park. Baseball, soccer and softball fields offer wide open spaces for some afternoon frolicking. Bring along a biscuit basket and enjoy a laid-back picnic.

Directions: Located at 56th Street and Sweetwater, between Cactus and Thunderbird Roads.

SHAW BUTTE TRAIL HIKE - Leashes

Intermediate/8.0 miles/5.0 hours

Info: Kick back under a shaded ramada in a lazy desert landscape or kick up some dust on a strenuous 8-miler. Before starting out, fill up your water bottles at the fountain, you're about to embark on a rustic journey. Beginning at an elevation of nearly 1,400 feet, you'll ascend mountainside to the summit at 1,890 feet. The views from the top will make the effort worthwhile. Bring a wide angle lens, it's the only way to capture the far reaching vistas. You'll need about five hours to complete the hike. Travel with a watch, the Park Rangers ask that all trails be cleared by sundown.

Directions: Take Central south of Thunderbird for access into the Phoenix Mountain Preserve.

Note: Hours 6 AM - Sundown.

SOLANO PARK - Leashes

Info: Located behind the Christown Shopping Center, this eight-acre park offers plenty of romping room for you and Bowser.

Directions: Enter the park through the shopping center at 17th Avenue and Bethany Home Road. Or from 19th Avenue. Or take Missouri Avenue east from 19th Avenue to 17th Avenue.

SONRISA PARK - Leashes

Info: Over five acres of serene green can belong to you and your pooch at this small park. Laze the day away reading under the shade of a tree, try a game of fetch/catch or do lunch paper-sack style.

Directions: Located on 52nd Street at Sweetwater, between Thunderbird and Cactus Roads.

SOUTH MOUNTAIN PARK/PRESERVE - Leashes

Info: Comprised of more than 17,000 acres, South Mountain is the world's largest dog-friendly and adventure-filled municipal park. It would take more than a few visits to come close to experiencing all that this enormous region has to offer. City park or not, remember you're in a rustic environment. Carry plenty of water and some high energy snacks as you explore this area.

Make a dent in your wanderlust mode on one of the pawdestrian trails scattered throughout the mountainous landscape. You might get lucky and hit upon a sampling of petroglyphs - these ancient Indian rock inscriptions are abundant. You might also experience a little of the Far East in your travels. South Mountain is home to its own Wall of China. A wall which bears a striking resemblance to the manmade legacy in China, only this one is carved solely by Mother Nature. Geology buffs, don't miss Fat Man's Pass, where the wind has created a smooth fissure in rock. Or combine local legend with natural history and check out the Marcos de Niza Rock, where according to legend, Father Marcos de Niza left his inscription 400 years ago.

For some awesome views of Phoenix and the Valley of the Sun, climb to Dobbins Lookout and be dazzled by the sweeping panoramas. Directional markers will help you locate Valley landmarks while the elevation will give you a feel for the fast growing city.

Look around as you mosey about. Over 300 species of plant life exist within the park's boundaries as well as an amazing array of wildlife. Wherever your travels take you and your canine companion, one thing's certain - the two of you will have a howling good time at this unusual parkland.

Directions: South Mountain Park is bordered by Dobbins and Baseline Roads to the north, 48th Street to the east and 27th Avenue to the west. South on Central Avenue is a main entrance but there are a number of other entrances to the park. For more information: (602) 495-0222.

SOUTH MOUNTAIN PARK/PRESERVE THUMBNAIL DESCRIPTIONS OF HIKING TRAILS:

ALTA TRAIL HIKE:
Mileage: 9.0 miles
Elevation: 1,320 feet to 1,570 feet
Difficulty Rating: Intermediate to Expert

HOLBERT TRAIL HIKE:
Mileage: 5.0 miles
Elevation: 1,350 feet to 2,255 feet
Difficulty Rating: Intermediate

KIWANIS TRAIL HIKE:
Mileage: 2.0 miles
Elevation: 1,590 feet to 1,990 feet
Difficulty Rating: Intermediate

MORMON TRAIL HIKE:
Mileage: 2.2 miles
Elevation: 1,290 feet to 1,960 feet
Difficulty Rating: Intermediate

NATIONAL TRAIL HIKE: (aka SUN CIRCLE TRAIL)
Mileage: 29.0 miles
Elevation: 1,200 feet to 2,400 feet
Difficulty Rating: Intermediate to Expert

RANGER TRAIL HIKE:
Mileage: 2.8 miles
Elevation: 1,460 feet to 2,260 feet
Difficulty Rating: Intermediate

SQUAW PEAK CIRCUMFERENCE HIKE - Leashes

Intermediate/3.7 miles/1.5 hours

Info: If gorgeous scenery tops your list of hike attractions, you'll want to pack your binoculars and camera and head out to this trail. User-friendly and dog-friendly, this area is one of the most breathtaking sections of the Phoenix Mountain Preserve. Sonoran Desert vegetation flourishes along the pathway and presents a smorgasbord of nature set against a backdrop of extraordinary views. Please stay on the trail. This fragile ecosystem cannot withstand heavy traffic. For more information: (602) 262-7901.

Directions: Take Lincoln to 22nd Street and go north on Squaw Peak Drive to the trailhead.

Note: Hours 6 AM - Sundown.

Locate Other Dog-Friendly Activities...Check Nearby Cities

SQUAW PEAK MOHAVE TRAIL HIKE - Leashes

Beginner/0.8 miles/0.5 hours

Info: This popular trail is promoted as multiple use, so watch out for mountain bikers and equestrians. Many animal species can still be seen along this short but fulfilling hike in the Squaw Peak area of the Phoenix Mountain Preserve. Enjoy some quiet time with your pal as you marvel at the distant cityscape. Although it may be tempting, please don't stray from the trail - much of this area is closed for revegetation. For more information: (602) 262-7901.

Directions: Take Lincoln to 22nd Street and go north on Squaw Peak Drive to the trailhead.

Note: Hours 6 AM - Sundown.

SQUAW PEAK NATURE TRAIL HIKE - Leashes

Intermediate/3.0 miles/1.5 hours

Info: Pick up the Squaw Peak Nature Trail Guide at the Ranger Station before you venture out on this hike. With the guide in hand, you'll be able to design a tour of the flora and fauna as you follow the numbered posts along the pathway. The diversity of the region will surprise you and you'll learn a thing or two about the wildlife inhabitants. This area is part of a delicate ecosystem. Make sure Fido is on his best behavior. Take particular care not to travel off the trail. For more information: (602) 262-7901.

Directions: Take Lincoln to 22nd Street and go north on Squaw Peak Drive to the trailhead.

Note: Hours 6 AM - Sundown.

SQUAW PEAK RECREATION AREA - Leashes

Info: Enjoy the desert landscape from a shady ramada or lace up your hiking boots, pick up a free guidebook at the Ranger Station and learn as you sojourn. Listen for the eerie howling of coyotes and the soothing serenade of songbirds. Dogs are permitted in all areas of this park except for the Summit Trail. For more information: (602) 262-7901.

Directions: Located at 2701 East Squaw Peak Lane. Take Lincoln to 22nd Street and go north on Squaw Peak Drive.

Note: Hours 6 AM - Sundown.

STARLIGHT PARK - Leashes

Info: Tucked away on the western edge of Phoenix, this park offers lots of spacious grounds for your bowser buddy to nab a low flying frisbee.

Directions: Located between Indian School and Thomas Roads to the north and south and 75th and 83rd Avenues to the east and west.

SUENO PARK - Leashes

Info: More than 20 acres of open fields await your puppy playmate. Or your four-footed, sure-footed friend can accompany you on the exercise course for an aerobic workout.

Directions: Located on 43rd Avenue at Encanto Boulevard, between McDowell and Thomas Roads.

SUMIDA PARK - Leashes

Info: This small neighborhood park is nestled in an out-of-the-way corner and frequented by locals. It's a definite escape route from the crowds. More than likely, you and the pupster will have the place to yourselves.

Directions: From Northern Avenue west of the Squaw Peak Parkway, take 16th Street south to Morten Avenue. Turn east (left) and drive to Dreamy Draw Drive. Turn south (right) onto Dreamy Draw and drive one block to the park.

SUNBURST PARADISE PARK - Leashes

Info: Off the beaten path, this 10-acre neighborhood greenbelt is the perfect setting for some park peace. Bring along a frisbee - there's a good chance you'll be the only visitors.

Directions: Located on Paradise Lane, (south of Bell Road) between 43rd and 51st Avenues.

SURREY PARK - Leashes

Info: Located a few blocks east of the ASU West Campus, you and the canine can find shade under a ramada and work on your thesis or spend the time tossing a tennis ball. Hmm - which sounds like more fun?

Directions: From Thunderbird, take 39th Avenue south three blocks to Joan d'Arc Avenue and the park.

SWEETWATER PARK - Leashes

Info: Give your credit cards a rest while you and the pooch enjoy a grassy knoll at this medium size park. Located across from the Paradise Valley Mall, you'll find over 10 acres including some leg-stretching sports fields. There's also an exercise course where you can burn off those lunchtime calories.

Directions: From Thunderbird Road take 44th Street south to the park. The southern end of the park connects with Paradise Village Parkway across from the northwest side of the Paradise Valley Mall.

TELEPHONE PIONEERS OF AMERICA PARK - Leashes

Info: Small, but quaint, this was one of the first barrier-free parks in the nation.

Directions: Located at 1946 West Morningside Drive.

Note: Hours 8 AM - 9 PM.

VENTUROSO PARK - Leashes

Info: Over 20 acres of soft sod beckon you and your canine companion. A fast moving tennis ball will have lots of bouncing room on the wide open lawn.

Directions: Located on 32nd Street between Thunderbird and Greenway Roads.

VISTA CANYON PARK - Leashes

Info: Another southern area park hidden from metro Phoenix. Over 15 acres of this secret green scene are just waiting for your frolicking Fido.

Directions: From the Tucson bound Interstate 10 take the Chandler Boulevard offramp and head west on Chandler. After about 3 miles you'll reach 28th Street. Turn south (left) and follow it around where it curves and heads into the park.

WASHINGTON PARK - Leashes

Info: 40 acres of stomping ground can be found at this park where strolling the perimeter is a popular pastime.

Directions: Located at 23rd Avenue and Maryland.

WEST PLAZA PARK - Leashes

Info: Five acres of grass and trees in a community setting provide a perfect locale for you and Fido to catch up on some doggie doings.

Directions: Located at 43rd Avenue and Maryland.

WHITE TANK MOUNTAIN REGIONAL PARK - Leashes

Info: This park encompasses more than 26,000 acres of staggering scenery. The largest park in the Maricopa County system, it is definitely worth a visit. Several hiking trails lace the park making their way to waterfalls, lookouts and remote areas. The park's unusual name comes from a natural phenomenon. The tanks are depressions in white granite rock resulting from water erosion and they present a fascinating sight. Petroglyphs are common to the region so play seek and find as you amble along the pathways.

You might be close to the city but the environment is decidedly rustic and quite dry. If you're spending the day, don a hat, some sunscreen and carry plenty of water. The leash law is meant to protect Fido and the wildlife. Avoid the temptation to set Fido free. Day use areas 1-11 are free for people and their pooches. For more information: (602) 955-2505 or (602) 272-8871.

Directions: Located 15 miles west of Peoria via Olive/Dunlap Avenue.

Note: Areas 3 and 4 may require a fee when posted.

Other Neighborhood Parks in Phoenix:

CENTRAL PARK - Leashes
Located at 1st Street and Tonto, north of Buckeye.

DESERT STORM PARK - Leashes
Located on 16th Street between Camelback and Bethany Home Roads.

EASTLAKE PARK - Leashes
Located at 16th and Jefferson Streets.

INDIAN BEND PARK - Leashes
Located at Thunderbird Avenue and 37th Place (just east of 36th Street).

LEWIS PARK - Leashes
Located at 1238 S 13th Place.

SMITH PARK - Leashes
Located at 41st Avenue and Grant.

TOWNSEND PARK - Leashes
Located at McDowell Road and 5th Street.

Locate Other Dog-Friendly Activities...Check Nearby Cities

VERDE PARK - Leashes
Located at 9th and Polk Streets

WESTERN STAR PARK - Leashes
Located at 4th Street and Western Star Boulevard.

WESTOWN PARK - Leashes
Located at 32nd Avenue and Corine Drive.

WILLOW PARK - Leashes
Located at 28th Avenue and Polk Street.

PINE

(See Strawberry and Payson for lodging and additional recreation.)

RECREATION
PINE CANYON TRAIL HIKE - Leashes
Intermediate/1.0-14.4 miles/0.5-7.5 hours

Info: This lovely hike in cool Rim Country escorts you through a dense forestland of ponderosa pine. Well shaded by mature trees, you can't beat this trail on a warm summer day. The region is home to diverse wildlife and sightings of elk herds are not uncommon. Listen to the sweet trill of songbirds that fill the pine scented air. Once you reach Dripping Springs, the trail becomes more difficult to follow. Turn around at any point and retrace your steps. Pack some high energy goodies for you and fur-face and don't forget to tote a supply of water. For more information: (520) 474-7900.

Dogs May Be Unleashed Unless Otherwise Indicated

Directions: About 1 mile south of Pine on Highway 87 turn left to the trailhead. From the trailhead parking lot, proceed through the gate and up the hill about 100 yards. As you intersect the Highline Trail, turn left to the Pine Canyon Trail.

PINETOP

LODGING

BEST WESTERN INN OF PINETOP
404 S White Mountain Blvd (85935) Rates: $50-$89;
Tel: (520) 367-6667; (800) 528-1234

BUCK SPRINGS RESORT COTTAGES
P. O. Box 130 (85935) Rates: $48-$65;
Tel: (520) 369-3554

DOUBLE B LODGE & CABINS
P. O. Box 747 (85935) Rates: $34-$62;
Tel: (520) 367-2747

ECONO LODGE OF PINETOP
458 E White Mountain Blvd (85935) Rates: $49-$99;
Tel: (520) 367-3636; (800) 424-4777

MEADOW VIEW LODGE
P. O. Box 325 (85935) Rates: $48+;
Tel: (520) 367-4642

MOUNTAIN HACIENDA LODGE
P. O. Box 713 (85935) Rates: $31-$47;
Tel: (520) 367-4146

NORTHWOODS RESORT
165 E White Mountain Blvd (85935) Rates: $62-$99;
Tel: (520) 367-2966

Recreation

COUNTRY CLUB TRAIL HIKE - Leashes

Intermediate/9.5 miles/5.0 hours

Info: This fairly level loop trail within a fragrant ponderosa forest eventually leads to Whitcomb Springs and a marvelous sprawling meadow. If you're a mountain topper, a side trail leads to the peak of Pat Mullen Mountain. If you and Fido have the time, this trail is worth the trip. For more information: (520) 368-5111.

Directions: From the Lakeside Ranger Station, head south on Highway 260. Take a left onto Buck Springs Road. From Buck Springs Road, turn left onto FR 182 and continue for two miles until you reach FR 185. Turn right on FR 185 and the trailhead will be in front of you.

MOGOLLON RIM NATURE TRAIL HIKE

Beginner/1.0 miles/0.5 hours

Info: The ease and beauty of this self-guided nature trail will be sure to make your top ten list. Simple, flat and pretty account for the popularity of this looping trail. But perhaps the most memorable part of the hike is the section that guides you to the edge of the awe-inspiring Mogollon Rim. This short but sweet trail encompasses the most diverse display of vegetation in the area: Douglas fir, ponderosa and pinyon pine, gambel and scrub oak, Rocky Mountain, Utah and alligator juniper, mountain mahogany, buck brush and whew! manzanita. Don't be a trailblazer. Stay on the designated path and avoid trampling the delicate natural shrubbery. For more information: (520) 368-5111.

Directions: Take Highway 260 northwest, just past the Lakeside Ranger Station. Once past Camp Tatiyee, watch for the Mogollon Rim Overlook sign. Park in the available lot and follow the signs to the trailhead.

SPRINGS LOOP TRAIL HIKE

Beginner/3.5 miles/2.0 hours

Info: Partake of an afternoon delight with your pooch hiking this easy, looping trail. As you circle the springs and creeks, keep alert for signs of the area's wildlife inhabitants. Remain on the designated trail to avoid disturbing the sensitive flora and fauna. For more information: (520) 368-5111.

Directions: Take Highway 260 east from Pinetop-Lakeside to Buck Springs Road (Pinetop Lakes Entrance) and turn left (north). Go .6 miles to Road 182 (Sky Hi Retreat), turn left. Drive for 1.3 miles to the trailhead on the left (west).

WOODLAND LAKE PARK

Info: Smack dab in the middle of town, this park is an absolute gem. Center your attention on the fun-filled activities available for you and the pupster. Frolic with Fido through sunlight and shadows on tree-lined paths. Birdwatch, peoplewatch or do some canine socializing. There are several hikes covering varying distances - more than enough to satisfy all your walking wishes. Troopers should try the 2-mile Hitching Post Loop Trail while wet waggers might prefer the 1.25 Lake Loop Trail. Whatever your pleasure, this park gets two paws up.

Directions: From Highway 260 in Pinetop, follow Woodland Lake Road south to the park entrance.

1) EAGLE SCOUT TRAIL HIKE

Beginner/0.5 miles/0.5 hours

Info: Sofa loafers rejoice, this trails for you. Even though this cinchy trail is practically over before it begins, you'll still feel like you've touched nature, if only for a brief moment. For more information: (520) 368-6700.

Directions: From Highway 260 in Pinetop, follow Woodland Lake Road south to Woodland Lake Park. The trail begins just past the park's ball field.

2) HITCHING POST LOOP TRAIL HIKE - Leashes

Beginner/3.0 miles/1.5 hours

Info: If you thought that the soft whisper of the wind through pine trees and the cushiony feel of pine needles beneath your feet was reserved for east coast dwellers, you'll want to hop along this trail. The wind sings a wild song as it rustles and shakes the oaks and pines in this scenic woodsy setting. Massive and stretching to the sky, the trees create a rustic milieu, perfect for a relaxing getaway. For more information: (520) 368-6700.

Directions: From Highway 260 in Pinetop, follow Woodland Lake Road south to Woodland Lake Park. The trailhead is located on the north side of the ball field in the park.

3) TURKEY TRACK TRAIL HIKE - Leashes

Beginner/3.0 miles/1.5 hours

Info: Delight in a pleasant stroll with Rover on this trail through an oak and pine forest - just perfect for a warm summertime hike. For more information: (520) 368-6700.

Dogs May Be Unleashed Unless Otherwise Indicated

Directions: From Highway 260 in Pinetop, follow Woodland Lake Road south to Woodland Lake Park. The trail begins near the park's boat dock.

4) WALNUT CREEK TRAIL HIKE - Leashes

Beginner/1.0 miles/0.5 hours

Info: Hiking creekside through a walnut-clad canyon is something you'll want to do over and over again. As you stroll through this riparian oasis, there's a chance you might spot a squirrel or a herd of elk. Birdwatchers report dozens of species within the canyon as well. For more information: (520) 368-6700.

Directions: From Highway 260 in Pinetop, follow Woodland Lake Road south to Woodland Lake Park. The trail begins near the park's boat dock..

PORTAL

RECREATION
SILVER PEAK TRAIL HIKE

Expert/9.2 miles/4.5 hours

Info: First make sure that you and the dawgus are up to the challenge and then arrange a double masseuse appointment. You'll both need it after this hike. The 3,000-foot ascent to the summit of 7,975-foot Silver Peak will leave you weak in the knees while the views will leave you breathless. The trail begins at the cottonwood-clad bottom of Cave Creek Canyon and climbs into a deciduous forest. If you visit in fall, you'll be treated to a landscape colored in hues of red and yellow. Closer to the summit, oak and juniper woodlands give way to a dense forest of ponderosa pine and woodsy ferns. When you top out at Cave Creek Canyon - aka the Southwest's Little Yosemite - the bird's-eye views should ease your calf pain. Take a good long break - the downhill return can turn rubbery legs to mere Jello. For more information: (520) 364-3468.

Directions: Take Forest Road 42 west for 1 mile to the Forest Service Ranger Station in Cave Creek Canyon. The marked trailhead is .2 miles south of the Ranger Station.

Notes

PRESCOTT

LODGING

ANTELOPE RESORT ESTATES
6200 N Hwy 89 (86301)
Rates: 2 month rental, (66 days) for $2950.00;
Tel: (520) 776-2600

ANTELOPE HILLS INN SUITES
6000 Willow Creek Rd (86301) Rates: $48-$64
Tel: (520) 778-6000

APACHE MOTEL
1130 E Gurley St (86301) Rates: $39-$59;
Tel: (520) 445-1422

BEST WESTERN PRESCOTTONIAN MOTEL
1317 E Gurley St (86301) Rates: $44-$125;
Tel: (520) 445-3096; (800) 528-1234

CASCADE MOTEL
805 White Spar Rd (86303) Rates: $30-$80;
Tel: (520) 445-1232

FOREST VILLAS HOTEL
3645 Lee Cir (86301) Rates: $69-$119;
Tel: (520) 717-1200; (800) 223-3449

HERITAGE HOUSE
819 E Gurley St (86301) Rates: $36-$85;
Tel: (520) 445-9091

HI-ACRE RESORT
1001 White Spar Rd (86303) Rates: $29-$110;
Tel: (520) 445-0588

LYNX CREEK FARM BED & BREAKFAST
P. O. Box 4301, SR 69 (86302) Rates: $75-$140;
Tel: (520) 778-9573

MOTEL 6
1111 E Sheldon St (86301) Rates: $37-$45;
Tel: (520) 776-0160; (800) 440-6000

MT. VERNON INN B&B & COUNTRY COTTAGES
204 N Mt Vernon Ave (86301) Rates: $110-$130;
Tel: (520) 778-0886; (602) 990-0682; (800) 456-0682

NINE PINES COTTAGE
P. O. Box 2099 (86302) Rates: $55-$85;
Tel: (520) 778-3620

PINE VIEW MOTEL
500 Copper Basin Rd (86303) Rates: $20-$60;
Tel: (520) 445-4660

PRESCOTT RESORT-CONFERENCE CENTER & CASINO
1500 Hwy 69 (86301) Rates: $118-$170;
Tel: (520) 776-1666; (800) 967-4637

PRESCOTT SIERRA INN
809 White Spar Rd (86303) Rates: $34-$95;
Tel: (520) 445-1250

SENATOR INN
1117 E Gurley St (86301) Rates: $35-$145;
Tel: (520) 445-1440

SKYLINE MOTEL
523 E Gurley St (86301) Rates: $32-$65;
Tel: (520) 445-9963

RECREATION

ASPEN CREEK TRAIL HIKE
Beginner/4.4 miles/2.0 hours

Info: This hike's a breeze. You and Fido can enjoy the outdoors without breaking a sweat. The trail offers some outstanding views of Prescott, including Mount Union and Spruce Mountain. And if you're lucky, you may catch sight of the elk and deer which inhabit the area. The trail ends after meeting up with Trail #260. For more information: (520) 445-7253.

Directions: Take Montezuma Street (Highway 89) south from Prescott for 1.1 miles to Copper Basin Road, turn right. Follow Copper Basin for 4.75 miles to the trailhead on the left side of the road.

BULLROAD TRAIL HIKE - Leashes

Expert/15.2 miles/9.0 hours

Info: Strap on the odometer and click off some miles along this rough and tumble trail. Watch for an amazingly lush area around Hidden Tunnel Spring and look for the dammed entrance to an old mine tunnel. Once you're out of the woods, you'll be greeted by sweeping panoramas of Mingus Mountain, the San Francisco Peaks and the Mogollon Rim. You've paid your dues on this one so enjoy a leisurely gander from the top. For more information: (520) 445-7253.

Directions: Take Highway 69 southeast to Mayer, following Main Street through Mayer. Head east to the junction with Antelope Creek Road, then head southeast for nine miles to Cordes. Take FR 259 approximately 16 miles to Crown King. Take FR 259A south .5 miles to the junction with FR 52. Go west on FR 52 3.2 miles to FR 52C. Take 1 mile to Eagle Tail Mine. The road turns northwest for .6 miles to Wildflower Saddle. Go east on FR 92 for 1.1 miles to trailhead. The trailhead is on private property about .5 miles west of turnoff for Gladiator Mine.

CEDAR SPRINGS TRAIL HIKE

Intermediate/5.6 miles/3.0 hours

Info: This old transportation road now serves as a hiking trail into the Granite Mountain Wilderness. As you and your best buddy make your way to Red Hill Tank use caution, the road is not in great condition. For more information: (520) 445-7253.

Directions: From Prescott take Iron Springs Road west about 15 miles to Contreras Road (Forest Road 102), turn north (right). Drive 7 miles to FR 41. Take FR 41 east (right) for .25 miles to an unnumbered access road and veer right. Take this road .25 miles to FR 671 and turn left (north) onto this high clearance vehicle road. Take FR 671 to the Granite Mountain Wilderness boundary (FR 671 is a high clearance vehicle road for about 1 mile to the trailhead). The trailhead is at the boundary on the southside of the road.

CLARK SPRING TRAIL HIKE

Intermediate/3.4 miles/2.0 hours

Info: This popular hike begins with a level journey from Granite Basin Lake to Clark Spring. The trail then gradually climbs to the pass between Two Rock Mountain and Little Granite Mountain and ends at the Trail #37 junction. For a change of scenery, loop back to the trailhead on Trail #37. For more information: (520) 445-7253.

Directions: From Prescott take Iron Springs Road west for 7 miles to the Granite Basin Lake (FR 374) and turn right. Drive north 3.25 miles to the Recreation Area. Pass the campground and at the next junction, veer left, staying on FR 374. Drive to the trailhead.

E&L TRAIL HIKE - Leashes

Intermediate/9.6 miles/5.0 hours

Info: This is one of the most interesting hikes within the Prescott National Forest. Allow enough time to visit the old Palace Station. It's currently a Forest Service Administration and Information Site but until 1910, it was a stage stop for weary travelers and their thirsty mounts. The trail is riddled with evidence of early settlers. See what you and the pup can sniff out. Stick to the trail though, the old mine shafts in this region can be extremely dangerous. There are also times when the trail can be difficult to follow. When you reach the ridge, steal a view of Crook's Canyon. For more information: (520) 445-7253.

Directions: Take Senator Highway (FR 52) south from Prescott for 11 miles to the Mt. Union turnoff (FR 261) but don't turn. Continue on FR 52 another .3 miles until you reach FR 52B. Travel .3 miles to FR 81. Go south on FR 81 for .3 miles to FR 70. Go southeast on FR 70 about .4 miles to the trailhead.

GOLDWATER PARK - Leashes

Info: If waterways still the savage beast within you, this 40-acre park has got your name on it. A 15-acre lake equipped with a dock and boat launch is ideal for a little toe dipping and the grounds are just right for a leisurely stroll.

Directions: Located at 1000 Goldwater Lake Park Road.

GRANITE CREEK PARK - Leashes

Info: Take a quick jog on the half mile path or just enjoy 15 acres of scenic stomping ground with your pooch pal.

Directions: Located at 500 N. 6th Street.

GRANITE MOUNTAIN TRAIL HIKE

Intermediate/8.0 miles/4.0 hours

Info: Whether you hike a mile of this trail or all eight, you and your furry friend will be surrounded by dazzling Mother Nature. Groves of mountain oak, pinyon pine, manzanita and ponderosa pine compete for attention with giant prickly pear, making for an aesthetically pleasing sojourn to the Granite Mountain summit.

After the first mile, you'll reach Blair Pass, an intersection of three trails. Continue north on #261 where you'll encounter a switchback course that climbs 1,400 feet in 1.3 miles. At 7,000 feet, there's a fork in the road, providing you with two options. To the left (north), magnificent vistas of the valley and cloud-capped mountains beckon. To the right (south), panoramas of the sky-kissing Bradshaws, Skull Valley and Prescott can be yours. Either way, you won't be disappointed. For more information: (520) 445-7253.

Directions: From downtown Prescott (Courthouse Square at Gurley and Montezuma Streets) go west on Gurley to Grove Avenue. Turn right and go 1.5 miles to Iron Springs Road. Turn left onto Iron Springs and continue 3 miles. A sign will say "Granite Basin 4 miles." Just past the sign is Forest Road 374. Turn right onto FR 374 and travel for 3.5 miles. The road forks into what is a big loop at the stop sign. Stay to the left and drive .5 miles until you come to another fork. Again take the left fork and drive another .5 miles to the parking area at the trailhead.

GROOM CREEK LOOP TRAIL HIKE

Intermediate/11.0 miles/6.0 hours

Info: If you crave a sense of history, take a voyage back in time to the days when dreams of "striking it rich" were a reality. This trail crosses over land that was once replete with gold and silver, the basis of Prescott's economy for 60 years.

Today, most hikers and pooches simply enjoy the beautiful dense woodlands of Spruce Mountain, which are actually Douglas fir and ponderosa pine and not spruce. This rather steep, looping trail tops out at a viewpoint and picnic area, perfect for a midday snack, before returning to your starting point. This trail is very popular on weekends. For more information: (520) 445-7253.

Directions: From Prescott, take Gurley Street east to Mt. Vernon Avenue. Go south on Mt. Vernon (Senator Highway/FR 52) for 6.5 miles to Groom Creek. Continue on to the trailhead at the Groom Creek Horse Camp.

HERITAGE PARK - Leashes

Info: Commune with other canines and humans at this large, sports-oriented park which comes complete with snack bar.

Directions: Located at 1497 Heritage Park Road.

Dogs May Be Unleashed Unless Otherwise Indicated

HYDE MOUNTAIN TRAIL HIKE

Expert/4.0 miles/2.0 hours

Info: Surefooted and fit - if the words don't apply, this hike's not for you. A steep, demanding trail, you'll be climbing to the highest point in the Santa Maria Mountains - 7,272-foot Hyde Mountain Lookout. Catch your breath at the top and drink in the sweeping panoramas. Avoid this hike on days of extreme temperatures. For more information: (520) 636-2302.

Directions: From Prescott, take Williamson Valley Road (Forest Road 6) north 22 miles to the Camp Wood turnoff (FR 21). Take FR 21 west for 16 miles to both Camp Wood and FR 95. Take FR 95 north for .3 miles to FR 95C. Take FR 95C west for 1.75 miles to the trailhead and limited parking.

JUNIPER SPRINGS TRAIL HIKE

Expert/7.4 miles/5.0 hours

Info: Only die-hard hikers and hearty hounds should attempt this long, arduous trek through the isolated Juniper Mesa Wilderness. The trail climbs steeply along the edge of Juniper Mesa affording fantastic vistas of the surrounding landscape. Juniper Springs marks the end of the trail and your downhill journey. For more information: (520) 636-2302.

Directions: Take Williamson Valley Road (Forest Road 6) north from Prescott for about 38 miles to FR 95 (the last 12 miles are unpaved). Take FR 95 west for 1.5 miles to the Juniper Springs/Old Military Trailheads, just shy of the Walnut Creek Station.

Note: High clearance vehicles only. Inform someone of your plans and carry a map.

LITTLE GRANITE MOUNTAIN TRAIL HIKE

Intermediate/6.6 miles/3.5 hours

Info: En route, you'll see signs of the damaging Doce fire of 1990 and the efforts made by the Forest Service to restore the area. This trail is just one of the many connecting trails throughout the Granite Mountain Wilderness. For more information: (520) 445-7253.

Directions: Take Iron Springs Road west for 7 miles. The trailhead is 3.2 miles past the turnoff for Granite Basin Lake (FR 374).

LYNX LAKE TRAIL HIKE

Beginner/3.0 miles/1.5 hours

Info: Stroll beside the lake on this simple trail. Or pack a biscuit basket and fishing gear and make an afternoon of it.. You're bound to enjoy a leisurely interlude at this quiet area. For more information: (520) 445-7253.

Directions: Take Highway 69 east approximately 5 miles to Walker Road (FR 197) and go south. Follow to the Lynx Lake turnoff, then proceed to the boat ramp area. There is no designated trailhead. Access the trail through the Lynx Lake picnic area.

MINT WASH TRAIL HIKE

Intermediate/6.0 miles/3.0 hours

Info: Trek across the rocky bottom of Mint Wash and then make your way amidst a pinyon-juniper forest. Plan ahead and leave a picnic lunch in your car - there are shaded picnic tables at the Granite Basin picnic area. For more information: (520) 445-7253.

Directions: From Prescott, take Iron Springs Road north to FR 374 and turn right. Follow to the trailhead at Granite Basin Lake.

PIONEER PARK - Leashes

Info: Restless Rovers will love this park which encompasses a total of 400 acres. Spectate at a couple of sporting events and then take your wagger for some exercise on the 6-mile walking course.

Directions: Located at 1200 Commerce Drive.

PRESCOTT ACTIVITY CENTER AREA - Leashes

Info: Military buffs can explore this old armory with their buddy. Dogs are allowed inside the building and there's a small turf area for outdoor sniffing.

Directions: Located at 824 E. Gurley Street.

RANCH TRAIL HIKE

Intermediate/6.0 miles/3.0 hours

Info: When you and old brown eyes are overcome by the need to spend some time in the great outdoors, try your hand at this rugged, mountain hike. Overall, the trail covers a 1,000-foot change in elevation which is marked by varying species of trees - chaparral covers the southern slopes, while ponderosa pine claims the northern ones. The higher you climb, the prettier the views. For more information: (520) 445-7253.

Directions: Take Highway 69 east to Walker Road (FR 197), turn south. Follow to the trailhead.

ROUGHRIDER PARK - Leashes

Info: Don't let the name fool you - it'll be smooth strolling for you and your furry fellow at this 25-acre sports-oriented park, complete with a snack bar.

Directions: Located on N. Washington Street.

THUMB BUTTE TRAIL HIKE - Leashes

Intermediate/1.75 miles/1.0 hours

Info: This trail traverses 1.75 miles of juniper and chaparral. Head out to your right and pick up the trail to the top. You'll pass through a turnstile and gradually ascend to the first vista point - Groom Creek, where cactus grow beside lichen-encrusted boulders and pine trees - truly high chaparral country. The views are beautiful, lush rolling hills, the town of Prescott, the San Francisco Peaks, Granite, Mingus, Bradshaw and Sierra Prieta Mountains and the prominent Thumb Butte. There's a bench atop the vista point where you can take a biscuit break while you and the pooch enjoy your lofty perch. When you continue the loop, look for the turnout on your left to Granite Vista where a different perspective of your surroundings awaits.

This is a great year-round hike. Visit in the winter after a snowfall and find yourself in a white wonderland where pooch can frolic trailside in fluffy snowdrifts. Do a little time traveling when your hiking day is done with a visit to Prescott and the charm and friendliness of a 1950's American town.

Directions: Take Gurley Street west through town. Approximately 3 miles after Gurley Street turns into Thumb Butte Road, you'll reach the Thumb Butte picnic area and trailhead on your left.

UPPER PASTURE TRAIL HIKE

Beginner/6.4 miles/3.0 hours

Info: This easy-does-it trail gives you the best of both worlds. A wilderness adventure with the ease of a city stroll. For more information: (520) 445-7253.

Directions: Take Iron Springs Road west from Prescott for 9.25 miles to Forest Road 102A. Turn north (right) and drive .75 miles to the trailhead located just before the bend.

WATSON LAKE PARK - Leashes

Info: Don't be surprised to see a tent or two scattered along the lake as this park is a favorite for happy campers.

Directions: Located 9 miles north of Prescott on Highway 89.

WEST SPRUCE TRAIL HIKE

Intermediate/6.0 miles/3.0 hours

Info: Gambel oak, Douglas fir and pine surround you as you hike the crest of the Sierra Prieta Range to the top of 7,100-foot West Spruce Mountain. Despite the name, no spruce trees exist.

Snoopy will love the feeling of power he'll experience at the summit - master of all he purveys - including Skull Valley, the Mingus Mountains and Copper Basin. When you reach FR 47B, turn around and retrace your route. For more information: (520) 445-7253.

Directions: From Prescott, head west on Gurley Street, which turns into Thumb Butte Road, to the Thumb Butte Recreation Area. About 1 mile past the recreation area, turn left at Aloma Camp for .6 miles to FR 373, go left. Follow FR 373 for approximately 3 miles. After you make a large horseshoe-shaped turn to the right, the trailhead is to the right of the cattle guard.

WILLOW CREEK PARK - Leashes

Info: Spend some quality playtime with your pooch on 9 acres of developed land.

Directions: Located at 3181 Willow Creek Road.

YANKEE DOODLE TRAIL HIKE - Leashes

Intermediate/2.5 miles/1.25 hours

Info: This section of the Yankee Doodle Trail (from FR 52 to FR 261) is dandy for anyone interested in ecology. Burned in the 1972 Battle Fire, this once dense ponderosa forest is now predominately scrub oak and manzanita. When you're seeking a bit of quiet, this pleasant walk will fit the bill. For more information: (520) 445-7253.

Directions: Take Senator Highway south for 11 miles to Palace Station. Go East on FR 52 for 1 mile to Orofino Mine where the trail crosses FR 52. Take the trail north to where it intersects with FR 261 and turn back.

Other Neighborhood Parks in Prescott:

KEN LINDLEY PARK - Leashes
Located at 700 E. Gurley Street.

Dogs May Be Unleashed Unless Otherwise Indicated

PRESCOTT VALLEY

LODGING

PRESCOTT VALLEY MOTEL
8350 East Hwy 69 (86314) Rates: $35+;
Tel: (520) 772-9412

RECREATION

SMITH RAVINE TRAIL HIKE
Intermediate/5.5 miles/2.5 hours

Info: Spend the afternoon with your furry sidekick exploring the rugged terrain of the Bradshaw Mountains. Be prepared for some rough going - sections of the trail are rather steep. Thanks to the towering ponderosa pines that shade your mountainous ascent, this hike spells cool year-round. For more information: (520) 445-7253.

Directions: Follow Senator Highway east to FR 52A south. The trailhead is off FR 52A.

WOODCHUTE TRAIL HIKE
Intermediate/6.0 miles/3.0 hours

Info: Solitude and gentle terrain combine to make this a great day hike. From Powerline Tank, a gradual 800-foot ascent takes you and Fido to the peak of Woodchute Mountain. Break some bread and biscuits, you've earned the pretty views of Red Rock Sedona, the San Francisco Peaks and the Verde Valley. For more information: (520) 567-4121.

Directions: Take Highway 89A east to Potato Patch Campground and Forest Road 106. Take FR 106 northwest for .3 miles to Powerline. The trailhead is under the powerlines, just beyond the pond. The road can be rough. Consider parking near the campground and hiking the last .3 of a mile to the trailhead.

RIO RICO

LODGING

RIO RICO RESORT & COUNTRY CLUB
1069 Camino Caralampi (85648) Rates: $95-$150;
Tel: (520) 281-1901; (800) 288-4746

ROOSEVELT

RECREATION

CHILLICUT TRAIL HIKE - Leashes
Expert/1.0-11.6 miles/0.5-6.0 hours

Info: Either follow the road for an easy 1/2 mile jaunt or tough it out for the whole round trip on this challenging hike. Sniff your way down the trail through the thick and varied vegetation. Proud and majestic, the surrounding mountains are seemingly endless. Pack some energizing trail mix and plenty of water if you plan to do it all.

Directions: Take Highway 188 north to FR 445, turn left. Follow to FR 445A, turn right. The trailhead is in Rock Creek which parallels FR 445A.

COTTONWOOD CANYON TRAIL HIKE - Leashes

Intermediate/8.0 miles/4.0 hours

Info: If lush landscapes wag your tail, then head out to Cottonwood Canyon. This interesting trail leads you and your pooch through a variety of settings as you gradually ascend Cottonwood Canyon. FR 83 is your turnaround point. The return hike presents such a different glimpse of the scenery you'll feel like you've hiked two trails instead of one. For more information: (520) 467-3200.

Directions: The trailhead is located .75 miles east of Roosevelt Visitor Center on Highway 88.

TULE CANYON TRAIL HIKE - Leashes

Intermediate/9.0 miles/4.5 hours

Info: Kick up a cloud of dust on this high chaparral Sonoran Desert hike. You'll encounter rougher, steeper terrain once you enter the Superstition Wilderness. This off-the-beaten-track trail offers plenty of seclusion as it climbs among thick forests of chaparral and pinyon/juniper. When it's time for a break, cop a squat at a lookout and pick you views. For more information: (520) 467-3200.

Directions: Take Highway 88 east to FR 449. Follow FR 449 south for 2.5 miles and turn right to the trailhead.

SAFFORD

LODGING

BEST WESTERN-DESERT INN OF SAFFORD
1391 W Thatcher Blvd (85546) Rates: $57-$80;
Tel: (520) 428-0521; (800) 528-1234

COMFORT INN
1578 W Thatcher Blvd (85546) Rates: $42-$64;
Tel: (520) 428-5851; (800) 221-2222

SANDIA MOTEL
520 E Hwy 70 (85546) Rates: $46+;
Tel: (520) 428-5000; (800) 578-2151

RECREATION

ARCADIA TRAIL HIKE - Leashes
Intermediate/10.2 miles/5.0 hours

Info: This trail has been designated a National Scenic Recreation Trail because of its stunning views of distant peaks and craggy canyons. Douglas fir, Englemann spruce and aspen dot the trail at higher elevations while tall stands of ponderosa pine and silverleaf oak veil the lower slopes. A truly treemarkable area, box elder and bigtooth maple are also firmly rooted in the varying terrain. One of the most outstanding trails in the nation, this picturesque hike will cram your RAM and stay with you and the dawgus long after your journey has ended. For more information: (520) 428-4150.

Directions: Take Highway 191 south for 8 miles until you reach Highway 366. Turn right on Highway 366 and follow for 22 miles to the campground and trailhead.

BEAR CANYON TRAIL HIKE - Leashes
Intermediate/12.0 miles/6.0 hours

Info: This adventure-filled trail has a little something for everyone. Check out Sulphur Springs Valley in the distance. As you climb, Dos Cabezas and Greasewood Mountains also come into view. See if Snoopy snoops out the millions upon millions of ladybugs that literally cover the rocky, tree-filled terrain of aptly named, Ladybug Peak. In addition to marvelling at the sheer numbers of these ecologically correct buggers, you'll be dazzled by outstanding views of the southern peaks of the Pinalenos. For more information: (520) 428-4150.

Directions: Take Highway 191 south for 8 miles until you reach Highway 366. Go right on Highway 366 and follow for 17 miles to the trailhead at Ladybug Saddle.

BLUE JAY RIDGE TRAIL HIKE
Intermediate/6.4 miles/3.25 hours

Info: Besides providing an afternoon escape into the great outdoors, this hike gets an A for incredible, far-reaching panoramas of the surrounding landscape. Go the distance and your gradual ascent will take you from Turkey Springs to Blue Jay Peak. The hardest part of the hike is staying on the trail while weaving through thickets of New Mexico locust. For more information: (520) 428-4150.

Directions: Take Highway 70 north through Pima to FR 286. Follow FR 286 south to the trailhead at Turkey Springs.

BONITA CREEK TRAIL HIKE

Intermediate/12.0 miles/6.0 hours

Info: You definitely want to include binoculars when planning for this hike. The trail through the Gila Box Riparian National Conservation Area is home to many rare and endangered raptors. You just might catch sight of a razorback sucker (oh what fun it is to hike), a Gila chub or a zone-tailed hawk on the prowl.

The moment you set paw in this red-walled box canyon, you and the tail wagger will forget that you're in the desert. Cactus are quickly replaced by cottonwoods and mesquite as you make your way upstream along an old jeep trail. Gila Box is a work of art that nature has carved out with the help of Bonita Creek. In summer and winter, it's hard to imagine the power of this gentle creek come spring. From March to May, the snowmelt of faraway mountains swells placid Bonita Creek to a width of 12 feet with ferociously gushing waters that measure nearly a foot deep.

History buffs will be delighted to learn that the red rock cliffs of this region were once home to the Anasazi, now a vanished people. Bonita was also used as an escape route by famous Indians like Geronimo, Chato and Nachez. When you reach the San Carlos Indian Reservation, turn tail and head back. For more information: (520) 428-4040.

Directions: From the intersection of Highway 191 and Highway 70 in Safford go north to Eighth Avenue and turn right. Follow for 1.5 miles, crossing a bridge to a fork in the road. Take the right fork and continue on Airport Road for 5 miles until it dead ends at Sanchez Road (north of the closed bridge over the Gila River) and turn left (northeast). Continue for approximately seven miles to the Bonita Creek sign, turning left. After 3.8 miles, bear left again at the "Y". Continue for a mile, turning left at the yellow cattle guard for 4.6 miles to the corral. Either park here or 4-wheel it the next .75 miles to the trailhead.

Note: A high clearance vehicle is required for the last .75 miles of road. Avoid during monsoon season.

DEADMAN TRAIL HIKE

Intermediate/6.8 miles/3.5 hours

Info: Don't be intimidated by the name of this trail. If you and your hiking hound are interested in exploring the rugged terrain of Deadman Peak, Deadman Trail is the best way to experience this isolated mountain. Make tracks along the drainage of Deadman Creek to the canyon's bottom and pay particular attention to the changing vegetation - typical Sonoran Desert plantlife gives way to a riparian delight. If you love waterfalls, visit in spring when the creek is full and cascading waterfalls are everywhere. For more information: (520) 428-4150.

Directions: From Safford, take 20th Avenue to Golf Course Road. Follow Pipeline Road around the golf course.

DOS ARROYOS TRAIL HIKE - Leashes

Beginner/3.5 miles/1.5 hours

Info: Easy, level and scenic. What more can you ask for in a trail? This path loops around the Dankworth Ponds and over two washes, affording terrific vistas of the Pinaleno Mountains and Mt. Graham. Plan ahead, pack a picnic lunch and make an afternoon of it. For more information: (520) 428-6760.

Directions: Take Highway 191 south of Safford to Roper Lake State Park - the Dankworth Ponds Unit.

Note: $3.00 per vehicle entrance fee.

FRYE CANYON TRAIL HIKE

Beginner/5.6 miles/2.5 hours

Info: Delightful best describes this trail which parallels the stream under a canopy of willows, sycamores and cottonwoods. The hike involves an elevation change of almost 1,800 feet but the ascent is very gradual. It's easy to lose track of the trail amongst the rocks, but keep following the streambed and you'll rediscover your route in no time. The trail ends at the junction of the Round the Mountain Trail #302. Do an about-face of if you're still in the walking mode, extend your hike by following Trail #302 for as long as you like. For more information: (520) 428-4150.

Directions: Take Highway 70 northwest to Thatcher. From Thatcher, go left on Stadium Street to FR 103 south. Follow FR 103 to the trailhead approximately 10 miles past Frye Mesa Reservoir.

Note: High clearance vehicles only.

Dogs May Be Unleashed Unless Otherwise Indicated

HELIOGRAPH TRAIL HIKE

Intermediate/4.0 miles/2.0 hours

Info: Go the distance on this fairly simple hike and you and brown eyes will earn the spectacular bird's-eye views atop 10,022-foot Heliograph Peak - one of the state's highest southeastern mountains. It's a fairly simple 2-mile hike to the peak. The 100-foot steel tower at the top allows fire rangers far-reaching views of several mountain ranges. For more information: (520) 428-4150.

Directions: From Safford, take Highway 191 south for 8 miles to Highway 366 and turn right (west). Follow Highway 366 for 22 miles to the Shannon Campground. Access the Arcadia Trailhead at the end of the campground. Follow this trail for 1 mile to the Heliograph Trail.

Note: Highway 366 is closed in winter.

HIGH CREEK TRAIL HIKE

Expert/3.4 miles/2.0 hours

Info: Get your juices flowing on this trek of a trail which climbs 2,000 feet in just 1.7 miles. Your journey begins along the High Creek drainage and quickly ascends verdant, oak-clad bluffs where you'll witness changes in tree species along with some outstanding views. You and Rover will have to tough it out at the end where the last section of trail involves a steep, switchbacking climb to the east ridge of Galiuros Range. If you still crave more, there are several connecting trails. Otherwise, ridgetop signals your turnaround point. For more information: (520) 428-4150.

Directions: From Safford, take Highway 191 south to Highway 266 west (right). Follow Highway 266 for 19 miles to Bonita. From Bonita, drive west on Sunset Road (FR 651) for 13 miles to FR 159 west. Continue on FR 159 to the trailhead.

MUD SPRING to SYCAMORE TRAIL HIKE - Leashes

Intermediate/2.0 miles/1.0 hours

Info: For a scenic, short trip, hike into the woods as far as Mud Spring, take a quickie break and then retrace the pawprints.

If you decide to continue further up the Sycamore Trail, be prepared for a very steep, very demanding 4-mile climb.

Directions: From Safford, take Highway 191 south 17 miles to Highway 266. Turn right and follow 19 miles to Bonita. From Bonita continue north on Aravaipa Road about 19 miles to FR 253 (Deer Creek Ranch Road). Turn left and travel 8.4 miles to the East Divide Trailhead. Take this trail about one mile to the Mud Spring turnoff.

ROPER LAKE STATE PARK - Leashes

Info: When you're yearning for some quality time with your canine, hightail it to Roper Lake State Park for a day of do-nothing pleasure. Gasoline-powered boats are banned to preserve the quietude and peacefulness of this delightful area. No rentals are available, so BYOB if you have one. If you've got fishing on your mind, try your luck at Dankworth Ponds, a lovely day use area. Who knows, you and the pooch might wind up dining on catfish, bass, bluegill or crappie.

Bring your binoculars along too - several mammal, bird and reptile species inhabit this lake area. When it's time for Frisky's constitutional, saunter among the exotic trees and visit the natural history stations dotted here and there. Just avoid the natural hot springs and beach areas, no dogs allowed. The elevation of 3,100 feet maintains comfortable temperatures even during those dog days of summer. For more information: (520) 428-6760.

Directions: From Safford, head south on Highway 191 for six miles to reach the park entrance.

SHAKE TRAIL HIKE - Leashes

Expert/10.2 miles/5.5 hours

Info: Only athletically-fit hikers and lean, mean hounds should attempt this extremely challenging, seldom-traversed trail. But if you venture forth on this high-energy voyage, you'll have the opportunity to study different life zones and species that call this place home. Make it to the top and your hiking bonus will be beautiful views of the Greasewood Mountains and Sulphur Springs Valley. For more information: (520) 428-4150.

Directions: To upper trailhead: Take Highway 191 south to Highway 366, following Highway 366 for 17.5 miles until you spot the trailhead on the left. The upper trailhead is only accessible in spring and fall. To lower trailhead: Take Highway 191 south to Highway 266 and follow Highway 266 for 12 miles to Stockton Pass picnic area. The trailhead is in the northwest corner of the picnic area beyond the fence.

Note: If snow is a possibility, use lower trailhead as a starting point. If you encounter snow on the trail, turn around and head back.

WEBB PEAK TRAIL HIKE

Beginner/2.0 miles/1.0 hours

Info: All that separates you from the spectacular vistas is a short, easy hike through a lush forest to Webb Peak Lookout. Actually a fire tower, it provides sweeping panoramas in every direction. Along the way you'll encounter several side trails which can extend the length of your hike. For more information: (520) 428-4150.

Directions: From Safford, take Highway 191 south to Highway 366. Make a right on Highway 366 for 29 miles to the Columbine Information Station and the trailhead. Park in the public horse corrals just past the station.

Note: Highway 366 is closed in winter.

SCOTTSDALE

<u>LODGING</u>

ADOBE APARTMENT HOTEL
3635 N 68th St (85251) Rates: $54-$89;
Tel: (602) 945-3544

DAYS INN-SCOTTSDALE FASHION SQUARE RESORT
4710 N Scottsdale Rd (85251) Rates: $42-$125;
Tel: (602) 947-5411; (800) 329-7466

EMBASSY SUITES RESORT HOTEL-SCOTTSDALE
5001 N Scottsdale Rd (85250) Rates: $155 +;
Tel: (602) 949-1414; (800) 528-1456

GARDINER'S RESORT ON CAMELBACK
5700 E McDonald Dr (85253) Rates: $195+;
Tel: (602) 948-2100; (800) 245-2051

HOLIDAY INN-OLD TOWN SCOTTSDALE
7353 E Indian School Rd (85251) Rates: $69-$149;
Tel: (602) 994-9203;
(800) 465-4329 (US); (800) 695-6995 (AZ)

HOSPITALITY SUITE RESORT
409 N Scottsdale Rd (85257) Rates: $49-$149;
Tel: (602) 949-5115; (800) 445-5115

HOWARD JOHNSON HOTEL
5101 N Scottsdale Rd (85250) Rates: $43-$88;
Tel: (602) 945-4392; (800) 446-4656

INN AT THE CITADEL
8700 E Pinnacle Peak Rd (85255) Rates: $89-$265;
Tel: (602) 585-6133; (800) 927-8367

INN SUITES OF SCOTTSDALE AT EL DORADO PARK
7707 E McDowell Rd (85257) Rates: $62-$86;
Tel: (602) 941-1202; (800) 238-8851

MARRIOTT'S CAMELBACK INN
RESORT, GOLF CLUB & SPA
5402 E Lincoln Dr (85253) Rates: $130-$340;
Tel: (602) 948-1700; (800) 242-2635

MARRIOTT'S MOUNTAIN SHADOWS
RESORT & GOLF CLUB
5641 E Lincoln Dr (85253) Rates: $175-$325;
Tel: (602) 948-7111; (800) 228-9290 (US);
(800) 835-6205 (AZ)

MOTEL 6
6848 E Camelback Rd (85251) Rates: $34-$40;
Tel: (602) 946-2280; (800) 440-6000

PARK INN INTERNATIONAL
2934 N Scottsdale Rd (85251) Rates: $35-$98;
Tel: (602) 947-5885; (800) 599-5885

THE PHOENICIAN RESORT
6000 E Camelback Rd (85251); Rates: $160-$445;
Tel: (602) 941-8200; (800) 888-8234

RAMADA HOTEL VALLEY HO
6850 E Main St (85251) Rates: $45-$135;
Tel: (602) 945-6321; (800) 272-6232

RED LION'S LA POSADA RESORT HOTEL & INN
4949 E Lincoln Dr (85253) Rates: $99-$229;
Tel: (602) 952-0420; (800) 547-8010

RESIDENCE INN BY MARRIOTT
6040 N Scottsdale Rd (85253) Rates: $129-$210;
Tel: (602) 948-8666; (800) 331-3131

SAFARI RESORT
4611 N Scottsdale Rd (85251) Rates: $42-$150;
Tel: (602) 945-0721; (800) 845-4356

SCOTTSDALE PIMA MOTEL SUITES
7330 N Pima Rd (85258) Rates: $45-$229;
Tel: (602) 948-3800; (800) 344-0262

STOUFFER RENAISSANCE COTTONWOODS RESORT
6160 N Scottsdale Rd (85253) Rates: $109-$295;
Tel: (602) 991-1414; (800) 468-3571

RECREATION

AGUA LINDA PARK - Leashes

Info: Drop in for a picnic and catch some afternoon fun in the sun. Basketball, baseball and volleyball make this park a happening place for sports fans.

Directions: Located at 8732 E. McDonald Drive.

AZTEC PARK - Leashes

Info: You'll have to sniff out your own stomping ground over these seven acres. The park is mainly geared for tennis players so no pathway is provided for pooch walkers.

Directions: Located on 100th Street east of 96th Street.

CACTUS PARK - Leashes

Info: You'll find more than enough grass for a healthy romp or a game of fetch at this 17-acre park which is popular with locals who make use of the indoor fitness facilities. You and the pooch can also get your daily dose of exercise along the well maintained bike path.

Directions: The park is located at the corner of Scottsdale and Cactus Roads.

CAMELBACK MOUNTAIN HIKE - Leashes

Intermediate/3.5 miles/2.0 hours

Info: For a bonafido great hiking experience, don't miss this calorie burning, mountain trek A popular trail, you'll watch the "Camelback regulars" literally jog from top to bottom. But you can take your time and enjoy the scenery. On the particularly steep sections, the trail is equipped with a steel rail to help your ascent. Along the trail, you'll find many ridgetops perfect for breath catching and thirst quenching. Do the distance on this sometimes difficult trail and you'll get to see the surrounding city from a hawk's perspective. Tote plenty of water, some high energy snacks, a couple of biscuits and a pair of binoculars and enjoy the beauty around you. On weekends, parking can be an adventure in itself. Good luck and happy trails to you.

Directions: From Scottsdale Road take McDonald Drive west to just before the Tatum intersection. The entrance and parking is signed and on the left.

CHAPARRAL PARK - Leashes

Info: This huge, 74-acre park is a great place to spend a dog-day afternoon. Bring a blanket and relax with Rover lakeside or take a jog along the extensive pathway. You'll meet lots of pooches and their people - out for a leg stretcher, a miler or a bit of socializing.

Directions: Located at the corner of Hayden and Chaparral Roads.

CHESNUTT PARK - Leashes

Info: Geared toward picnickers, this 5-acre park is good sniffing ground for you and your hound.

Directions: Located at 4565 N. Granite Reef Road, just past Camelback Road.

CHOLLA PARK - Leashes

Info: Plenty of stomping ground and other canines make this a social, dog-friendly park.

Directions: Take Pima Road north to Via Linda. Turn right and continue for approximately 3 miles to the park on the righthand side.

CIVIC CENTER COMPLEX - Leashes

Info: Smack dab in the middle of downtown Scottsdale, a tail wagging park experience can be yours on over 34 acres of developed parkland. Stroll or window shop, find a shady grassy knoll and peoplewatch or study the swans as they go

Dogs May Be Unleashed Unless Otherwise Indicated

about their daily routines. On many weekends throughout the year, fairs and festivals cover the grounds with stalls and artware, yummy food and lots of entertainment. You might get lucky and catch a free outdoor concert under clear blue skies. There are several restaurants offering take-out food if you and the pupster want to make a picnic day of it. Lots of locals bring their dogs for an afternoon of sniffing and friendly chitchat.

Directions: The Civic Center Complex is located on Civic Center Boulevard just south of Indian School Road.

COMANCHE PARK - Leashes

Info: Drop in for your pooch's daily constitutional or lollygag along the bike path. Or pull up some grass and watch neighborhood hoopsters battle it out on the courts.

Directions: Located at 7639 Via de los Ninos just east of Hayden Road and south of Mountain View Road.

ELDORADO PARK - Leashes

Info: Perk up those ears and listen for songbirds as you make your way through 55 acres of desert oasis. Put some biscuits in your basket and head for a picnic spot lakeside. This is definitely a dog-gone good way to spend an afternoon.

Directions: Located on the east side of Miller Road, just north of McDowell.

INDIAN SCHOOL PARK - Leashes

Info: Take a promenade along the pathway winding through 60 acres of greenery. Brown bag lunch by the lake and watch ducks waddle or simply chill out in the shade of a covered ramada. Indian School Park provides a huge outdoor playground for humans and canines alike. You're sure to meet some locals at this lovely neighborhound park.

Directions: Located on the northeast corner of Hayden and Indian School Roads.

McCORMICK RAILROAD PARK - Leashes

Info: All aboard! This theme park with a train and carousel is a wonderful way to spend some time. If you choo-choose to walk in a quieter setting, there is a short nature trail along the canal for your pleasure.

Directions: Located at the corner of Scottsdale and Indian Bend Roads.

McDOWELL EXHIBIT AREA - Leashes

Info: Show off your dog in this 8-acre park as you walk him along the bike path provided for exercise hounds.

Directions: Located on McDowell Road just west of Hayden Road.

McDOWELL MOUNTAIN REGIONAL PARK - Leashes

Info: Geographically located between the Fort McDowell Indian Reservation on the east, Fountain Hills on the south, and Scottsdale on the west, this regional park is easily accessible from Scottsdale and Fountain Hills. It harbors some of the most picturesque terrain within the county park system. If a road trip appeals to you, the drive to and through the park is beautiful. The slight rise in elevation on the drive from Scottsdale to Fountain Hills gives you some pretty, desertscapes, as well as a feel for the vastness of the Valley which stretches across citified desert land to distant mountain ranges.

If your intentions lean more to enjoying the outdoors on foot, over 50 miles of hiking trails lace this lush, desert landscape. Pick a trail and pick your pleasure. Some trails to consider are: Lousley Hill, Pemberton, Stoneman Historic and Scout Trails. Check Fountain Hills for listings and always pack enough water, this is desert country.

Directions: Access to the park is from McDowell Mountain Road, 4 miles north of Fountain Hills. The park is 15 miles northeast of Scottsdale.

Note: Entry fee for weekend use. Picnic area closes at sunset. Campgrounds closed Memorial Day-Labor Day. Call (602) 471-0173.

McKELLIPS LAKE - Leashes

Info: Don't forget your doggie bag. McKellips Lake is a lovely let's-do-lunch spot. There's also a jogging path for restless Rovers to move on out to the doggie beat.

Directions: Take McKellips Road east. The lake will be on the north side, past Miller Road.

Locate Other Dog-Friendly Activities...Check Nearby Cities

MOUNTAIN VIEW PARK - Leashes

Info: Nestled in a friendly neighborhood, you're bound to meet some local hounds at this 20-acre park where the green scene is very serene.

Directions: Take Pima Road to Mountain View Road and head west on Mountain View to just before Granite Reef Road.

NATURE AREA - Leashes

Info: Treat your best buddy to six acres of nature in this mellow fellows area.

Directions: Located at 6801 N. Hayden Road between Indian Bend Road and Lincoln Drive.

NORTHSIGHT PARK - Leashes

Info: A large, 20-acre park, you'll find lots of opportunity for exercise, but use caution, the horsy set likes this pathway too.

Directions: Take Pima Road to Thunderbird Road. The park is located just east on Thunderbird Road.

OSBORN PARK - Leashes

Info: This 3-acre park is a lovely little spot for a grassy stroll.

Directions: The park is located on Osborn Road, east of Miller Road.

PAIUTE PARK - Leashes

Info: You and the pupster can frolic along and enjoy eight acres of activity-filled fun at this neighborhood park. Catch a match of tennis or a game of hoops as you lead your lad along the paved pathway.

Dogs May Be Unleashed Unless Otherwise Indicated

Directions: Located at 3210 N. 66th Street south of Osborn Road.

PAPAGO PARK - Leashes

Info: Stop and go at Papago. One acre makes for a quick, but satisfying leg stretch.

Directions: Located at 73rd Street and Garfield Road west of Miller Road.

PIMA PARK - Leashes

Info: Give in to those big, pleading brown eyes and get out for some exercise. Pima Park offers five acres of land to wander and gad about.

Directions: Located on the northwest corner of Pima and Thomas Roads.

ROTARY PARK - Leashes

Info: Definitely Rosie and Maxwell's favorite bark park, chill out in the shade of a ramada or pound the paws along the jogging path which circles this spacious green scene. Or get in some aerobic walking on the trail at the rear of the park - it winds its way between gated Gainey Ranch and an area of walled houses. Shaded and peaceful, it runs about a mile roundtrip. If you're in the mood for canine capers and conversation, check out the AM and PM pooch playgroups at this quaint neighborhood park. And if you visit when we don't, give the high five to some of Rosie and Maxwell's pals, namely Paolo, his sibling Nico, Chelsea, Ripley, Buster, Bunky, Barkley, Shadow, Pooch, Apache, whew!, that's just part of the gang. Have fun and make friends.

Directions: Take Scottsdale Road north to Doubletree Ranch Road and go east (right). Continue to Gainey Ranch Road and make a left. The parking area will be directly on your right before the gated entrance.

SCOTTSDALE RANCH PARK - Leashes

Info: Walk off the kibble on the well-designed exercise course of this thirty-acre parkland. Geared to sports, you can still find your doggie space.

Directions: Located at 10400 E. Via Linda.

SHOSHONE PARK - Leashes

Info: Padded paws will love stomping along the jogging path in this small and quiet 3-acre park.

Directions: Located at 8300 Via Dorado Road between Doubletree Ranch and Indian Bend Roads.

THOMAS BIKE STOP - Leashes

Info: For a quick stop and a wee leg stretcher, this one-acre area is a popular resting ground for weary pedalers.

Directions: Located at 7801 E. Thomas Road east of Miller Road.

THUNDERBIRD PARK - Leashes

Info: Keep that leash taut - soccer balls, volleyballs and softballs are common here in this 5-acre park, and a temptation for any canine.

Directions: Take Pima Road to Thunderbird Road. Turn right on Thunderbird Road and follow to the park entrance.

Dogs May Be Unleashed Unless Otherwise Indicated

VISTA DEL CAMINO PARK - Leashes

Info: When walktime calls and tails are wagging, head out to the 52-acre Vista del Camino Park for an afternoon delight lakeside or a jaunt on the popular jogging trail.

Directions: Take Miller Road to Roosevelt Road, turning east on Roosevelt. Park is on the north side at 7700 E. Roosevelt Road.

ZUNI PARK - Leashes

Info: Zuni Park is a suitable solution for sofa loafers. A small neighborhood park of 3 acres, it's a great place for a romp or a playful stroll.

Directions: Located at 7343 Via del Elemental, just north of Doubletree Ranch Road.

SEDONA

LODGING

BEST WESTERN INN OF SEDONA
1200 Hwy 89A (86336) Rates: $70-$120;
Tel: (520) 282-3072;
(800) 528-1234 (US); (800) 292-6344 (AZ)

CANYON MESA COUNTRY CLUB
500 Jacks Canyon Rd (86351) Rates: $125-$200;
Tel: (520) 284-2176

COURTHOUSE BUTTE VILLA BED & BREAKFAST
2451 Red Rock Loop Rd (86336) Rates: $70-$95;
Tel: (520) 204-1505

DESERT QUAIL INN
6626 Hwy 179 (86336) Rates: $49-$140;
Tel: (520) 284-1433; (800) 385-0927

FOREST HOUSES RESORT-OAK CREEK CANYON
HC 30, Box 250 (86336) Rates: $75-$120;
Tel: (520) 282-2999

GREYFIRE FARM BED & BREAKFAST
1240 Jacks Canyon Rd (86351) Rates: $80-$200;
Tel: (520) 284-2340; (800) 579-2340

LO LO MAI SPRINGS
Page Springs Rd (86340) Rates: $40-$50;
Tel: (520) 634-4700

MATTERHORN MOTOR LODGE
230 Apple Ave (86336) Rates: $49-$89;
Tel: (520) 282-7176

NEW EARTH LODGE VACATION COTTAGES
665 Sunset Dr (86336) Rates: $75-$100;
Tel: (520) 282-2644

OAK CREEK TERRACE RESORT
Star Rt 3, Box 1100 (86336) Rates:$65-$160;
Tel: (520) 282-3562; (800) 224-2229

QUAIL RIDGE RESORT
120 Canyon Circle Dr (86351) Rates: $64-$93;
Tel: (520) 284-9327

QUALITY INN-KING'S RANSOM MOTOR HOTEL
771 SR 179 (86336) Rates: $75-$120;
Tel: (520) 282-7151; (800) 221-2222

RAILROAD INN AT SEDONA
2545 W Hwy 89A (86336) Rates: $45-$66;
Tel: (520) 282-1533; (800) 858-7245

SKY RANCH LODGE MOTEL
SR 89A, Airport Rd (86336) Rates: $55-$135;
Tel: (520) 282-6400

SUGAR LOAF LODGE
1870 W Hwy 89A (86340) Rates: $36-$60;
Tel: (520) 282-9451

Dogs May Be Unleashed Unless Otherwise Indicated

WHITE HOUSE INN
2986 W Hwy 89A (86336) Rates: $35-$95;
Tel: (520) 282-6680

<u>RECREATION</u>

A.B. YOUNG TRAIL HIKE
Expert/4.8 miles/2.5 hours

Info: A strenuous hike through Oak Creek Canyon rewards you with superb views before, during and after your aerobic workout. This hike, aka East Pocket Trail, steeply switchbacks to the top of a scenic plateau. Time for a Kodak moment and a little breather before heading back. For more information: (520) 282-4119.

Directions: Take Highway 89A north to the Bootlegger Campground, just north of Junipine Resort. The trailhead is located across the creek from the campground.

ALLEN'S BEND TRAIL HIKE
Beginner/1.0 miles/0.5 hours

Info: Don't forget to pack your swimming trunks and a picnic lunch before setting out on this simple sojourn along picturesque Oak Creek. Paw and tootsie dipping can't be beat at this refreshing water oasis. Look around and in back as you glide through this pristine landscape. The towering cliffs of the red-walled canyon change with the lighting and the beauty of any particular moment can be inspiring. Or just pick a rock and be soothed and mesmerized by the twinkling, crystal clear waters.

A visit in fall has its own special rewards. The deciduous trees decorate the landscape in vibrant reds and yellows, first on the trees and then on the leaf littered trail. Trying to capture the golden leaves, sunlight streaming upon them, is like trying to capture the brilliance of an Arizona sunset - it's just about impossible. Unless of course your name just happens to be Muensch. For more information: (520) 282-4119.

Directions: Two miles north of Sedona on Highway 89A is the Grasshopper Point Recreation Area. The trailhead is at the north end of the parking area.

BACK O' BEYOND TRAIL HIKE - Leashes

Intermediate/1.2 miles/0.75 hours

Info: Brush up on those bushwhacking skills and sniff your way through the chaparral cover amid scattered junipers and Arizona cypress. The trail leads to the base of Cathedral Rock where you can gaze up at the towering spires, some as tall as 1,000 feet. Follow the shallow slope for a top-dog view of other notable features including Bell Rock, Courthouse Butte, and Airport Mesa. If Fido's ears are perked, he might be listening to the screech of a red-tailed hawk. Look skyward, you might catch a glimpse of one of these majestic birds. When you're ready to end this pleasant interlude, backtrack to your starting point. This is high desert country, pack enough water for you and the pupster. For more information: (520) 282-4119.

Directions: From the "Y" in Sedona (intersection of Highway 89A and Highway 179), go south 3.1 miles on Highway 179 to Back O' Beyond Road. Make a right and drive 2.5 miles to the parking area on the left. There is a gate with an unsigned trail that leads to Cathedral Rock.

BEAR MOUNTAIN TRAIL HIKE - Leashes

Expert/4.0 miles/2.0 hours

Info: Fill those water bottles and get ready to cram your RAM with the sights you'll encounter on this outing. Photo hounds can indulge their passion with shots of Boynton Pass, Capitol Butte, lovely leas and unending vistas. Continue your journey to a sprawling plateau where you'll be rewarded with views of Courthouse Butte to the south and Casner Mountain to the west. Let Snoopy snoop his way to the chaparral covered plateau and then on to the summit and to-die-for-serenery. You've earned this time - enjoy the landscape before retracing your steps. For more information: (520) 282-4119.

Directions: From the "Y" in Sedona (intersection of Highway 89A and Highway 179), head west on Highway 89A for about three miles to Dry Creek Road. Turn right and head north for 2.8 miles until you come to a "T" in the road. Turn left on Boynton Pass Road and go 2.7 miles to the parking area for Bear Mountain Trail.

BOYNTON CANYON TRAIL HIKE

Beginner/3.0 miles/1.5 hours

Info: Even mellow fellows will adore this level hike through a magical, majestic red-cliffed canyon. The multi-colored sandstone bluffs and spires are absolutely amazing and almost inspirational. There isn't a season when the beauty of this area can't be appreciated. Always pack sufficient water. For more information: (520) 282-4119.

Directions: Take Highway 89A west for three miles to Dry Creek Road (Forest Road 152C). Turn right (north) and go about 2.5 miles. Turn left (southwest) on Boynton Pass Road (FR 152D) and drive for about a mile. When the road forks, turn right (north) towards the Enchantment Resort. The trailhead is off to the right, a short distance before the resort.

BRINS MESA TRAIL HIKE

Beginner/6.0 miles/3.0 hours

Info: Lazy dogs and couch potatoes, listen up. This hike is the most scenic and the least demanding trail leading to the heart of spectacular Red Rock Country. Photo opportunities are endless. Before you head out, pick up an area map to help you identify the various rock formations. The only drawback to the trail - it's unshaded. Avoid on hot days. And as always, pack plenty of thirst quenchers for you and the dawgus. For more information: (520) 282-4119.

Directions: From Highway 89A in Sedona, take Jordan Road west about 1 mile to the trailhead.

Note: The last .25 miles of this road are rough. If you're not in a high clearance vehicle, park and hike instead.

BROKEN ARROW TRAIL HIKE - Leashes

Intermediate/5.0 miles/2.5 miles

Info: Where can you see a submarine creeping through an impressive stand of cypress, praying nuns along the pathway or a sleeping whale on land? The Broken Arrow Trail, that's where. These are just some of the intriguing rock formations that punctuate this area. And don't miss the chance to picnic with your pooch in the Devil's Dining Room.

This aptly named sinkhole isn't really a dining room but it's interesting to peruse. At the half-mile point, follow the old jeep road (blocked now by boulders) on your right for this quick sidetrip. The sinkhole is surrounded by a wire fence but there are a number of sandstone sitting/viewing/lunching rocks perfect for tushies and tails.

Back on the trail, another two miles brings you to stunning viewpoints. Lefties can climb to the deck of Submarine Rock for their camera snapping, while righties can wind up to Chicken Point. When you see the dropoff from Chicken Point, you'll understand the name. The trail winds among the region's largest stand of cypress. Kick back and enjoy the shade anywhere along the path. Hike in the morning when it's quiet. In the afternoon, jeep tours can sometimes detract from the peace and quiet. For more information: (520) 282-4119.

Directions: From the "Y" (intersection of Highway 89A & Highway 179) head south on Highway 179 for 1.3 miles to Morgan Road. Turn left and drive .5 miles to the Forest Service gate on the right and park inside. The path inside the gate is the unsigned trail.

CASNER CANYON TRAIL HIKE

Expert/4.0 miles/2.5 hours

Info: You and the tail wagger may need a long hot bath after this hike, but you'll have fun memories to recall when the sore muscles set in. Oak Creek is a wet and wild adventure - wading is part of the excitement. Not that you'll mind, particularly if you're doing this trail on a warm day. The refreshingly cold water of the creek will numb your senses while it numbs your feet.

Shortly after crossing the creek, you'll have to step lively up the canyon's steep north slope to the canyon rim. The shade is sparse so avoid this trail during hot summer months. And always carry lots of water for you and brown eyes. When the demands of the arduous trail start to get you down, lighten up with a look around. This kind of beauty is hard to find. Store the visuals in your memory bank for one of those blah days. For more information: (520) 282-4119.

Directions: Take Highway 89A north to the Grasshopper Point Recreation Area. The Allen's Bend Trailhead is at the north end of the parking area. Follow it to its intersection with the Casner Canyon Trail.

COOKSTOVE TRAIL HIKE

Expert/1.4 miles/1.0 hours

Info: This hike is short, but steep. Definitely not for the fair of paw or out of shape. Beginning at the bottom of Oak Creek Canyon, the trail switchbacks up and tops out at the east canyon rim. Openings in the groves of gambel oaks, alligator junipers and mixed conifers provide great peeks of the breathtaking terrain. For more information: (520) 282-4119.

Directions: Take Highway 89A 12 miles north of Sedona to the Pine Flat Campground. The trailhead is at the north end of the campground, near milepost 387.

DEVIL'S BRIDGE TRAIL HIKE

Intermediate/1.8 miles/1.0 hours

Info: Don't let the shortness of this trail fool you or Fido. The hike to the natural stone bridge is on the demanding side. Pack your camera and plenty of film - the vistas eat Fuji. For more information: (520) 282-4119.

Directions: From Sedona, take Highway 89A west to a right on Dry Creek Road (FR 152) north. The road splits after 2 miles, keep right on FR 152. In approximately 1.5 miles, you'll see a sign for the trailhead. The parking area is 100 feet off the road.

DOE MOUNTAIN TRAIL HIKE

Intermediate/1.4 miles/1.0 hours

Info: For picture book views of Sedona's Red Rock Country, hightail it to the top of this 400-foot high mesa. On a cloudy day, stretch out atop the mesa and watch cumulus float by the red-walled backdrop. Short on distance, this hike is long on effort. For more information: (520) 282-4119.

Directions: Take Highway 89A west to Dry Creek Road, turning right (north). Follow Dry Creek Road (FR 152C) for 3 miles to the Boynton Canyon intersection and turn left. Continue approximately one mile to the trailhead.

FAY CANYON ARCH TRAIL HIKE - Leashes

Intermediate/2.2 miles/1.0 hours

Info: Warm up your muscles along the level path for the first .75 miles, then boogie with Bowser up the hillside to your final destination - Fay Canyon Arch. The largest arch in Sedona, it's 20 feet wide and 15 feet high, an incredible, nature-made picture window for the colorful walls of Fay Canyon. Take note of the reconstructed Indian ruin that rests beside the arch. When you've finished ogling, retrace your steps. For more information: (520) 282-4119.

Directions: From the "Y" in Sedona (intersection of Highway 89A and Highway 179), head west on Highway 89A for about three miles until you reach Dry Creek Road. Turn right and drive for 2.8 miles until you reach a "T" in the road. Turn left on Boynton Pass Road and drive 2.7 miles to the parking area for Fay Canyon Trail.

HARDING SPRINGS TRAIL HIKE

Intermediate/1.4 miles/1.0 hours

Info: For a quick glimpse of sensational red-walled Oak Creek Canyon, head out on this short, shaded hike. From bottom to rim, your journey gradually ascends the canyon's east slope and provides unending views. For a longer, looping hike, you and your canine companion can continue north to Cookstove Trail (Expert/1.4 miles) or south to Thomas Point Trail (Expert/2.0 miles). For more information: (520) 282-4119.

Directions: Take Highway 89A 10 miles north of Sedona to the Cave Springs Campground entrance at Milepost 385.5. The trailhead is on the east side of the highway. The Harding Springs Trail leads uphill.

HOT LOOP TRAIL HIKE - Leashes

Intermediate/9.0 miles/4.5 hours

Info: If you hike this trail in the summer, you'll have one hot Spot on your hands. But any other time of the year, the weather should be anywhere from warm to chilly - perfect temperatures to enjoy the outstanding landscape and incredible red rocks.

In winter, thin layers of ice cling to the red rocks in the streambed and create a glittering ice feast for the eyes. The views also include an authentic western ranch complete with high chaparral flora and steep-walled pink tinted canyons. Kodak moments abound. Keep your snouts out for the cairns and turn around when they no longer mark the path. For more information: (520) 282-4119.

Directions: From the "Y" (intersection of Highway 89A and Highway 179) head south on Highway 179 for about 8 miles to the gate for Woods Canyon Trail (FS 93.) Follow that trail for 1.5 miles until you reach the Hot Loop Trailhead (FS 94).

LITTLE HORSE TRAIL HIKE - Leashes

Intermediate/4.2 miles/2.0 hours

Info: Like an outdoor music concert, the sounds of songbirds fill the air as you and your pooch journey along this pretty, view-filled trail. Religious Rovers will be inspired by Cathedral Rock, church spires, the Madonna rock formation and the Chapel of the Holy Cross. This trail is definitely a place for peace-seeking hikers and their pals. If time permits, find a comfortable boulder and catch a sunset. The glowing sun against the red rocks paints a picture of indescribable beauty. Sedona at dusk is truly a slice of heaven. For more information: (520) 282-4119.

Directions: From The "Y" (intersection of Highway 179 & Highway 89A) in Sedona, take Highway 179 south for 2.7 miles to Chapel Lane. Turn left and travel .9 miles to the parking area for Chapel of the Holy Cross. Look closely for the trail at the lower end of the lot, the trailhead is unmarked.

LONG CANYON TRAIL HIKE

Beginner/4.4 miles/2.0 hours

Info: In descriptive terms, this hike is easy to do and pretty to behold - ideal for sofa loafers with a passion for photography. Pack the Kodak - once in a lifetime photo opportunities abound as you wander among the breathtaking red rock cliffs and lofty spires. The trail ends on a bluff with ancient rock petroglyphs and Indian ruins. Do not touch, these are sacred relics. Leave only footprints, take only memories. For more information: (520) 282-4119.

Directions: Take Highway 89A west to Dry Creek Road and turn right (north). Follow for 1.5 miles to Sterling Canyon Road (FR 152D). Make a right (north) on Sterling Canyonand travel approximately .5 miles to the trailhead.

MARG'S DRAW TRAIL HIKE - Leashes

Intermediate/2.4 miles/1.5 hours

Info: Fascinating geometric rock formations draw hikers to this trail. See if Spot can spot the sleeping Snoopy near the beginning of the hike, the first of many chiseled rock sculptures along this picturesque trail. Made solely by nature, you'll be surprised how many of these mountain formations resemble man-made creations. Use your imagination and see what visions come to mind as you continue your sojourn through Sedona's magical, mystical landscape. For more information: (520) 282-4119.

Directions: From the "Y" (intersection of Highway 89A and Highway 179), take Highway 179 south .4 miles to Sombart Lane. Turn left on Sombart Lane and proceed for .2 miles to a gate. Look for the unmarked trailhead.

MIDGELY BRIDGE to WILSON MOUNTAIN SUMMIT HIKE -
Leashes

Expert/10.0 miles/5.0 hours

Info: Rugged Rovers will love this hike. When you reach First Bench, you'll notice some old cattle trails and a small tank. Pawse for a break and sniff out the other relics, like a rusted plow and an old foundation left by homesteaders. Carouse with care and avoid the barbed wire, a reminder of times gone by.

Now comes the rugged part. Endurance-testing switchbacks ascend the chaparral-blanketed south face of the mountain and separate the pups from the dogs. Once you reach the top, you'll be stunned by the remarkable vistas. No matter where you stand on the plateau, awesome beauty envelops you, your reward for perseverance. Look due south and you'll see Steamboat Rock, Sedona and Airport Mesa; to the southwest, Teapot Rock and Thumb Butte. For more information: (520) 282-4119.

Directions: At the "Y" (intersection of Highway 89A and Highway 179) take Highway 89A north for 1.8 miles to the lot on the north side of Midgely Bridge. Wilson Mountain Trail (FS 10) begins next to the ramada.

NORTH WILSON MOUNTAIN TRAIL HIKE

Expert/4.0 miles/2.0 hours

Info: A three-tier hike, it goes from easy to butt-kicking. This canyon trail lulls you into laziness with an easy beginning. But get ready for a mean punch in the middle and then an effortless ending. The trail winds amidst a lush, side canyon before terminating at the junction with the Wilson Mountain Trail (#10). You and your hiking buddy can either head back the way you came or extend your hike along TR #10 (Expert/11.2 miles). For more information: (520) 282-4119.

Directions: Take Highway 89A north to the Encinoso Picnic Area. The trailhead is just east of the parking lot at the bottom of the ridge.

PENDLEY HOMESTEAD TRAIL HIKE - Leashes

Beginner/0.5 miles/0.5 hours

Info: Take a pleasant stroll through the apple haven of Oak Creek Canyon - Pendley Homestead. Simply follow the trail as it moseys along a section of the historic homestead founded in the early 1900's. Too bad this hike is over before you know it. Summertime at the homestead means crowds, so plan accordingly. For more information: (520) 282-3034.

Directions: Take Highway 89A north for 7 miles to Slide Rock State Park. The trailhead is at the north end of the parking area.

Note: $5 per vehicle entrance fee.

Dogs May Be Unleashed Unless Otherwise Indicated

SECRET CANYON TRAIL HIKE - Leashes

Intermediate/10.0 miles/5.0 hours

Info: It's no secret that this trail is one of the most exceptional and interesting in all of Sedona. The first two miles trace a sandstone streambed that has carved a postcard pretty landscape. The views of Secret Mountain and Sedona will dazzle the eyes. Two miles in, you'll reach an ancient woodland of ponderosa, oak, maple and box elder. Hike in the fall and see if your camera can capture the crayola colors. Or just sit back and be entertained by Fido's antics as he frolics through the colorful and crackly autumnal leaves. For more information: (520) 282-4119.

Directions: From the "Y" (intersection of Highway 89A and Highway 179) in Sedona, head west on Highway 89A for about three miles until you reach Dry Creek Road. Turn right and go approximately 2 miles to FS Road #121. Turn right and head northeast on FR 152 for 3.4 miles until you reach the parking area for Secret Canyon.

Note: FS #121 may be difficult to travel after 1.5 miles due to erosion in the area.

SOLDIER PASS TRAIL HIKE - Leashes

Intermediate/4.4 miles/2.0 hours

Info: Amazing geology and unusual land formations embody the terrain along this trail. After .25 miles, you and fur-face will encounter a sinkhole. Another short distance brings you to a series of pools that dot the rock-strewn landscape. A few more pawsteps and you'll arrive at an intriguing series of natural rocky arches. Keep stomping down the trail for picture worthy panoramic views. While you're eyeballing these amazing vistas, you may notice that Fido is sniffing like crazy - a sure sign of wildlife. If it's your lucky day, you might catch a glimpse of several species that inhabit the area.

The trail continues further and takes an interesting turn leading you through a calming canyon shaded by juniper and pinyon pine. Time for a high energy snack, you'll need it. Flex your muscles and get ready for the final ascent up the canyon and out to Soldier Pass. Avoid hiking in summer. And carry your own water supply. For more information: (520) 282-4119.

Directions: From the "Y" in Sedona (intersection of Highway 89A and Highway 179), head west on Highway 89A for 1.2 miles until you reach Soldier Pass Road. Turn right and go 1.4 miles to Rim Shadow Drive. Turn right and travel .2 miles to the parking area on the left and head out on the Soldier Pass Trail.

STERLING PASS TRAIL HIKE

Expert/4.8 miles/3.0 hours

Info: Canyon hopping is the objective of this steep, strenuous hike. You'll huff and puff up and out of Oak Creek Canyon along an unnamed drainage, and through a forest of mixed conifers, dwarf canyon maples and towering orange-barked ponderosa pine before topping out at Sterling Pass. Once at the pass, you'll have to slip between sandstone monoliths before descending into Sterling Canyon. The climb out of Oak Creek Canyon affords the best panoramas, so be sure to stop at the various overlooks - your pooch will thank you for the hiking break. For more information: (520) 282-4119.

Directions: Take Highway 89A 5 miles north of Sedona to the Manzanita Campground. The trailhead is on the west side of the highway near milepost 380, approximately 100 yards north of the campground entrance. Park on the east side of the highway, just south of the campground entrance.

THOMAS POINT TRAIL HIKE

Expert/2.0 miles/1.5 hours

Info: Not for the fair-of-paw or weak-of-knees. Daily conditioning and plenty of carbohydrates will prove extremely beneficial on this rigorous hike through Oak Creek Canyon. The trail makes a steep climb from the canyon bottom to the top of the east rim. You can't beat the vistas of Sedona and the surrounding Red Rock Country, the San Francisco Peaks or West Fork Canyon from atop the rim - they're one of a kind. Avoid in summer, shade is only found on the first stretch of trail. For more information: (520) 282-4119.

Directions: The trailhead is located just past mile marker 384 on the east side of Highway 89A, about 9.5 miles north of the intersection of Highway 89A and Highway 179 in Sedona. Additional parking can be found .25 miles north of the trailhead at the Call O' The Canyon day area. The trail starts across the road.

VULTEE ARCH TRAIL HIKE

Beginner/4.0 miles/2.0 hours

Info: A simple hike through verdant, red-walled Sterling Canyon is a delightful way to spend the afternoon. Set your sights on Vultee Arch, an awesome 40-foot natural arch of red sandstone, a popular hiking destination.

This lush canyon provides an easy, shaded walk through a forest of juniper, scrub oak, ponderosa and manzanita. After 1.5 miles, the trail forks to the left and to a sandstone ledge with the most spectacular view of the arch. Unpack the camera and start clicking. For more information: (520) 282-4119.

Directions: From the intersection of Highway 179 and Highway 89A, head west on Highway 89A approximately 3 miles to Dry Creek Road, turn right. Follow for 2 miles to the trail sign at FS Road #152 and go right. Drive slowly for the next 4.5 miles (4-wheel drive is recommended in wet weather) to the parking area. A sign indicates the trailhead.

WEST FORK TRAIL HIKE - Leashes

Beginner/6.0 miles/3.0 hours

Info: This is a numero uno hike - don't miss the experience. Oak Creek Canyon is a masterpiece of nature - a lush canyon and riparian oasis guarded by towering pink and grey streaked cliffs.

Your trip begins in an area of tall, green grasses and woodsy shrubs. The sound of the creek splashing over the rocks is with you from start to finish - sometimes fading to a mere whisper, sometimes loud and clear, a reminder that this perennial creek never stops. Just an hour beside the creek would make any dog's day. This is definitely puppy paradise. As you travel further along the trail, you'll cross the creek many times. Balance definitely counts - but even a little paw wetting is fun and part of the adventure.

The slight ups and downs of the trail lead past cliffs and coves, forests of ponderosa, fields of ferns and of thick pine covered earth. The sights and smells are overwhelming and soothing at the same time. In summer, you can stretch out on a flat white rock and sunbathe, dangle your toes in the chilly waters or find a deep pool and do the doggie paddle with your water-loving pooch.

In autumn, the contrast of reds, oranges and yellows against the pink cliffs, the blue sky and the verdant evergreens will be indelibly stamped in your memory. There isn't a season you can't find a reason to visit this glorious canyon. One day in this mystical wonderland and your RAM will never by the same.

Hike as long as you like, it's all beautiful. Just use caution crossing the creek. The wet, moss-covered rocks can be very slippery. For more information: (520) 282-4119.

Directions: Take Highway 89A north approximately 10 miles. The trailhead is between Mileposts 384 and 385 on the west side of the road, about 100 feet north of the "Dos Pinos" sign. Parking is on the left a little further up the road.

WILSON CANYON TRAIL HIKE - Leashes

Intermediate/3.0 miles/1.5 hours

Info: Some boulder hopping skills are required for this shaded path that climbs a gentle grade along a seldom-filled streambed. Tails will definitely be wagging when you climb out of the canyon to the camera snapping views of Wilson Canyon, Teapot Rock and Thumb Butte in far off Prescott. For more information: (520) 282-4119.

Directions: From the "Y" (intersection of Highway 89A and Highway 179), take Highway 89A north for 1.8 miles across Midgley Bridge. Turn left into a lot on the north side of the bridge. Wilson Canyon Trail (FS#49) follows the canyon from the picnic ramada.

WILSON MOUNTAIN TRAIL HIKE - Leashes

Expert/11.2 miles/5.5 hours

Info: This energizing, albeit tough hike will take you through several distinctive landscapes before reaching the summit. You'll climb amid forests of Arizona cypress, pinyon juniper, oak and ponderosa pine. In springtime, the meadows along the trail explode in a profusion of color. From atop the summit, give Bowser a bone while you partake of some exceptional views of Oak Creek and Sterling Canyons. For more information: (520) 282-4119.

Directions: Take Highway 89A north for two miles. The trailhead is north of Midgley Bridge on the west side of the highway.

WOODS CANYON TRAIL HIKE - Leashes

Intermediate/6.0 miles/3.0 hours

Info: Pack plenty of water for you and your buddy before venturing onto this trail. If you're hiking in March, you might be treated to the rushing waters of winter runoff that flow down the streambed. In fall, cottonwoods and sycamores paint the trail with brilliant colors. The trail fades out after three miles. Boulder hoppers, you might decide to travel further along the stream and find the ideal picnic spot for you and Spot. For more information: (520) 282-4119.

Directions: From the "Y" (intersection of Highway 89A and Highway 179) in Sedona, head south on Highway 179 for 8.3 miles until you see a gate on the east side of the road with a marker for Woods Canyon (FS#93). Turn there and continue driving for about a mile before parking. The trailhead is one mile further but you will need a high clearance vehicle to continue further.

SELIGMAN

LODGING
CANYON SHADOWS MOTEL
114 E Chino (86337) Rates: $35+;
Tel: (520) 422-3255

SUPAI MOTEL
134 W Chino (86337) Rates: $35+;
Tel: (520) 422-3663

SHOW LOW

LODGING
DAYS INN
480 W Deuce of Clubs Ave (85901) Rates: $51-$63;
Tel: (520) 537-4356; (800) 329-7466

HOLIDAY INN EXPRESS
151 W Deuce of Clubs Ave (85901) Rates: $70-$75;
Tel: (520) 537-5115; (800) 465-4329

KIVA MOTEL
261 E Deuce of Clubs Ave (85901) Rates: $32-$48;
Tel: (520) 537-4542

SNOWY RIVER MOTEL
13640 E Deuce of Clubs Ave (85901) Rates: $34-$38;
Tel: (520) 537-2926

SUPER 8 MOTEL
1941 E Deuce of Clubs Ave (85901) Rates: $45+;
Tel: (520) 537-7694; (800) 800-8000

RECREATION

BEAR CANYON LAKE TRAIL HIKE

Beginner/4.0 miles/2.0 hours

Info: Enhance your memory banks. This hike is perfect for an impromptu afternoon outing with your pooch - short, sweet and scenic. The Douglas fir and ponderosa pine-clad trail skirts the west bank of Bear Canyon Lake from the dam to the headwaters. Begin or end the hike with a scrumptious picnic lunch lakeside and a game of fetch afterwards. For more information: (520) 289-2471.

Directions: Take Highway 60 south to Forest Road 300 west. Follow FR 300 to FR 89, turn north (right). Take FR 89 for two miles to the turnoff for Bear Canyon Lake. The road forks - either fork leads to parking and the trail.

BLUE RIDGE TRAIL HIKE

Intermediate/9.5 miles/5.0 hours

Info: Spend a quiet afternoon with your nature loving pup on this long, but fairly simple looping trail. A sense of peace and tranquility washes over you as you hike through this dense, verdant forest, the air filled with the sounds of chattering birds and murmuring creeks. This trail is a bonafido escape from the hustle and bustle of everyday life.

The first three miles escalade over rocky terrain, topping out at Blue Ridge Mountain, where sweeping panoramas of Lakeside, Pinetop and the Mogollon Rim are yours for the taking. Continue through a medley of juniper, gambel oak, pinyon, yellow pine and jackpine before looping around and finishing the last leg of the trail creekside. A

Dogs May Be Unleashed Unless Otherwise Indicated

great puppy playtime place for ball chasing or paw splashing - your pooch will love every minute. For more information: (520) 368-6700.

Directions: Take Highway 260 south eleven miles to the Baptist Church between the towns of Pinetop and Lakeside. Turn north onto Moonridge Drive for .3 miles to Billy Creek Drive. Turn right for another .3 miles to Meadow Drive. Turn left, cross the bridge and turn right on Pine Shadow Drive. At the top of the hill (at the water tank) turn right onto Forest Road 187. Follow for one mile to the trailhead.

BUENA VISTA TRAIL HIKE - Leashes

Intermediate/9.0 miles/4.5 hours

Info: This trail is not for the padded of paw but if you're up to the endeavor, you'll be rewarded with some terrific scenery. This loop trail laces among pine, oak and manzanita on several muscle-tensing uphill climbs. Look to the east for a great view of Mt. Baldy. For more information: (520) 368-5111.

Directions: Head south on Highway 60 for about 4.5 miles until you reach FR 300. Take a left on FR 300 and look for the trailhead on the lefthand side.

GHOST OF THE COYOTE TRAIL HIKE - Leashes

Intermediate/28.0 miles/14.0 hours

Info: This do-your-own-thing hike lets you decide how long or short your excursion will be. You're surrounded by pretty country so time won't matter. You might encounter meadows or come across an abandoned railroad. The main tree species is juniper but you'll spot others as well. And wherever you walk you'll be serenaded by songbirds and surprised by picture-perfect vistas. Have fun! For more information: (520) 368-5111.

Directions: From Highway 260 south, head north on FR 129 for the west trailhead, or turn north on FR 134 for the east trailhead.

LAND-OF-THE-PIONEERS TRAIL HIKE - Leashes

Intermediate/14.0 miles/7.0 hours

Info: This looping trail offers hikers and hounds a combination of flat terrain with some steep climbs thrown in. Do the distance on this one and find yourself atop Ecks Mountain where you can savor the stunning scenery from your lofty aerie. The trail follows fire roads and then becomes a single-track trail. You may have to move Rover over to accommodate an occasional equestrian. For more information: (520) 368-5111.

Directions: Take Highway 60 east, exiting at Vernon. Head south through Vernon, turning right on FR 5. The trailhead is on the right.

Note: Winter travelers are advised to contact the Lakeside Ranger District at (520) 368-5111.

LOS CABALLOS TRAIL HIKE - Leashes

Intermediate/11.0 miles/5.5 hours

Info: Enjoy a hearty workout with the pupster along eleven miles of extraordinary, often steep terrain. The trail loops back, passing 3 tanks that are readily accessible from the trail: Joe, Fence and Morgan Tank. For more information: (520) 368-5111.

Directions: Head west on Highway 260 for three miles, turning south on FR 136. The trailhead is located on the west side of FR 136.

TELEPHONE RIDGE TRAIL HIKE

Intermediate/2.0 miles/1.0 hours

Info: Lace up your boots and get ready for a bit of fun with the pupster on this hiking adventure into Chevelon Canyon. As you tackle the steep descent to Chevelon Creek, sections of loose gravel and fallen trees add a touch of excitement. When you reach the creek, pull up a rock, and let fur-face have a wet and wild frolic. For more information: (520) 289-2471.

Directions: Take Highway 260 west to the Tonto/Apache-Sitgreaves Forest boundary and turn north on FR 300. Follow FR 300 to FR 169 and make a right. Take FR 169 to FR 119, making another right to the trailhead at the end of the road.

SIERRA VISTA

LODGING

MOTEL 6
1551 E Fry Blvd (85635) Rates: $27-$33;
Tel: (520) 459-5035; (800) 440-6000

RAMADA INN
2047 S Hwy 92 (85635) Rates: $55-$86;
Tel: (520) 458-1347;
(800) 272-6232 (US); (800) 825-4645 (AZ)

SIERRA SUITES
391 E Fry Blvd (85635) Rates: $44-$77;
Tel: (520) 459-4221

SUN CANYON INN
260 N Garden Ave (85635) Rates: $50-$55;
Tel: (520) 459-0610; (800) 822-6966

Locate Other Dog-Friendly Activities...Check Nearby Cities

THUNDER MOUNTAIN INN
1631 S Hwy 92 (85635) Rates: $44-$70;
Tel: (520) 458-7900; (800) 222-5811

VISTA INN
201 W Fry Blvd (85635) Rates: $29+;
Tel: (520) 458-6711

WYNDMERE HOTEL & CONFERENCE CENTER
2047 S Hwy 92 (85635) Rates: $74;
Tel: (520) 459-5900

RECREATION

BROWN CANYON TRAIL HIKE
Intermediate/6.0 miles/3.0 hours

Info: When the summer doldrums get you down, perk up and step lively on this pretty trail into the Huachuca Mountains. The dawgus will howl with delight at the thought of this interlude with nature. As you traverse Brown Canyon, you'll experience a dramatic change of landscape - from typical desert terrain to a beautiful riparian oasis.

After .5 miles, the trail climbs to a small ridge before descending along old mining roads into the black-walled canyon. Maple, sycamore and ash create a canopy of cool shade on this relatively simple hike. Continue upstream to Brown Canyon Box. You and your buddy will have to clamber up and over a 15-foot rockfall but a refreshing pool awaits on the other side. Pack a picnic lunch and some biscuits and make an afternoon of it in this puppy paradise. For more information: (520) 378-0311.

Directions: Head south on Highway 92 for a few miles watching closely for the small sign on the right (west) for Ramsey Canyon. Turn right (west) on Ramsey Canyon Road for 2.1 miles to a Forest Service gate. Unless you have a high clearance vehicle, park here and hike the last half mile to the trailhead.

Note: Do not attempt in rainy weather - flash floods are common.

COMFORT SPRINGS TRAIL HIKE

Expert/4.6 miles/2.25 hours

Info: Complete this butt-kicker of a hike and you and your sidekick will earn one guilt-free week of sweets and treats. Along the trail through Ramsey Canyon, you'll admire the views of Carr Canyon. This once beautiful area is presently in a state of regeneration. Destroyed by a forest fire in 1977, it's humbling to witness the comeback of the trees and wildflowers. Mother Nature never gives up. For more information: (520) 378-0311.

Directions: Take Highway 92 south to FR 368 south. Follow for 7.8 miles to the trailhead at the Ramsey Vista Campground.

CREST TRAIL HIKE - Leashes

Intermediate/1.0-22.0 miles/0.5-12.0 hours

Info: For optimum viewing, plan your outing for a cloudless day when you'll be able to see forever or at least espy all the mountain ranges that constitute the Coronado National Forest. Northern Mexico is also visible from a number of vistas along the trail. You and Frisky can frolic among a variety of settings as the trail takes you on an interesting voyage through desert and woodlands. Views are everywhere, providing wonderful photo ops of valleys and lowlands. But the beauty of this trail doesn't come easy. Remember, your walk out will be as far as your walk in. Keep track of time, turning back whenever you or the pupster have had enough. Pack plenty of Perrier. For more information: (520) 364-3468.

Directions: Take Highway 92 south out of Sierra Vista for 13 miles to Coronado National Memorial Road (FR 61). Turn right and drive 8.2 miles through the Coronado National Memorial to the top of Montezuma Pass. The trailhead will be across from the parking lot.

LUTZ CANYON TRAIL HIKE

Expert/5.8 miles/3.0 hours

Info: You and the Schnauzer will need a snoozer after this one. A high-energy trail, it climbs 3,000 feet in elevation before ending at the junction with Crest Trail #103, your turnaround point. Take note of the changing trees along the way. The trail begins in a forest of juniper and oak and ends in a woodland of Douglas fir. For more information: (520) 378-0311.

Directions: Take Highway 92 south 12 miles to FR 59 (Ash Canyon Road). Follow FR 59 south to the trailhead at road's end.

OVERSITE CANYON TRAIL HIKE

Expert/5.0 miles/4.25 hours

Info: In addition to being physically demanding, this trail requires excellent reconnoitering skills. Once the trail leaves the mining road and enters the streambed it becomes difficult to follow. Pay close attention, or you'll miss the point where the pathway leaves the canyon floor and begins upward on a switchbacking adventure. This next section is overgrown with many confusing spur trails. For a change of scenery and a somewhat longer hike, return by looping around on the Ida Canyon Trail #110. For more information: (520) 378-0311.

Directions: Take Highway 92 south to FR 61 west. Follow FR 61 to FR 771 (through Coronado National Memorial). Take FR 771 north to the fork and bear right to the trailhead.

SAN PEDRO RIVER HIKE

Beginner/4.0 miles/2.0 hours

Info: Tree species range from glorious Fremont cottonwoods to Goodding willows and fragrant acacias. Binoculars, particularly in summer, will provide rainbow-like glimpses of yellow-billed cuckoos, gray hawks, green kingfishers and vermilion flycatchers while warblers provide the musical entertainment. This area is also home to a plentitude of wildlife including raccoons, deer, pocket gophers, bobcats, foxes and pallid bats. And there's something for history buffs too - ancient Indian petroglyphs. Volunteer docents lead interpretive tours on Saturday and Sunday mornings. For more information: (520) 458-3559.

Directions: Take Charleston Road east approximately 7.7 miles to the one-lane bridge. Park at the Mormon Battalion marker just east of the bridge. Hike north along the railroad tracks and down an embankment to the river.

SPRINGERVILLE

LODGING

EL-JO MOTOR INN
425 E Main St (85938) Rates: $24-$36;
Tel: (520) 333-4314

REED'S MOTOR LODGE
514 E Main St (85938) Rates: $24-$40;
Tel: (520) 333-4323

RECREATION

BUFFALO TRAIL HIKE - Leashes

Beginner/4.2 miles/2.0 hours

Info: This piece-of-cake trail has a unique distinction - it affords the opportunity of seeing a herd of buffalo in a natural setting. The buffalo are owned by the St. Johns Chamber of Commerce. Pretty vistas of Lyman Lake and the surrounding landscape are yours and the pupsters as you continue on the trail. For more information: (520) 337-4441.

Directions: From Springerville, go north on Highway 81 to Lyman State Park. The trailhead is just inside the entrance of the park.

Note: $3.00 per vehicle entrance fee.

LYMAN LAKE TRAIL HIKE - Leashes

Beginner/2.4 miles/1.0 hours

Info: This trail furnishes a quick and easy way to enjoy an outdoor adventure with the dawgus. Head to Lyman Lake State Park and hop on the looping trail around Lyman Lake for your daily dose of exercise and fresh air. For more information: (520) 337-4441.

Directions: From Springerville, go north on Highway 81 to Lyman State Park. The trailhead is just inside the entrance of the park.

Note: $3.00 per vehicle entrance fee.

PETROGLYPH TRAIL HIKE - Leashes

Beginner/2.0 miles/1.0 hours

Info: As the name implies, ancient petroglyphs adorn this short, cinchy trail. Not just for history hounds, fishing fiends will also like the area. Pack your rod and reel. This trail maneuvers past several popular fishing holes. Bring your waterdog's chew along - it'll keep him busy while you catch dinner. For more information: (520) 337-4441.

Directions: From Springerville, go north on Highway 81 to Lyman State Park. The trailhead is just inside the entrance of the park.

Note: $3.00 per vehicle entrance fee.

Notes

Notes

_____

_____

_____

_____

_____

_____

_____

_____

_____

_____

_____

_____

_____

STRAWBERRY

Lodging

THE STRAWBERRY LODGE

HCR 1, Box 331 (85544) Rates: $42-$52;
Tel: (520) 476-3333

Recreation

THE CABIN LOOP TRAIL

Info: The Cabin Loop Trail is a must-see, must-do hike combining both history and beauty as it stretches through the impressive Mogollon Rim. The trail is a connective loop to three log cabins - Pinchot Cabin, General Springs Cabin and Buck Springs Cabin and a great just-for-the-fun-of-it hike.

In the early 1900s, these cabins were fire guard stations and home to Forest Service Rangers during periods of high fire danger. This lengthy trail system is divided into four sections - four good reasons to visit this wonderland of nature. Trails are accessible from April to November. For more information: (520) 477-2255.

Directions: From Strawberry, head north on Highway 87 for 9 miles to Forest Road 300. Turn right (east) onto FR 300. The road forks almost immediately with one road heading south to Milk Ranch Point. Take the northern route (FR 300) instead and travel to the trailhead of your choice.

1) BARBERSHOP TRAIL HIKE

Intermediate/9.0 miles/4.5 hours

Info: If your favorite season is fall, plan to hike this section of the Cabin Loop Trail and color your world with red, yellow and orange, compliments of the deciduous trees which blanket the terrain. Rover will find ecstasy frolicking in crunchy piles of leaves. You might get lucky and spot a herd of mule deer or elk, perhaps even a wild Tom turkey.

Directions: There are two ways to reach this trail. The first is to take FR 300 east to the Houston Brothers Trailhead. The Barbershop Trail branches off about .75 miles in. The second route allows you to drive to the trailhead. Take Forest Road 300 about 7 miles past the Fred Haught Trailhead to FR 137. Turn north (left) and drive about 2.25 miles to the Barbershop Trailhead.

2) FRED HAUGHT TRAIL HIKE

Intermediate/12.0 miles/6.0 hours

Info: Peace and quiet are yours on this trail through the beautiful high country of the Rim. As you and your hound traverse the lush canyons and forested ridges, keep an eye out for wildlife, especially elk and mule deer. Follow the blazes to keep on the trail and imagine as you hike that this trail was once a main commerce route.

Directions: From Highway 87, take FR 300 east for about six miles to the Fred Haught Trailhead.

3) HOUSTON BROTHERS TRAIL HIKE

Intermediate/14.0 miles/7.5 hours

Info: Time and endurance permitting, you and water-loving Bowser won't regret hiking this trail in its entirety. The first section passes through pastoral Houston Draw, a small pine-clad canyon and home to a perennial stream, the perfect place for splashdown. Continue further and you'll find yourself on a ridgetop with sweeping landscape vistas. But the most breathtaking panorama of all is at the southernmost end of the trail, where the Rim takes a dramatic 2,000-foot plunge. The spectacle is absolutely picture-book perfect. The trail fades at times, making blaze following a necessity.

Directions: Take FR 300 east for about eight miles to the Houston Brothers Trailhead.

4) U-BAR TRAIL HIKE

Intermediate/13.0 miles/7.0 hours

Info: There's no better way to spend some quality time with your best buddy than along this trail through the dense forests and lush canyons of the beautiful Mogollon Rim. Who could ask for anything more? The views from 7,000 feet are breathtaking. The greenery is serenery. Summertime, you'll be cool. In the fall, you'll be color-blinded. And if you could access in winter, you'd be up to your knees (or a lot higher) in white powdery snow. Wow! When it's time to head back, do an about-face and retrace your steps. At times when the trail seems to disappear, follow the blazed trees.

Directions: Take Forest Road 300 about 7 miles past the Fred Haught Trailhead to FR 137. Turn north (left) and drive about 2.25 miles to the Barbershop Trailhead. The U-Bar Trail branches off from the Barbershop Trail about .25 miles in.

FLUME ROAD TRAIL HIKE - Leashes

Expert/8.0 miles/4.0 hours

Info: History hounds will want to sniff out this hike. But make sure hiker and hound are up to the challenge. This trail is not for powder-pups. It's a high-energy climb along a road once used as a passage for delivering materials to construct the dam and flume that still divert and provide water to the Irving Power Plant. Listed in the National Register of Historic Places, the flume and power plant have been in existence since 1916. Take a splash in the springs, one million gallons of water an hour percolate from the ground and form the lovely stream that runs through the area. Tote some munchies and plan a leisurely waterside rest. For more information: (520) 567-4501.

Directions: Take FR 708 west from Strawberry for 12 miles to reach parking lot just before the Irving Power Plant.

HIGHLINE TRAIL to RED ROCK SPRING HIKE

Intermediate/5.0 miles/4.5 hours

Info: For a cool retreat from the summer heat, grab your backpack and make tracks for the beautiful countryside just below the Mogollon Rim. The Highline Trail runs for 51 miles and crosses through dense woodlands beneath the Rim. Lush ponderosa, maple, oak, juniper and pinyon forests make this a delightfully shaded, wonderfully scented journey.

The opportunities for backpacking and camping are extraordinary, but this 5-mile stretch makes for an exceptional day hike. Red Rock Spring is the turnaround point, unless you and Bowser are still going strong. Then you can continue as long as you like. Just remember, the hike out will take as long as the hike in. Plan accordingly.

Directions: Take Highway 87 south to the trailhead about a half mile after the community of Pine. Or turn east onto Forest Road 64 and drive to another trailhead at Camp Geronimo.

HORSE CROSSING TRAIL HIKE

Intermediate/3.0 miles/1.5 hours

Info: Everything in life should be as delightful as this hike through the beautiful countryside of the Mogollon Rim. The trail traverses a verdant forest of pine and oak as it gradually descends to East Clear Creek. If you've got a water-loving pooch, he'll have a ball splashing the day away in the cool waters of the creek. For more information: (520) 477-2255.

Directions: Take Highway 87 north to FR 95. Go south on FR 95 for 4 miles to FR 513B and turn left. Follow FR 513B approximately 3 miles to the trailhead.

Note: **High clearance vehicles only.**

KINDER CROSSING TRAIL HIKE

Intermediate/6.0 miles/3.0 hours

Info: Hop on this creek crossing trail with your aquatic pooch and make all his water dreams come true. The creek is filled with trout, ideal if fish fantasies fill your dreams. A cool retreat in summer, you might even plan to enjoy some creekside wading or just some toe dipping. This picturesque trail is rocky and steep in certain sections. For more information: (520) 477-2255.

Directions: Head north on Highway 87 to the Blue Ridge Ranger Station, head south on FR 95. Follow to the Kinder Crossing sign, turning east for approximately .75 miles to the parking area.

MAXWELL TRAIL HIKE

Intermediate/1.2 miles/0.5 hours

Info: Switchback down West Clear Creek Canyon along this very steep and demanding trail. As you descend, typical canyon vegetation of gambel oak, ponderosa pine and Douglas fir surround you and then give way to riparian vegetation of willow, canyon grape, ash, box elder, red-osier dogwood, wild rose and "egad" poison ivy - remember, leaves of three, let it be.

Plan to spend the afternoon. Pack a picnic lunch and pull up a boulder creekside and watch as your aquatic pup enjoys the invigorating cold waters of the fast running creek. Relax and prepare yourself for the uphill trek out of the canyon. And don't be a trailblazer. Tread lightly, this is a delicate region. For more information: (520) 567-4501.

Directions: Take Highway 87 north for about 17 miles to Clints Well and Forest Highway 3. Take Forest Highway 3 north towards Flagstaff for 7 miles until you reach FR 81, turn left (west). There are several forks, stay on 81 until you reach FR 81E and go left. At the FR 693/81E fork, go left (east). It becomes a high clearance vehicle road from there. Stay on 81E until it ends at the trailhead.

Note: High clearance vehicles only.

TRAMWAY TRAIL HIKE

Intermediate/1.5 miles/1.0 hours

Info: Think about the cool and inviting creek at the bottom of the canyon as you make your way along this somewhat difficult trail. As you tackle the rigorous descent, enjoy the beautiful views of this lush, riparian canyon. The trail snakes along scrub oak, yucca and agave and then yields the ground to pine, ash, oak, white fir and Douglas fir. Creekside flora includes cattails, willows, wild sunflowers, locust, box elder and wild grape. At the canyon bottom, you and Fido can splish-splash in the always cool, sometimes icy waters of the creek. Sunbathe on a flat rock or find a shady spot under a fragrant pine - you've earned the rest. And you'll need your strength for the uphill trek. For more information: (520) 567-4501.

Directions: Take Highway 87 north for about 17 miles to Clints Well and Forest Highway 3. Take Forest Highway 3 north towards Flagstaff for 7 miles until you reach FR 81, turn left (west). There are several forks, stay on FR 81 until you reach FR81E. Take FR 81E (left) for about 4 miles to FR 693, a high clearance vehicle road. Take the right fork and travel less than a mile to the Tramway Trailhead.

Note: High clearance vehicles only.

Dogs May Be Unleashed Unless Otherwise Indicated

WILLOW CROSSING TRAIL HIKE

Beginner/2.6 miles/1.5 hours

Info: When you and the dawgus yearn for peace, seclusion and a sense of nature, this trail in Willow Valley is the one for you. An easy journey through woodlands and a riparian canyon exposes you to a variety of flora and fauna without much effort. Shaded by ponderosa pine, gambel oak, locust, willow and wild grape, you'll soon forget your everyday cares. There's also poison ivy so remember - leaves of three, let it be. For more information: (520) 567-4501.

Directions: Take Highway 87 north for about 17 miles to Clints Well and Forest Highway 3. Take Forest Highway 3 north for about 4 miles to FR 122A. Turn right and follow for 2 miles to the trailhead.

Note: Remember to close the gate by Peck's Point Tank.

SUMMERHAVEN

LODGING

SUMMERHAVEN SUITES & SWEETS

P. O. Box 757 (85619) Rates: $135;
Tel: (520) 576-1542

RECREATION

ASPEN-MARSHALL GULCH LOOP HIKE

Beginner/3.75 miles/4.0 hours

Info: Cool your heels along this delightfully shaded hike in the Santa Catalina Mountains. Visit in summer and explore meadows and aspen forests. Visit in springtime and catch a wildflower show of paintbrush, yellow columbine and penstemon. In fall, the golden shimmer of white barked aspen brightens the landscape.

The first half mile is quite level and easy but then it becomes somewhat steep and a little rugged as you proceed along switchbacks to Marshall Gulch. At the trail's halfway point, you'll reach Lunch Ledge, an aptly named flat-topped bluff with stunning views of the Wilderness of Rocks. Break some bread and biscuits and then continue through a dense aspen forest to Marshall Saddle, your eventual descent into Marshall Gulch and the end of a wonderful outdoor excursion. For more information: (520) 749-8700.

Directions: From Summerhaven, turn south and follow the paved road for a mile to the end. The trailheads are clearly marked.

MARSHALL GULCH TRAIL HIKE

Intermediate/2.6 miles/1.5 hours

Info: If you love trees, you won't want to miss this popular hike into the Pusch Ridge Wilderness. The treemarkable trail laces among a grab bag forest of madrone, aspen, gambel and silverleaf oak and white and Douglas fir. Imagine what colorful fun this trail would be in autumn. For more information: (520) 749-8700.

Directions: Follow FR 10 through Summerhaven to the Marshall Gulch Picnic Area. The trailhead is on the west side of the picnic area.

SUN CITY

LODGING

BEST WESTERN INN OF SUN CITY
11201 Grand Ave (85373) Rates: $38-$88;
Tel: (602) 933-8211; (800) 528-1234

RECREATION

CHAPPARAL PARK - Leashes

Info: You and your canine crony can find many things to do in this 11-acre park. Sports fields are abundant and provide lots of leg-stretching room. Picnic areas with grills and benches under shady trees offer more relaxed pastimes. Visit in early evening and plan a kibble cookout.

Directions: Take Bell Road east into Glendale. At 57th Avenue turn north (left) and drive to the park.

SUNSITES

RECREATION

COCHISE TRAIL HIKE - Leashes
Expert/9.0 miles/4.5 hours

Info: Travel through time on this trail once used as an escape route by Cochise and his tribe. Before attempting this demanding hike, make sure you and the pupster are in excellent physical condition. The majestic rock formations will remind you of every Western you've ever seen and the extraordinary scenery will give you an understanding of why the Indians fought so hard to keep their land. For more information: (520) 364-3468.

Directions: Go southbound on Highway 191. Take a right on Ironwood Road to FR 84. Follow for 8 miles to the campground and the trailhead.

SUPERIOR

RECREATION

BOYCE THOMPSON SOUTHWESTERN ARBORETUM - Leashes

Info: This very special expanse is a must-see, must-do for botanists, biologists and nature lovers. Thousands of desert plants cover 1,076 acres of Sonoran Desert for your viewing pleasure. Visitors will enjoy the well-marked, self-guided nature trails that lead the way through gardens of desert plantings. Perhaps Snoopy's keen snout will snoop out the unique Boojum tree while you admire some of the oldest saguaros within the state.

Perk up your ears and listen to the chirping of over 174 species of birds that flutter about. Look down too, you might catch a glimpse of a three-inch shrew scurrying beneath your feet. Tote your binocs and try to catch sight of some of the other 72 animal species that inhabit the area.

Pack a picnic lunch and enjoy the peacefulness you'll find at this nature wonderland that is beautifully backdropped by Picket Post Mountain. Pick up a pamphlet and learn about the rich history behind the Arboretum. This educational and inspirational park is open every day except Christmas. For more information: (520) 689-2723.

Directions: Take Highway 60 west through Superior. The park entrance is on the south (left) side of the highway, 3 miles west of town.

Note: $5-adult; $2-children; dogs and kids under 5-free.

HIGH TRAIL HIKE - Leashes

Beginner/1.0 miles/0.5 hours

Info: See the Boyce Thompson Arboretum from a bird's-eye perspective. This simple, relatively level trail ascends ridgetop to an overlook with views of the Arboretum and the Superstition Mountains. The interpretive signs provide an education on the area's flora and fauna. You'll come away enlightened. For more information: (520) 689-2723.

Directions: Take Highway 60 west to the Boyce Thompson Southwestern Arboretum, just 3 miles west of Superior. The trailhead is at the visitor center.

Note: $5-adult; $2-children; dogs and kids under 5-free.

MAIN LOOP TRAIL HIKE - Leashes

Intermediate/2.5 miles/1.5 hours

Info: Pack a scrumptious picnic lunch, Fido's favorite biscuits and those trusty binoculars and make a day of it at this enchanting state park. As you stroll along the looping trail, you'll pass interpretive kiosks which detail the interesting flora and fauna of the region. You can even detour to Queen Creek where you and the pup can enjoy a bit of water fun. Birdwatchers, be alert and you won't be disappointed. For more information: (520) 689-2723.

Directions: Take Highway 60 west to the Boyce Thompson Arboretum State Park, just 3 miles west of Superior. The trailhead is near the visitor center.

Note: $5-adult; $2-children; dogs and kids under 5-free.

SURPRISE

LODGING

WINDMILL INN AT SUN CITY WEST
12545 W Bell Rd (85374) Rates: $50-$99;
Tel: (602) 583-0133; (800) 547-4747

RECREATION

FORD CANYON TRAIL HIKE

Intermediate/5.8 miles/3.0 hours

Info: After the first two miles, you'll find yourself at the mouth of Ford Canyon and a scenic wonderland of fascinating rock formations which continue as you ascend to the old stone masonry dam. The ranchers who lived and the cattle that grazed in this area are long gone so you and your buddy boy can enjoy a quiet moment or two before turning around and heading back the way you came. For more information: (520) 935-2505.

Directions: Take Olive Avenue west of Phoenix to White Tank Mountain Road. Follow White Tank Mountain Road to Ford Canyon Road. The trail marker is at the far end of Ford Canyon Road.

GOAT CAMP TRAIL HIKE

Expert/6.0 miles/3.0 hours

Info: Don't be fooled by the first mile, a mere leg stretcher for the tough uphill climb which comes next. Your climb will snake through rock spires and along sheer rock face until you reach your final destination. Take a breather at Goat Camp and take some time to explore the old corral and interesting stonework. Naturally, what goes up must come down. Your descent will give you plenty of time to admire the surrounding terrain and enjoy what you might have missed amid all that huffing and puffing. For more information: (520) 935-2505.

Directions: Take Olive Avenue west of Phoenix to White Tank Mountain Road. Follow White Tank Mountain Road north to Black Canyon Drive. The trailhead is located at the far northwestern end of the loop.

WATERFALL TRAIL HIKE

Beginner/1.8 miles/1.0 hours

Info: This Kodak-worthy trail is peppered with petroglyphs - an ideal stroll for history lovers and their hounds. On this casual hike you'll be amazed at the beautiful scenery. Plan a visit in spring when an 80-foot waterfall marks the end of the trail. Erosion has created the park's namesake white tanks, an astounding phenomenon which attracts many enthusiastic sightseers each year. For more information: (520) 935-2505.

Directions: Take Olive Avenue west of Phoenix to White Tank Mountain Road. Follow White Tank Mountain Road to Waterfall Canyon Road and continue for about .5 miles northwest to the trailhead.

Locate Other Dog-Friendly Activities...Check Nearby Cities

WILLOW SPRINGS TRAIL HIKE

Intermediate/5.8 miles/3.0 hours

Info: The first mile of the hike is the most difficult as it ascends the steep and rocky terrain, but don't be discouraged. Continue trekking through Mesquite and Willow Canyons until you drop into the wash. Follow the wash upstream to the remains of a cabin, stock tank and corral. The surroundings will soon make you forget your initial workout. Actually, you'll forget just about everything except having a doggone good time. Absorbing and stimulating, this hike offers hours of exploration for eager hikers. For more information: (520) 935-2505.

Directions: Take Olive Avenue west of Phoenix to White Tank Mountain Road. Follow White Tank Mountain Road to Waterfall Canyon Road. Go about .7 miles to trailhead.

TAYLOR

LODGING

WHITING MOTOR INN

825 North Highway 77 (85939) Rates: $48-52;
Tel: (520) 536-2600

TEMPE

LODGING

THE BUTTES

2000 Westcourt Way (85282) Rates: $100-$235;
Tel: (602) 225-9000; (800) 843-1986

COMFORT INN
5300 S Priest Dr (85283) Rates: $40-$90;
Tel: (602) 820-7500; (800) 228-5150

COUNTRY SUITES BY CARLSON
1660 W Elliot Rd (85283) Rates: $49-$92;
Tel: (602) 345-8585; (800) 456-4000

EMBASSY SUITES HOTEL
4400 S Rural Rd (85282) Rates: $65-$145;
Tel: (602) 897-7444; (800) 362-2779

FIESTA INN
2100 S Priest Dr (85282) Rates: $55-$138;
Tel: (602) 967-1441; (800) 528-6481

HOLIDAY INN-PHOENIX-TEMPE/ASU
915 E Apache Blvd (85281) Rates: $55-$82;
Tel: (602) 968-3451;(800) 465-4329 (US);
(800) 238-5754 (AZ)

INNSUITES HOTEL TEMPE/PHOENIX AIRPORT
1651 W Baseline Rd (85283) Rates: $52-$119;
Tel: (602) 897-7900; (800) 841-4242

LA QUINTA MOTOR INN
911 S 48th St (85281) Rates: $44-$74;
Tel: (602) 967-4465; (800) 531-5900

MOTEL 6
513 W Broadway Rd (85282) Rates: $30-$36;
Tel: (602) 967-8696; (800) 440-6000

MOTEL 6
1720 S Priest Dr (85281) Rates: $32-$38;
Tel: (602) 968-4401; (800) 440-6000

MOTEL 6
1612 N Scottsdale Rd (85281) Rates: $30-$36;
Tel: (602) 945-9506; (800) 440-6000

PARAMOUNT HOTEL
225 E Apache Blvd (85281) Rates: $42-$99;
Tel: (602) 967-9431

Locate Other Dog-Friendly Activities...Check Nearby Cities

RAMADA SUITES TEMPE/SCOTTSDALE
1635 N Scottsdale Rd (85281) Rates: $39-$139;
Tel: (602) 947-3711; (800) 272-6232

RESIDENCE INN BY MARRIOTT
5075 S Priest Dr (85282) Rates: $145-$195;
Tel: (602) 756-2122; (800) 331-3131

RODEWAY INN PHOENIX AIRPORT EAST
1550 S 52nd St (85281) Rates: $49-$109;
Tel: (602) 967-3000; (800) 228-2000

SUPER 8 MOTEL
1020 E Apache Blvd (85281) Rates: $41-$87;
Tel: (602) 967-8891; (800) 800-8000

TEMPE MISSION PALMS HOTEL
60 E Fifth St (85281) Rates: $109+;
Tel: (602) 894-1400

TRAVELODGE-UNIVERSITY
1005 E Apache Blvd (85281) Rates: $46-$85;
Tel: (602) 968-7871; (800) 578-7878

RECREATION

ARREDONDO PARK - Leashes

Info: Get some Rexercise along the four acres of this cozy urban park.

Directions: Located on Dorsey Lane and Carson Drive.

BIRCHETT PARK - Leashes

Info: One acre offers an opportunity for a brief but paw pleasing trip to the park.

Directions: Corner of Mill Avenue and Apache Boulevard.

CAMPBELL PARK - Leashes

Info: Eight acres provide lots of leg stretching room for you and the pooch. Brown bag it at lunch and share a relaxing hour with the hound.

Directions: Corner of Beck Avenue and Yvonne Lane.

CANAL PARK - Leashes

Info: Wag a tail for Canal Park. Spend the day fishing with Fido lakeside or frolic in the wide open space at this delightful recreation area. You can also hop on a nature trail or two and learn while you burn. Go ahead, make your dog's day.

Directions: Corner of McKellips Road and College Avenue.

CELAYA PARK - Leashes

Info: If the playing fields are empty, a game of catch or fetch with Fido will make for a fun break at this 5.5-acre park.

Directions: Corner of Roosevelt and Vaughn Streets.

CLARK PARK - Leashes

Info: Although this park is geared more toward indoor recreation, there are still 10 acres of dog-friendly outdoor terrain where you and the pupster can take an afternoon stroll.

Directions: Corner of 19th Street and Roosevelt Street.

COLE PARK - Leashes

Info: Enjoy a fresh air interlude and take Rover to this 3.7-acre school park.

Directions: Located at Country Club Way and Carson Drive.

CORBELL PARK - Leashes

Info: Eleven acres of open space and ball fields can be found at this park - ideal for you and your pal to roam.

Directions: Located at Lakeshore and Chilton Drives.

CYPRUS PARK - Leashes

Info: Share some quality time with the wagger at this small dog-friendly park.

Directions: Located at Dorsey Lane and Malibu Drive.

DALEY PARK - Leashes

Info: This 17-acre expanse is a social dog's dreamwalk. You're sure to meet locals and their pups out for their daily dose. Or spectate at one of the sports fields with your best buddy beside you.

Directions: Located at Encanto Drive and College Avenue.

DAUMLER PARK - Leashes

Info: Enjoy a bit of fresh air as you do a couple of turns around this four-acre park.

Directions: Located at Evergreen and Balboa Drives.

DWIGHT PARK - Leashes

Info: If you're in the neighborhood, this four-acre park offers pleasant strolling grounds for padded paws.

Directions: Located at Roosevelt Street and Manhattan Drive.

EHRHARDT PARK - Leashes

Info: Pack some biscuits and saunter around the grounds of this 6.5-acre park.

Directions: Located at Evergreen and Riviera Drives.

ESCALANTE PARK - Leashes

Info: This school park has 10 acres of developed desertland for you and your pal to put your best paws forward and go for a walk.

Directions: Located at River Road and Orange Street.

ESTRADA PARK - Leashes

Info: Take a good read and a rawhide chew and relax with your hound in this 8-acre park.

Directions: Located at McClintock Road and Palamino Drive.

GAICKI PARK - Leashes

Info: Two acres of land is still big enough for you and Fido to take a quickie stroll.

Directions: Located at Cornell Drive and McClintock Road.

Locate Other Dog-Friendly Activities...Check Nearby Cities

GOODWIN PARK - Leashes

Info: This park offers five acres of frolicking space for you and the pupster.

Directions: Located at Taylor Drive and Caroline Lane.

HANGER PARK - Leashes

Info: The dawgus will have a tailwagging good time playing and roaming about on the grounds of this 15-acre park.

Directions: Located at Rural and Knox Roads.

HARELSON PARK - Leashes

Info: This 11-acre school park provides a pleasant area for your pup's constitutional.

Directions: Located at Warner Ranch Drive and Myrna Lane.

HAYDEN BUTTE PARK - Leashes

Info: Nature trails and plenty of open space make this park a great place to spend some quality time with your buddy while you enjoy the outdoors. Brown bag it and take pleasure in the scenery as you laze the day away in this spacious 25-acre park.

Directions: Located at Mill Avenue and First Street.

HUDSON PARK - Leashes

Info: Short on time? You can still satisfy old brown eyes with a walk in this 3-acre park.

Directions: Located at Cedar Street and Spence Avenue.

INDIAN BEND CANAL TRAIL HIKE

Beginner/2.2 miles/1.0 hours

Info: Even urban areas have their get-away-from-it-all places. On this easy trail you and fur-face will wander through a variety of vegetation. The landscape has been enhanced by surface water and seepage of canals which have filled the terrain with desert shrubs and young trees. After you kick up some dust along the trail, kick back and relax in the shade of one of the mature mesquite trees that shade the north-south portion of the trail. For more information: (602) 350-8587.

Directions: Take Mill Avenue to Curry Road. The park will be off of Curry Road, west of Mill Avenue.

INDIAN BEND PARK - Leashes

Info: Reward Rover's loyalty with a stroll through this 8-acre urban park.

Directions: Located at Miller Road and Marigold Lane.

INDIAN BEND WASH - Leashes

Info: Happy days are here again. You and your pooch can frolic and play in the natural open space of this 10-acre undeveloped area. Nature trails provide hiking hounds with a chance to enjoy the day while working off the kibble.

Directions: Located at 1600 E. McKellips Road.

JAYCEE PARK - Leashes

Info: This 7-acre park is a pleasant place for a jaunt and a bit of fresh air.

Directions: Located at 5th Street and Hardy Drive.

Locate Other Dog-Friendly Activities...Check Nearby Cities

JOYCE PARK - Leashes

Info: Give the Bowser an education on the outdoors at this 4.6-acre school park.

Directions: Located at Hermosa and Laguna Drives.

KIWANIS COMMUNITY PARK - Leashes

Info: A little something for everyone including pooches, this spacious 125-acre park is fun-filled and pretty. You and Fido can try your fly in the lake, or pack a picnic, a blanket, a chew and find yourselves a tree-shaded spot. Or do some fast-paced walking around the expansive and scenic recreation area.

Directions: Located at Mill Avenue and All-American Way.

MEYER PARK - Leashes

Info: Watch a softball match or do a couple of laps around this 8-acre school park.

Directions: Located at Dorset Lane and Alameda Drive.

MITCHELL PARK

Info: Run, doggie, run. This secluded neighborhood park is the perfect place for friendly Fidos to run, play and mingle. Delight in Fido's frolicking as he plays with friends in the enclosed dog run. There are benches for human counterparts, water fountains for all, and doggie bags for easy clean up. This fun- time, anytime park can be used at night too, the dog run is well lit.

Directions: Located at Mitchell Drive and 9th Street.

MOEUR PARK - Leashes

Info: If your dog isn't a disc chaser, why not leash him up and head out for a round of frisbee golf? If you think that disc is for the dogs, you can still enjoy a pleasant stroll or picnic in this spacious park of 11 acres.

Directions: Located at Mill Avenue and Curry Road.

OPTIMIST PARK - Leashes

Info: This 9-acre park offers plenty of stomping room for you to enjoy with your pooch.

Directions: Located at Cornell Drive and Kenwood Lane.

PALMER PARK - Leashes

Info: Spectate at a game of hoops or just opt for a leisurely stroll through this 4.5-acre park.

Directions: Located at College Avenue and Carson Circle.

PAPAGO PARK - Leashes

Info: Shared by Tempe and Phoenix, the park offers 300 acres of land laced with numerous hiking trails, ideal avenues for you and your pooch to enjoy. If you've got a water hound, bring a blanket and laze lakeside with the lad. Aside from an 18-hole golf course, the park also houses the Phoenix Zoo and the Desert Botanical Gardens. Go ahead, roam away and give the pooch something grand to bark about. Make a day of it with a kibble cookout.

Directions: Located at Curry Road and College Avenue.

Locate Other Dog-Friendly Activities...Check Nearby Cities

PAPAGO PARK TRAIL SYSTEM HIKE

Beginner/5.6 miles/2.5 hours

Info: Archaeologists will certainly dig this hike. It's easy and informational. Twelve sites are contained within the area, the most astounding being the Loma Del Rio, the remains of a seven-room Hohokam dwelling. And there's more - natural rock formations, desert washes and scenic overlooks comprise some of the trail's charm. The flora and fauna are particularly interesting. Cactus and low desert shrubs thrive everywhere and are home to jackrabbits, cottontails and lizards aplenty. This trail provides a quick escape from city life and an easy way to observe the diverse offerings of the desert. For more information: (602) 350-5200.

Directions: Go west from Curry and College Avenues in Tempe to locate trailhead.

PETERSEN PARK - Leashes

Info: Plan a picnic with your precious pooch and head to this 5-acre expanse.

Directions: Located at Southern Avenue and Priest Drive.

REDDEN PARK - Leashes

Info: This 4-acre school park provides a lovely setting for an afternoon interlude with Fido.

Directions: Located at Redfield and Lakeshore Drives.

ROTARY PARK - Leashes

Info: Make it a habit for you and the hound to get your daily dose of exercise in this 5-acre park.

Directions: Located at Country Club Way and Hermosa Drive.

SCUDDER PARK - Leashes

Info: Enjoy some fresh air and a stroll in this 4-acre park.

Directions: Located at Lakeshore and Watson Drives.

SELLEH PARK - Leashes

Info: Plan a picnic waterside with your pup in this 6.3-acre park.

Directions: Located at Los Feliz and Aspen Drives.

STROUD PARK - Leashes

Info: Watch that tail wag as you and the mutt strut through this 5.6-acre park.

Directions: Located at Taylor and Redfield Drives.

SVOB PARK - Leashes

Info: Set on 7.8 acres, this park offers basketball and soccer for your viewing pleasure as you lead the lad over the turf.

Directions: Located at Vineyard Road and Park Drive.

WAGGONER PARK - Leashes

Info: Spend some quality playtime in this 8-acre school park.

Directions: Located at Lakeshore Drive and Carver Road.

TOLLESON

LODGING
ECONO LODGE
1520 N 84th Dr (85353) Rates: $44-$79;
Tel: (602) 936-4667; (800) 424-4777

TOMBSTONE

LODGING
BEST WESTERN LOOKOUT LODGE
Hwy 80 W (85638) Rates: $51-$75;
Tel: (520) 457-2223; (800) 528-1234

RECREATION
COCHISE TRAIL HIKE
Expert/3.5 miles/2.0 hours

Info: This butt-kicker of a hike is definitely not for sofa-loving types. If you and your faithful sidekick are up to the challenge, tackle the steep 1,000-foot ascent up the Dragoon Mountains to Stronghold Divide. Once atop the pass, you'll have a new appreciation for the physical strength of the Apache Indians who built their fortress in the upper confines of this canyon.

Jello may appropriately describe your legs, while spectacular describes the commanding vistas of this craggy, boulder-strewn terrain. Either retrace your ascent or if you've got the stamina, extend the hike with a 3-mile descent to the canyon bottom and the Cochise Stronghold. For more information: (520) 364-3468.

Directions: Take Highway 80 north to the community of St. David. From the post office in St. David, it's about 2 miles to the Holy Trinity Monastery. Opposite the Monastery is FS Road 688. Follow this road for 15 miles to the trailhead. Be sure to bear left at the first fork in FS 688.

Note: High clearance vehicles only.

TUBA CITY

LODGING
TUBA CITY MOTEL
P.O. Box 247 (86045) Rates: $85-$90;
Tel: (520) 283-4545

TUBAC

LODGING
TUBAC GOLF RESORT
1 Otero Rd (85646) Rates: $62-$142;
Tel: (520) 398-2211; (800) 848-7893

RECREATION

DUTCH JOHN TRAIL HIKE

Intermediate/3.6 miles/1.5 hours

Info: Evergreen and silverleaf oaks, alligator junipers and white-barked sycamores all work together to keep this trail well-shaded and cool - perfect for those hot, summer days. The trail steadily slithers up the Santa Ritas and into Dutch John Canyon, topping out at Dutch John Spring. About halfway through your hike, you'll encounter a spring marked Dutch John, but don't be fooled - this isn't the hike's destination, unless you make it so. As you hike, keep your eyes open for a glimpse of white-tailed deer. You may want to leash Rover if he likes to chase after Bambis. Black bears also inhabit the area. For more information: (520) 281-2296.

Directions: Take Interstate 19 north to FR 62 east. Follow FR 62 east to FR 70 and head east for 12.5 miles to the Bog Springs Campground. The trailhead is near the parking area at the back of the campground.

QUANTRELL MINE TRAIL HIKE

Intermediate/4.6 miles/2.25 hours

Info: An area once rich with gold and silver ore, it's now a favorite trail with hikers and pooches who love a good workout backdropped by incredible vistas. The trail follows a steep, switchbacking course through the Santa Ritas providing sweeping area panoramas the entire way. You may want to bring your camera along for this one. For more information: (520) 281-2296.

Directions: Take Interstate 19 north, exiting at Amado. Head east on Canoa Road for 3 miles to Elephant Head Road. Turn east for 1.6 miles to Mt. Hopkins Road, continuing east for 4.5 miles to FR 183. Take FR 183 north for 2.4 miles to the parking area. Park and hike down to the mountain bike trail. Hike this trail one mile to the trailhead.

TUCSON

Lodging

BEST WESTERN EXECUTIVE INN
333 W Drachman (85705) Rates: $40-$115;
Tel: (520) 791-7551;
(800) 528-1234 (US); (800) 255-3371 (AZ)

BEST WESTERN GHOST RANCH LODGE
801 W Miracle Mile (85705) Rates: $39-$98;
Tel: (520) 791-7565; (800) 528-1234

BEST WESTERN INNSUITES-CATALINA FOOTHILLS
6201 N Oracle Rd (85704) Rates: $49-$149;
Tel: (520) 297-8111; (800) 528-1234

BEST WESTERN TANQUE VERDE INN
7007 E Tanque Verde Rd (85715) Rates: $40-$99;
Tel: (520) 298-2300; (800) 528-1234

CANDLELIGHT SUITES
1440 S Craycroft Rd (85711) Rates: $39-$69;
Tel: (520) 747-1440; (800) 223-1440

THE CAT AND THE WHISTLE BED & BREAKFAST
22nd St & Kolb Rd (85710)
Rates: $65-$75; Monthly: $850-$1000;
Tel: (602) 990-0682; (800) 456-0682

CHATEAU SONATA
550 S Camino Seco (85710) Rates: $39-$111;
Tel: (520) 886-2468

CLARION HOTEL TUCSON AIRPORT
6801 S Tucson Blvd (85706) Rates: $49-$106;
Tel: (520) 746-3932;
(800) 221-2222 (US); (800) 526-0550 (AZ)

COUNTRY SUITES BY CARLSON
7411 N Oracle Rd (85704) Rates: $49-$100;
Tel: (520) 575-9255; (800) 456-4000

THE COVE BED & BREAKFAST
Tucson Blvd & Norton (85713)
Rates: $60-$80; Weekly: $350-$400;
Tel: (602) 990-0682; (800) 456-0682

DAYS INN-PALOVERDE/TUCSON AIRPORT
3700 E Irvington Rd (85714) Rates: $45-$90;
Tel: (520) 571-1400; (800) 329-7466

DOUBLETREE HOTEL
445 S Alvernon Way (85711) Rates: $64-$101;
Tel: (520) 881-4200; (800) 222-8733

EMBASSY SUITES HOTEL &
CONFERENCE CENTER/AIRPORT
7051 S Tucson Blvd (85706) Rates: $89-$139;
Tel: (520) 573-0700;
(800) 362-2779 (US); (800) 262-8866 (AZ)

EMBASSY SUITES HOTEL TUCSON/BROADWAY
5335 E Broadway (85711) Rates: $79-$139;
Tel: (520) 845-2700; (800) 362-2779

FLYING V RANCH
6800 N Flying V Ranch Rd (85715) Rates: $50-$110;
Tel: (520) 299-4372

FRANCISCAN INN
1165 N Stone Ave (85705) Rates: $26-$60;
Tel: (520) 622-7763

HAMPTON INN-AIRPORT
6971 S Tucson Blvd (85706) Rates: $52-$75;
Tel: (520) 889-5789; (800) 426-7866

HOLIDAY INN-CITY CENTER
181 W Broadway (85701) Rates: $50-$160;
Tel: (520) 624-8711;
(800) 465-4329 (US); (800) 448-8276 (AZ)

HOLIDAY INN-PALOVERDE
4550 S Paloverde Blvd (85714) Rates: $52-$128;
Tel: (520) 746-1161; (800) 465-4329

LA QUINTA INN-EAST
6404 E Broadway (85710) Rates: $40-$74;
Tel: (520) 747-1414; (800) 531-5900

LA QUINTA INN-WEST
665 N Freeway (85745) Rates: $40-$74;
Tel: (520) 622-6491; (800) 531-5900

THE LODGE ON THE DESERT
306 N Alvernon Way (85711) Rates: $54-$177;
Tel: (520) 325-3366; (800) 456-5634

MOTEL 6
1031 E Benson Hwy (85713) Rates: $28-$34;
Tel: (520) 628-1264; (800) 440-6000

MOTEL 6
755 E Benson Hwy (85713) Rates: $28-$34;
Tel: (520) 622-4614; (800) 440-6000

MOTEL 6
960 S Freeway (85745) Rates: $30-$36;
Tel: (520) 628-1339; (800) 440-6000

MOTEL 6
4950 S Outlet Ctr Dr (85706) Rates: $34-$40;
Tel: (520) 746-0030; (800) 440-6000

Locate Other Dog-Friendly Activities...Check Nearby Cities

MOTEL 6
4630 W Ina Rd (85741) Rates: $36-$42;
Tel: (520) 744-9300; (800) 440-6000

MOTEL 6
1222 S Freeway (85713) Rates: $30-$36;
Tel: (520) 624-2516; (800) 440-6000

MOUNTAIN VIEWS BED & BREAKFAST
E Tanque Verde Rd (85749)
Rates: $65-$75; Weekly: $390-$450;
Tel: (602) 990-0682; (800) 456-0682

PARK INN CLUB & BREAKFAST-SANTA RITA
88 E Broadway (85701) Rates: $41-$45;
Tel: (520) 622-4000; (800) 437-7275

PUEBLO INN
350 S Freeway (85745) Rates: $68-$76;
Tel: (520) 622-6611

QUALITY INN-UNIVERSITY & CONFERENCE CENTER
1601 N Oracle Rd (85705) Rates: $45-$88;
Tel: (520) 623-6666; (800) 228-5151

RADISSON SUITE HOTEL TUCSON
6555 E Speedway Blvd (85710) Rates: $59-$165;
Tel: (520) 721-7100; (800) 333-3333

RAMADA INN FOOTHILLS
6944 E Tanque Verde Rd (85715) Rates: $50-$120;
Tel: (520) 886-9595; (800) 272-6232

RAMADA INN PALOVERDE 1
5251 S Julian Dr (85706) Rates: $70-$120;
Tel: (520) 294-5250; (800) 272-6232

RED ROOF INN
3700 E Irvington Rd (85714) Rates: $100+;
Tel: (520) 571-1400; (800) 843-7663

RESIDENCE INN BY MARRIOTT
6477 E Speedway Blvd (85710) Rates: $85-$174;
Tel: (520) 721-0991; (800) 331-3131

RODEWAY INN-BENSON HWY & PARK
810 E Benson Hwy (85713) Rates: $38-$99;
Tel: (520) 884-5800; (800) 424-4777

RODEWAY INN I-10 & GRANT RD
1365 W Grant Rd (85745) Rates: $42-$90;
Tel: (520) 622-7791; (800) 424-4777

SHERATON EL CONQUISTADOR
GOLF & TENNIS RESORT
10000 N Oracle Rd (85737) Rates: $130-$260;
Tel: (520) 544-5000; (800) 325-7832

SMUGGLER'S INN HOTEL
6350 E Speedway Blvd (85710) Rates: $42+;
Tel: (520) 296-3293; (800) 525-8852

THE TILLINGHAST PLACE BED & BREAKFAST
N Oracle Rd & Rt 89 (85705) Rates: $65-$105;
Tel: (602) 990-0682; (800) 456-0682

TRAVELODGE-FLAMINGO
1300 N Stone Ave (85705) Rates: $47-$142;
Tel: (520) 770-1910; (800) 578-7878 (US);
(800) 300-3533 (AZ)

TRAVELODGE SUITES
401 W Lavery Ln (85704) Rates: $140+;
Tel: (520) 797-1710; (800) 578-7878

TUCSON EAST HILTON
7600 E Broadway (85710) Rates: $49-$89;
Tel: (520) 721-5000; (800) 648-7177

UNIVERSITY INN
950 N Stone Ave (85705) Rates: $32-$59;
Tel: (520) 791-7503

WAYWARD WINDS LODGE
707 W Miracle Mile (85705) Rates: $39-$89;
Tel: (520) 791-7526; (800) 791-9503

WESTWARD LOOK RESORT
245 E Ina Rd (85704) Rates: $70-$130;
Tel: (520) 297-1151; (800) 722-2500

Locate Other Dog-Friendly Activities...Check Nearby Cities

WINDMILL INN AT ST. PHILLIP'S PLAZA
4250 N Campbell Ave (85718) Rates: $60-$103;
Tel: (520) 577-0007; (800) 547-4747

RECREATION

ARROYO CHICO TRAIL to REID PARK

Beginner/4.0 miles/2.0 hours

Info: Take Rover for a wonderful walk through the wash to reach Tucson's largest urban park. Pack a snack for you and biscuits for the pooch and enjoy a picnic lunch before backtracking to the car. The diversity of the plant species in the Arroyo Chico Wash may surprise you, so take your time and take notice of your surroundings. On this hike, you can experience nature without leaving the city limits, a delightful way to get those urban tails wagging. For more information: (520) 791-4372.

Directions: There are several access points to the trailhead on the University of Arizona campus.

BELLOTA TRAIL HIKE

Intermediate/4.4 miles/2.0 hours

Info: If you and your pooch are socializing types, this high traffic trail's for you. The popularity of this hike stems from the fact that it's part of the renowned Arizona Trail. Remember to leave only footprints, take only memories. For more information: (520) 749-8700.

Directions: Head east on Tanque Verde Road to Redington Road (FR 371). Take Redington Road east to Bellota Ranch junction. To lengthen your hike, you can park here. Otherwise, continue on for 2.5 miles to lakes, park and wash basin. The signed trailhead is to the left of the basin.

Dogs May Be Unleashed Unless Otherwise Indicated

BUTTERFLY TRAIL HIKE to NOVIO SPRING

Intermediate/5.6 miles/3.0 hours

Info: Tranquility and beauty greet you from the get-go on this hike. One of the best kept secrets of the Santa Catalinas, the trail is well shaded with ponderosa pine and gambel oak, making for a cool escape on a hot desert day.

A somewhat demanding trek, the first part of the journey plunges into the confines of a lush canyon via a series of switchbacks. As you and the pupster traverse this area, you'll be serenaded by the melodic songs of jays, thrushes and hummingbirds. Keep an eye out for the trail's namesake. Fido might just take off on a butterfly chase. Your final destination is Novio Spring. If yours is an aquatic pup, he'll be splish-splashing in no time at this refreshing water hole. If you're feeling energetic, the trail continues another 2.9 miles to Soldier Camp. Whenever you've had enough, retrace your steps. For more information: (520) 749-8700.

Directions: Take Catalina Highway (which becomes Mt. Lemmon Hwy) north to the Santa Catalina Mountains. The trailhead is at Milepost 19 at the Palisade Visitor Station on the north side of the road. Or continue north another 2.5 miles to the second trailhead at the Soldier Camp turnoff - bear left at the fork.

CATALINA STATE PARK - Leashes

Info: Nestled in the Coronado National Forest, this park offers a variety of outdoor adventures for hikers and their hiking hounds. Legends of buried gold and tall tales of ancient travelers create an air of mystery and make a visit to the park intriguing. From a nature hike to a birdwatching pathway, this park in the Tucson Foothills offers a little something for everyone. All hiking areas are dog-friendly, but the wilderness areas are off limits to pooches. For more information: (520) 628-5798.

Directions: Take Highway 77 north to the park entrance.

Note: $3.00 per vehicle entrance fee.

1) CANYON LOOP TRAIL HIKE - Leashes

Intermediate/1.0 miles/0.5 hours

Info: As you loop through this riparian section of the park, you'll be privy to some outstanding views of the Santa Catalina Mountains and the Pusch Ridge Wilderness. If you and your hiking sidekick aren't ready to call it quits after this short jaunt, hop on one of the other scenic trails within the park's boundaries. For more information: (520) 628-5798.

Directions: Take Highway 77 north to Catalina State Park. The trailhead is at the end of park road.

Note: $3.00 per vehicle entrance fee.

2) CATALINA BIRDING TRAIL HIKE - Leashes

Beginner/1.0 miles/0.5 hours

Info: Birdwatchers, this trail is avian heaven. Ready those binoculars and aim for the skies and trees as you wander along this pretty looping trail. A popular trail with Tucsonians, you and your best buddy might make some new friends. For more information: (520) 628-5798.

Directions: Take Highway 77 north to Catalina State Park. The trailhead is at the end of park road.

Note: $3.00 per vehicle entrance fee.

3) CATALINA EQUESTRIAN TRAIL HIKE - Leashes

Beginner/2.8 miles/1.5 hours

Info: As the name implies, this trail is popular with the horsy set and, as you traverse the path, you'll understand why - the views are exceptional. Just make sure Rover doesn't get too close to the back end of Hi Ho Silver. If you want to extend your hiking day, three other park trails connect with this one - Canyon Loop, Catalina Birding and Catalina Nature. For more information: (520) 628-5798.

Directions: Take Highway 77 north to Catalina State Park. The trailhead is at the equestrian center just past the campground.

Note: $3.00 per vehicle entrance fee.

4) CATALINA NATURE TRAIL HIKE - Leashes

Beginner/1.0 miles/0.5 hours

Info: This trail offers yet another hiking option in the 5,500-acre state park. Once you complete this flat, scenic loop, chill out with a picnic lunch or make tracks on another trail. For more information: (520) 628-5798.

Directions: Take Highway 77 north to Catalina State Park. The trailhead is at the end of the park road.

Note: $3.00 per vehicle entrance fee.

THE DAVID YETMAN TRAIL HIKE

Intermediate/12.0 miles/6.0 hours

Info: Located along the hills of Tucson Mountain Park, this trail provides a hearty workout for you and the pupster. The semi-looping trail winds through open, cactus-studded hillsides. A visit in springtime will reward you with vibrant orange, yellow and purple wildflowers. Popular with mountain cyclists and equestrians, be prepared to share your space. You might also want to keep a leash handy. For more information: (520) 740-2690.

Directions: Immediately west of the intersection of Speedway Boulevard and West Anklam Road, turn left (south) on Camino de Oeste and follow to one of the two trailheads. Or continue west past the intersection on Gates Pass Road (the name changes past Camino de Oeste) to the second trailhead just after the road crosses the pass.

FLORIDA SADDLE TRAIL HIKE

Intermediate/6.0 miles/3.0 hours

Info: Bird lovers will want to plan a hike in springtime, prime nesting season in the Santa Rita Mountains. Home to canyon wrens, painted redstarts, cardinals, Mexican jays, verdins and white-winged doves, the mountain air sings with the music from its noisy residents.

A strenuous hike, you'll climb a steep 2,000 feet in elevation and pass through a patchwork of woodlands including specimens of oak, mesquite, juniper, ponderosa pine and Douglas fir. Shaded and aromatic, this is an excellent summertime hike. Once you reach the saddle, retrace your steps. In winter, it's not unusual to encounter snow on the mountainside. In any season, you and the dawgus are sure to have an invigorating adventure. For more information: (520) 281-2296.

Directions: Take Interstate 19 south to the Continental Road off-ramp. At the bottom, turn left (east) and drive for one mile to the Madera Canyon turnoff (Forest Service Road 62). Take FR 62 for 7.5 miles to where FR 62 and FR 70 (to Madera Canyon Recreation Area) split, remaining on FR 62. Drive to FR 62A, the Florida Canyon turnoff. Take FR 62A for 3 miles to the trailhead.

GATES PASS TRAIL HIKE

Intermediate/4.4 miles/2.25 hours

Info: If you're torn between spending the afternoon hanging out at a park or hiking, head for Tucson Mountain Park where you can do both. Enjoy a picnic lunch and a game of fetch with Rover and then head for the hills. This trail wanders through the beautiful terrain of the Sonoran Desert. For more information: (520) 740-2690.

Directions: Head west on Speedway Boulevard to Gates Pass Road. Continue west to the trailhead at Tucson Mountain Park.

LEMMON ROCK TRAIL HIKE

Expert/4.0 miles/2.0 hours

Info: Only experienced hikers and their fearless canines should attempt this steep, rugged, demanding hike. In just two miles, you'll climb 1,500 feet in elevation. Rewards for the physically fit who embark on this trail are breathtaking vistas of the Wilderness of Rock that peek through the pines on your ascent. Make an about-face whenever you and Fido have had enough and do the descent thing. For more information: (520) 749-8700.

Directions: From Tucson, take Catalina Highway northwest past the Mt. Lemmon Ski Valley to the power substation. Hike west to a dirt road and down the road to the trailhead.

MERCER SPRING TRAIL HIKE

Intermediate/2.6 miles/1.5 hours

Info: Plan a springtime hike and experience this trail at its best - when sweet madrigals fill the air and rainbowlike wildflowers blanket the terrain. When you reach the junction with the Sycamore Reservoir Trail (#39) you're at the end of your journey. Either head back the way you came of if you're up to more hiking miles, continue a few miles further on #39 and retrace your steps when you've had enough. For more information: (520) 749-8700.

Directions: From Tanque Verde Road, take Catalina Highway approximately 10 miles to the trailhead at Molino Basin Campground.

OLD SPANISH TRAIL HIKE - Leashes

Beginner/1.0-31.4 miles/0.5-15 hours

Info: Take the pooch for a drive up Broadway Road and watch his tail wag with anticipation as you leash him up for a day hike along the trail. You'll intersect roadways about every half-mile, so keeping track of distance won't be difficult. Definitely an exciting alternative to your everyday walking routine. For more information: (520) 791-4372.

Directions: Trailhead is located off of Broadway Road east of Pantano Road. There are numerous entrances between Broadway and Colossal Cave Park.

PICACHO PEAK STATE PARK - Leashes

Info: Civil war aficionados will love this area which hosted one of the only civil war battles fought in the southwest. A memorial plaza in the park proudly displays plaques and markers detailing the historic event. The park is ideal for naturalists too. In springtime, lucky dogs might get a chance to behold a breathtaking display of colorful poppies. Bring your camera and a keen mind and get ready to absorb a dollop of history and a heap of scenery.

The park's namesake is actually a 1,500 foot volcanic spire that rises abruptly from the Santa Cruz River Valley. This landmark seems to touch the sky and offers amazing photo opportunities for amateurs and professionals alike. Although the park is dog-friendly, for pooch's sake, avoid the Hunter Trail and the Sunset Vista Trail. Due to the rough terrain, these trails are not paw-friendly. For more information: (520) 466-3183.

Directions: Take Interstate 10 northwest for 40 miles to the park entrance.

Note: $3.00 per vehicle entrance fee.

PIMA AIR & SPACE MUSEUM - Leashes

Info: A back to the future experience awaits you and your Red Baron pooch at this dog-friendly museum. From the Wright Flyer and a SR-71 Blackbird to an X-15 and the Mercury Space

Capsule, over 200 exhibits provide a first-hand peek at the past, present and future of aviation and space travel. Grab your bomber jacket and your astro-pup's leash and take off on a nonstop adventure of flying fun. For more information: (520) 574-9658.

Directions: Take Interstate 10 east to the Valencia Road exit and continue 2 miles to the museum.

Note: $6.00 entrance fee; hours are 9:00 AM - 4:00 PM.

RED RIDGE TRAIL HIKE - Leashes

Expert/10.0 miles/5.0 hours

Info: This beautiful forest hike among pines and firs is a sure antedote for the summer blues, but it's definitely not the for the soft of paw. If you and your canine are experienced hikers, make tracks for this refreshingly scented trail along the Oracle Ridge. Water-loving pooches will especially like a little paw dipping in the cold, rushing waters of the East Fork of the Canada del Oro. When you reach the crossing of the East Fork Trail #24A, it's time for an about-face and your return trip.

Directions: From Tucson, take Tanque Verde Road to Catalina Highway. Go north to FR 38. Take FR 38 for .4 miles to the trailhead.

RILLITO RIVER TRAIL HIKE - Leashes

Beginner/8.0 miles/ 4.0 hours

Info: Your city weary pooch will adore you forever after a brisk walk along this energizing riverside trail. Perhaps there'll even be time for some splish-splashing fun. For more information: (520) 740-6340.

Directions: Trailheads are located on Campbell Avenue or Oracle Road north of Grant Road. Also accessible from La Cholla Boulevard south of Orange Grove Road.

SKY CLUB WASH INTERPRETIVE TRAIL HIKE

Intermediate/3.0 miles/1.5 hours

Info: An urban wildlife refuge - is this for real or an oxymoron? It's definitely a nature trail and definitely one you and the pupster will relish. This trail loops around the scenic Sky Club Wash Natural Area at the local high school. Sweet smelling acacia, paloverde and mesquite trees canopy the trail, while desert plant life borders the wash. What a pretty combo. The success of such an unusual refuge is due to the efforts of community and government agencies. For more information: (520) 577-5090.

Directions: Take Pontatoc Road north to Sunrise Drive east. Follow to the parking area in Catalina Foothills High School.

SOLDIER TRAIL HIKE

Intermediate/5.2 miles/2.5 hours

Info: This trail doesn't rate a ten on the difficulty scale, but it's not just a walk in the park either. You're bound to work up a sweat as you tackle the 1,700-foot elevation change on your mountainside ascent and descent into Soldier Canyon. If you and your Snoopy are adventurous types, head off and snoop around one of the well worn side trails. They're sure to make your excursion more interesting. For more information: (520) 749-8700.

Directions: Take Catalina Highway north to Old Prison Camp Road (Milepost 7), turn left. Follow this road to the trailhead.

SYCAMORE RESERVOIR TRAIL HIKE

Intermediate/5.0 miles/2.5 hours

Info: Once you reach the trailhead, it's another mile to the trail's destination - Sycamore Reservoir. Brown bag an afternoon picnic and nibble the kibble while admiring sweeping panoramas. FYI - the reservoir was constructed to provide water to the prison camp. For more information: (520) 749-8700.

Directions: Take Catalina Highway approximately 3 miles north of the Molino Basin Picnic Area to the Federal Honor Camp. If you don't have a high-clearance vehicle, park and hike the dirt road west of the prison for 1.5 miles to the trailhead.

TUCSON MOUNTAIN PARK - Leashes

Info: Is the pupster panting for a true desert experience? Then take old brown eyes to Tucson Mountain Park. Sprawling over 22,000 acres, this park is home to some of the most outstanding examples of saguaros you'll find in the state. Kick up some dust on one of the trails in this Sonoran Desert region and get your fill of an amazing variety of flora and fauna. Numerous sandwashes slice through the landscape and create intensely scenic backgrounds. You'll find plenty of Kodak moments along the 26 miles of trails. This park gets two paws up for scenery and serenity.

Directions: Take Speedway Boulevard west to Gates Pass Road West. The park will be off Gates Pass.

Dogs May Be Unleashed Unless Otherwise Indicated

VENTANA CANYON TRAIL HIKE to MAIDEN POOLS

Intermediate/5.0 miles/2.5 hours

Info: Depending on the time of year you visit, you might encounter cascading waterfalls, gushing streams and overflowing pools. This water wonderland in the middle of the Sonoran Desert isn't a mirage, but it is seasonal. Try to plan a trip after a heavy rainfall and you'll behold the magical effect rain has on this canyon. Tote a picnic repast - you can't beat the Maiden Pools for a scenic lunch site. Ventana Creek is usually dry summer through winter, but in springtime, it transforms itself into a wet and wild adventure, the perfect oasis for your aquatic pup. The trail crosses the creek eight times each way on your journey through the canyon to the incredible Maiden Pools where, in the heart of the desert, you'll experience a water scene of rivers and 50-foot cascading waterfalls. Spread out a blanket, break out the biscuit basket and do lunch in a mesmerized state. When you've quenched your scenic thirsts, begin the return trip. For more information: (520) 299-3272.

FYI: The trail continues past the pools to The Window, a viewpoint through rock, but the area is part of the Big Horn Sheep Preserve and dogs are not permitted.

Directions: To reach Ventana Canyon in northeastern Tucson, take Kolb Road north from where it meets Sunrise Drive. Kolb Road curves left (west) to the Loews Ventana Canyon Resort. Park in the west parking lot and walk west to Canyon View Apartments. Turn left at the leasing office, right at the recreation building and left again past the tennis courts to the trailhead.

Note: Contact the Flying V Guest Ranch at (520) 299-4372 before heading out. They'll need your name and size of your hiking party.

WEST SPRING TRAIL HIKE - Leashes

Intermediate/4.4 miles/2.5 hours

Info: In order to reach a trail less traveled, you'll have to cross a road more traveled. Use caution, speeding cars are common so keep a tight hold on your pooch. You and Bowser will make tracks for about two miles until you come to West Spring, the perfect place to kick back and enjoy the serenery. On your return journey, you'll partake of a different visual experience. The sun's shifting position in the sky creates looming, moving shadows which change the appearance of the woodlands. Breathe deeply and enjoy the invigorating walk, the woodsy aromatic scents and changing scenery all about you. For more information: (520) 749-8700.

Directions: Take Mount Lemmon Road in Tucson 10 miles to the Molino Basin Campground. The trailhead is on the east side of Mount Lemmon Road which is also known as the Catalina Highway.

WILD HORSE CANYON TRAIL HIKE

Intermediate/5.0 miles/3.0 hours

Info: Hidden within the Rincon Mountains lie some of the best low elevation desert hikes to be found in this area of the state - namely lush, trail-laced Wild Horse Canyon. The canyon is a maze of trails so an area map would be handy and will keep you on course through this incredibly scenic descent through exotic desert flora. Visit in early spring for a prismatic display of wildflowers. Desert dandelion, Mojave aster, agave, Cooper's paper flower, ocotillo and cholla are just some of the dazzling blooming plants you and flower-loving Fido can sniff out along your journey.

You'll cross several small drainages and pass through a gate before bottoming out at a stream. Fascinating Little Wild Horse Tank, a natural phenomenon, is a water sculpted pool just a mere boulder scramble away. Or opt for the easier approach and continue on the path to the pools. Depending on recent rains, the water level of the streams and pools can vary. Take a biscuit break and enjoy some paw dipping before heading back the way you came.

Directions: Head east on East Speedway Boulevard to the dead end. From the sign-in station, take the trail to the south. The trail north is the Douglas Spring Trailhead, a popular equestrian trail.

TUMACACORI

RECREATION

JUAN BAUTISTA DE ANZA TRAIL HIKE - Leashes

Intermediate/9.0 miles/4.5 hours

Info: This 1,200-mile historic trail provides hiking and water fun for you and the pupster. Captivating and picturesque, the Santa Cruz River skirts the trail and offers hikers and their hounds excellent opportunities for contemplation, recreation and photographic memories. Over the course of this trail, you'll cross the river several times. The lighting and shadows on the water and terrain are ideal for photographers. And tote a pair of binoculars. This hike is recognized by the Audubon Society for it's diversity of bird species - you won't want to miss a close-up of your favorite tweeter. For more information: (520) 398-2522.

Directions: Trailheads are located in Tubac Presidio State Historic Park, or north of Tumacacori National Historic Park.

WENDEN

<u>RECREATION</u>

ALAMO LAKE STATE PARK - Leashes

Info: Enrich your memory bank with a visit to this parkland where there's something special for everyone. Fishing fiends, pack your gear. This remote but popular area is known for bass, catfish and bluegill. Tow your own or rent a boat and relax the day away - your line in the water, your best buddy by your side. But keep your aquapup in the boat, underwater hazards such as trees, brush and cactus aren't conducive to dog paddling.

Calling all nature lovers - the park's unusual landscape offers a diverse experience for naturalists. Rockhounds will think they've found hounding heaven. With a little luck, you might uncover a specimen or two to add to your collection. Wildlife watchers, deer sightings are common and of course, there are always the antics of a squirrel or two to entertain and amuse. And birdwatchers won't be disappointed. A plentitude of waterfowl make their home in these environs, the park is the only permanent open water for miles.

For a rare opportunity to see Joshua trees and saguaros nestled together, plan a side excursion and drive sixteen miles east of the park. Look for a dirt road which leads to Highway 93 where you'll see the two specimens growing side by side.

Directions: From Highway 60 in Wenden, head north for 38 miles.

Note: $3.00 per vehicle entrance fee

Dogs May Be Unleashed Unless Otherwise Indicated

WICKENBURG

LODGING

BEST WESTERN RANCHO GRANDE MOTOR HOTEL
293 E Wickenburg Way (85358) Rates: $53-$95;
Tel: (520) 684-5445; (800) 528-1234

WESTERNER MOTEL
680 W Wickenburg Way (85358) Rates: $35-$50;
Tel: (520) 684-2493

RECREATION

VULTURE PEAK TRAIL HIKE

Intermediate/2.0 miles/1.0 hours

Info: A steep, switchbacking adventure to the summit of Vulture Mountain challenges you and the pup to a calorie burning trek as you make your way over the rugged terrain to the top. At the peak, delight in the beautiful views before beginning your downward journey. If you'd rather hike the jeep road, you'll be adding an additional four miles and two hours to the length of your trip. For more information: (520) 650-0509.

Directions: From Wickenburg, take Vulture Mine Road south for 9 miles to a jeep road on the left side of the road. The road leads east to the trailhead at the base of Vulture Mountain. This road is for four-wheel drive vehicles only. Otherwise, park at the roadside turnout and hike 2 miles to the trailhead.

Note: High clearance vehicles only for last 2 miles.

WILLCOX

LODGING

BEST WESTERN PLAZA INN
1100 W Rex Allen Dr (85643) Rates: $50-$80;
Tel: (520) 384-3556; (800) 528-1234

ECONO LODGE
724 N Bisbee Ave (85643) Rates: $40-$78;
Tel: (520) 384-4222; (800) 221-2222

MOTEL 6
921 N Bisbee Ave (85643) Rates: $27-$33;
Tel: (520) 384-2201; (800) 440-6000

ROYAL WESTERN LODGE
590 S Haskell Ave (85643) Rates: $24-$38;
Tel: (520) 384-2266

RECREATION

BOOTLEGGER TRAIL HIKE
Expert/4.0 miles/2.0 hours

Info: Describing this trail as steep is an understate-
ment. Be prepared for a tough workout on this connector trail which climbs 500 feet in under a half-
mile. This trail is for experienced hikers and hiking
hounds only. But if you've got the stuff, you'll
enjoy it enough. You can turn the hike into a looping adventure by hooking up with Crest Trail #270
at two points, one at the beginning and one at the
end. For more information: (520) 364-3468.

Directions: Head south on Highway 186 to
Highway 181, turn left. Follow Highway 181 to FR
42. Take FR 42 south for 12 miles to FR 42D and go
south to the Rustler Park Campground. To access
Bootlegger Trail, you need to hike along the Crest
Trail #270 for .4 miles.

Dogs May Be Unleashed Unless Otherwise Indicated

CLARK PEAK TRAIL HIKE

Beginner/2.0 miles/1.0 hours

Info: This trail covers the three beginner basics - short, simple and scenic. Sofa loafers are sure to give this excursion two paws up. The hike begins at 8,985 feet and then climbs a short distance to 9,006 feet. Lazy day level, the scenery is beautiful and you can't beat the pure mountain air.

In springtime, the meadows along the trail to aspen-clad Clark Peak come alive in a brilliant display of flower power. In the fall, the aspens take center stage, their leaves quaking and shaking in golden splendor.

At the beginning of the trail, you'll have a short upward climb and then it's smooth sailing to the peak. The turnoff is unmarked so be alert for a rock cairn and a dead tree marking the point where the trail branches off to Clark Peak. You'll know you missed the turnoff if you begin a descent along a maze of switchbacks. Merely turn around the look again - it's there and it's worth the effort to find it. Good hunting and great hiking! For more information: (520) 428-4150.

Directions: Take Interstate 10 east to Highway 191 northbound. Follow to the Swift Trail turnoff (State 366) on the left. Continue on Swift Trail for 35 miles (vehicles over 26 feet are not recommended on this road). The trailhead is approximately 1.5 miles past the Riggs Lake turnoff. Depending upon weather conditions, the road is closed from mid-November to Memorial Day.

CREST TRAIL HIKE

Expert/8.0 miles/5.0 hours

Info: You'll have to make tracks up the mountainside on this hike in the Chiricahua Wilderness as this trail climbs to 9,797-foot Chiricahua Peak. The trail is not for the padded of paw, so be prepared for rough going. But the goodies along the way and atop the peak should provide the impetus to make this trek.

You'll traverse dense ponderosa and aspen woodlands and be serenaded by robins and whippoorwills along the way. You'll also encounter a number of parklike areas, perfect for a game of fetch. Pack a frisbee or a favorite tennis ball - this is definitely green scene territory. In the springtime, the meadows of the grassy areas are strewn with vibrant wildflowers. But for a wildflower display that is certain to knock your socks off, visit in mid-June when the mountainsides explode with Rocky Mountain iris. Look for the most dramatic display at Round Park. When you finally reach the crest, and proudly stand atop the heaven-kissing peak, you'll be rewarded with seemingly endless, breathtaking vistas. If you don't mind hiking with a full load, tote your camera and binoculars too. You won't want to miss any of it. Chill out, enjoy your efforts and then take it nice and easy on the return voyage. For more information: (520) 364-3468.

Directions: Take Highway 186 southeast to Highway 181 east. Head south on Pinery Canyon Road approximately 10 miles to Onion Saddle. Go south for about 4 miles to Long Park's parking area. Four-wheel drive is recommended for the last 2 miles. Remember to use caution, mountain roads are winding and narrow.

Note: A high clearance vehicle is required for last 2 miles.

Dogs May Be Unleashed Unless Otherwise Indicated

IDA PEAK TRAIL HIKE

Expert/5.4 miles/3.0 hours

Info: This trip is strenuous and demanding, yet beautifully unforgettable. A 2,000-foot switchbacking climb culminates with great vistas of Pinery Canyon. The beginning of the hike leads through yucca, juniper and scrub oak. The middle section passes through an area devastated by the Ida Burn Fire in 1953. Take a moment to marvel at the rebirth of the terrain. The final part of the hike journeys through pine woodlands. Once atop Ida Saddle, either retrace your steps or if you and your sidekick are up to more, continue another mile to Barefoot Park. For more information: (520) 364-3468.

Directions: Take Highway 186 south 23 miles to Highway 181. Head east on Highway 181 for 4 miles to FR 42 south. Follow FR 42 for 6 miles to FR 42C. FR 42C leads to the trailhead.

MIDDLEMARCH CANYON TRAIL HIKE

Expert/4.6 miles/2.5 hours

Info: A no-nonsense butt-kicker of a hike, don't even attempt it unless you and Hercules are up to the challenge. The trail escalades over the rugged terrain of the Dragoon Mountains - an historic route used by Native Americans, the military, miners and ranchers. It is not well-maintained and sometimes difficult to follow. Don't end up on one of the cow paths. Do an about-face whenever you've had enough. For more information: (520) 364-3468.

Directions: Take Interstate 10 west to Highway 191 south. Follow Highway 191 for 13 miles, turning right on FR 345 (Middlemarch Road) for 7 miles to FR 4388. The trailhead is at the end of FR 4388.

MORSE CANYON TRAIL to JOHNSON SADDLE HIKE

Intermediate/4.0 miles/2.0 hours

Info: For a healthy dose of Rexercise, try this steep trail which climbs through the Chiricahua Mountains. You'll journey amidst a dense ponderosa pine forest before reaching your destination - Johnson Saddle. This hike offers a great escape from the summer heat. Or visit in autumn when orange, red and yellow splash the mountainous terrain in a riot of color.

If the views from the Saddle have just whet your appetite, continue another two miles to Monte Vista Peak where some of the finest panoramas in southeastern Arizona can be found. But the trail is precipitous and the trek demanding so be sure you and Rex are up to the challenge. Whenever you've had your fill, turn around and do the descent thing. For more information: (520) 364-3468.

Directions: Take Highway 186/181 south from Willcox approximately 43 miles to the West Turkey Creek Road (FR 41) turnoff. Follow this road for about 11 miles to the trailhead.

SLAVIN GULCH TRAIL HIKE

Intermediate/5.4 miles/2.5 hours

Info: Tackle the descent through the Dragoons and find yourself in a riparian oasis. Step lightly on the steep 1,800-foot descent to the bottom of Slavin Gulch and listen for the sweet tweets of the resident songbirds that nest in the cottonwoods and sycamores. A teeming wildlife habitat, you might spot a Bambi or two. You'll also be treated to some extraordinary views of China Peak, Tombstone and the Huachuca Mountains. If you're traveling with more than just your canine buddy, consider the shuttle system as an option - the other trailhead is located at the end of FR687A. For more information: (520) 364-3468.

Directions: Take Interstate 10 west to Highway 191 south. Follow Highway 191 for 13 miles, turning right on FR 345 (Middlemarch Road) for 8 miles to FR 345A. The trailhead is at the end of FR 345A.

Note: High clearance vehicles only.

WILLIAMS

LODGING

BIG SIX MOTEL
134 E Bill Williams Ave (86046) Rates: $25+;
Tel: (520) 635-4591

BUDGET HOST INN
620 W Bill Williams Ave (86046) Rates: $20-$79;
Tel: (520) 635-4415; (800) 283-4678

CANYON MOTEL
Old E Hwy 66 (86046) Rates: $20-$45;
Tel: (520) 635-9371

DOWNTOWNER HOTEL
201 E Bill Williams Ave (86046) Rates: $30+;
Tel: (520) 635-4041

FAMILY INN
200 E Bill Williams Ave (86046) Rates: $17-$50;
Tel: (520) 635-2562

GATEWAY MOTEL
219 E Bill Williams Ave (86046) Rates: $25-$40;
Tel: (520) 635-4601

GRAND MOTEL
234 E Bill Williams Ave (86046) Rates: $24-$40;
Tel: (520) 635-4601

HIGHLANDER MOTEL
533 W Bill Williams Ave (86046) Rates: $25-$48;
Tel: (520) 635-2541

9 ARIZONA MOTEL
831 W Bill Williams Ave (86046) Rates: N/A;
Tel: (520) 635-4552

PARK INN INTERNATIONAL
710 W Bill Williams Ave (86046) Rates: $35-$85;
Tel: (520) 635-4464; (800) 733-4814

QUALITY INN-MOUNTAIN RANCH & RESORT
Rt 1, Box 35 (86046) Rates: $65-$102;
Tel: (520) 635-2693; (800) 221-2222

RAMADA INN-AT THE MOUNTAIN SIDE
642 E Bill Williams Ave (86046) Rates: $65-$125;
Tel: (520) 635-4431; (800) 272-6232

SUPER 8 MOTEL
2001 E Bill Williams Ave (86406) Rates: $45-$100;
Tel: (520) 635-4700; (800) 800-8000

TRAVELODGE
430 E Bill Williams Ave (86046) Rates: $29-$169;
Tel: (520) 635-2651; (800) 578-7878

WESTERNER MOTEL
530 W Bill Williams Ave (86046) Rates: $85+;
Tel: (520) 635-4312; (800) 385-8608

Dogs May Be Unleashed Unless Otherwise Indicated

Recreation

BENHAM TRAIL HIKE

Intermediate/9.0 miles/5.0 hours

Info: Escape the summer heat with a hike on this cool trail among pine, oak and mixed conifer woodlands on your way to the top of Bill Williams Mountain. Cover the distance on this one for a certified workout and reward yourself with panoramic views along the way and from the top. Take it easy on the return portion and enjoy the visuals from a descending perspective. For more information: (520) 635-2633.

Directions: From Williams, take 4th Street (Country Road 173) south for about 4 miles to FR 140. Take FR 140 right (west) for .2 miles to the trailhead.

BILL WILLIAMS MOUNTAIN TRAIL HIKE

Intermediate/6.0 miles/3.5 hours

Info: Boogie with Bowser up this mountainside trail. You'll climb 2,000 feet in just three miles - talk about exercise. One thing's for certain, you'll be cool as you make your way through groves of Douglas fir and aspen. At the 9,256-foot summit, you'll want to take it all in - the Verde Valley, the north rim of the Grand Canyon and distant San Francisco Peaks. This is rugged mountain country, smell the air, feel the power. For more information: (520) 635-2633.

Directions: Take Historic Route 66 west from Williams for two miles to the Camp Clover Ranger Station and the trailhead.

BIXLER SADDLE TRAIL HIKE

Intermediate/4.0 miles/2.0 hours

Info: Get an early start and spend the morning hiking this pleasant trail along the west slope of Bill Williams Mountain. You'll hike through stands of ponderosa pine, Douglas and white fir, gambel oak and aspen as you climb 1,000 feet in elevation. Shading trees and high elevation make this a great summertime outing for you and your sidekick. This is a relatively new trail and it may not be included on most area maps. Visit in early fall and experience an autumnal extravaganza. For more information: (520) 635-2633.

Directions: Take Interstate 40 west to the Devil Dog Interchange. Turn south (left) and take FR 108 for about a mile to FR 45. Turn left (east) onto FR 45 and go to the trailhead.

DAVENPORT HILL TRAIL HIKE

Intermediate/5.0 miles/2.5 hours

Info: Ascend to the top of Davenport Hill and you and the dawgus will witness changing plantlife along with changing elevation as you pass from forests of pine to fir to groves of aspen. The hike to the summit is a gradual one so that you and your hiking hound will have time to cram your RAM with the pretty scenery. Sweeping panoramas of Dogtown Lake and the picturesque countryside beckon from the hilltop knoll. For more information: (520) 635-2676.

Directions: Take Country Road 73 south for 4 miles to FR 140. Turn left (east) for 3 miles to FR 132. Turn left (north) on FR 132 and follow for one mile to the campground. Take the Nature Walk east to where the Davenport Trailhead intersects with the loop from the east.

DOGTOWN LAKE TRAIL HIKE

Beginner/1.8 miles/1.0 hours

Info: Treat Rover to a pleasant, lakeside stroll along this flat, easy trail. The hike is such a breeze that you may opt for seconds. Speaking of seconds, a picnic lunch can be a perfect ending to a perfect hike. Please remain on the designated trail - do not disturb the fragile shoreline terrain. For more information: (520) 635-2676.

Directions: Take Country Road 73 south for 4 miles to FR 140. Turn left (east) for 3 miles to FR 132. Turn left (north) on FR 132 and follow for one mile to the Dogtown Recreation Area.

I-40 PARKS MULTI-USE TRAIL HIKE

Beginner/1.0 miles/0.5 hours

Info: A great leg-stretcher, you'll want to pick up a trail pamphlet before you and the pupster start out on this self-guided interpretive trail. Learn while you explore - the pamphlet and trail signs will provide some insight into the area.

Directions: Take Interstate 40 east to the Bellemont exit. Here you have to circle back to Interstate 40 and head west to the Parks Rest Area and the trailhead.

KENDRICK MOUNTAIN TRAIL HIKE

Intermediate/8.0 miles/5.0 hours

Info: For a spectacular peek from Kendrick Peak, lace up your hiking boots and have a go at this high energy trail to 10,418-foot Kendrick Peak. Views of the Grand Canyon, San Francisco Peaks, Oak Creek Canyon and the Little Colorado River Gorge should be reasons enough to meet the challenge of this difficult hike.

Locate Other Dog-Friendly Activities...Check Nearby Cities

The trail escalates through the Kendrick Mountain Wilderness, climbing over 2,000 feet in 4 miles. As you hike, the elevation change is evident as ponderosa woodlands pave the way to forests of fir and spruce. Mule deer and elk call these forests home and toward dusk, they'll often be observed grazing, usually in herds of half a dozen or more. Keep Rover's leash handy if you think he might be tempted for a better look. For more information: (520) 635-2633.

Directions: Take Interstate 40 east to the Parks exit. Make a left back across the overpass, then left again at the "T" intersection. Go right (north) on FR 141 for eight miles to the fork with FR 194. Take FR 194 northeast (right) for 4.5 miles to FR 171. Turn right (southeast), go about two miles to FR 190, turn left (north) and go one mile to the trailhead.

KEYHOLE SINK TRAIL HIKE

Beginner/4.0 miles/2.0 hours

Info: Journey back in time - 1,000 years to be exact - to the age of prehistoric artists. The volcanic walls of this beautiful box canyon are covered with ancient petroglyphs and contain the memories and stories of the long ago inhabitants of the canyon. If you and the pupster want to be enlightened, devote some extra time to wander throughout the canyon. See what you can learn about the people who etched their history upon the canyon walls. For more information: (520) 635-2676.

Directions: Take Interstate 40 east to the Pitman Valley exit. Turn left and proceed across the overpass. Turn right (east) on Route 66 for two miles to the Oak Hill Snowplay Area. Park in the lot, the trailhead is on the north side (left).

OVERLAND ROAD HISTORIC TRAIL HIKE - Leashes

Intermediate/1.0-60.0 miles/0.5-30.0 hours

Info: Leash up your best lad and journey along an old wagon trail. Cover a mile or ten along this historic road and simply enjoy your surroundings. Keep track of the time, the trail is extremely long. Retrace the pawprints for your return trip.

Directions: Take FR 141 to FR 109 and look for the trailhead at Pomeroy Tanks.

SPRING VALLEY X-COUNTRY SKI TRAILS - Leashes

Intermediate/6.5-8.0 miles/3.0-4.0 hours

Info: Sofa loafers may prefer to follow the R.S. Hill Loop, an easy 6.7 mile excursion through ponderosa pine. But if you're seeking a wee bit more of a challenge, head out to Eagle Rock Saddle, where you'll encounter a few hundred feet of steep going along the 8-mile trail. No matter which trail beckons, you and the pup will experience a pleasant afternoon in this unusual, picturesque landscape. For more information: (520) 635-2676.

Directions: Head east on Interstate 40 to the Parks exit. Go north over the interstate and turn left at the "T" intersection. At the Parks Country Store, turn right onto FR 141 and head north for 6 miles. Look for the signs on your left.

SYCAMORE RIM TRAIL HIKE - Leashes
Beginner/11.0 miles/5.5 hours

Info: This loop trail wanders amid a wooded area which is intersected by several streams and dotted with pretty ponds. Water loving pooches won't be able to resist a paw dip or two along the way in this charming area. You and Rover can ooh and aah at the stunning views of Sycamore Canyon as you mosey here and there on the trail. For more information: (520) 635-2676.

Directions: Head east on Interstate 40 to Parks exit, then go south on FR 141 for about 11 miles to FR 56. Take a right on FR 56 and follow 1.5 miles to the trailhead.

WINDOW ROCK

LODGING
NAVAJO NATION INN
48 W Hwy 264 (86515) Rates: $55-$70;
Tel: (520) 871-4108; (800) 662-6189

WINSLOW

LODGING
BEST WESTERN ADOBE INN
1701 N Park Dr (86047) Rates: $47-$66;
Tel: (520) 289-4638; (800) 528-1234

BEST WESTERN TOWN HOUSE LODGE
1914 W Third St (86047) Rates: $36-$56;
Tel: (520) 289-4611; (800) 528-1234

Dogs May Be Unleashed Unless Otherwise Indicated

COMFORT INN
520 Desmond St (86047) Rates: $44-$68;
Tel: (520) 289-9581; (800) 221-2222

ECONO LODGE
1706 N Park Dr (86047) Rates: $32-$49;
Tel: (520) 289-4687; (800) 424-4777

SUPER 8 MOTEL
1916 W Third St (86047) Rates: $37-$57;
Tel: (520) 289-4606; (800) 800-8000

RECREATION

HOMOLOVI II RUIN TRAIL HIKE - Leashes

Beginner/1.0 miles/0.5 hours

Info: More accessible than a time capsule, hop aboard this trail for a journey back in time to the 14th century - the golden age of the ancient Hopi. This historic path will guide you through Homolovi Ruins State Park to the largest pueblo ruins, the ancestral homes of the Hopi people. Stop by the visitor center for more detailed information on the history of this intriguing area. For more information: (520) 289-4106.

Directions: From Winslow, drive east on Interstate 40 to Highway 87 north. Follow Highway 87 for 1.3 miles, turning left at the visitor center for Homolovi Ruins State Park.

Note: $3 per vehicle entrance fee

LITTLE PAINTED DESERT PARK - Leashes

Info: Red, green, violet and gray vistas carved by the desert winds await your exploration at this little known park. Take in the view from the scenic overlook, or view and do lunch in the picnic area.

Directions: Drive east on Interstate 40 to Highway 87 north. Take Highway 87 for 13 miles to the park and turn off just before the Reservation.

SOLDIER TRAIL HIKE

Expert/4.0 miles/2.5 hours

Info: Not only is this hike physically challenging, it's also navigationally difficult at times. But if you or your hiking hound possess a keen sense of direction, you should be able to find your way. For the most part, this trail traverses the bottom of East Clear Creek before climbing the west canyon wall of the creek. Kodak moments can be captured along the trail. Pack your camera and lots of film for the stunning vistas you'll encounter. For more information: (520) 477-2255.

Directions: Head south on Highway 87 to FR 319E west. Follow to FR 319D and head south to the trailhead.

Note: This trail is impassable during high water.

YOUNG

RECREATION

MURPHY RANCH TRAIL HIKE - Leashes

Intermediate/2.2 miles/1.0 hours

Info: Downward ho and back up you go. This trail plummets 800 feet in 1.1 miles until it intersects with the Rim Trail, the end of the line for you and Rover and the beginning of your rigorous upward climb. Plan a midway pawse and do lunch - make the most of your wilderness experience. For more information: (520) 462-3311.

Directions: Take Highway 288 South to FR 487. Go east on FR 487 for 4.5 miles to FR 487A. Take a right and go .5 miles until you reach Murphy Ranch.

PLEASANT VALLEY VISTA TRAIL HIKE

Beginner/0.8 miles/0.5 hours

Info: Aptly named, this trail is definitely pleasant and extremely scenic. Bring your camera and lots of film. For more information: (520) 462-3311.

Directions: Take Highway 88 approximately 2 miles south of the town of Young.

RIM TRAIL HIKE - Leashes

Beginner/1.0-15.2 miles/0.5-7.5 hours

Info: This is a definite tail wagger of a hike and a definite must for nature lovers. It's easy to reach, simple to do and beautiful in every way. As you stroll through the aromatic, plush pine forestland, you'll be startled by the unexpected beauty of the surrounding landscape. Tote a camera and lots of film, the view of box canyons and graded cliffs will overwhelm you and eat your Fuji. It's easy to lose track of time, so travel with a watch and allow enough daylight hours for your return trip. For more information: (520) 462-3311.

Directions: Take Highway 288 south to FR 487. Take 487 to 487A to Murphy Ranch. From Roosevelt or Globe, take Highway 88 to Highway 288. Go north to FR 487 and drive about 4 miles to reach the trailhead.

YOUNGSTOWN

LODGING

MOTEL 6
11133 Grand Ave (85363) Rates: $35-$41;
Tel: (602) 977-1318; (800) 440-6000

YUMA

LODGING

BEST WESTERN CHILTON INN & CONFERENCE CENTER
300 E 32nd St (85364) Rates: $59-$99;
Tel: (520) 344-1050; (800) 528-1234

BEST WESTERN CORONADO MOTOR HOTEL
233 4th Ave (85364) Rates: $35-$90;
Tel: (520) 783-4453; (800) 528-1234

BEST WESTERN INNSUITES HOTEL YUMA
1450 S Castle Dome Ave (85365) Rates: $59-$119;
Tel: (520) 783-8341;
(800) 528-1234 (US); (800) 922-2034 (AZ)

Dogs May Be Unleashed Unless Otherwise Indicated

CARAVAN OASIS MOTEL
10574 Fortuna Rd (85365) Rates: $25-$43;
Tel: (520) 342-1292

HOLIDAY INN EXPRESS
3181 S 4th Ave (85364) Rates: $55-$85;
Tel: (520) 344-1402; (800) 465-4329

INTERSTATE 8 INN
2730 S 4th Ave (85364) Rates: $33+;
Tel: (520) 726-6110; (800) 821-7465

MOTEL 6
1640 S Arizona Ave (85364) Rates: $25-$31;
Tel: (520) 782-6561; (800) 440-6000

MOTEL 6
1445 E 16th St (85365) Rates: $27-$33;
Tel: (520) 782-9521; (800) 440-6000

PARK INN INTERNATIONAL
2600 S 4th Ave (85364) Rates: $66-$96;
Tel: (520) 726-4830; (800) 437-7275

ROYAL MOTOR INN
2941 S 4th Ave (85364) Rates: $40-$110;
Tel: (520) 344-0550; (800) 729-0550

SHILO INN-YUMA CONVENTION RESORT
1550 S Castle Dome Rd (85365) Rates: $83-$105;
Tel: (520) 782-9511; (800) 222-2244

TRAVELODGE-YUMA AIRPORT
711 East 32nd St (85365) Rates: $41-$65;
Tel: (520) 726-4721; (800) 578-7878

YUMA CABANA MOTEL
2151 S 4th Ave (85364) Rates: $25-$65;
Tel: (520) 783-8311; (800) 874-0811

Locate Other Dog-Friendly Activities...Check Nearby Cities

RECREATION

BETTY'S KITCHEN INTERPRETIVE TRAIL HIKE

Beginner/1.0 miles/0.5 hours

Info: Education is the main objective of this scenic, interpretive trail. As you and your pooch stroll along the Colorado River, you'll learn interesting tidbits about the area's flora and fauna. Black willow, honey mesquite, screw bean, arrowweed and Fremont cottonwood are native to this riparian area. Pick up a trail guide before setting out - it'll make the hike even more interesting and enjoyable. For more information: (520) 726-6300.

Directions: Head east on Highway 95 for 7 miles to Avenue 7E, turn north. Follow this road to Laguna Dam. Just past the dam, make a left at the sign for Betty's Kitchen Wildlife and Interpretive Area.

CABALLERO PARK - Leashes

Info: Sports facilities, picnic areas and a small grassy section comprise this park which adjoins Desert Sun Stadium and Complex.

Directions: Take A Avenue south to 34th Street.

CARVER PARK - Leashes

Info: Even though this park is sports-oriented, you and the pupster can make your own fun at this 17-acre stretch of land.

Directions: Located on the corner of 5th Street and 13th Avenue.

J.F. KENNEDY MEMORIAL PARK - Leashes

Info: You'll be able to find enough of a green scene at this sports-galore park to make for a pleasurable jaunt.

Directions: Located at 24th Street and Kennedy Lane.

JOE HENRY MEMORIAL PARK - Leashes

Info: This pleasant 12-acre shaded park fills the bill for your pooch's constitutions.

Directions: Take 1st Street to 23rd Avenue. Turn north to Colorado Street and the park.

LIBRARY PARK - Leashes

Info: This quiet, picturesque park surrounds the Yuma City Library. Offering 4.5 acres of grass, shade, benches and tables, it's a nice getaway from the highway buzz.

Directions: Located on 3rd Street between 3rd and 4th Avenues.

PAINTED DESERT TRAIL HIKE

Beginning/1.0 miles/1.0 hours

Info: Peace and tranquility can be yours on this short looping trail through the Imperial National Wildlife Refuge. But remember you're still in desert country - dry, hot and thorny. Keep an eye on Snoopy, because if he is snooping under rocks and between crevices, he might uncover an unwanted find.

The first section of trail stretches alongside a wash and leads into an area of lava and unusual rock formations, compliments of a volcanic eruption over 25 million years ago. You'll traverse ridgetops and collect magnificent vistas before looping around and beginning your return via another scenic wash. This part of the Sonoran Desert is home to bighorn sheep, wild burros and mule deer. It's also hot and dry. Avoid in summer and always carry sufficient water for you and the pupster. Pick up a trail guide at the trailhead and make your hike more interesting and educational. For more information: (520) 783-3371.

Directions: On Highway Route 95, 26 miles north of Yuma is the Martinez Lake/Imperial National Wildlife Refuge turnoff. It's about ten miles up to Martinez Lake - take Red Cloud Mine Road to the Imperial Wildlife Refuge. It is about three miles north on a maintained dirt road to the Refuge. There the road forks, to the left leads to the Refuge headquarters where you can get information and pamphlets. To the right, three more miles on a now unmaintained road is the Painted Desert Trailhead.

RIVERSIDE PARK - Leashes

Info: Just below the famous Yuma Territorial Prison on the banks of the Colorado River, this small park provides a break from the drive across the desert.

Directions: Take Giss Parkway east to Prison Hill Road. Follow Prison Hill north to the parking area.

SANGUINETTI MEMORIAL PARK - Leashes

Info: This 5-acre park is good for a quickie stop and look-see.

Directions: Located at 23rd Street and 6th Avenue.

SMUCKER PARK - Leashes

Info: Put on your jogging shoes for this park. There's a track where you and the dawgus can get your Rexercise or find a shady spot and chill out.

Directions: Located on the corner of A Avenue and 28th Street.

YUMA RIVERWALK HIKE - Leashes

Beginner/1.8 miles/1.0 hours

Info: Treat Fido to a pleasant jaunt beside the Colorado River and a little cool off time. In addition to the plentitude of birds and birdwatchers that this riparian oasis attracts, this area has some historic significance as well. Aside from the prison and quartermaster depot, you'll saunter along Yuma Crossing, a section once traversed by early pioneers, explorers, Indians and armies. For more information: (520) 783-4771.

Directions: Located at the guard tower of Yuma Territorial Prison State Historic Park off Interstate 8.

LET'S GET READY TO TRAVEL BY CAR

"Kennel Up"...the magical, all-purpose command

When Rosie and Maxwell's training began, I used a metal kennel which they were taught to regard as their spot, their sleeping place. Whenever they were left at home and then again when they were put to bed at night, I used the simple command, "Kennel Up," as I pointed to and touched their kennel. They quickly learned the command. As they outgrew the kennel, the laundry room became their "kennel up" place. As full-grown dogs, the entire kitchen became their "kennel up" spot. Likewise, when they began accompanying me on trips, I reinforced the command each time I told them to jump into the car. They soon understood that being in their "kennel up" place meant that I expected them to stay quietly and behave, whether they were at home, in the car or in a hotel room. There isn't a better tip I can pass along.

Old dogs can learn new tricks

When we first began vacationing with Rosie and Max, some friends decided to join us on a few of our local jaunts. Their dog Brandy, a ten-year old Cocker Spaniel, had never traveled with them. Other than trips to the vet and the groomer, she'd never been in the car. The question remained... would Brandy adjust? We needn't have worried. She took to the car immediately. Despite her small size, she quickly learned to jump in and out of the rear of their station wagon. She ran through the forests with Rosie and Max, playing and exploring as if she'd always had free run. To her owners and to Brandy, the world took on new meaning. Nature as seen through the eyes of their dog became a more exciting place of discovery.

Can my pooch be trained to travel?

Dogs are quite adaptable and responsive and patience will definitely have its rewards. Your pooch loves nothing more than to be with you. If it means behaving to have that privilege, he'll respond.

Now that you've decided to travel and vacation with your dog, it's probably a good idea to get him started with short trips. Before you go anywhere, remember two of the most important items for happy dog travel, a leash for safety and the proper paraphernalia for clean up. There's nothing more frustrating or scary than a loose, uncontrolled dog. And nothing more embarrassing than being without clean-up essentials when your dog unexpectedly decides to relieve himself.

Make traveling an enjoyable experience. Stop every so often and do fun things. As you lengthen travel times, don't think that you have to stop every hour or so. Handle your dog as you would at home. He won't have to walk any more frequently. But when you do stop to let him out, leash him before you open the car doors.

When the walk or playtime is over, remember to use the "Kennel Up" command when you tell your pooch to get into the car or into his kennel. And use lots of praise when he obeys the command.

You'll find that your dog will most likely be lulled to sleep by the motion of the car. When I travel with Rosie and Maxwell, after less than fifteen minutes, they're both asleep. When we vacation together, I stop every few hours to give them water and let them "stretch their legs." They've become accustomed to these short stops and anticipate them. The moment the car is turned off and the hatch-back popped open, they anxiously await their leashes. When our romping time is over and we're back at the car, a simple "kennel up" gets them into their travel area.

To kennel or not to kennel?

Whether or not you use a kennel for car travel is a personal choice. Safety should be your primary concern. Yours and your dog's. Whatever method of travel you choose, be certain that your dog will not interfere with your driving. If you plan to use a kennel, line the bottom with an old blanket, towel or shredded newspaper. Include a treat or chew toy to keep him amused. When you're vacationing by car and not using a kennel, consider a car harness.

If it's your habit not to use a kennel or harness, confine your dog to the back seat and command him to "kennel up." Protect your upholstery by covering the rear seat with an old blanket. The blanket will make clean up that much easier at the end of your trip. To keep my car fresh smelling and free from doggie odors, I keep a deodorizer tucked under the front seat.

How often should I stop?

Many people think that when their dogs are in the car, they have to "go" more often. Not true. Whenever you stop for yourself, let your pooch have a drink and take a walk. It's not necessary to make extra stops along the way unless your dog has a physical problem and must be walked more often. Always pull your car out of the flow of traffic so you can safely care for your pooch. Never let your dog run free. Use a leash at all times. Since your pooch is in unfamiliar territory, he can bolt into traffic, be injured, become lost or run away.

Can my dog be left alone in the car?

Even if you think you'll only be gone a few minutes, that's all it takes for a dog to become dehydrated. Even if all the windows are open, even if your car is parked in the shade, even when the outside temperature is only 85° the temperature in a parked car can reach 100° to 120° in thirty minutes. Exposure to high temperatures, even for short periods, can cause brain damage and possibly death.

NEVER LEAVE YOUR DOG UNATTENDED IN WARM WEATHER.

During the winter months, you should also be aware of hypothermia, a life threatening condition when an animal's body temperature falls below normal. In particular, short-haired dogs and toys are very susceptible to illness in extremely cold weather.

What about carsickness?

Just like people, some dogs are queasier than others. And for some reason, puppies suffer more frequently from motion sickness. It's best to wait a couple of hours after your dog has eaten before beginning your trip. Or better yet, feed your dog after you arrive at your destination. Keep the windows open enough to allow in fresh air. If your pooch has a tendency to be carsick, sugar can help. Give your dog a tablespoon of honey or a small piece of candy before beginning your trip (**NO CHOCOLATE**).

That should help settle his stomach. If you notice that he looks sickly, stop and allow him some additional fresh air.

What about identification if my dog runs off?

As far as identification, traveling time is no different than staying at home. Never allow your pooch to be anywhere without proper identification. ID tags should provide your dog's name, your name, address and phone number. Most states require dog owners to purchase a license every year. The tag usually includes a license number that is registered with your state. If you attach the license tag to your dog's collar and you become separated, your dog can be traced. There are also local organizations that help reunite lost pets and owners. The phone numbers of these organizations can be obtained from local police authorities.

MY POOCH'S IDENTIFICATION

In the event that your dog is lost or stolen, the following information will help describe your pooch. Before leaving on your first trip, take a few minutes to fill out this form, make a duplicate, and then keep them separate but handy.

Answers to the name of: _____

Breed or mix: _____

Sex: _____ Age: _____ Tag ID#: _____

Description of hair (color, length and texture): ____

_____

Indicate unusual markings or scars: _____

_____

_____

TAIL: ( ) Short   ( ) Screw-type   ( ) Bushy   ( ) Cut

EARS: ( ) Clipped   ( ) Erect   ( ) Floppy

Weight: _____ Height: _____

If you have a recent photo of your pet, attach it to this form.

27
Things To Know
When Driving To Your Destination

1. Keep your dog confined with either a crate, barrier or car seat.

2. To avoid sliding in the event of sharp turns or sudden stops, be certain that your luggage, as well as your dog's crate are securely stored or fastened.

3. Be certain your vehicle is in good working order. Check brakelights, turn signals, hazard and headlights. Clean your windshield and top off washer fluid whenever you fill up. You'll be driving in unfamiliar territory so keep an eye on the gas gauge. Fill up when your tank goes below half full. And fill up during daylight hours or at well-lit service stations.

4. A first aid kit, an extra blanket, and sweets like hard candy will come in handy. When packing, include a flashlight, tool kit, paper towels, an extra leash, waterproof matches and a handy supply of plastic bags. If you'll be traveling during the winter months, include an ice scraper, snow brush and small shovel in your car.

5. Never drive tired. Keep the music on, windows open. Fresh air can help you remain alert.

6. Keep your windshield clean, inside and out.

7. Avoid using sedatives or tranquilizers when driving.

8. Don't drink and drive.

9. Never try to drive and read a map at the same time. If you're driving alone, pull off at a well-lit gas station or roadside restaurant and check the map. If you're unsure of directions, ask for assistance from a safe source.

10. Wear your seatbelt. They save lives.

11. Keep car doors locked.

12. Good posture is especially important when driving. Do your back a favor and sit up straight. For lower back pain, wedge a small pillow between your back and the seat.

13. If you're the driver, eat frequent small snacks rather than large meals. You'll be less tired that way.

14. Don't use high beams in fog. The light will bounce back into your eyes as it reflects off the moisture.

15. When pulling off to the side of the road, use your flashers to warn other cars away.

16. Before beginning your drive each day, do a car check. Tire pressure okay? Leakage under car? Windows clean? Signals working? Mirrors properly adjusted? Gas tank full?

17. Roads can become particularly slippery at the onset of rain, the result of water mixing with dust and oil on the pavement. Slow down and exercise caution in wet weather.

18. Every so often, turn off your cruise control. Overuse can often lull you into inattention.

19. If you'll be doing a lot of driving into the sun, put a towel over the dashboard. It will provide some relief from the heat and brightness.

20. Even during the cooler months, your car can become stuffy. Keep your windows or sun roof open and let fresh air circulate.

21. Kids coming along? A small tape or CD player can amuse youngsters. Hand-held video games are also entertaining. And action figures are a good source for imaginary games. Put together a travel container and include markers or colored pencils, stamps, stickers, blunt safety scissors, and some pads of paper, both colored and lined.

22. If your car trip requires an overnight stay on route to your destination, pack a change of clothing and other necessities in a separate bag. Keep it in an accessible location.

23. When visiting wet and/or humid climates, take along insect repellent.

24. Guard against temperature extremes. In hot weather, protect your skin from the effects of the sun. Hazy days are just as dangerous to your skin as sunny ones. Pack plenty of sun-screen. Apply in the morning and then again in the early afternoon. The sun is strongest midday so avoid overexposure at that time. To remain comfortable, wear lightweight, loose fitting cotton clothing. Choose light colors. Dark ones attract the sun. In dry climates, remember to drink lots of liquids. Because the evaporation process speeds up in arid areas, you won't be aware of how much you're perspiring.

25. In cold climes, protect yourself from frostbite. If the temperature falls below 32° fahrenheit and the wind chill factor is also low, frostbite can occur in a matter of minutes. Layer your clothing. Cotton next to your skin and wool over that is the best insulator. Wear a hat to keep yourself warm - body heat escapes very quickly through your head.

26. Changes in altitude can cause altitude sickness. Whenever possible, slowly accustom yourself to the altitude change. Don't overexert yourself either. Symptoms of high altitude sickness occur more frequently over 8,000 feet and include dizziness, shortness of breath and headaches.

27. Store your maps, itinerary and related travel information in a clear plastic container (shoe box storage type with a lid works best). Keep it in the front of your vehicle in an easy-to-reach location.

WHAT YOU SHOULD KNOW ABOUT DRIVING IN THE DESERT

Water: Check your radiator before journeying into the desert. Outside of metropolitan areas, service stations are few and far between, even on major roads. Always carry extra water.

Gasoline: Since you'll be traveling through sparsely populated areas, fill up before beginning your desert adventure. When you have half a tank or less, refuel whenever you come upon a service station - you never know when you'll come across another.

Flashfloods: Summer thunderstorms can wreak havoc on the Arizona road system, especially where roads dip into washes. The run-off quickly fills the washes, creating hazardous driving conditions and impassable roads. Heed the warning signs which pinpoint flash flood areas.

Duststorms: When a duststorm approaches, pull your vehicle off the road as far as possible, switch off your headlights and wait until the storm passes.

Breakdowns: Put on your hazard lights or raise the hood of your vehicle and remain with your vehicle until help arrives. Keep doors locked and do not open doors except for police officers. If you break down on a secluded back road and must seek help, retrace your route. Don't take any short cuts.

Desert survival

Acquiring the skills necessary to survive in the desert isn't the responsibility of just hikers and campers - any one of us could end up lost or stranded in the desert. All it takes is a flat tire, a wrong turn or a sprained ankle/paw and suddenly you're faced with a dire situation which requires survival skills you may or may not have. Remain calm. Think through your options. Use common sense and remain focused. Survivalists recommend that you stay with your vehicle. Do not attempt to walk through the desert. Dehydration, exposure and exhaustion are killers.

The best way to handle survival situations is to avoid them. But when you find yourself in a survival situation, the following tips may help.

- Pre-plan your hike and become familiar with the area.

- Know where the water sources are in the area you're hiking.

- Familiarize yourself with the local weather conditions.

- Avoid intense desert heat by taking early morning or evening hikes.

- Always carry a topographical map of the area you're hiking.

- Avoid sidetrips, they may only confuse you and cause you to lose your bearings.

- Carry as much drinking water as possible - it can save your life.

- If you're planning an overnight, establish camp near water.

- Inform a third party where you're going and when you'll be home. And then contact the person upon your return.

- Never overestimate your hiking abilities - know your limits.

Heat Stroke / Exhaustion

Both newcomers and longtime desert dwellers are susceptible to these potentially serious medical conditions. Early heat exhaustion indicators include: weakness, pale skin, dizziness, nausea, dehydration, muscle cramping and profuse sweating. Heat stroke symptoms include the above along with hot, dry, red skin. In either case, seek shade, cool off by fanning and apply damp cloths to face, neck and ears. Cases of heat stroke demand immediate medical attention.

Hypothermia

Although hypothermia is a serious medical condition most commonly associated with mountain hiking, desert hikers and campers are also susceptible. Temperatures do not have to dip below freezing for exposure to occur. In fact, hypothermia strikes most often in the 30-50° temperature range - a common temperature for winter nights in the desert. Damp clothing and a cool breeze can sometimes be enough to cause the body to lose heat faster than it can be replaced - causing cold shivers. If you experience unstoppable shivering, it's imperative that you put on dry clothes, wrap yourself in a blanket and drink hot liquids. Without these precautions, you can lapse into the second, and often fatal stage of hypothermia. When that occurs, there is little chance of the body rewarming itself without the aid of internal heating, conventional heating methods and immediate medical attention.

Keep your cool

- When traveling with Fido, it's a good idea to keep a cooler of cold towels in the car. Cold towels help to bring down a dog's body temperature after a long afternoon of hiking

- A wet handkerchief wrapped around your neck can keep you and Fido cool while hiking.

TRAVEL TRAINING

A well-trained, well-behaved dog is easy to live with and especially easy to travel with. There are basics other than "sit," "down," "stay" which you might want to incorporate into your training routine. Whenever you begin a training session, remember that your patience and your dog's attention span are the key elements. Training sessions should be 5-10 minutes each. Don't let yourself become discouraged or frustrated. Stick with it. After just a few lessons, your dog will respond. Dogs love to learn, to feel productive and accomplished. Training isn't punishment. It's a gift. A gift of love. You'll quickly see the difference training can make. Being with your dog will become a pleasant experience, something you'll anticipate, not dread. Most of all, keep a sense of humor. It's not punishment for you either.

Throughout this section, many references are made to puppies. But it's never too late for training to begin. The adage that you can't teach an old dog new tricks just isn't true. Patience and consistency combined with a reward system will provide excellent results.

Let's get social

When it comes to travel training, not enough can be said about the benefits of socialization. I regard the lessons of socialization as the foundation of a well-trained, well-behaved dog.

Whenever possible socialize your dog at an early age. Allow your puppy to be handled by many different people. Include men and children since puppies are inherently more fearful of both. At three months, you can join a puppy class. These classes are important because they provide puppies with the experience of being with other dogs. Your puppy will have the opportunity of putting down other dogs without inflicting harm and he'll also learn how to bounce back after being put down himself. Socialization can also be accomplished through walks around your neighborhood, visits to parks frequented by other dogs and children, or by working with friends who have dogs they also want to socialize.

Bite inhibition

The trick here is to keep a puppy from biting in the first place, not break the bad habit after it's formed, although that too can be accomplished. Your puppy should be taught to develop a soft mouth by inhibiting the force of his bites. As your dog grows into adolescence, he should continue to be taught to soften his bite and as an adult dog should learn never to mouth at all.

Allow your puppy to bite but whenever force is exhibited, say OUCH! If he continues to bite, say OUCH louder and then leave the room. When you return to the room, let the puppy come next to you and calm down. Your pup will begin to associate the bite and OUCH with the cessation of playtime and will learn to mouth more softly. Even when your puppy's bites no longer hurt, pretend they do. Once this training is finished, you'll have a dog that will not mouth. A dog who will not accidentally injure people you meet during your travels.

Chewing

Most dogs chew out of boredom. Teach your dog constructive chewing and eliminate destructive chewing. Teach your dog to chew on chew toys. An easy way to interest him in chewing is to stuff a hollow, nonconsumable chew toy with treats such as peanut butter, kibble or a piece of hard cheese. Once the toy is stuffed, attach a string to it and tempt your dog's interest by pulling the toy along. He'll take it from there.

Until you're satisfied that he won't be destructive, consider confining your pooch to one room or to his crate with a selection of chew toys. This is a particularly important training tool for dogs who must be left alone for long periods of time, and for dogs who travel with their owners. If your pooch knows not to chew destructively at home, those same good habits will remain with him on the road.

Walking on a leash

The same "paying attention" rules apply here. It's only natural for a puppy to pull at his leash. Instead of just pulling back, stop walking. Hold the leash to your chest. If your dog lets the leash slacken, say GOOD DOG. If he sits, say GOOD SIT. Then begin your walk again. Stop every ten feet or so and tell your dog to sit. Knowing he'll only be told to sit if he pulls, he'll eventually learn to pay attention to the next command. It makes sense to continue your training while on walks because your dog will learn to heed your commands under varying circumstances and environments. This will be especially important when traveling together. The lack of "tug of war" can mean the difference between enjoying or disliking the company of your pooch at home or away.

Jumping dogs

Dogs usually jump on people to get their attention. A fairly simple way to correct this habit is to teach your dog to sit and stay until released. When your dog is about to meet new people, put him in the sit/stay position. Be sure to praise him for obeying the command and then pet him to give him the attention he craves. Ask friends and visitors to help reinforce the command.

Come

The secret to this command is to begin training at an early age. But as I've said before, older dogs can also learn. It might just take a little longer. From the time your pup's brought home, call him by name and say COME every time you're going to feed him. The association will be simple. He'll soon realize that goodies await him if he responds to your call. Try another approach as well. Sit in your favorite armchair and call to your dog every few minutes. Reward him with praise and sometimes with a treat. Take advantage of normally occurring circumstances, such as your dog approaching you. Whenever you can anticipate that your dog is coming toward you, command COME as he nears you. Then reward him with praise for doing what came naturally.

NEVER order your dog to COME for a punishment. If he's caught in the act of negative behavior, walk to him and then reprimand.

Pay attention

Train your dog to listen to you during his normal routines. For example, when your dog is at play in the yard, call him to you. When he comes, have him sit and praise him. Then release him to play again. It will quickly become apparent that obeying will not mean the end of playtime. Instead it will mean that he'll be petted and praised and then allowed to play again.

Communication - talking to your dog

Training isn't just about teaching your dog to sit or give his paw. Training is about teaching your pooch to become an integral part of your life. To fit into your daily routine. And into your leisure time. Take notice of how your dog studies you, anticipates your next move. Incorporate his natural desire to please into your training. Let him know what you're thinking, how you're feeling. Talk to him as you go about your daily routines. He'll soon come to understand the differences in your voice, your facial expressions, hand movements and body language. He'll know when you're happy or angry with him or with anyone else. If you want him to do something, speak to him. For example, if you want him to fetch his ball, ask him in an emphatic way, stressing the word ball. He won't understand at first, so fetch it yourself and tell him ball. Put the ball down and then later repeat the command. He'll soon know what you want when you use the term ball with specific emphasis.

Training Do's & Don'ts

1. Never hit your dog.

2. Praise and reward your dog for good behavior. Don't be embarrassed to lavish praise upon a dog who's earned it.

3. Unless you catch your dog in a mischievous act, don't punish him. He will not understand what he did wrong. And when you do punish, go to your dog. Never use the command COME for punishment.

4. Don't repeat a command. Say the command in a firm voice only once. If your dog doesn't obey, return to the training method for the disobeyed command.

5. Don't be too eager or too reticent to punish. Most of all, be consistent.

6. Don't encourage fearfulness. If your dog has a fear of people or places, work with him to overcome this fear rather than ignoring it, or believing it can't be changed.

7. Don't ignore or encourage aggression.

8. Don't use food excessively as a reward. Although food is useful in the beginning of training, it must be phased out as the dog matures.

8
Ways To Prevent Aggression in Your Dog

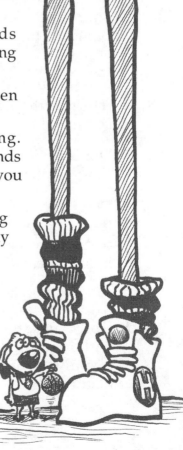

1. Socialize him at an early age.

2. Under your supervision, let him play with children.

3. Never be abusive towards your dog by hitting or yelling at him.

4. Offer plenty of praise when he's behaving himself.

5. Be consistent with training. Make sure your dog responds to your commands before you do anything for him.

6. Don't handle your dog roughly or play aggressively with him.

7. Neuter your dog.

8. Your dog is a member of the family. Treat him that way. Tied to a pole is not a life.

Lodging Guidelines For You and Your Pooch

Conduct yourself in a courteous manner and you'll continue to be welcome anywhere you travel. Never do anything on vacation with your pooch that you wouldn't do at home. Some quick tips that can make traveling with your pooch more enjoyable.

1. Don't allow your dog to sleep on the bed with you. If that's what your dog is accustomed to doing, take along a sheet or favorite blanket and put that on top of the bedding provided by your lodging.

2. Bring a towel or small mat to use under your dog's food and water dishes. Feed your dog in the bathroom where cleanup is easier should accidents occur.

3. Try to keep your dog off the furniture. Take along a washable lint and hair remover to remove unwanted hairs.

4. When you walk your dog, carry plastic bags and/or paper towels for clean up.

5. Always keep your dog on a leash on the hotel and motel grounds.

Can my pooch be left alone in the room?

Only you know the answer to that. If your dog is not destructive, if he doesn't bark incessantly, and the hotel allows unattended dogs, you might consider leaving him in the room for short periods of time — say when you dine out. In any case, hang the "Do Not Disturb" sign on your door to alert the chambermaid or anyone else that your room shouldn't be entered.

Consider doing the following when you plan to leave your dog unattended:

1. Walk or otherwise exercise your pooch. An exercised dog will fall asleep more easily.

2. Provide a chew or toy.

3. Turn on the TV or radio for audio/visual companionship.

4. Make sure there is an ample amount of fresh water available.

5. Calm your dog with a reassuring goodbye and a stroke of your hand.

Take your dog's temperament into account:

- Is he a pleaser?
- Is he the playful sort?
- Does he love having tasks to perform?
- Does he like to retrieve? To carry?

Dogs, like people, have distinct personalities... mellow, hyper, shy or outgoing. Take advantage of your dog's unique characteristics. A hyper dog can amuse you with hours of playful frolicking. A laid-back pooch will cuddle beside you offering warm companionship. An outgoing dog will help you make friends.

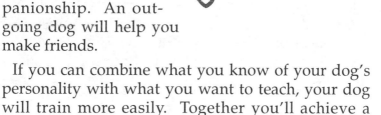

If you can combine what you know of your dog's personality with what you want to teach, your dog will train more easily. Together you'll achieve a unique compatibility.

WHAT AND HOW DO I PACK FOR MY POOCH?

Be prepared

Dogs enjoy the adventure of travel. If your dog is basically well behaved and physically healthy, he will make an excellent traveling companion. But traveling times will be more successful with just a little common sense and preparation.

Just as many children (and adults I might add) travel with their own pillow, your pooch will also enjoy having his favorites with him. Perhaps you'll want to include the blanket he sleeps with or his favorite toy or chew. Not only will a familiar item make him feel more at ease but he'll have a toy along to keep him occupied and give him something to do.

To keep things simple from vacation to vacation, I use two travel bags which I restock at the end of each vacation. That way, I'm always prepared for the next one. You'll want to include some or all of the following:

- A blanket to cover the back seat of your car.
- Two or three old towels for emergencies.
- Two bowls, one for water, the other for food.
- Plastic clean up bags (supermarket produce bags work well).
- Paper towels — for spills, clean up and everything in between.

- A long line of rope. You'll be surprised how often you'll use this very handy item.

- An extra collar and lead.

- Can opener and spoon.

- Flashlight.

- An extra flea and tick collar.

- Dog brush.

- Small scissors.

- Blunt end tweezers — great for removing thorns and cactus needles.

- Chew toys, balls, frisbees, treats — whatever your pooch prefers.

- Nightlight.

- A room deodorizer.

- A handful of zip-lock bags in several sizes.

- Pre-moistened towelettes. Take along two packs. Put one in your suitcase, the other in the glove compartment of your car. More than just great for cleaning your hands, they'll serve a dozen uses.

- Dog food — enough for a couple of days. Most brands are available throughout the country — either at pet stores, supermarkets or veterinary offices. But, you'll want to take enough to eliminate having to find a store that's open the first night or two of your vacation.

- Water — a full container from home — top off as needed to gradually accustom your dog to his new water supply.

Special tip: When hiking with your dog, large zip-lock bags make great portable water bowls. Just roll down the sides to form a bowl and add water.

Packing made easy...12 tips!

I've said it before but I'll say it again. No matter where your travels take you, whether it's to the local park or on a cross-country trip, never leave home without your dog's leash and a handful of plastic bags or pooper scooper. I still remember those awful moments when I ended up without one or both.

1. Whenever possible, consolidate. Even if you're traveling as a family, one tube of toothpaste and one hair dryer should suffice.

2. Avoid potential spills by wrapping perfume, shampoo and other liquids together and placing them in large zip-lock plastic bags.

3. When packing, layer your clothing using interlocking patterns. You'll fit more into your suitcase and have less shifting and wrinkling.

4. Keep a duplicate copy of your itinerary in a safe place. Record flight info, car rental confirmation numbers, travel agent telephone numbers, lodging info, etc.

5. Take along a night light, especially if you're traveling with a child.

6. Stash a supply of zip-lock plastic bags, moist towelettes, several trash bags, an extra leash (or rope) and a plastic container in an accessible place.

7. If you plan to hike and you're traveling with your children, give each a whistle to hang around their necks. They're great for signaling help.

8. Include a can opener and a flashlight.

9. Comfortable walking shoes are a must. If you plan on hiking, invest in a sturdy pair of hiking boots, but be sure to break them in before your trip. Take along an extra pair of socks whenever you hike.

10. Don't forget to include first aid kits. One for dogs and one for people.

11. Include an extra pair of glasses or contact lenses. And don't forget to take a copy of your eyeglass prescription.

12. Keep prescribed medications in separate, clearly marked containers.

CRATE TRAINING IS GREAT TRAINING

Many people erroneously equate the crate to jail. But that's only a human perspective. To a dog who's been properly crate trained, the crate represents a private place within your home where your dog will feel safe and secure. It is much better to prevent behavioral problems by crate training than to merely give up on an unruly dog.

4 REASONS WHY CRATE TRAINING IS GOOD FOR YOU

1. You can relax when you leave your dog home alone. You'll know that he is safe, comfortable and incapable of destructive behavior.

2. You can housebreak your pooch faster. The confinement encourages control and helps establish a regular walk-time routine.

3. You can safely confine your dog to prevent unforseen situations. For example, if he's sick, if you have workers or guests that are either afraid or allergic to dogs, or if your canine becomes easily excited or confused when new people enter the scene.

4. You can travel with your pooch. Use of a crate eliminates the potential for distraction and assures that your dog will not get loose during your travels.

5 REASONS WHY CRATE TRAINING IS GOOD FOR THE POOCH

1. He'll have an area for rest when he's tired, stressed or sick.
2. He'll be exposed to fewer bad behavior temptations which can result in punishment.
3. He'll have an easier time learning to control calls of nature.
4. He'll feel more secure when left alone.
5. He'll be thrilled to join you in your travels.

SOME DO'S AND DONT'S

- DO exercise your dog before crating and as soon as you let him out.
- DO provide your pooch with his favorite toy and blanket.
- DO place the crate in a well-used, well-ventilated area of your home.
- DO make sure that you can always approach your dog while he is in his crate. This will insure that he does not become overly protective of his space.
- DON'T punish your dog in his crate or banish him to the crate.
- DON'T leave your pooch in the crate for more than four hours at a time.
- DON'T let curious kids invade his private place. This is his special area.

- DON'T confine your dog to the crate if he becomes frantic or completely miserable.
- DON'T use a crate without proper training.

Hiking...
a walk through nature

Hiking conjures up images of rugged outdoor types, standing tall on mountaintops, wind in their hair, outfitted with sturdy, specially designed vests, pockets filled with intriguing paraphernalia.

While there might have been a time when hiking was an activity with limited appeal, America's obsession with physical fitness has changed all that. Hiking has become a popular pastime. In addition to the physical benefits associated with hiking, consider the pleasures to be found in nature. And other than the simple gear and supplies you might want to include, hiking is free.

There's something special about hiking, particularly with a canine companion. It's truly time of the highest quality. Time when the phone isn't ringing, when hours seem endless and when a little dirt is part of the experience, not a disaster. Share an invigorating hike with your pooch. It will be an experience you'll want to repeat again and again.

Hiking on a marked trail provides a sense of fulfillment and security. Both goal-oriented types who like to feel they've accomplished something and novices who want to know what to expect will appreciate marked hiking trails. Knowing the length of the trail, the time required, a bit about the terrain and the sights to be expected also adds to the pleasures of hiking.

Hiking can be a total exploration of a defined area or merely a slice of nature. You set the distances and the time. Hike in for half an hour and then retrace your steps. Do a loop trail with predetermined mileage. Or do it all, see it all.

Some words of advice for novice hikers

Begin with easy trails. Learn what to take along, what to leave at home. Find a pace that suits your walking style. For that's what hiking is — walking with a purpose. Easy trails are usually found in low lying areas. Although the terrain might change from level, even ground to more hilly contours, for the most part, you'll experience a trail without obstacles.

Intermediate level trails are more rugged. Typically, they might be found in mountainous areas. Along the trail you might have to wade through shallow streams, make your way through brush, among rocks and fallen trees. You can expect changes in elevation that will require some exertion and provide more of an aerobic workout. If you're new to hiking but in good physical condition, you shouldn't have difficulty with intermediate hiking trails. Set a comfortable pace and rest whenever you feel tired.

Expert trails are usually steeper and more challenging. Stamina, agility and fitness all come into play. You might have to scale boulders, ascend and descend precipitous escarpments or maintain your balance on slippery rocks. Expert trails should not be attempted by beginner hikers. Even intermediates should only hike the more difficult trails after they've accumulated some "hiking points" in the intermediate arena. Take into account your dog's ability as well as your own when deciding where to hike. In any case, don't hike expert trails alone, and let someone know where you're hiking and when to expect your return.

Hiking is an experience that's enjoyable to share. With your pooch, with your friends. That's not to say that solitary hikers don't enjoy themselves — many solitary hikers prefer the peacefulness of nature without the distractions of other people.

Eileen's "BE PREPARED" approach to hiking

The day hikes I've detailed in *Doin' Arizona With Your Pooch!* will be more pleasurable if you travel with a light load. Invest in a well-made, light-weight fanny pack with built-in water bottles and several zippered compartments, large enough to hold the following items.

1. Penlight size flashlight with fresh batteries and bulb.

2. A small box of waterproof matches - the type that light when scratched on just about any-thing.

3. A large trash bag, folded into a small square. This serves three purposes. It's an instant rain-coat (just punch out arm and head holes), a receptacle for trash and a seat covering for cold/wet ground.

4. A bandana. This simple cotton garment serves as a washcloth, headband, cool compress, etc. It folds up into nothing or can be worn around your neck to save fanny pack room.

5. Lip balm with UV protection.

6. Small travel size tube of sunscreen. Use in sunny or hazy weather, especially at high alti-tudes.

7. Nylon windbreaker. Many sporting goods stores sell the type that fold up and fit into their own case.

8. Soft felt hat. Great protection from the sun, it's easily stored or safety pinned to your pack.

9. A whistle. Wear it around your neck on a tripled piece of string which is also handy to have along. Three whistle blasts are the signal for help.

10. Small map magnifier (doubles as a fire starter).

11. Water bottle(s) with squirt top. If water supplies run low, a squirt in your mouth or your dog's will temporarily relieve thirst.

12. Sunglasses with UV protective lenses can be worn or left dangling on an eyeglass holder.

13. Travel-size first aid kit.

14. An extra pair of socks.

15. Grocery produce bags. They're great for doggie clean up and as an emergency barrier between wet socks and dry feet.

16. A small, non-aerosol spray can of insect repellent. Spray yourself and your pooch before the hike and leave the can in the car.

17. A couple of safety pins.

18. A multi-use, swiss army-type knife.

19. A compass if you know how to use one.

20. A map of the area or a copy of the trail description/information.

Depending on conditions, weather and personal preferences, you might also want to include:

• A walking stick for the extra balance it provides (ski poles are great).

• An extra sweater or jacket. Two or three lighter layered articles of clothing are better than one heavy garment. Layering locks in air between garments, warms the air and then warms you.

What about the pooch

Your pooch can be outfitted with side saddle bags — small but roomy enough to carry all his needs. When you pack his saddle bags, keep the weight even on both sides for balance. Include the following:

1. Water bottles with spritzer tops
2. Bones, biscuits or treats
3. Small grooming brush
4. A chamois for drying
5. An extra leash
6. A line of rope
7. A ball, soft frisbee or other favorite toy

100

Ways To Be A Better Hiker

The following tips and info will add to your enjoyment of the outdoors and help prepare you for the unexpected.

1. Never hike in a new pair of hiking boots. Always break in boots before hiking.

2. Buy smart. To get a good fit, try boots on with the type of socks you'll be wearing. COMFORT is the key word in boot selection. After comfort, look for support and traction. For day hikers, a lightweight, well-made, sturdy boot is the number one choice.

3. Water, water everywhere, but not a drop to drink. Drink plenty of water before you begin and pack enough to last through your hike. Although there may be water available trailside in the form of lakes and streams, unless you're experienced and properly prepared to purify the water, don't drink it.

4. Carry a generous supply of grocery-type plastic bags for clean up. Keep extras in your car and suitcase.

5. Dress in layers. Peel off or add clothing as weather dictates. Cotton next to the skin with wool over it is the most comfortable. The exception is during wet weather when cotton is a negative because it takes too long to dry and offers little insulation.

6. Pack extra clothing, most importantly a second pair of socks and a nylon windbreaker.

7. If your feet are cold, put on a hat. Body heat escapes through the head.

8. Before you begin your trip, make sure all hiking apparel is in good repair. Check for loose buttons, open seams, stuck zippers. Lubricate zipper slides and teeth with wax or a spray lubricant.

9. Don't litter, carry out your trash.

10. Leave only footprints, take only memories.

11. Carry a small first-aid kit and learn some basic skills.

12. Avoid wet, soggy socks and boots. If you know the trail includes crossing streams or creeks, pack a pair of all-terrain sandals to use instead of your boots. Or use plastic grocery bags under your wool socks.

13. Carry your own water and top off at every opportunity.

14. In warm weather hiking, freeze your filled water bottles the night before your trip, leaving room for expansion. Your water supply will remain cooler.

15. Take along an extra leash or line of rope for unforeseen emergencies.

16. Set a comfortable pace. Don't overexert yourself, there's always tomorrow.

17. Ski poles make great walking sticks.

18. Before you begin any hiking trip, tell a reliable person your plans. Include an estimated time for your return and make sure you let them know when you've returned.

19. Pack picnic goodies in reusable containers or plastic zip-lock bags.

20. For an instant water bowl, include a large size zip-lock bag. With the sides rolled down, it makes a terrific water bowl for your pooch.

21. Spray exposed arms, legs and face area with insect repellent. Spray your pooch too but remember to avoid spraying near the eyes.

22. Sites containing Native American relics should be treated with respect. Do not disturb or remove anything.

23. Nature is soft and serene - behave accordingly.

24. Blend in with your surroundings.

25. Wear light colored clothing. When it's warm and sunny, dark colors attract the sun and mosquitoes.

26. Every hour or so, take a ten-minute break. In warm weather, select a shady spot. In cooler weather, find a sunny, wind-protected area. In cold weather, sit on something other than the ground.

27. Should a lightning or thunderstorm occur, find shelter away from mountain peaks or exposed slopes.

28. Stow some high energy snacks in your pack. Include some biscuits and a chew for your pooch.

29. A small roll of duct tape can repair just about anything.

30. Consider your dog's age and physical capabilities when you plan trips.

31. Stop and look around and in back of you as you hike. The views are always different.

32. A large garbage bag can double as an emergency rain coat. Just punch holes for your head and arms.

33. Some basic geology knowledge will go a long way towards enhancing your outdoor experience.

34. View your surroundings as if you're in an out-door museum, you'll see and enjoy more.

35. Wear sunglasses to protect your eyes and a hat to protect your scalp from UV rays and direct sunlight.

36. Apply a minimum 15 SPF sunscreen to all exposed parts of your body, particularly your face. Reapply after swimming or after several hours.

37. Carry a UV-protected lip balm and apply frequently.

38. Always clean up after your pooch. The fact that dog owners don't clean up after their dogs is the number one complaint to federal, state and local agencies governing public lands. In some areas, dogs have been banned because of these complaints. Do your share so dogs will continue to be welcome.

39. A box of waterproof matches can be a lifesaver.

40. Keep a multi-purpose knife in your hiking gear.

41. Remember you have to walk out as far as you've walked in.

42. Don't begin a hike towards evening. Hiking in darkness is dangerous.

43. Practice trail etiquette. Allow fast-walking hikers to pass you.

44. Carry your dog's leash even in areas where he is permitted to run free.

45. Keep your dog on a leash in wildlife areas, for his protection and the protection of wildlife.

46. Dogs must be leashed in all developed camp-grounds.

47. Dogs are not permitted to swim in public pools.

48. Control your dog at all times. One unruly dog can cause problems for every dog.

49. Unless your dog responds to voice commands, keep him leashed in crowded areas or on well-used trails.

50. Certain breeds of dogs are inclined to chase wildlife. Know your own dog. If you feel he might do harm to the wildlife, the terrain or himself, keep him leashed.

51. Get into shape before your trip. Start with short walks and lengthen them, increasing your pace as you do. Take your dog along and get him in shape too.

52. Make exercise an integral part of your daily routine. Whenever there's a choice, take the stairs. Park a few streets from your destination and then walk.

53. Ten minutes of easy stretching before any physical activity will minimize the chance of injury. Avoid jerky movements. Stretch the hamstrings, shoulders, back, legs, arms and Achilles tendon.

54. Go for comfort. Avoid tight constrictive clothing.

55. Socks should fit well and be clean. Loose, ill-fitting or dirty socks can cause blisters.

56. Educate yourself on the area's flora and fauna and you'll have a more interesting hike.

57. During warmer months or in desert terrain, drink plenty of water before and during your hike. You won't always know when your body is becoming dehydrated because perspiration dries very quickly. You might not feel thirsty but your body will be.

(DON'T FORGET TO WATER THE POOCH!)

58. If you use a backpack, buy one with wide straps so it won't dig into your skin.

59. Pack a whistle - a series of three blasts is the recognized distress signal.

60. Even if you intend to begin and end your hike during daylight hours, pack a small flashlight with fresh batteries and bulb for emergencies.

61. Wear a watch or keep one handy. Time flies by without reference points. Remember, it's going to take as long to hike out as it did to hike in.

62. As the name implies, trail mix makes a great hiking snack.

63. Be prepared for unexpected weather changes. Tune in to a local radio station before beginning your hiking.

64. Hypothermia is the number one outdoor killer. As soon as you feel chilled, put on an extra layer of clothing. Don't wait until you're cold.

65. Feeling warm, remove a layer.

66. If you're hiking and rain or wet conditions are expected, don't wear cotton. Synthetic fabrics and wool offer the best insulation when wet.

67. A long time favorite of hikers are wool rag socks. Thick and absorbent, they'll keep your feet warm even when wet. They'll also provide cushioning. Take along an extra pair.

68. Liner socks are also popular. Similar to the thin socks worn under ski boots, they're usually made of wool, silk or a synthetic. Liner socks are softer to the touch and can be worn under heavier socks.

69. When hiking in cooler temperatures, two light sweaters are better than one heavy sweater.

70. Slow your pace when descending a trail to avoid potential injury.

71. If the weather turns unpredictably cold but you still want to hike, plastic produce bags can be used to keep your feet warm. Put them on your bare feet, wrap the top around your ankles and put on your socks. The plastic becomes a barrier and prevents body heat from escaping.

72. Wide brimmed soft felt hats are great for hiking. They fold up into nothing and even in hot summer months, they can be comfortable. Simply air condition them by cutting out hearts or triangles with a pair of scissors.

73. Disposable polyethylene gloves, the kind sold in paint stores, make great glove liners. They'll keep your hands toasty warm in the coldest climes.

74. An old-fashioned bandana can become a washcloth, head-band, cool compress, napkin and a dozen other useful items. Wrap one around your dog's neck too.

75. Consider side saddle bags for your pooch to wear. He'll feel productive and help carry the load.

76. A small map magnifier can double as a fire starter.

77. Disposable cameras are lightweight and easy to include on a day hike. The panoramic-type captures Arizona the best.

78. In the summer, fannypacks are cooler to use than backpacks.

79. Fruit, fresh or sun dried, is a quick energy source. Peel a couple of oranges or tangerines before your hike and store in zip-lock baggies. You'll always have a light snack at your fingertips.

80. Cut your toenails a few days before your hike or trip. Long toenails can cripple a hiker, especially descending a steep trail.

81. Before your trip, wear your pack at home with a typical load until you're certain it's comfortable.

82. If your feet or hands begin to feel swollen during your hike, find a shady tree and elevate your feet higher than your head. Hold your arms up in the air at the same time. Three minutes ought to do the trick and redistribute the blood throughout your body.

83. Begin a hike wearing only enough clothing to keep you just shy of comfortable. After the first ten minutes of exertion, you'll feel warmer and be happier with less on.

84. After walking through mud, loose dirt, sand or other clogging substances, clear your boot's cleats and restore their traction with a sharp kick at a sturdy tree or boulder.

85. Use your arms to make hiking more controlled and aerobic. Don't let them hang limply beside you. Swing them as you walk; use them for balance.

86. Take along a package of pre-moistened towelettes and travel-size tissues.

87. Take a trash bag along and clean the trail on your way out.

88. Puffy cumulus clouds usually mean fair weather.

89. A ring around the moon forecasts rain or snow.

90. Bad weather warnings — a red sky at dawn, the absence of dew on the grass or an early morning rainbow.

91. When bad weather threatens, avoid high, open places, lakes, meadows, exposed slopes and lone or towering trees. Seek shelter in caves, canyon bottoms or areas of the forest with shorter, relatively equal sized trees.

92. To gauge lightning- every five seconds between flash and boom equals a mile in distance.

93. When cumulus clouds blend together and the bottoms darken, a storm is on the way.

94. Yellow sunsets and still moist air can signal bad weather.

95. Make your own folding cup. Flatten a waxed paper cup or a paper cone cup and tuck into your pocket. Unfold when needed.

96. Carry safety pins.

97. To prevent spillage, store your canteen or water bottle in a plastic bag.

98. Do not undertake more than you can handle. Recognize your limitations and the limitations of your canine.

99. While you're hiking, if you become too hot, too cold, too tired, too anything, other than ecstatic, take a rest or begin your return.

100. High altitude sickness can occur in elevations over 7,000 ft. Whenever possible, slowly accustom yourself to changes in altitude. Symptoms include lightheadedness, faintness, headaches and dryness. If you experience any of these symptoms, stop, rest, seek shade, and drink plenty of water.

CANINE CAMPER

Traditionally canine campers have been welcome in our national forests. Owners however should be aware that problems with dogs in many recreation areas have increased in recent years. The few rules that apply to dogs are meant to assure that you and other visitors have enjoyable outdoor experiences. Although it's fun to treat Rover to a day or night in the forest, not everyone appreciates his behavior.

In a study done several years ago in developed recreation areas, one of every eight dogs was involved in either a complaint as a result of their behavior or a warning to the owner for not observing rules. If the situation worsens, more rules and stronger enforcement action will be necessary, possibly resulting in a ban on pets in some areas. Dog owners must be responsible for their pets.

Your fellow visitor's reaction will be a major factor in determining whether or not dogs continue to be welcome in national forest recreation and wilderness areas. To avoid complaints from other visitors, please follow these rules:

- When you bring your dog, assume responsibility for him. Be courteous and remember not all visitors like dogs in their campsites and that dogs are not permitted on beaches that are designated for swimming.

- Leave vicious or unusually noisy dogs at home. If they disturb or threaten anyone, they will not be allowed in public recreation areas.

- The law requires that you have your dog on a leash at all times in developed areas.

- Developed campgrounds are for people, not animals. Please do not bring more than two dogs or other pets into any one campsite.

- Make preparations for your dog before bringing him into wilderness areas. Remember that you have hiking boots to protect your feet. Consider your dog's pads and feet. Keep your pet leashed in the wild. Dogs are predators by nature and will chase wildlife and stock animals. Any dog found running at large in national forest areas may be captured and impounded.

After you return home from a backcountry trip, keep an eye on your pet for any signs of illness. If your pet develops diarrhea, have a vet check him for giardia. This small parasite is often found in streams and lakes. Check your pooch for ticks, foxtails and burrs as well.

ROCKHOUNDING WITH THE HOUND

Arizona is a rockhound's dream. From agate to multi-colored onyx, quartz crystals to jasper, garnet clusters to chalcedony roses, gold nuggets to azurite, obsidian to geode, chrysocolla to selenite clusters, Arizona is world renowned as a rockhounder's heaven. For more detailed information on houndable gems and minerals, along with the top hounding hotspots, contact your local gem and mineral club or the Arizona Mining and Mineral Museum at (602) 255-3795.

Since most rockhounding adventures take you into remote areas, it's a good idea to hound with a group. But if you and Digger are treasure seeking loners, inform a third party where you're going and when you'll be back. Also, pack plenty of drinking water along with an updated map of the area.

Regardless of the temptation, stay out of mines. They are deathtraps capable of caving in with the smallest disturbance. They are also home to rattlesnakes and other poisonous creatures. For the most part, mines are privately owned and marked with "No Trespassing" signs or surrounded by a fence. For your safety and your pooch's - keep out and keep safe. Leave things as they are unless you've been told that it is okay to remove rocks, or you're in an area designated specifically for rockhounding.

37

WAYS TO HAVE A BETTER VACATION WITH YOUR POOCH

Some tips and suggestions to increase your enjoyment when you and the pooch hit the road.

1. Don't feed or water your pooch just before starting on your trip. Feed and water your dog approximately two hours before you plan to depart. Or better still, if it's a short trip, wait until you arrive at your destination.

2. Exercise your pooch before you leave. A tired dog will fall off to sleep more easily and adapt more readily to new surroundings.

3. Take along a large container of water to avoid potential stomach upset. Your dog will do better drinking from his own water supply for the first few days. And having water along will mean you can stop wherever you like and not worry about finding water. Gradually accustom your pooch to his new source of water by topping off your water container with local water.

4. Plan stops along your trip. Just like you, your pooch will enjoy stretching his legs. Along your route, there will be many areas conducive to dog freedom. And you'll be surprised how satisfying these little stops will be for you as well. If you make the car ride an agreeable part of your trip, your vacation will begin the moment you leave home — not just when you reach your ultimate destination.

5. While driving, keep windows open enough to allow the circulation of fresh air but not enough to allow your dog to jump out. If you have air conditioning, that will keep your dog cool enough.

6. Vets advise against letting your dog hang his head out of the window. Eyes, ears and throats can become inflamed.

7. Use a short leash when walking your pooch through public areas — he'll be easier to control.

8. Take along your dog's favorite objects from home. If they entertain him at home, they'll entertain him on vacation.

9. Before any trip, allow your pooch to relieve himself.

10. Cover your back seat with an old blanket or towel to protect the upholstery.

11. A room freshener under the seat of your car will keep it smelling fresh. Take along an extra deodorizer for your room.

12. If your dog has a tendency for carsickness, keep a small packet of honey (many restaurants offer them with toast) in the glove compartment or carry a roll of hard candy — like Lifesavers — with you. Either of these might help with carsickness.

13. Use a flea and tick collar on your pooch.

14. When traveling in warm weather months, drape a damp towel over your dog's crate. This allows ventilation and the moist, cooler air will reduce the heat.

15. Before you begin a trip, expose your pooch to experiences he will encounter while traveling; such as crowds, noise, people, elevators, walks along busy streets, and stairs (especially those with open risers).

16. Shade moves. If you must leave your dog in the car for a short period of time, make sure the shade that protects him when you park will be there by the time you return. As a general rule though, it's best not to leave your dog in a parked car. <u>NEVER LEAVE YOUR DOG IN THE CAR DURING THE WARM SUMMER MONTHS</u>. In the colder months, beware of hypothermia, a life threatening condition that occurs when an animal's body temperature falls below normal. Short-haired dogs and toys are very susceptible to illness in extremely cold weather.

17. Take along a clip-on minifan for airless hotel rooms.

18. When packing, include a heating pad, ice pack and a few safety pins.

19. A handful of clothespins will serve a dozen purposes, from clamping motel curtains shut to sealing a bag of potato chips... they're great.

20. A night light will help you find the bathroom in the dark.

21. Don't forget that book you've been meaning to read.

22. Include a journal and record your travel memories.

23. Pack a roll of duct tape. Use it to repair shoes, patch suitcases or strap lunch onto the back of a rented bicycle, to name just a few.

24. Never begin a vacation with a new pair of shoes.

25. Pooper scoopers make clean up simple and sanitary. Plastic vegetable bags from the supermarket are great too.

26. FYI, in drier climates, many accommodations have room humidifiers available for guest use. Arrange for one when you make your reservation.

27. Use unbreakable bowls and storage containers for your dog's food and water needs.

28. Don't do anything on the road with your pooch that you wouldn't do at home.

29. Brown and grey tinted sun lenses are the most effective for screening bright light. Polarized lenses reduce the blinding glare of the sun.

30. Before you leave on vacation, safeguard your home. Either ask neighbors to take in your mail and newspapers, or arrange with your mailman to hold your mail. Stop newspaper delivery. Use timers and set them so that a couple of lights go on and off. Unplug small appliances and electronics. Lock all doors and windows. Place steel bars or wooden dowels in the tracks of all sliding glass doors or windows. Ladders or other objects that could be used to gain entrance into your home should be stored in your garage or inside your home. Arrange to have your lawn mowed. And don't forget to take out the garbage.

31. Pack some snacks and drinks in a small cooler.

32. As a precaution when traveling, once you arrive at your final destination, check the yellow pages for the nearest vet and determine emergency hours and location.

33. NEVER permit your dog to travel in the bed of a pickup truck. If you must, there are safety straps available at auto supply stores that can be used to insure the safety of your dog. Never use a choke chain, rope or leash around your dog's neck to secure him in the bed of a pickup.

34. Take along a spray bottle of water. A squirt in your dog's mouth will temporarily relieve his thirst.

35. Heavy duty zip-lock type bags make great traveling water bowls. Just roll down edges, form a bowl and fill with water. They fold up into practically nothing. Keep one in your purse, jacket pocket or fanny pack. Keep an extra in your glove compartment.

36. Arrange with housekeeping to have your room cleaned while you're present or while you're out with your pooch.

37. Traveling with children too? Keep them occupied with colored pencils and markers. Avoid crayons — they can melt in the sun. Take along question cards from trivia games as well as a pack of playing cards. Travel size magnetic games like checkers and chess are also good diversions. Don't forget those battery operated electronic games either. Include a book of crossword puzzles, a pair of dice and a favorite stuffed animal for cuddling time. In the car, games can include finding license plates from different states, spotting various makes or colors of cars, saying the alphabet backwards, or completing the alphabet from roadsigns.

TRAVELING BY PLANE

Quick Takes:

- Always travel on the same flight as your dog. And personally ascertain that your dog has been put on board before you board the plane.

- Book direct, nonstop flights.

- Upon boarding, inform a flight attendant that your pooch is traveling in the cargo hold.

- Early morning or late evening flights are best in the summer, while afternoon flights are best in the winter.

- Fill the water tray of your dog's travel carrier with ice cubes rather than water. This will prevent spillage during loading.

- Clip your dog's nails to prevent them from hooking in the crate's door, holes or other openings.

Dog carriers/kennels

Most airlines require pets to be in specific carriers. Airline regulations vary and arrangements should be made well in advance of travel. Some airlines allow small dogs to accompany their owners in the passenger cabins. The carrier must fit under the passenger's seat. These regulations also vary and prior arrangements should be made. In addition, airlines require that your dog remain in the carrier for the duration of the flight.

Airlines run hot and cold on pet travel

Many airlines won't allow pets to travel in the cargo hold if the departure or destination temperatures are over 80°. The same holds true if the weather is too cold. Check with the airlines to ascertain policies.

What about the size of the carrier?

Your dog should have enough room to stand, lie down, sit and turn around comfortably. Larger doesn't equate to more comfort. If anything, larger quarters only increase the chances of your dog being hurt because of too much movement. Just like your dog's favorite place is under the kitchen desk, a cozy, compact kennel will suit him much better than a spacious one.

Should anything else be in the carrier?

Cover the bottom with newspaper sheets and cover that with additional shredded newspaper. This will absorb accidents and provide a soft, warm cushion for your dog. Include a soft blanket, or an old flannel shirt of yours, some article that will remind your pooch of home and provide a feeling of security. You might want to include a hard rubber chew. But forget toys. They can increase the risk of accidents.

How will my pooch feel about a kennel?

Training and familiarization are the key elements in this area. If possible, buy the kennel (airlines and pet stores sell them) several weeks before your trip. Leave it in your home in the area where your dog spends most of his time. Let him become accustomed to its smell, feel and look. After a few days, your pooch will become comfortable around the kennel. You might even try feeding him in his kennel to make it more like home. Keep all the associations friendly. Never use the kennel for punishment. Taking the time to accustom your dog with his traveling quarters will alleviate potential problems and make vacationing more enjoyable.

What about identification?

The kennel should contain a tag identifying your dog and provide all pertinent information including the dog's name, age, feeding and water requirements, your name, address and phone number and your final destination. In addition, it should include the name and phone number of your dog's vet. A "luggage-type" ID card will function well. Use a waterproof marker. Securely fasten the ID tag to the kennel. Your dog should also wear his state ID tag. Should he somehow become separated from his kennel, the information will travel with him. Using a waterproof pen, mark the kennel "LIVE ANIMAL" in large letters at least an inch or more. Indicate which is the top and bottom with arrows or more large lettering of "THIS END UP."

How can I make plane travel comfortable for my pooch?

If possible, make your travel plans for weekday rather than weekend travel. Travel during off hours. Direct and nonstop flights reduce the potential for problems and delays. Check with your airline to determine how much time they require for check in. Limiting the amount of time your dog will be in the hold section will make travel time that much more comfortable. Personally ascertain that your dog has been put on board your flight before you board the aircraft.

Will there automatically be room on board for my pooch?

Not always. Airline space for pets is normally provided on a first-come, first-served basis. As soon as your travel plans are decided, contact the airline and confirm your arrangements.

What will pet travel cost?

Prices vary depending on whether your dog travels in the cabin or whether a kennel must be provided in the hold. Check with the airlines to determine individual pricing policies.

What about food?

It's best not to feed your dog at least six hours before departure.

What about tranquilizers?

Opinions vary on this subject. Discuss this with your vet. But don't give your dog any medication not prescribed by a vet. Dosages for animals and humans vary greatly.

What about after we land?

If your pooch has not been in the passenger cabin with you, you will be able to pick him up in the baggage claim area along with your luggage. Since traveling in a kennel aboard a plane is an unusual experience, he may react strangely. Leash him before you let him out of the kennel. Having his leash on will avoid mishaps. Once he's leashed, give him a cool drink of water and then take him for a walk.

Dogs who shouldn't fly

In general, very young puppies, females in heat, sickly, frail or pregnant dogs should not be flown. In addition to the stress of flying, changes in altitude and cabin pressure might adversely effect your pooch. Also, pug-nosed dogs are definite "no flys". These dogs have short nasal passages which limit their intake of oxygen. The noxious fumes of the cargo hold can severely limit their supply of oxygen, leaving them highly susceptible to heatstroke.

Health certificates - will I need one?

Although you may never be asked to present a health certificate, it's a good idea to have one with you. Your vet can supply a certificate listing the inoculations your dog has received, including rabies. Keep this information with your travel papers.

Airlines have specific regulations regarding animal flying rights. Make certain you know your dog's rights.

29
TIPS FOR TRAVEL SAFETY

Whether you're at home doing errands or on a far-flung travel adventure, you should practice travel safety. A few minutes of preparation and an extra moment of prevention can help you from becoming a statistic, no matter where you travel.

Safety Tips:

1. When returning to your room late at night use the main entrance of your hotel.

2. Don't leave your room key within sight in public areas, particularly if it's numbered instead of coded.

3. Store valuables in your room safe or in a safety-deposit box at the front desk.

4. Don't carry large amounts of cash; use traveler's checks and credit cards.

5. Avoid flaunting expensive watches and jewelry.

6. When visiting a public attraction like a museum or amusement park, decide where to meet should you become separated from your traveling companions.

7. Use a fanny pack and not a purse when touring.

8. Make use of the locks provided in your room. In addition to your room door, be certain all sliding glass doors, windows and connecting doors are locked.

9. If someone knocks on your room door, the American Hotel and Motel Association advises guests to ascertain the identity of the caller before opening the door. If you haven't arranged for room service or requested anything, call the front desk and determine if someone has been sent to your room before you open the door.

10. Carry your money (or preferably traveler's checks) separately from credit cards.

11. Use your business address on luggage tags, not your home address.

12. Be alert in parking lots and underground garages.

13. Check the rear of your car before getting inside.

14. In your car, always buckle up. Seatbelts save lives.

15. Keep car doors locked.

16. When you stop at traffic lights, leave enough room (one car length) between your vehicle and the one in front so you can quickly pull away.

17. AAA recommends that if you're hit from behind by another vehicle, motion the other driver to a public place before getting out of your car.

18. When driving at night, stay on main roads.

19. Fill your tank during daylight hours. If you must fill up at night, do so at a busy, well-lit service station.

20. If your vehicle breaks down, tie a white cloth to the antenna or the raised hood of your car to signal other motorists. Turn on your hazard lights. Remain in your locked car until police or road service arrives.

21. Don't pull over for flashing headlights. Police cars have red or blue lights.

22. Lock video cameras, car phones and other expensive equipment in your trunk. Don't leave them in your vehicle.

23. Have car keys ready as you approach your car.

24. At an airport, allow only uniformed airport personnel to carry your bags or carry them yourself. Refuse offers of transportation from strangers. Use the services of the airport's ground transportation center or a uniformed taxi dispatcher.

25. Walk purposefully.

26. When using an ATM, choose one in a well-lit area with heavy foot traffic. Look for machines inside establishments — they're the safest.

27. Avoid poorly lit areas, shrubbery or dark doorways.

28. When ordering from an outside source, have it delivered to the front desk or office rather than to your room.

29. Trust your instincts. If a situation doesn't feel right —it probably isn't.

11
TIPS THAT TAKE THE STRESS OUT OF VACATIONS

Vacations are intended to be restful occasions but sometimes the preparations involved in "getting away from it all" can prove stressful. The following are proven stress reducers to help you cope before, during and after your trip.

1. Awaken fifteen minutes earlier each day for a couple of weeks before your trip and use that extra time to plan your day and do "vacation" chores.

2. Write down errands to be done. Don't rely on your memory. The anticipation of forgetting something important can be stressful.

3. Don't procrastinate. Whatever has to be done tomorrow, do today. Whatever needs doing today, do NOW.

4. Take stock of your car. Get car repairs done. Have your car washed. Your journey will be more pleasant in a clean car. Fill up with gas the day before your departure. And check your tires and oil gauge. Summertime travel, check your air conditioning. In the winter, make sure your heater and defroster work. Make sure wiper blades are in good working condition.

5. Learn to be more flexible. Not everything has to be perfect. Compromise, you'll have a happier life.

6. If you have an unpleasant task to do, take care of it early in the day.

7. Ask for help. Delegating responsibility relieves pressure and stress. It also makes others feel productive and needed.

8. Accept that we are all part of this imperfect world. An ounce of forgiveness will take you far.

9. Don't take on more tasks than you can readily accomplish.

10. Think positive thoughts and eliminate negativism, like, "I'm too fat, I'm too old, I'm not smart enough."

11. Take 5-10 minutes to stretch before you begin your day or before bedtime. Breathe deeply and slowly, clearing your mind as you do.

9
TIPS ON MOVING WITH YOUR DOG

During this coming year, one out of five Americans will be moving. Of those, nearly half will be moving with their pets. If you're part of the "pet half", you should understand that your dog can experience the same anxiety as you. The following tips can make moving less stressful for you and your dog.

1. Although moving companies provide information on how to move your pet, they are not permitted to transport animals. Plan to do so on your own.

2. Begin with a visit to your vet. Your vet can provide a copy of your dog's medical records. Your vet might even be able to recommend a vet in the city where you'll be moving.

3. If you'll be traveling by plane, contact the airlines ASAP. Many airlines offer in-cabin boarding for small dogs, but only on a first-come, first-served basis. The earlier you make your reservations, the better chance you'll have of securing space.

4. If you'll be driving to your new home, use *Doin' Arizona With Your Pooch!* (or our national lodging directory, *Vacationing With Your Pet!)* for your lodging reservations. By planning ahead, your move will proceed more smoothly .

5. Buy a special toy or a favorite chew that's only given to your dog when you're busy packing.

6. Don't feed or water your pooch for several hours before your departure. The motion of the ride might cause stomach upset.

7. Keep your dog kenneled up on moving day to avoid disasters. Never allow your pet to run free when you're in unfamiliar territory.

8. Pack your dog's dishes, food, water, treats, toys, leash and bedding in an easy-to-reach location. Take water and food from home. Drinking unfamiliar water or eating a different brand of food can cause digestion problems. And don't forget those plastic bags for clean-up.

9. Once you've moved in and unpacked, be patient. Your pooch may misbehave. Like a child, he may resent change and begin acting up. Deal with problems in a gentle and reassuring manner. Spend some extra time with your canine during this upheaval period and understand that it will pass.

FIRST-AID EMERGENCY TREATMENT

Having a bit of the Girl Scout in me, I like being prepared. Over the years, I've accumulated information regarding animal emergency treatment. Although I've had only one occasion to use this information, once was enough. I'd like to share my knowledge with you.

Whether you're the stay-at-home type who rarely travels with your dog, or a gadabout who can't sit still, every dog owner should know these simple, but potentially lifesaving procedures.

The Basics

Assemble your own first-aid kit by including some or all of the following:

- Two-inch bandages
- Antibiotic ointment
- Scissors
- Rectal thermometer
- Boric acid
- Baking soda
- Lighter fluid
- 3% hydrogen peroxide
- Blunt tweezers
- Tomato juice
- Cotton gauze
- Flea powder
- Flashlight (with new batteries)
- Extra flea and tick collar

The following are only guidelines to assist you during emergencies. Whenever possible, seek treatment from a vet if your animal becomes injured and you don't feel qualified to administer first aid. I have not personally experienced any of the emergencies outlined but these tips may help you with initial treatment.

Allergies: One in five dogs suffers from some form of allergy. Sneezing and watery eyes can be an allergic reaction caused by pollen and smoke. Inflamed skin can indicate a sensitivity to grass or to chemicals used in carpet cleaning. See your vet.

Bites and stings: Use ice to reduce swelling. If your animal has been stung in the mouth, take him to the vet immediately. Swelling can close the throat. If your dog experiences an allergic reaction, an antihistamine may be needed. For fast relief from a wasp or bee sting, dab the spot with plain vinegar and then apply baking soda. If you're in the middle of nowhere, a small mud pie plastered over the sting will provide relief. Snake bites: seek veterinary attention ASAP.

Bleeding: If the cut is small, use a tweezers to remove hair from the wound. Gently wash with soap and water and then bandage (not too tightly). Severe bleeding, seek medical attention ASAP.

Burns: <u>First degree burns:</u> Use an ice cube or apply ice water until the pain is alleviated. Then apply vitamin E, swab with honey or cover with a freshly brewed teabag.

Minor burns: Use antibiotic ointment.

Acid: Apply dampened baking soda.

Scalds: Douse with cold water. After treatment, bandage all burns for protection.

Earache: A drop of warm eucalyptus oil in your dog's ear can help relieve the pain.

Eye scratches or inflammation: Make a solution of boric acid and bathe eyes with soft cotton.

Falls or impact injuries: Limping, pain, grey gums or prostration need immediate veterinary attention. The cause could be a fracture or internal bleeding.

Fire: Friends of Animals, Inc. will send you a decal for your window alerting fire fighters to the presence of a pet and the area in your home where the pet may be found. Charge for one decal is $1. Write to them at 1841 Broadway, #212, New York, NY 10023 or call 212-247-8120.

Fleas: Patches of hair loss, itching and redness are common signs of fleas, particularly during warm months. Use a flea bath and a flea collar to eliminate and prevent infestation. Ask your vet about new oral medication now available for flea control.

Heatstroke: Signs include lying prone, rapid breathing and heartbeat, difficulty in breathing, rolling eyes, panting, high fever, a staggering gait. Quick response is essential. Move your pooch into the shade. Generously douse with cold water or if possible, partially fill a tub with cold water and immerse your dog. Remain with him and check his temperature. Normal for dogs: 100°-102°. Don't let your dog's temperature drop below that.

Prevent common heatstroke by limiting outdoor exercise in hot or humid weather, provide plenty of fresh, cool water and access to shade. Never leave your dog in a car on a warm day, even for "just a few minutes."

Poisons: Gasoline products, antifreeze, disinfectants, and insecticides are all poisonous. Keep these products tightly closed and out of reach. Vomiting, trembling, and convulsions can be symptoms of poisoning. If your dog suffers from any of these symptoms, get veterinary attention. (See listings on Poison Control Centers in section "Everything You Want to Know About Pet Care...".)

Poison ivy: Poison ivy or oak on your dog's coat will not bother him. But the poison can be passed on to you. If you believe your dog has come in contact with poison ivy or oak use rubber gloves to handle your dog. Rinse him in salt water, then follow with a clear water rinse. Shampoo and rinse again.

Shock: Shock can occur after an accident or severe fright. Your animal might experience shallow breathing, pale gums, nervousness or prostration. Keep him still, quiet and warm and have someone drive you to a vet.

Skunks: Hopefully, you and your pooch will never encounter one of Rover's favorite furry friends during your travels. But, unfortunately, dogs and skunks have a way of sniffing each other out and establishing a very smelly relationship. Here are some tips if you encounter a skunk on the trail. You'll be surprised at how persistent the little black and white fellows can be, even when Fido is perfectly behaved.

1. Try to keep your pooch quiet. Skunks have an unforgettable way of displaying their dislike of barking.

2. Try to ignore the little critter. Distract Rover, and hasten your pace down the pathway.

3. Don't try to scare the skunk away, they'll spray!

If you end up in a very stinky situation, here are three home remedies recommended by groomers. (Of course, it is always a good idea to consult with a veterinarian before dousing your dog with foreign substances.) Time is of the essence for your nose's sake and for Fido's sake. So, if possible, act quickly.

1. The old tomato juice method might work for you. Saturate Fido's fur with the juice and wait for it to dry. Brush and shampoo later. This method may prove effective, but is quite messy.

2. A 5-part water, 1-part vinegar ratio is an alternative. Pour the solution over Rover and let it soak for 10-15 minutes. Shampoo.

3. Use 1 quart 3% hydrogen peroxide, 1/4 cup baking soda and a small amount of liquid soap. Apply on your pal and let him sit for 15 minutes. Shampoo.

Note: Immediately wash eyes with boric acid solution. Always apply any solution with care around the eyes and face.

Snake bites:

1. Immobilization and prompt medical attention are key elements to handling a poisonous snake bite. Immediate veterinary care is essential to recovery this means within 2 hours of the bite. DO NOT try to treat this yourself.

2. If the bite occurs while in a remote location, immediately immobilize the bitten area and carry the dog to the vehicle. If the dog walks on his own, the venom will spread quicker.

3. Most snake bites on dogs occur in the head or neck area, especially on the nose. The front leg is the second most common place.

4. Severe swelling within 30 to 60 minutes of the bite is the first indication that your dog is suffering from a venomous snake bite.

5. Excessive pain and slow, steady bleeding are other indicators- hemotoxins in the venom of certain snakes prevent the clotting of blood.

6. If your dog goes into shock or stops breathing, CPR (cardiopulmonary resuscitation) is your only option. CPR for dogs is the same as for humans- push on the dog's chest to compress his heart and force blood to the brain, then hold his mouth closed and breathe into his nose.

7. DO NOT apply ice to the bite- venom constricts the blood vessels and ice only compounds the constriction.

8. DO NOT use a tourniquet - the body's natural immune system fights off the venom and by cutting off the blood flow you'll either minimize or completely eliminate this fight.

Ticks: Use lighter fluid (or other alcohol) and loosen by soaking. Then tweeze out gently. Make sure you get the tick's head.

Winter woes: Rock salt and other commercial chemicals used to melt ice can be very harmful to your dog. Not only can they burn your dog's pads, but ingestion by licking can result in poisoning or dehydration. Upon returning from a walk through snow or ice, wash your dog's feet with a mild soap and then rinse. Before an outdoor excursion, you can also try spraying your dog's paws with cooking oil to deter adherence.

Notes

_____

_____

_____

_____

_____

_____

_____

_____

_____

_____

STEPS TO BETTER GROOMING

Grooming is another way of saying "I love you" to your pooch. As pack animals, dogs love grooming rituals. Make grooming time an extension of your caring relationship. Other than some breeds which require professional grooming, most canines can be groomed in about 10 minutes a day.

1. Designate a grooming place, preferably one that is not on the floor. If possible, use a grooming table. Your dog will learn to remain still and you won't trade a well-groomed pooch for an aching back.

2. End every grooming session with a small treat. When your dog understands that grooming ends with a goodie, he'll behave better.

3. Brush out your dog's coat before washing. Wetting a matted coat only tightens the tangles and makes removal more difficult.

4. Using a soft tissue, wipe around your dog's eyes daily, especially if his eyes tend to be teary.

5. When bathing a long-haired dog, squeeze the coat, don't rub. Rubbing can result in snarls.

6. To gently clean your dog's teeth, slip your hand into a soft sock and go over each tooth.

Grooming tips...sticky problems

Chewing gum: There are two methods you can try. Ice the gum for a minimum of ten minutes to make it more manageable and easier to remove. Or use peanut butter. Apply and let the oil in the peanut butter loosen the gum from the hair shaft. Leave on about 20 minutes before working out the gum.

Tar: This is a tough one. Try soaking the tarred area in vegetable or baby oil. Leave on overnight and then bathe your dog the following day. The oil should cause the tar to slide off the hair shaft. Since this method can be messy, shampoo your dog with Dawn dishwashing soap to remove the oil. Follow with pet shampoo to restore the pH balance.

Oil: Apply baby powder or cornstarch to the oily area. Leave on 20 minutes. Shampoo with warm water and Dawn. Follow with pet shampoo to restore the pH balance.

Burrs:

1. Burrs in your dog's coat may be easier to remove if you first crush the burrs with pliers.
2. Slip a kitchen fork under the burr to remove.
3. Soak the burrs in petroleum jelly before working them out.

Keep cleaning sessions as short as possible. Your dog will not want to sit for hours. If your dog's skin is sensitive, you might want to simply remove the offending matter with a scissors. If you don't feel competent to do the removal yourself, contact a grooming service in your area and have them do the job for you.

FITNESS FOR FIDO

A daily dose of exercise is as important for the pooch's health as it is for yours. A 15-30 minute walk twice daily is a perfect way to build muscles and stamina and get you and the dogster in shape for more aerobic workouts. If you're a summer hound, beat the heat by walking in the early hours of the morning or after sundown. Keep in mind that dogs don't sweat, so if you notice your pooch  panting excessively or lagging behind, stop in a cool area for a water break.

Be especially careful when beginning an exercise program with a young dog or an overweight pooch. Consult with your veterinarian about a fitness program that would be best for your furry friend before leashing him up and pooping him out. Obese dogs may have other health problems which should be considered before taking to the trail. Young dogs are still developing their bones and may not be ready for rigorous programs. Use common sense when beginning any exercise program.

MASSAGE, IT'S PETTING WITH A PURPOSE

After a tough day of hiking, nothing is more appealing than a soak in a hot tub. Since that won't work for your pooch, consider a massage. All it takes is twenty minutes and the following simple procedures:

1. Gently stroke the head.
2. Caress around the ears in a circular fashion.
3. Rub down both the neck and the shoulders, first on one side of the spine, and then the other continuing down to the rump.
4. Turn Rover over and gently knead the abdominal area.
5. Rub your dogs legs.
6. Caress between the paw pads.

After his massage, offer your pooch plenty of fresh, cool water to flush out the toxins released from the muscles.

Massages are also therapeutic for pooches recovering from surgery and/or suffering from hip dysplasia, circulatory disorders, sprains, chronic illnesses and old age. Timid and hyperactive pooches can benefit as well.

10
REASONS WHY DOGS ARE GOOD FOR YOUR HEALTH

Adding a dog to your household can improve your health and that of your family. In particular, dogs seem to help the very young and seniors. The following is based on various studies.

1. People over 40 who own dogs have lower blood pressure. 20% have lower triglyceride levels. Talking to dogs has been shown to lower blood pressure as well.

2. People who own dogs see their doctor less than those who don't.

3. Dogs have been shown to reduce depression, particularly in seniors.

4. It's easier to make friends when you have a dog. Life is more social with them.

5. It's healthier too. Seniors with dogs are generally more active because they walk more.

6. Dogs are friends. Here again, seniors seem to benefit most.

7. Dogs can help older people deal with the loss of a spouse. Seniors are less likely to experience the deterioration in health that often follows the stressful loss of a mate.

8. Dogs ease loneliness.

9. Perhaps because of the responsibility of dog ownership, seniors take better care of themselves.

10. Dogs provide a sense of security to people of all ages.

ARIZONA'S NATIONAL FORESTS AND WILDERNESS AREAS

Sunrise in the San Francisco Peaks. As morning's glow lights up the mountain snowpack, a jumping trout sends ripples across the still surface of a mountain lake. Sunset in the desert mountains, the rocks, heated by the midday sun, are warm to the touch as the sun drops below the western horizon and the dry air cools. Uncountable stars, unseen by those who remain in the city, fill the sky. A coyote howls in the distance as darkness brings the desert to life. Wilderness areas in Arizona's national forests range from woodlands in the north to desert mountains in the south. Visitors are welcome to enjoy Arizona's wilderness areas and national forests, but are asked to leave only footprints and take only memories.

With care our children's grandchildren will be able to cherish the same sight of a crystal clear mountain lake or elk crossing a meadow. To preserve wilderness areas for future generations, the Forest Service asks people to be sensitive to their surroundings and observe the rules and guidelines designed to protect the wilderness areas. Unfortunately, rules alone can't preserve a wilderness. Users need to make protection of these areas a personal ethic.

Green forests and tumbling rivers, small mountain lakes tucked behind towering peaks, desert vistas stretching as far as the eye can see, these scenes and a multitude of others greet visitors to forest service wilderness areas in Arizona. The Wilderness Act of 1964 set aside wilderness areas "where the earth and its community of life are untrammeled by man, where man himself is a visitor who does not remain."

You enter the wilderness at your own risk and must be prepared to take care of yourself. There are no bathrooms, rest stops, food or drink. In turn, however, you will find unspoiled vistas, solitude and escape from the fast pace of civilization. Although many non-wilderness areas in the national forests provide similar opportunities for camping and hiking in an isolated, undeveloped setting, wilderness areas in particular are managed to preserve their natural conditions.

Recreation use of national forest wilderness areas in Arizona averages about 2 million visitors a year, but varies according to weather and travel conditions that affect access to the areas. Preserving the wilderness quality of these unique lands while accommodating increased recreation use is one of the major challenges faced by national forest managers.

What Is Wilderness?

Land designated by Congress as wilderness:

- Is affected primarily by the forces of nature; people visit, but don't remain. It may contain ecological, geological or other features with scientific, educational, scenic or historical values.
- Has outstanding opportunities for solitude or primitive recreation.
- Is large enough so continued use won't change its unspoiled, natural condition.

Preserving Wilderness

The forest service manages wilderness areas to:

- Perpetuate a high-quality wilderness system that represents natural ecosystems.
- Maintain native plants and animals by protecting complete biological communities.
- Preserve healthy watersheds.
- Protect threatened or endangered species.
- Maintain the primitive character of wilderness as a benchmark for developed lands.

Permits

A visitor permit may be required to enter some national forest wilderness areas. Some have a quota system for peak season use that admits visitors gradually in order to reduce adverse impacts on the wilderness quality of the areas. The forest service offices listed for the areas you intend to visit will provide you with information about permit requirements and permit application forms. A campfire permit is required if you plan to build a wood fire or use a portable stove during your trip. During periods of severe fire danger, campfires may be prohibited and some areas or parts of areas closed to public entry. Be sure to inquire at the forest service office at your point of entry for complete information about any fire restrictions in effect. Group size is limited. No matter how careful, very large groups tend to compact campsites and have a greater impact on wilderness than small groups.

Fishing and hunting are permitted in season in many wilderness areas. State fish and game laws apply to all national forest land. If you don't want to camp in an area during hunting season, be sure to inquire about the effective dates when you plan your trip.

To ensure preservation of this unique area and a quality experience for all who visit it, please abide by the Forest Service guidelines.

Pooch Rules & Regulations:

THEY CAN'T BE AVOIDED. AND THEY'RE REALLY QUITE EASY TO LIVE WITH. BE A RESPONSIBLE DOG OWNER AND OBEY THE RULES.

- Clean up after your dog even if no one has seen him do his business.
- Leash your dog in areas that require leashing.
- Train your dog to be well behaved.
- Control your dog in public places so that he's not a nuisance to others.

Camp With Courtesy

- Burn all paper.
- Pack out all cans, bottles and metal foil.

Refuse & Garbage

- Don't bury your trash, animals dig it up.
- Don't leave leftover food for the next party, it teaches bears to rob camps.

Smoking

Don't smoke on trails. You may smoke at your campsite - sit down and dig a small area to be used as an ashtray. Always take your cigarette butt with you - filters don't easily decompose.

Bicycles

Motor vehicles and bicycles are prohibited. Travel is restricted to foot or horseback.

Small Groups

Travel in groups of 15 or fewer. Give others as much privacy as possible. Leave radios and tape players at home.

Stay On Trails

To preserve plants and prevent erosion, don't take shortcuts. Don't cut your own trails. This contributes to trail erosion and destroys plant life. Stick to marked trails. Whenever possible, walk on rocks or dry ground. Tread lightly in meadows which are home to many sensitive plants.

Horses

Some restrictions exist, check with the ranger district.

Hunting

Hunting is allowed with the proper permits. Check with the Arizona Department of Fish and Game for regulations.

Fishing License

The state of Arizona requires that any person 14 years or older possess a valid fishing license in order to partake in any fishing activity throughout the state (a license is not required of those persons under the age of 14). To purchase a license, contact the Arizona Game and Fish Department at (602) 942-3000 for an order form. The average cost of an annual, class A resident license is $12, while the average cost of an annual, class A non-resident license is $38. Varying class options and license additions, such as the $10 trout stamp, affect the cost of the license and are listed on the order form. State licenses and permits are not required on Indian Reservations; however, you must obtain a special license or permit from the individual Reservation. Additional information is available through the Arizona Game and Fish Department. For the latest fishing reports call (602) 789-3701.

Notes

_____

_____

_____

_____

_____

_____

_____

_____

_____

_____

_____

TRAIL MANNERS & METHODS

Trails are both a convenience for wilderness users and a way to minimize human impact on an area. Cutting switchbacks or cutting through trail sections can cause serious erosion. Walking on the shoulder of a wet or muddy trail creates ruts along the trail. If you aren't following the trail, stay well away from it. Use caution when crossing dangerous sections, such as swampy areas, potential slide areas, deep snowdrifts, slippery trails on slopes or rapid streams.

For everyone's safety, hikers should stand quietly on the downhill side to allow horses to pass. Don't try to touch the pack animals or hide from them. Startled horses can be dangerous.

Be prepared

Be sure you and your fellow campers are in shape. Take weekend hikes and exercise with a full backpack for several weeks before your trip. Clothing is the most important precaution against hypothermia, exhaustion and exposure. Pack a waterproof poncho for stormy weather. Dressing in layers lets you adapt to temperatures that

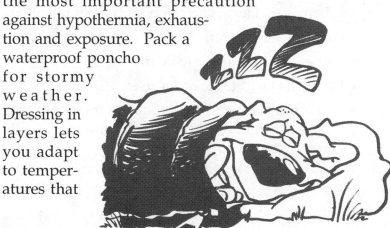

can change as much as 80° between day and night in mountainous areas. Be sure your sleeping bag keeps you warm when outdoor temperatures are well below freezing. Your boots should be sturdy, well insulated and waterproof, fit comfortably over two pairs of socks (cotton inner, wool outer), protect the ankle and support the foot. Break them in before you go, but don't wear them out. You'll need plenty of traction on mountain slopes. Bring a hat or wool beanie. Exposure and heat loss are greatest through the head, and sunstroke and hypothermia are major hazards. Plan menus carefully. Take food that is simple, nutritious and lightweight.

Arizona hiking etiquette

- Respect the land--don't shortcut the trail.
- Avoid wet trails if possible, and avoid cutting new trails.
- Keep to the right of the trail- left is for passing.
- Downhill traffic yields to uphill traffic.
- Adjust your pace when approaching other users.
- When overtaking a hiker, announce your intentions.
- Don't block the trail. Allow room for others.
- Joggers yield to trail stock and hikers.
- Bicyclists yield to all other users.
- Some trails have steep grades, natural hazards, variable terrain conditions, and limited visibility. Observe and heed all signs.

Trip checklist

You will find greater enjoyment in the wilderness if you are properly prepared. The following check-list is important for your safety and enjoyment.

- Clothing and shelter for rain, wind and cold

- Map and compass

- First-aid kit

- Sunglasses or hat

- Flashlight

- Knife

- Waterproof matches

- Nylon twine or cord

- Sun lotion and lip ointment

- Mosquito repellent

- Notification of your trip route and time

First aid

Blisters, headaches or other ailments can ruin a trip. Wilderness users should carry a first-aid kit to treat common medical problems. The following supplies should handle most cases. Additional supplies should be carried based on the size of the party and specific needs.

- Pain medication such as aspirin (25 tablets)
- Antacid (25 tablets)
- Antihistamine (12 tablets)
- Bandages (12, 1-inch size)
- Sterile gauze pads (6, 4-inch squares)
- Adhesive tape (2-inch roll)
- Elastic bandages (3-inch)
- Tweezers (1 pair)
- Mole skin (1/2 package)
- Antibacterial soap (small bottle)
- Roll gauze (2, 2-inch rolls)
- Oral thermometer
- Personal prescription drugs
- Space blanket
- Pencil and paper
- Change for a telephone
- Arm and leg inflatable splints (1 each)
- Safety pins (3 large)

Get ready to go

Plan your trip from start to finish at home. Use topographic maps and trail guides, and get the advice of experienced backcountry travelers. Check elevations and total distance to be traveled **up and down**. Allow plenty of time for moving over hilly, rugged terrain. Before entering the wilderness, leave your itinerary with a relative or friend. Write a full account of who is going, where you are going, when you will be back, where you will exit, and the approximate location of each overnight campsite. Carry a map and compass and stick to the planned route. It is wise never to travel alone, but if you must, stick to frequently used trails in case you become sick or injured.

Buying Equipment

Acquiring equipment requires a little research and the advice of experienced backpackers. You can refer to the many camping guides commercially available, but don't rely on printed information alone. Talk to an experienced backpacker or your local camping supplier. They can help you select basic equipment.

Wildlife

Many of the hikes will bring you in close proximity to wildlife. Please do not disturb the natural habitat or get too close to the animals. If you know that you will encounter wildlife and you do not feel you have total voice control over your dog, leash him to prevent mishaps. Elk, for example, have been known to charge when they sense danger or feel threatened.

When hiking in a marshland or other bird sanctuary, keep your dog leashed, particularly if he's a hunting or bird dog. It's up to you to protect our wildlife.

Regardless of where you hike, whether it's through a red-walled canyon, in a heavily wooded forest or on granite mountaintops, clean up after your dog. Let's work together to preserve dog-friendly attitudes and policies.

Bears are not cuddly

Most large mammals stay away from anything that smells of humans, but some bears are exceptions. Bears are intelligent, adaptable animals, and some have changed their natural foraging habits to take advantage of hikers bringing food into wilderness areas. Some basic rules - stay away from bears and don't harass them. Here are some additional suggestions when traveling in bear country:

Keep your camp clean and counterbalance anything that has an odor, including soap, toothpaste and trash. To counterbalance your load, place the items in two bags so they weigh about the same. Find a tree with a good branch about 20 feet off the ground. Toss a rope over the branch far enough from the trunk so cubs can't crawl along the branch and reach the bags. Tie the first sack on one end of the rope and hoist the sack up to the branch. Tie the second sack to the other end of the rope. The rope should be about 10 feet long, tuck any excess in the bag. Tie a loop in the rope near the second bag. Toss the second bag into position so both bags are hanging about 12 feet off the ground. To retrieve them, hook the loop with a long stick and pull the bags down.

Don't hang packs in trees. Leave them on the ground with zippers and flaps open so bears can nose through them without doing any damage.

If a bear approaches your camp, yell, bang pans and wave coats in the air. In many cases, the bear will retreat. If the bear doesn't retreat, get yourself out of camp.

Bears may only enter camp looking for food, but they still are potentially dangerous. Never try to take food away from a bear. Never approach a bear, especially a cub. You may lose a meal to animals, but they pay a higher price for human carelessness. Bears that become accustomed to getting food from campers sometimes become too aggressive and have to be destroyed. Animals that spend the summer getting food from campers also can be in trouble when the first snow falls and their food supply quits for the year.

Rattlesnakes

Rattlesnakes inhabit much of Arizona but they prefer dry, rocky areas below the 6,000 ft. elevation. Active in warmer months, they will not normally attack unless they are cornered or touched. Be aware of your surroundings. If a bite occurs, do not panic. Remain calm, immobilize the bitten area below the level of the heart and get to a hospital ASAP for an anti-venom shot.

Don't get ticked off

Ticks are prevalent in many areas of Arizona. They prefer brushy areas and tall grass so avoid both whenever possible and keep your dog away as well. When hiking in tick country, wear long pants and a long sleeve shirt to minimize contact. It's also easier to spot a tick on light colored clothing. At the end of your outing or hike, carefully inspect yourself and your canine for ticks. Deep Woods OFF!, an insect repellent, can help repel ticks. To remove a tick, use lighter fluid (or other alcohol) and loosen by soaking. Then tweeze out gently, being sure to remove the tick's head.

Poison oak

Found throughout Arizona, poison oak can be either a vine or a shrub. The leaves are red in fall, green in spring and summer. They usually form clusters of three. If you come into contact with poison oak, wash with soap and cool water ASAP. Remove and wash all clothing as well. Over-the-counter medicines are available to help relieve symptoms. If your dog comes in contact with poison oak, he won't experience any ill effects, but the poison will remain on his coat. Do not pet him. Use rubber gloves to handle your dog. Rinse him in salt water, followed with a clear water rinse. Then shampoo and rinse again.

Foxtails

Foxtails are those annoying, prickly shafts of dried grass which always seem to fasten themselves to your clothing. Unfortunately, pooches are more susceptible to foxtails and they don't have the added protection of clothing. If you happen to be hiking through dry grass, be certain to thoroughly check your pooch for this nasty grass, especially his paws, eyes, nose, mouth and ears. Left untreated, foxtails can cause serious medical problems.

The Arizona deserts

Desert education and familiarity are recommended before any desert excursion. The following are some basics: Dress in light colored/lightweight clothing. Wear a hat, and sunscreen and reapply as needed. Carry plenty of water. And don't overdo it. These guidelines and a heavy dose of common sense will go a long way toward helping you enjoy and appreciate the grandeur and beauty of the desert.

Take it easy

Once in the wilderness, take it easy for a day or two. Getting out of your living room and into the wild takes some adjustment. Walk slowly and steadily, and eat dried fruit or other quick energy food from time to time.

Remember, if you overexert yourself at high elevations you may experience altitude sickness or hyperventilation. Most of the time these attacks are the result of traveling too fast. Never joke about a person's ability to keep up when traveling in the wild. A good principle of wilderness travel is to take it slow, rest often and snack frequently to restore body energy.

Stoves & fire

Take a lightweight camping stove specifically designed for backpackers, and plenty of fuel. Don't rely on finding firewood for cooking. Cutting wood from standing trees is prohibited, and heavy use of dead and down wood means that many areas don't have a reliable supply of wood fuel. Standing dead trees are used by cavity nesting birds, small mammals and other wilderness inhabitants. Pulling limbs off trees also scars campsites for future users. In addition, wood fires may be prohibited in some wilderness areas. A portable stove cooks efficiently and reliably, and never gets so wet it won't burn.

If you plan to use a portable stove or build a wood fire you must obtain an Arizona campfire permit from the forest service office listed for the area you plan to visit. Some areas restrict the use of campfires or portable stoves.

Use only dead and down wood. Never break branches from standing trees, even if they look dead. The trees may be alive and breaking branches can cause injury. To build the fire, select a level spot away from overhanging trees, bushes or dry grass. Keep away from the base of steep hills; fire travels uphill fast. With your shovel, clear a circle 10 feet across down to

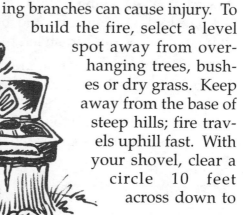

bare dirt. Hollow out a firehole 2 feet across and 5 to 6 inches deep. Pile the soil around the edge of the firehole. Keep the fire small and never start a fire in windy weather. Put out your fires at least a half hour before you start to break camp. First let it die down. Then pour water over the wood and ashes, and spread soil over that. Mix soil, water and ashes until the fire is OUT.

No trace camping

Camp on mineral soil, never in meadows or soft grassy areas that compact easily. Locate your campsite at least 100 feet from water or trail. Pick a place where you won't have to clear vegetation or level a tent site. Do not bury trash. Burn it or pack it out. You must pack out cans, bottles or metal foil. If you bury trash, animals will dig it up. Keeping trails and campsites clean helps preserve the wilderness experience for all.

Before leaving camp, naturalize the area. Scatter any rocks and wood you used, and scout the area to be sure you're leaving nothing behind. Try to make the site look as if no one had been there. Even if you have to pack out trash left by careless campers.

The natural balance of an area around a campsite can be destroyed by such things as building rock walls or cutting branches. Plants and animals depend on the micro-habitats for their survival, and the actions alter the area for the next camper.

Water

Lakes and streams are gathering points for wilderness users, so protecting water quality becomes more critical with growing wilderness use. Hikers and hounds can contract diseases such as giardiasis from drinking impure water. Improper disposal of human waste can contaminate water supplies. Soaps and other wastes add nutrients that can upset the biological balance of water bodies. Water problems can be reduced by following these guidelines.

- Camp at least 100 feet from any water source.

- Carry water to camp for cooking and washing.

- Protect water sources by keeping wash water, food scraps, fish entrails and other wastes at least 100 feet from water.

- Don't use soaps, including "biodegradable" soap near lakes and streams.

- Waste sites should be at least 100 feet from the nearest water supply. Dig a hole 8 to 10 inches wide and 6 to 8 inches deep. After use, fill the hole with loose soil and tamp in the sod.

- Purify even clear, running water before drinking. A recommended treatment is to bring water to a rolling boil for five minutes.

Notes

_____

_____

_____

_____

_____

_____

_____

_____

_____

_____

_____

_____

THUMBNAIL DESCRIPTIONS OF ARIZONA'S NATIONAL FORESTS

The Mission of the National Forests of the United States:

"Caring for the land and serving people."

Apache-Sitgreaves National Forest

Dense pine forests, lush mountain meadows, shimmering lakes, scenic drives and breathtaking vistas are a sampling of what this vast 2 million acre national forest offers. Stretching from the southern end of the relatively flat Colorado Plateau to the White Mountains, the forest experiences an 8,000-foot elevation change.

More than 800 miles of hiking trails usher you and the pupster into three wilderness areas - Mount Baldy, Bear Wallow and Escibulla - as well as the Blue Range Primitive Area. Deer, bear, elk and antelope are some of the wildlife species which inhabit this region. With 400 miles of rivers and streams and 24 lakes and reservoirs, the forest is an angler's dream.

Nearby cities with dog-friendly accommodations include: Alpine, Eagar, Holbrook, Pinetop-Lakeside, Show Low, Springerville, and Winslow.

See the NATIONAL FOREST HIKING TRAIL LOCATOR for a complete list of dog-friendly hikes in the Apache-Sitgreaves National Forest.

Coconino National Forest

Grandeur and beauty go hand in hand at this spectacular 1.8 million acre national forest. Oak Creek Canyon, "Red Rock" Sedona, the Mogollon Rim and towering San Francisco Peaks are just the tip of the panoramic iceberg. Kodak moments are endless as the forest climbs from 3,500 feet to the 12,670-foot peak of Mount Humphreys - the highest point in Arizona. The Verde River and a handful of lakes and streams offer fishing and boating opportunities. Nine wilderness areas - Kendrick Mountain, Kachina Peaks, Strawberry Crater, Sycamore Canyon, Munds Mountain, Red Rock-Secret Mountain, Wet Beaver, West Clear Creek and Fossil Springs combine rolling terrain and deep canyons. Scenic drives are yet another fun alternative. But be alert to wildlife. Antelope, turkey, deer and elk are abundant in these areas.

Nearby cities with dog-friendly accommodations include: Camp Verde, Cottonwood, Flagstaff, Lake Montezuma, Payson, Sedona, Williams and Winslow.

See the NATIONAL FOREST HIKING TRAIL LOCATOR section for a complete list of dog-friendly hikes in the Coconino National Forest.

Coronado National Forest

Nearly 1.8 million acres of diverse terrain comprise Arizona's southernmost national forest. Within the twelve scattered divisions, the forest's elevation ranges from 3,000 feet to the 10,720 foot Mount Graham. These elevation extremes add up to a potpourri of adventure. Desert or mountain hiking, lake hopping, rugged scenic drives, canyon explorations and snowhounding are just a few of the outdoor activities you can enjoy. From flat, cactus-strewn deserts to rugged, pine-clad mountains, it will be hard to comprehend that you're still in the same forest, let alone the same state.

The Chiricahua, Galiuro, Santa Teresa, Pusch Ridge, Rincon Mountain, Mt. Wrightson, Miller Peak and Pajarita Wilderness Areas can be found in the Coronado National Forest. Wildlife includes javelina, deer, mountain lion, dove and quail.

Nearby cities with dog-friendly accommodations include: Douglas, Nogales, Patagonia, Safford, Tombstone, Tucson and Willcox.

See the NATIONAL FOREST HIKING TRAIL LOCATOR section for a complete list of dog-friendly hikes in the Coronado National Forest.

Kaibab National Forest

Kaibab National Forest is a 1.5 million acre wonderland of nature divided by the awesome Grand Canyon. Encompassed within its borders are limestone plateaus, dense forests, volcanic cones, towering mountains, sun-drenched lakes and alpine meadows. Explore this panoramic forest along 370 miles of hiking trails or along 44 miles of the nation's most beautiful roadway - the North Rim Parkway. Pack your binoculars and camera, birdwatching and wildlife sightings are a bonus from May to November. Wildlife might include black bear, elk, North Kaibab deer, pronghorn antelope, wild buffalo, the unique Kaibab squirrel and the majestic bald eagle.

Kendrick and Saddle Mountains, Kanab Creek and Sycamore Canyon constitute the wilderness areas of the forest. Kendrick Peak at 10,418 feet is the forest's highest point.

Nearby cities with dog-friendly accommodations include: Ash Fork, Fredonia, Grand Canyon National Park, Marble Canyon, Page and Williams.

See the NATIONAL FOREST HIKING TRAIL LOCATOR section for a complete list of dog-friendly hikes in the Kaibab National Forest.

Prescott National Forest

With 450 miles of trails, 2,500 miles of roadway and 104,000 acres of wilderness at your fingertips, your options are limitless in this 1.2 million acre forest. Lace up for an invigorating hiking excursion through dense forests and rugged terrain or buckle up for a fourwheelin' adventure along scenic offroads. Either way, your travels will take you from an elevation of 3,000 feet to 8,000 feet, so dress and pack appropriately.

The forest encompasses eight wilderness areas: Sycamore Canyon, Juniper Mesa, Apache Creek, Wood Chute, Granite Mountain, Cedar Bench, Pine Mountain and Castle Creek.

Nearby cities with dog-friendly accommodations include: Camp Verde, Cottonwood, Jerome, Prescott and Prescott Valley.

See the NATIONAL FOREST HIKING TRAIL LOCATOR section for a complete list of dog-friendly hikes in the Prescott National Forest.

Tonto National Forest

"Weighing in" at 2.9 million acres, Tonto National Forest is the reigning champ of Arizona's national forests. Travel through this colossal region and be drawn into a world of beauty where cactus-clad deserts give way to dense piney woodlands as you ascend from 1,300 to 7,900 feet. The gateway to this outdoor wonderland is an 800-mile network of hiking trails and a handful of scenic roadways.

Eight spectacular wilderness areas - Pine Mountain, Mazatzal, Hellsgate, Salome, Sierra Ancha, Salt River Canyon, Four Peaks and Superstition are brimming with 16,000 acres of lakes, rivers and reservoirs, a fact that should bring a smile to the faces of all fishermen. Javelina, deer, mountain lion, turkey and bear inhabit the forest.

Nearby cities with dog-friendly accommodations include: Apache Junction, Carefree, Fountain Hills, Globe, Mesa, Miami, Payson, Phoenix, and Scottsdale.

See the NATIONAL FOREST HIKING TRAIL LOCATOR section for a complete list of dog-friendly hikes in the Tonto National Forest.

THUMBNAIL DESCRIPTION OF ARIZONA WILDERNESS AREAS

Apache Creek Wilderness

Rolling hills of juniper and pinyon interspersed with granite outcrops characterize this small, remote and relatively rugged wilderness. Established in 1984, the 5,420-acre Apache Creek Wilderness features three natural springs and several important riparian areas including Apache Creek. Elevations range between 5,200 feet and 7,200 feet and the area provides excellent habitat for mountain lion and numerous bird species.

There are no maintained wilderness trails or public access points currently in existence. It is recommended that topographic maps be studied prior to a visit.

Additional information concerning the Apache Creek Wilderness may be obtained from the Prescott National Forest Supervisor's Office in Prescott or the Chino Valley Ranger District, P. O. Box 485, Chino Valley, AZ 86323, Phone: (520) 636-2302.

Bear Wallow Wilderness

This newly established wilderness in eastern Arizona boasts some of the largest acreage of virgin ponderosa pine in the Southwest. Only a few trails provide access into and within this area, and only limited grazing of domestic livestock in the western half has kept this area unspoiled.

Beautiful Bear Wallow Creek flows throughout the year, providing suitable habitat for the endangered Apache trout. Wildlife is abundant throughout the area. A majestic view from atop Mogollon Rim is available to the hiker from the Rim Trail on the southern boundary of the wilderness.

Additional information concerning this 11,080-acre wilderness is available from the Apache-Sitgreaves National Forest, Alpine Ranger District, P. O. Box 469, Alpine, AZ 85920, Phone: (520) 339-4384.

Castle Creek Wilderness

Castle Creek Wilderness is situated on the eastern slopes of the Bradshaw Mountains and is characterized by extremely rugged topography with prominent granite peaks that overlook the Agua Fria River.

Created in 1984, Castle Creek Wilderness contains approximately 29,770 acres which range in elevation between 2,800 feet and 7,000 feet. At the lower elevations, saguaro cactus, paloverde, and mesquite are the principal vegetative species. As the elevation increases, grassland species change into the chaparral community and the highest elevations have ponderosa pine, Arizona white oak, and alligator juniper.

Additional information concerning Castle Creek Wilderness may be obtained from the Prescott National Forest Supervisor's Office in Prescott or the Bradshaw Ranger District, 2230 E. Hwy. 69, Prescott, AZ 86031, Phone: (520) 445-7253.

Cedar Bench Wilderness

Located along a broad northwest-southeast trending ridge, the 14,840 acres that comprise the Cedar Bench Wilderness occupy the dividing line between the Verde and Agua Fria drainages. Elevations range between 4,500 feet and 6,700 feet with the principal vegetative cover being chaparral as well as lesser amounts of pinyon pine and Utah juniper. The Verde Wild and Scenic River forms a portion of the eastern boundary of the Cedar Bench Wilderness.

Additional information concerning the Cedar Bench Wilderness may be obtained by contacting the Prescott National Forest Supervisor's Office in Prescott or the Verde Ranger District, P. O. Box 670, Camp Verde, AZ 86322-0670, Phone: (520) 567-4121.

Chiricahua Wilderness

Established in 1933 at 18,000 acres, Chiricahua Wilderness was greatly expanded by the 1984 Arizona Wilderness Act and now encompasses 87,700 acres within the Chiricahua Mountains. There is wide variation in elevation, exposure, slope, moisture, and related plant and animal life. There are many unusual birds which are more common in Mexico.

More than a century ago the mountains were hunting grounds for Cochise and Geronimo. From here Cochise and his followers defended their homeland with surprise attacks on pioneer settlements, travelers, and Army troops. Later, the mountains were part of the short-lived Chiricahua Apache Reservation.

Because of dense brush and timber, steep slopes, precipitous canyons and uncertain water, travel is difficult except on the well-developed trail system. Campgrounds outside the boundaries provide good access for day hiking. The wilderness is administered by the Douglas Ranger District, Coronado National Forest.

Further information can be obtained from the Douglas Ranger District, R.R. 1, Box 228-R, Douglas, AZ 85607, Phone: (520) 364-3468.

Escudilla Wilderness

Escudilla Wilderness, designated in 1984 and containing 5,200 acres, lies atop Arizona's third highest peak, Escudilla Mountain. Its 10,912-foot elevation provides marvelous vistas. It is home to several pristine, high elevation meadows which are comprised of relatively rare plant species. Notable landmarks in or just outside the wilderness include Profanity Ridge, Terry Flat, Toolbox Draw, and the Punchbowl.

A trail takes the visitor to Escudilla Lookout where vistas many miles distant can be absorbed. Because of the relative scarcity of water and the small size of this wilderness, day use is encouraged.

Information on trail conditions, maps, water, and other matters of interest to visitors are available from the Apache-Sitgreaves National Forest, Alpine Ranger District, P. O. Box 469, Alpine, AZ 85920, Phone: (520) 339-4384.

Fossil Springs Wilderness

The springs are located at the bottom of a steep, wide canyon approximately 1,600 feet down at the edge of the Colorado Plateau, approximately 60 miles south of Flagstaff.

The Fossil Springs Botanical Area adjacent to the wilderness has been described as one of the most diverse riparian areas in the state. Over 30 species of trees and shrubs provide striking contrast to the surrounding desert shrub zone. The vegetative diversity creates many wildlife niches for deer, javelina, and hundreds of species of birds.

This area has retained its integrity as an outstanding, pristine site. The Mail Trail and Fossil Spring Trail are within the Fossil Springs Wilderness.

Additional information can be obtained from Beaver Creek Ranger District, H.C. 64, Box 240, Rimrock, AZ 86335, Phone: (520) 567-4501.

Four Peaks Wilderness

Four Peaks Wilderness was established in 1984, and contains approximately 60,740 acres with a major mountain rising up in its center from the desert foothills. The Four Peaks themselves are visible for many miles, and the rapid change in elevation produces interesting plant combinations. Elevations range from 1,900 feet near Apache Lake to 7,600 feet on Brown's Peak.

Visits to some parts of this wilderness can be made throughout the year, using a rather extensive trail system. A Recreation Opportunity Guide is available which gives directions to trailheads and describes each trail. Copies are available from the Tonto National Forest, Mesa Ranger District, P. O. Box 5800, 26 N. MacDonald, Mesa, AZ 85211-5800, Phone: (602) 835-1161.

Galiuro Wilderness

Located about 50 airline miles northeast of Tucson, the remote Galiuro Wilderness is accessible only by dirt roads. Congress set aside 52,717 acres in 1932 and then enlarged it to 76,317 acres in 1984. Administered by the Safford Ranger District of the Coronado National Forest, the Galiuro Mountains are a very steep, rugged range.

In spite of the fact that the Galiuros are lower in elevation than some surrounding mountain ranges, they offer a surprisingly, rich variety of plant life. Grasses and evergreen oaks extend to the lower slopes, and ponderosa pines cloak the higher peaks. Douglas fir and maple grow in the limited cooler, moist sites, and one grove of aspen exists on the northern side of 7,663-foot Bassett Peak, the Galiuros' highest point.

Maintained trails should be followed, since off-trail hiking is extremely difficult due to rough terrain and dense vegetation. This remote wilderness offers a truly rugged outdoor experience.

Additional information is available from the Safford Ranger District, P. O. Box 709, Safford, AZ 85548-0709, Phone: (520) 428-4150.

Granite Mountain Wilderness

The 9,700 acres that comprise the Granite Mountain Wilderness are characterized by the rugged vision of granite boulders, some the size of a house, stacked one atop the other to elevations that exceed 7,600 feet. Created in 1984, Granite Mountain Wilderness is an easily identifiable landmark located on the outskirts of Prescott.

Campground and picnic facilities are located at the base of Granite Mountain and a trailhead facility there provides easy access to the wilderness.

Additional information concerning Granite Mountain Wilderness may be obtained from the Prescott National Forest Supervisor's Office or the Bradshaw Ranger District, 2230 E. Hwy. 69, Prescott, AZ 86301, Phone: (520) 445-7253.

Hellsgate Wilderness

This wilderness was established in 1984, and contains approximately 37,440 rough acres with a major canyon and perennial stream extending its entire length. Deep pools of water are sometimes separated by impassable falls. Elevations range from 3,000 feet along the lower end of Tonto Creek to 6,400 feet on Horse Mountain. Spring and fall are ideal times to visit this area, however trails are scarce and access is limited.

A Recreation Opportunity Guide is available from the Payson Ranger District of the Tonto National Forest, 1009 E. Highway 260, Payson, AZ 85541, Phone: (520) 474-2269.

Juniper Mesa Wilderness

Established in 1984, the 7,640-acre Juniper Mesa Wilderness is characterized by the flat-topped mesa from which the wilderness derived its name. The steep southern slopes are covered principally with pinyon pines and Utah juniper, and the northern slopes are predominantly vegetated by ponderosa pine and alligator juniper.

A great variety of wildlife can be found in the area. Black bear, mule deer, bobcat, and Abert's squirrel are relatively common. There are no perennial water sources present, and the reliability of springs may be questioned during long periods of dry weather.

There are maintained wilderness trails and public access points currently in existence. It is recommended that topographic maps be studied prior to a visit. Additional information concerning the Juniper Mesa Wilderness may be obtained from the Prescott National Forest Supervisor's Office in Prescott or the Chino Valley Ranger District, P. O. Box 485, Chino Valley, AZ 86323, Phone: (520) 636-2302.

Kachina Peaks Wilderness

Located just north of Flagstaff, the Kachina Peaks Wilderness is part of a large, heavily vegetated composite volcano 7,400 to 12,643 feet high including Humphreys Peak, the highest point in Arizona. The "Peaks" exhibit a rich diversity of past geologic events such as lava flows, violent volcanic explosions, glaciation, erosion, and frost action.

The only Arctic-Alpine vegetation in the state is found on the Peaks in a fragile 2-square mile zone and contains a threatened plant: Senecio franciscanus. Visitors must stay on designated trails and there is no camping allowed above timberline.

The Peaks are outstanding examples of past volcanic activity and preserve the best example of Ice Age glaciation in Arizona in lateral and medial moraines and former stream beds.

Recreational opportunities include day hiking, backpacking, cross-country skiing, snowshoeing, winter camping, snow and ice climbing, small and big game hunting, and natural history appreciation.

The Peaks are sacred to several western Indian tribes including the Zuni, Havasupai, Hopi and Navajo. A number of religious shrines have been documented. These shrines have historic and religious value and are currently used. Please respect these religious rights while visiting this wilderness and do not disturb any features.

Information and maps are available from the Peaks Ranger District, 5075 N. Hwy. 89, Flagstaff, AZ 86004, Phone: (520) 526-0866.

Kanab Creek Wilderness

Kanab Creek Wilderness lies in the southwestern corner of the North Kaibab Ranger District and abuts the western edge of the Kaibab plateau. Kanab Creek is one of the major tributaries of the Colorado River, with its origin some 50 miles north in southern Utah. Kanab Creek and its tributaries have cut a network of vertical-walled gorges deep into the Kanab and Kaibab plateaus. Within these walls lies a maze of water and wind carved fins, knobs, potholes and indescribable sculptured forms. Elevations range from about 2,000 feet at the river to 6,000 feet at rim's edge. The upper reaches serve as a winter range for the famed Kaibab mule deer. Vegetation is varied and sparse except for heavy riparian growth in the creek bottom. There is very little dependable water supply for man or beast during summer months when temperatures approach 120°. There are numerous trails in this rather hostile environment, but many are poorly marked and infrequently maintained. Limited and arduous access to the area adds a measure of remoteness that says this is wilderness.

Additional information is available from the Kaibab National Forest Supervisor's Office in Williams or the North Kaibab Ranger District, P. O. Box 248, Fredonia, AZ 86022, Phone: (520) 643-7395.

Kendrick Mountain Wilderness

Kendrick Mountain Wilderness is located on the eastern edge of the Chalender Ranger District, straddling a boundary with Coconino National Forest.

Kendrick Mountain is one of many remnants of the vast San Francisco Mountain volcanic field that stretches from Seligman on the west to beyond Flagstaff to Canyon Diablo in the east. Kendrick Mountain, with an elevation of 10,418 feet is forested to the very top with ponderosa pine, fir, spruce, oak and aspen. Much of the steeper parts of

Kendrick contain old growth forests that contribute valuable habitat for the spotted owl, bear, and goshawk. The north and west slope, with large meadows, is a preferred area for elk and deer. There are three well established trails on Kendrick Mountain that offer fantastic views of canyonlands on the north, striking panoramic views of the volcanic field, and to the south, the distant red rocks of the Oak Creek/Sycamore Canyon country.

Additional information is available from Chalender Ranger District in Williams, Phone: (520) 635-2676 or the Peaks Ranger District in Flagstaff, Phone: (520) 526-0866.

Mazatzal Wilderness

Known locally as the "Ma-ta-zel" Wilderness, this area embraces the north end of the Mazatzal Range. These are predominantly rough desert mountains, sometimes broken by narrow, vertical-walled canyons. Further west, below the brush-covered foothills, the Verde River flows through the Sonoran Desert found there. This river flows through Arizona's only Wild River Area, designated by Congress in 1984.

Mazatzal Wilderness now contains over 252,500 acres of the Tonto and Coconino National Forests. Established in 1932 and expanded to its present size in 1984, it is the oldest continuously designated wilderness in the Southwest.

Elevations range from 1,600 feet along the Verde River to 7,903 feet on Mazatzal Peak. There is an extensive system of trails; their conditions vary from very good to poor. Visitors may check with the Cave Creek Ranger District office, (520) 488-3441 for information about the west side of the wilderness or the Payson Ranger District, (520) 474-2269 for information on the east side. A Recreation Opportunity Guide is also available.

Miller Peak Wilderness

Located just six miles south of Sierra Vista in the southern half of the Huachuca Mountains, this 20,190-acre wilderness was established in 1984. Characterized by sheer cliffs many hundreds of feet in height, the area is also known for large, intense fires. A considerable area once covered by pine and Douglas fir has, at least temporarily, been converted to oak and grass vegetation.

Miller Peak Wilderness is one of the most rugged, wildlife-filled areas in all of southern Arizona. Elevations range from 5,200 feet to 9,466 feet at Miller Peak itself. Well-maintained trails go to the unit's major points of interest and lead to some of the most exceptional panoramas in southern Arizona. The Huachucas are famous as a haven for bird life, and more than 170 species, including 14 species of hummingbirds, have been observed. More than 60 species of reptiles and 78 species of mammals also are found in this range.

The area has a rich and colorful mining and ranching history, with some remains of old mining operations still visible. There are several parcels of private, patented mining claims within the wilderness.

Additional information is available from the Coronado National Forest, Sierra Vista Ranger District, 5990 S. Hwy. 92, Hereford, AZ 85616, Phone: (520) 378-0311.

Mount Baldy Wilderness

At 7,000 acres, Mount Baldy is one of the smallest wildernesses. This, coupled with its great popularity, has forced limits to be placed on the size of groups using the area. Hiking and riding groups should not exceed 12 persons and the maximum number in a group for overnight camping is 6.

Two trails, each approximately 7 miles long, lead into the wilderness and join each other near the top. The half-mile spur trail which leads to the summit and the summit itself are on the Fort Apache Indian Reservation. The Mt. Baldy summit has religious significance and has been closed by the Apaches. Anyone entering is subject to arrest by tribal law enforcement officers.

From 8,700 feet to 11,000 feet, the topography varies from gently sloping timbered benches to extremely steep, rockstrewn mountainsides cut by deep canyons. Big game is common and there are 5 miles of fishing streams. The wilderness is administered by the Apache-Sitgreaves National Forest, Springerville Ranger District, P. O. Box 640, Springerville, AZ 85938, Phone: (520) 333-4372.

Mount Wrightson Wilderness

Lying at the core of the Santa Rita Mountains about 30 miles south of Tucson, this 25,260-acre area was dedicated by the Arizona Wilderness Act of 1984.

Surrounded on all sides by semi-arid hills and sloping savannah, the center of the wilderness is striking Mt. Wrightson, which at 9,453 feet is the highest point in Pima and Santa Cruz Counties. Its majesty is accentuated by the fact that it rises a full 7,000 feet above the valley floor and can be seen from Tucson and surrounding communities.

Mt. Wrightson's stream-fed canyons are the source of an exceptional abundance of animal and plant life. Ponderosa pine and Douglas fir dominate the higher elevations. Rough hillsides, deep canyons, and lofty ridges and peaks characterize the wilderness throughout. It is an extremely well-known area to bird watchers, backpackers, and other outdoor enthusiasts. A developed recreation area in Madera Canyon lies at the foot of the wilderness, and the area is internationally renowned as a unique habitat for a variety of both common and rare birds.

The Nogales Ranger District of the Coronado National Forest manages the area and can be contacted for further information at 2251 N. Grand Avenue, Nogales, AZ 85621, Phone: (520) 281-2296.

Munds Mountain Wilderness

Munds Mountain Wilderness preserves many of the unique red rock formations just east of Sedona, as well as some of the traditional high mesas common to the area. Elevations range from 3,600 feet to 6,800 feet. The country is characterized by moderate to steep slopes along Mogollon Rim.

Munds and Lee Mountains are unique geologic areas along the Mogollon Rim with extensive outcroppings of Coconino and Supai sandstone on the cliff faces, and ramp basalt flows throughout.

There is a great diversity of vegetation and wildlife species and outstanding riparian habitat in upper Woods Canyon. Desert sagebrush, desert grass and short grass plains, oak brush, chaparral, oak woodland, and pinyon-juniper woodland types are common. There are small concentrations of ponderosa pine, and the major drainages contain vital riparian zones.

This wilderness is perfect for those who enjoy more primitive recreation such as hiking, backpacking, horseback riding, swimming, birdwatching, rock climbing and hunting. The area is a photographer's delight due to it's red rock formations and rugged vistas.

Information and maps are available from the Sedona Ranger District, P. O. Box 300, Sedona, AZ 86336, Phone: (520) 282-4119.

Pajarita Wilderness

Administered by the Nogales Ranger District of the Coronado National Forest, this area was established as wilderness in 1984. Located approximately 15 miles west of Nogales, the only access is Ruby Road which is unpaved for much of its length.

Although comprising only 7,420 acres, the area is extremely important to wildlife and plant life. Hugging the international border with Mexico, Pajarita's canyons - principally Sycamore Canyon - provide an important corridor for wildlife migration. Sycamore Canyon is widely known and esteemed both as a popular hiking spot and even more importantly, as the habitat for rare and unusual plants and animals.

Pajarita is the only non-mountainous wilderness within the Coronado National Forest. Although it is an area of rolling hills with elevations ranging from 3,800 to 4,800 feet, the terrain within the canyons is rough with steep slopes and vertical cliffs. Vegetation is largely oak woodland, with riparian zones along the narrow canyon bottoms. Abundant wildflowers put on an annual display of color extremely popular with photographers.

Additional information is available from the Nogales Ranger District, 2251 N. Grand Avenue, Nogales, AZ 85621, Phone: (520) 281-2296.

Pine Mountain Wilderness

This 20,100-acre wilderness straddles the boundary between the Prescott and Tonto National Forests. There are good trails in parts of the area, but water scarcity limits camping. Lying along the high Verde River rim, the area stands as an island of tall, green timber, surrounded by desert mountains with hot, dry mesas and deep canyons. The timber is predominantly ponderosa pine.

A great variety of wildlife and plants unfold as the hiker or rider climbs through several life zones en route to the top of Pine Mountain at 6,800 feet. Big game abounds in the heavy cover on steep slopes and canyons.

Maps and other information are available from the Verde Ranger District, P. O. Box 670, Camp Verde, AZ 86322-0670, Phone: (520) 567-4121.

Pusch Ridge Wilderness

Note: Dog policies vary, check with Santa Catalina Ranger District.

Pusch Ridge Wilderness extends from the desert floor adjacent to metropolitan Tucson to peaks covered with pine, fir, aspen, and maple. The great variety of vegetation and wildlife found as one ascends from 2,800 to 9,000 feet above sea level is truly remarkable. Lower elevations are extremely steep and rugged with spectacular rocky bluffs and peaks. Water is scarce, but several live streams originating on the highest peaks offer some relief from the essentially dry Santa Catalina Mountains.

There is an extensive trail system, and opportunities exist for day hiking as well as extended backpacking. Access can be gained easily at trailheads near the city, or by driving a paved highway to the upper elevations.

Part of the Coronado National Forest, this 56,933-acre wilderness was created in 1978 and is administered by the Santa Catalina Ranger District, 5700 N. Sabino Canyon Road, Tucson, AZ 85715, Phone: (520) 749-8700.

Red Rock - Secret Mountain Wilderness

Twenty miles south of Flagstaff, Red Rock-Secret Mountain Wilderness includes spectacular red, tan, and buff cliffs that mark the edge of the Colorado Plateau. The landscape plunges as much as 1,500 feet into canyons that drain into Oak Creek and the Verde River. Secret Mountain and Wilson Mountain are the high mesas jutting out into the lower country.

This is an area of great climatic variation. The high rims are cool and moist most of the year, except for May and June. The lower end of the unit near Sedona has a much warmer climate. The wide variety of vegetative types provides habitat for equally diverse wildlife populations. There are at least 250 species of vertebrates in the area including elk, mule and white-tail deer, javelina, coyote, rabbit, mountain lion, and bear. Of these, 60 percent depend on the riparian habitat during at least part of their life cycles. The wilderness offers outstanding solitude because of topography and vegetation. Opportunities for primitive recreation are many.

Contact the Peaks Ranger District, 5075 N. Highway 89, Flagstaff, AZ 86004, Phone: (520) 526-0866 for information on the north side. The Sedona Ranger District, P. O. Box 300, Sedona, AZ 86336, Phone: (520) 282-4119, can provide information on the south side.

Rincon Mountain Wilderness

Rising sharply, this mountainous wilderness of 38,590 acres was established in 1984 and is located just east of Tucson, embracing three sides of the Saguaro National Monument. One of the primary functions of the Rincon Wilderness is to complement the Saguaro National Monument and to protect the complete ecosystems found there.

Several trails cross the area, and hikers can quickly find total solitude in canyon bottoms or along ridge lines to the high elevations of the Rincons. However, access to the area is rather difficult. Only four-wheel drive roads lead to the area except on the east side in Happy Valley, served by Forest Road 35, which is generally passable to conventional vehicles. A well-developed trail system also provides access from the National Monument.

The area is dominated by very rocky, steep terrain with elevations ranging from 3,600 feet to 7,700 feet. At higher elevations, dramatic rock outcrops and deep canyons make many areas difficult to reach on foot and virtually impossible on horseback. Vegetation varies from desert grassland at the lower elevations to an oak-juniper-pinyon pine woodland at the higher elevations.

The wilderness is administered by the Santa Catalina Ranger District of the Coronado National Forest. Additional information is available from the District Office at 5700 N. Sabino Canyon Road, Tucson, AZ 95715, Phone: (520) 749-8700.

Saddle Mountain Wilderness

Saddle Mountain Wilderness is located in the extreme southeastern portion of the North Kaibab Ranger District. Elevations vary from 6,000 feet on Marble Canyon Rim to 8,000 feet on Saddle Mountain. The name originates from the profile of a prominent ridge that appears from the distance as a saddle, horn and all. The main ridge falls off into sheer walls on the south to form the Nankoweap Rim. Bounded on three sides by steep canyons, the terrain is very steep and rocky. A lightning-caused fire in 1960 consumed approximately 8,000 acres and set the stage for prime deer habitat. Regrowth has resulted in a dense mass of locust, oak, aspen, elderberry and the re-establishment of a young coniferous forest. The Saddle Mountain Trail that parallels the main ridge offers a sense of confinement, only to be rewarded with spectacular views of the Grand Canyon, Marble Canyon Gorge, Cocks Combs, House Rock Valley and Vermillion Cliffs from vantage points along the trail. The uniqueness of the wilderness is found in a perennial stream in North Canyon, habitat of the threatened Apache trout, and in the upper portion of House Rock Valley where a remnant herd of buffalo roam.

Additional information is available from the North Kaibab Ranger District, P. O. Box 248, Fredonia, AZ 86022, Phone: (520) 643-7395.

Salome Wilderness

This wilderness was established in 1984 and contains approximately 18,530 acres, with a major canyon running practically its entire length. The upper reaches of Salome Creek and Workman Creek are small perennial streams, snaking their way to the bottom of this scenic canyon. Inviting pools of water can be found nearly yearlong. Elevations range from 2,600 feet at the lower end of Salome Creek to 6,500 feet on Hopkins Mountain. Spring and fall are ideal times to visit this area; however, trails are few and access to the wilderness is limited.

Information is available from the Tonto National Forest, Pleasant Valley Ranger District, P. O. Box 450, Young, AZ 85554, Phone: (520) 462-3311.

Salt River Canyon Wilderness

This wilderness contains approximately 32,100 very rugged acres and was established in 1984. The Salt River and its spectacular canyon bisect the wilderness for its complete length. Elevations range from 2,200 feet at the canyon's lower end to 4,200 feet on White Ledge Mountain. This area can be visited practically any time; however, there are no maintained trails within the wilderness. Travel is basically by raft or kayak during the short and dangerous river-running season.

Information is available from the Tonto National Forest Supervisor's Office in Phoenix and the Globe Ranger District, Rt. 1, Box 33, Globe, AZ 88501, Phone: (520) 425-7189.

Santa Teresa Wilderness

The Santa Teresas are located in the Coronado National Forest, about 30 miles west of Safford. They are characterized by a network of rugged mountains, deep canyons and large mesas. Elevations rise from less than 4,000 feet in the canyon bottoms to nearly 7,500 feet at the summit of Cottonwood Peak.

The central part of the wilderness is dominated by Holdout and Mud Spring mesas. Holdout Canyon typifies the Santa Teresas because of its extreme ruggedness and abundance of caves and alcoves that provide extraordinary solitude. The area has several good foot trails leading to major points of interest, but is rarely used due to its remote location and somewhat difficult access over many miles of unpaved roads.

A wide variety of game and non-game animals are present, including black bear and peregrine falcon. The wilderness, consisting of 26,780 acres, is generally dominated by chaparral vegetation with stands of ponderosa pine and Douglas fir along the north flank and crest of Cottonwood Peak.

Additional information is available from the Safford Ranger District, P. O. Box 709, Safford, AZ 85548-0709, Phone: (520) 428-4150.

Sierra Ancha Wilderness

While not large in acres, this is a very special wilderness which includes precipitous box canyons, high vertical cliffs, and pine-covered mesas. The extremely rough topography limits (and in some places prohibits) cross-country travel; however, there is a good system of trails. A wide variety of plant and animal species are within the boundaries and vary from those found on the desert to those found at 8,000 feet.

First established in 1933, this 20,850-acre wilderness is full of surprises and a pleasure to explore. A Recreation Opportunity Guide is available. It is administered by the Pleasant Valley Ranger District, Tonto National Forest, P. O. Box 450, Young, AZ 85554, Phone: (520) 462-3311.

Strawberry Crater Wilderness

Located 20 miles northeast of Flagstaff, Strawberry Crater Wilderness is gently rolling pinyon-juniper, cinder terrain, about 5,500 to 6,000 feet in elevation. The wilderness is dominated at the southern tip by low cinder cones and cut at the northwestern corner by the rugged lava flow of Strawberry Crater.

Strawberry Crater is part of the San Francisco Mountain volcanic field, which contains some 600 craters and cones, and is about 50,000 to 100,000 years old.

This wilderness offers the visitor an excellent opportunity to experience a sense of time past and an endless horizon of pinyon-juniper zones. From the many low cinder cones, there are good views of the Painted Desert, Hopi Buttes, and mesas of the Little Colorado River Valley. The area offers opportunities for day hiking, backpacking, and camping. The region presents opportunities for solitude and exploration of interesting geological and archeological features. These features and the twisted, aesthetically pleasing junipers, are excellent subjects for the photographer.

For more information contact the Peaks Ranger District, 5075 N. Hwy. 89, Flagstaff, AZ 86004, Phone: (520) 526-0866.

Superstition Wilderness

This wilderness was first designated in 1939, and was expanded to its present size in 1984. It now contains approximately 160,200 acres. There is a well-developed trail system, and the western end of the wilderness receives heavy use during the cooler times of the year.

The area is starkly beautiful and often rugged, but can be inhospitable to those not equipped to meet nature on her own terms. Searing heat and a shortage of water are typical conditions in the summer. Bitter cold, torrential rains, and even snowstorms are not uncommon in the winter. To those hardy enough to meet the challenges, this wilderness offers scenic beauty, and a chance to study the many plants and animals indigenous to the area.

A Recreation Opportunity Guide is available from the Mesa Ranger District of the Tonto National Forest, P. O. Box 5800, 26 N. MacDonald, Mesa, AZ 85211-5800, Phone: (602) 835-1161.

Sycamore Canyon Wilderness

Established in 1935, this area contains a unique canyonland environment. The canyon cuts through the Mogollon Rim which forms the southern edge of the Colorado Plateau. It winds for 20 miles along Sycamore Creek and at places stretches 7 miles from rim to rim. Wind and water have exposed 7 geological associations of plants and animals set in a spectacular setting of red sandstone, white limestone, and brown lava.

Camping is limited by the often unreliable water sources. Visitors may get maps and information at Ranger District offices in Prescott, Williams, Flagstaff, and Sedona. Three National Forests, the Prescott, Kaibab and Coconino share the boundaries and spectacular beauty of this 55,937-acre area.

West Clear Creek Wilderness

Located 25 miles northwest of Camp Verde, West Clear Creek is one of the most rugged, remote canyons in northern Arizona. Clear Creek Canyon is the longest of the canyons that cut through the Mogollon Rim on the edge of the Colorado Plateau.

In spite of the short distance from the northern to southern boundary, the area offers outstanding opportunities for solitude and primitive recreation by virtue of the very steep canyon walls. A trail starts at Bull Pen Ranch and follows the creek eastward for a few miles and climbs the northern slope to the rim. This access is fairly easy, even for inexperienced hikers. The Maxwell and Tramway Trails provide access from the rim to the canyon bottom.

In the main, narrow part of the canyon, there are no trails. It is necessary to wade or swim in many places when hiking from one end of the canyon to the other so that even the most seasoned hiker will find lots of challenge. The canyon is wild and primitive. Visitors must plan trips carefully.

For more information, contact the Coconino National Forest, Long Valley Ranger District, HC 31, Box 68, Happy Jack, AZ 86024, Phone: (520) 354-2216 or the Beaver Creek Ranger District, HC 64, Box 240, Rimrock, AZ 86335, Phone: (520) 567-4501.

Wet Beaver Wilderness

Wet Beaver is a steep-walled canyon cutting into the rim of the Colorado Plateau. Supai sandstone and shale form striking red cliffs along the lower canyon. This wilderness is a benchmark of pristine riparian habitats and excellent water quality; an excellent example of one of Arizona's finest and rarest resources, a perennially flowing desert stream. Opportunities for primitive recreation are further enhanced by the narrow twisting character of the canyon which offers seclusion, even with relatively high use. Two major trails, Apache Maid and Bell Trail, offer easy access to the rim country portions of this wilderness.

For more information, contact the Coconino National Forest, Beaver Creek Ranger District, HC 64, Box 240, Rimrock, AZ 86335, Phone: (520) 567-4501.

Woodchute Wilderness

This small wilderness offers relatively easy access and spectacular views of the San Francisco Peaks and panoramic vistas of central Arizona. Created in 1984, the 5,700 acres that comprise the Woodchute Wilderness range in elevation from 5,500 feet to 7,800 feet. Ponderosa pine is the dominate species located at the upper elevations which gradually gives wax to pinyon pine and Utah juniper at the lower and relatively drier elevations.

There are maintained wilderness trails and public access points currently in existence. It is recommended that topographic maps be studied prior to a visit.

Additional information concerning Woodchute Wilderness may be obtained from the Chino Valley Ranger District office in Chino Valley at (520) 567-4121, and the Verde Ranger District office in Camp Verde at (520) 636-2302, or the Prescott National Forest Supervisor's Office in Prescott.

ARIZONA PRIMITIVE AREA

Blue Range Primitive Area

This 173,762-acre area, designated in 1933, is now completely within the state of Arizona. The other 29,304-acre portion in New Mexico became the new Blue Range Wilderness with passage of the 1980 New Mexico Wilderness Act.

Lying at the southern edge of the Colorado Plateau, the Blue Range is rugged and beautiful with many geologic and scenic attractions, including timbered ridges and deep canyons. The Mogollon Rim, made famous as the "Tonto Rim" in Zane Grey's books, crosses the area from west to east. This rim, unique from both geological and ecological standpoints, is further enhanced by the spectacular Blue River Canyon and River. There is spruce and fir in the high country, and ponderosa pine, pinyon and juniper in lower areas.

Deer, elk, and other big and small game find food and shelter in the primitive area's more remote reaches.

Trail access is fairly good, but prospective visitors are reminded that this is big, rough, generally dry country. Inquire at Ranger District offices at Clifton (520) 687-1301, or Alpine (520) 339-4384 and the Apache-Sitgreaves National Forests' offices in Springerville for seasonal information and maps.

National Forest Tips & Info

- April through July are the driest months, increasing the threat of forest fires.

- Be certain that your campfire is completely out. Use your hands to spread dirt and water over the coals.

- If you smoke, adhere to these precautions. Don't smoke on trails. Clear a small area to be used as an ashtray. Pack out your cigarette butts, filters don't easily decompose.

- Water hemlock, mushrooms and berries can be deadly. If you are unsure of a plant's identity, leave it alone.

- Afternoon thunderstorms are a common occurrence from July to summer's end.

- Flash floods are common after heavy rains, especially in canyons and washes.

- Carry tire chains. They are extremely helpful on mud slicked, snow covered and ice coated roads.

- When hiking into a forest, identify landmarks for your hike out. Build cairns along the way, except in wilderness areas.

- Inform a third party of your itinerary and when you expect to return. Upon your return, contact that person.

- From mid-May to July, deerflies and horseflies are troublesome above 7,000 feet.

- Summer rains bring a profusion of mosquitos.

- Learn to identify poison oak. Leaves are usually shiny, bright green in the spring, bright red, or maroon in the fall. In the winter, there are no leaves. Poison oak can look like a shrub or vine always with three-lobed leaves. Remember "Leaves of three, let it be."

- Dogs must be leashed in all developed areas.

- It's illegal to remove or disturb historic and/or prehistoric artifacts.

- Pack enough water to last the extent of your trip and then some - untreated stream or lake water can cause illness.

- Begin car travel with a full tank of gas.

- A shovel is an invaluable tool to store in your car.

- Don't litter. Litter lasts this long:

Cigarette butts	1 - 5 Years
Aluminum cans	80 - 100 Years
Orange peels	Up to 2 Years
Plastic bags	10 - 20 Years
Glass bottles	1 Million Years
Tin cans	50 Years
Wool socks	1 - 5 Years
Plastic bottles	Indefinitely

IF YOU PACK IT IN... PACK IT OUT

Mammals, Reptiles and Rodents of Arizona's National Forests and Deserts

Abert's Tree Squirrel

Otherwise known as tassel-haired squirrels, these beauties are quite large and are certainly among America's most unique tree squirrels. With tufts of long hair growing from the end of their ears, it's easy to see how their nickname originated. Dark gray with a reddish stripe along the middle part of the body, the fur on the underparts and tail is light gray to white. Increase your chances of observing an Abert's squirrel with a visit to a ponderosa pine forest, their favorite habitat - no small wonder since the inner bark of the ponderosa is their main food source. They also supplement their diet with mushrooms, acorns and pine seeds.

Acorn Woodpecker

They may not be as colorful as the lovable cartoon character Woody Woodpecker, but acorn woodpeckers are just as entertaining and noisy. Diminutive in size, this woodpecker packs a mean beak and a determined attitude. The acorn's philosophy: if it's wood, it's fair game. Although insects are the woodpeckers preferred delicacy, the acorn woodpecker diligently excavates and then plugs holes in trees with its namesake acorn, storing the nuts for nibbling emergencies.

Woodpeckers thrive on teamwork. They live in colonies and members help with the drilling and filling of holes, along with a variety of other chores.

Antelope

The number of people who have actually seen an antelope up close are few and far between. Aside from being human-shy, antelopes are the fastest land animals in North America, reaching speeds of 60MPH. A three-day old antelope can outrun a full-grown man. Bucks have forked horns which in mature animals extend well beyond the ears. Unlike deer, antelope do not shed their horns. Instead they shed only the outer sheath of the horn. Born in springtime, the offspring are often twins.

Arizona Pocket Mice

These adorable, white-bellied rodents are night-time creatures. During the day, they remain in burrows, jamming the entrances with earth to keep out unwanted visitors. Their diet consists of grass and weed seeds and they can exist months on only the meager water they extract from their food sources.

Bannertail Kangaroo Rats

Scientists believe the seed hoarding habit of the Bannertail Kangaroo Rat is the key element in maintaining and preserving our desert environment. These small, furry, long-tailed rodents are prevalent throughout the Southwestern deserts and have a striking resemblance to mice. They never drink water, relying on seeds as their only source of moisture. Their inner ear is tuned to low-frequency sound which can detect the presence of enemies - snakes and owls. They're nocturnal creatures but as always, nature provides - these critters have an incredible sense of smell allowing them to locate both food sources and soulmates in the dark.

Bats

Horror movies have created a negative, undeserved image of bats. Contrary to legend, they do not come in the night "to suck your blood" or become entangled in your hair. They are actually beneficial to the environment. It is through their pollination efforts that the saguaro survives and insect populations are contained.

There are over 900 species, from small creatures that fit in the palm of your hand to those with wing spans topping out at five feet. Although all are nocturnal, their habits vary greatly. Some migrate while others remain true to one cave for more than twenty years. Some may feed year round while others prefer hibernation. Some maintain coed societies while others believe in separation of the sexes. Their diets range from insects to fruit and pollen. One trait they all have in common is their reliance on high-frequency sounds to guide them through the night. As they have for millions of years, when darkness falls they emerge from their caves by the thousands, quickly darkening the sky with fluttering wings, satisfying their sometimes voracious appetites. To witness their flight is to witness primordial nature.

Black Bears

Despite their enormous size and "bad boy" reputations, black bears are shy, night dwelling animals who usually pose little threat to people. But any confrontation with a bear can prove fatal. And it has been documented that dogs can provoke these normally docile animals. Black bears are omnivorous, surviving on a diet of plants, berries, small mammals and garbage. The smallest of North American bears, the black bear stands 40 inches tall, can stretch 4-6 feet in length and weighs in at about 450 pounds. Contrary to their name, colors range from black, to light tan to reddish brown. Black bears dwell in dense woodlands or deep, cool canyons situated above 5,000 feet. Most cubs are born in January and twins are common.

Black-Tailed Jackrabbits

Contrary to popular belief, and the animal's name, jackrabbits are not really rabbits. They're large hares, averaging 24 inches in length. An interesting color combination, they're greyish on top, white on the bottom with black striped tails and long blacktipped ears. The jackrabbit's summer diet consists of various plants, while in the winter they chow on woody and dried vegetation.

Bobcats

At first sight, they'll remind you of winsome albeit oversized house cats. But don't be fooled by the innocent appearance and somewhat passive behavior of the most common wildcat in North America. Just catch sight of one perched atop a giant saguaro catching a few Z's and you'll quickly appreciate the bobcat's tenacity. Timid toward humans, they ruthlessly pursue their prey. Rabbits, mice, squirrels, bats, porcupines and even small deer top off a bobcat's menu.

Chuckwallas

These easily frightened lizards seek shelter and safety between rock crevices. Measuring in at 16 inches, chuckwallas have large bodies with rounded abdomens, loose folds of skin around the neck and thick, blunt tails. For protection against predators, they turn sideways, wedge themselves between rocks and inflate their bodies to insure a tight fit.

Coyotes

Extremely adaptable, the coyote is one of the only animals whose population has increased over the last hundred years. As predators and scavengers, coyotes thrive under most conditions. Weighing from twenty to fifty pounds and ranging in color from buff gray to reddish gray, they share a likeness with canines but there's something very distant and aloof that sets them apart. In early morning, they can often be seen nonchalantly strolling through residential neighborhoods that border the desert, tails down and tucked, possessing a slightly mangy, underfed look. At dusk, their plaintive cries and howls can send shivers up and down your spine. Normally, they live and hunt in packs, establishing lairs in mountain caves.

Desert Bighorn Sheep

The migration of the bighorn sheep began nearly 100,000 years ago when they crossed the Bering land bridge and then little by little migrated southward to Arizona. For more than 10,000 years they survived on the land, overcoming many obstacles until the arrival of miners and explorers in Arizona threatened their existence. Not only were they killed for food, but their numbers also dwindled due to contamination of water supplies and development of grazing land. Forced to flee their lowland habitat, the majestic bighorn sheep made their way to the remote confines of the Grand Canyon and other secluded mountain ranges. Although these areas afforded protection, they sorely lacked the one necessary ingredient for survival - a sufficient and reliable water supply.

It wasn't until 1967 that their plight was recognized and the Arizona Desert Bighorn Sheep Society was formed to save this species from extinction. Their motto, "Sine aqua mortis" meaning, "Without water, death," reflects their main concern. Untold man hours and more than a million dollars has been contributed to erect and secure reservoirs for the besieged animals. Without the dauntless efforts of the Society, the sight of the elusive bighorns, perched atop the rocky crags they prefer, would have been lost to all of us, for all time.

Desert Cottontails

Talk about cute! This brownish, desert dwelling rabbit measures about 15 inches with long ears, large eyes and an adorable "powder puff" white tail. Catch sight of one of these hopping critters, and you might start humming "Here Comes Peter Cottontail". The cottontails' primary defense against predators is their light-footedness and uncanny ability to remain motionless.

Their next best defense is their reproductive potential. Fertile Myrtles can give birth to a litter of 2 to 6 bunnies, 3 to 5 times a year. And within 3 days of giving birth, another litter can be expected in about 4 weeks.

Desert Tortoises

The survival of desert tortoises can be attributed to the burrows they dig to protect themselves from the scorching days of summer. In winter, during bone chilling nights, these reptiles hibernate in their burrows. Brown or reddish-brown with lighter color spots or blotches on their hard shells, a mature tortoise will measure ten to fourteen inches.

Diamondback Rattlesnakes

These slithering creatures of the night can attain lengths of six to seven feet. Females give live birth to as many as thirty young in late summer. They have large, distinct heads with dark diamond or hexagon-shaped body blotches, and black and white ringed tails. When cornered with no means of escape, this snake will raise its head and body off the ground and emit a loud rattling sound of warning. Hightail it out of reach - there is no second warning.

Digger Bees

Talk about tunneling, the English/French Chunnel Engineers could take a lesson or two from digger bees. Female bees burrow deep into the ground, build a nest, fill it with pollen and nectar and then lay an egg. Once hatched, the baby bee will dine on the pollen and nectar until adulthood when it begins the laborious process of tunneling out. This is where engineering know-how comes into play.

The male Digger Bee is armed with highly sensitive odor detectors, capable of sniffing out a female as she's digging her way to the surface. The male bee knows exactly where to dig and dig he will - with unlimited energy and unerring accuracy - to meet up with his female destiny, the first of many. There are even times that the male will have to do battle with other males on the same bee-scent. Once mating occurs, the female will start the digging and nesting process once again while the male will sniff his way to another tunnel of fun.

El Clarinete

Aptly named, the songs of el clarinetes are harmonious and sweet sounding. From the depths of the wilderness to inner city parks, these birds fill nature's airways with melodic tunes. If you're lucky enough to be in earshot of el clarinete, take a moment to enjoy the music - you won't be sorry. El clarinetes are large birds distinguishable by their blue-black color and keel-shaped tail which droops in flight.

Gambel's Quail

Ten to eleven inches tall, both the male and female have teardrop-shaped head plumes. Common throughout the deserts, you'll often see Mom and Dad Gambel running helter skelter with a covey of up to twelve teeny quail. The quail's loud, cackling call usually consists of three syllables.

Gecko Lizards

Gecko species number 750 worldwide but only two call Arizona home; the Western Banded, a native, and the Mediterranean, a comparative newcomer. Rarely seen because of their secretive, nocturnal nature, the Western Banded gecko is one of the most common animals in Arizona. Even when they venture out during daylight hours, their desert coloring provides a natural camouflage. Tiny in size, they're only about four inches long and barely an inch around. They have dark colored bands from neck to tail and walk as if on tippy-toe. Thanks to the fat storage in their tails, they survive and prosper in our desert environment.

The Mediterranean gecko took a shortcut through customs on nursery stock and other imports from Europe. These passportless critters have adapted well to Arizona, finding cohabitation with humans quite satisfying. Their colors run the gamut from pinkish to grayish with brown or gray blotches that become bands on their tails. A velcro-like pad on their feet enables them to defy gravity, sort of like Fred Astaire when he danced on the walls and ceilings in *DADDY LONG LEGS*. These darling lizards are harmless with an insatiable appetite for insects.

With their velvety bodies and large inquisitive eyes, geckos have a definite charm and appeal. Only one of two reptiles with a voice box, when frightened, the gecko will signal his fear with a Chihuahua-like bark.

Gila Monsters

"Don't bother me, I won't bother you," is the gila monster refrain. The only poisonous lizard species in the world, the venom is secreted by glands in the lower jaw. Gila monsters are plump, patterned in salmon, yellow, red and black. A blunt head, rounded snout, and thick tail make them easy to identify. But if you're that close, back off.

Gray Foxes

Normally nocturnal, the gray fox has large ears and a black-tipped bushy tail. Although rodents are the preferred food of choice, these adaptable creatures can survive on a vegetarian diet of berries, tubers and cactus fruit. Measuring a mere forty inches, the gray fox is smaller than a coyote and is tinged with red coloring at the sides and throat.

Ground Squirrels

Witness the antics of these cute furry fellows and you'll wish you had a video camera along. Morning rituals include stretching and yawning, kisses from mom, wrestling matches with siblings and then chow time. Hey, these could be my home videos!

The similarities to human families are uncanny. But there's more to mother's pecks than just affection. She's more or less smelling her young to make certain they're hers. Each squirrel family has a distinct odor and it's through "kisses" that this scent is exchanged. Squirrels have shown themselves to be affectionate and family-oriented. Mother is at the core of the family, shunning the father after mating.

When squirrels are of breeding age, their dependence and closeness quickly dissipates. Leaving home for squirrels who come of age is like kids leaving home for college - they stake out their own territory and begin to interact with non-family members. And the cycle continues.

Harris' Antelope Squirrels

Tiny is one way to describe this 9-inch ground squirrel. Talk about tall tails, this squirrel's wagger is one-third of its body size. These ground squirrels have uncovered the secret to desert survival- rest time. When the temperature rises, the squirrel takes to bed to conserve vital moisture. These squirrels are easy to identify by the white stripe along each side of their gray colored bodies and the white line defining their eyes.

Harvester Ants

Oops, there goes another harvester ant. These indomitable, indestructible inhabitants of the Arizona deserts have prospered for nearly 100 million years - and its hasn't always been a picnic. "Have seed, will succeed," could be their motto. Their methodical seed collecting and storage processes contribute to their longevity and sociability. Millions live together in a colony with one female as the queen of the nest (the nest is often buried as deep as 20 feet). They have but one purpose in life - to build up their seed supply. This teamwork definitely pays off. In the driest of the dry climes, harvester ants encompass nearly 95% of the ant species.

Javelina

Also called collared peccary, this animal may not go "oink, oink," but it sure looks as if it should. The javelina bears a strong physical resemblance to a pig, except that instead of a muddy sty, it makes its home in the desert. Darkish grey in color, the javelina has a lighter band of heavy, bristly hair around the neck that sometims erects into a mane. Most weigh 50 pounds and measure 30 inches in length. Nothing pleases them more than a meal of prickly pear cactus, a source of both food and water. By exuding a foul-smelling musk, the javelina keeps itself from becoming another critter's dinner. Want to catch a peek of a peccary? Try early morning or late afternoon.

Mountain Lions

Talk about loners- mountain lions (aka cougar) define the term. They live a solitary existence in the thickest, wildest, most rugged terrain of the state. Even biologists who have dedicated their lives to studying these large predators have never witnessed a free-roaming specimen. On occasion, they've observed a mountain lion who's been trapped by snares or treed by hounds. But even loners have the urge to propagate, and mating season is one of the rare times that these cats interact with one another. Tan or gray with a white belly, they weigh anywhere from 80 to 200 pounds. One of the most efficient predators of North America, they prey on elk, deer, javelina and at times, domestic livestock.

Mule Deer

Named for their long, mule-like ears, these deer inhabit both the mountainous regions and low-lying deserts of Arizona. If you're planning a visit to the Grand Canyon, walk around the grounds at the El Tovar Hotel at dusk. Although mule deer tend to be solitary, don't be surprised to encounter one or more strolling the grounds, grazing, oblivious to the humans who are oohing and aahing over them. Their sweet, innocent expressions and diminutive size will remind you of Bambi with Dumbo's ears.

Woody plants are their favorite munchies and they can always be found in forests that are experiencing new growth after severe burns. During mating season, the females will join the males for a bachelor party and after the breeding, the sexes separate and go their own way.

Porcupine

If it's porcupine mating season and you're taking an evening stroll through a brushy, forested area, you might just hear the groans, grunts and screams of the nocturnal porcupine. The quills which cover the porcupine's body, particularly the tail and rump are often sufficient defense against most predators - animal and human alike. But not against bobcats and cougars who have learned to slip the porcupine on its back before attacking, exposing its vulnerable underbelly.

Praying Mantis

In addition to first-rate camouflage techniques, and excellent eyesight, six out of ten praying mantis possess built-in "bat ear" survival mechanisms which make the praying mantis one of the most merciless predators in the insect world. Located on the insect's underside, this ear enables the mantis to hear the high-frequency cries of bats, their mortal enemy.

Mantis vs bat is an ongoing game of survival. Frogs and mice can also become "specialties of the day." Spiked, praying forearms trap prey while the mantis slowly, bite by bite, devours its dinner.

Talk about killjoys. The female mantis can teach the black widow a trick or two. In laboratory experiments, females bite off the male's head, causing his lovemaking desires to reach their peak. While in the throes of amour, the female eats her mate from the head down, providing herself with egg producing nutrients but certainly not a recipe for long lasting love.

Ramsey Canyon Leopard Frogs

According to scientists, the secluded water-filled canyons of Ramsey Canyon in southwestern Arizona are prime breeding locations for a new species of amphibians, the leopard frog, the only known species to communicate with underwater croaking.

Ringtails

A two pound bundle of fluff and energy, the ring-tail is a member of the raccoon family. Sometimes called a night monkey because it flies through the night with amazing speed and agility, its face is like a slender fox, its body catlike with a bushy, banded tail. Ringtails prefer meat but these predators will eat just about anything they can kill or find.

The envy of rock climbers, they can scramble up sheer slick rock surfaces using their retractable claws and soft footpads, while their busy tails provide the balance they need. It's their descent though that's most remarkable. By being able to rotate their hind feet a complete 180 degrees, they descend headfirst as quickly and adeptly as they ascend. When this critter can't find an easy way up, he uses a spring forward and ricochet action to bounce from stone wall to stone wall all the way to the peak. Pogo sticks could be named for these little guys. But don't count on seeing one of these little acrobats putting on a show - they're nocturnal creatures who hunt and frolic under the cover of darkness.

Roadrunner

Sometimes called the desert cuckoo, this clownish looking bird is known for its snake catching abilities. Growing to lengths of two feet, the roadrunner flies only when frightened or on a downhill course. You'll often see these birds in suburban desert neighborhoods, quickly crossing streets as if on an important, no-nonsense mission.

Rock Squirrels

Another tall tail - this ground dwelling rodent is twenty inches long - with a tail nearly half that size. This furry, grayish brown creature prefers morning and evening outings, munching away on seeds, nuts, fruits, berries and insects.

Rocky Mountain Elk

Merriam's Elk once flourished in Arizona. But by the early 1900's, these mammals had been hunted to extinction. A combined civic effort brought eighty Rocky Mountain Elk to Arizona from Montana, their native state. The Apache-Sitgreaves National Forest, located on the Mogollon Rim, became their new home. Throughout the next few years, additional elk were brought into various locations throughout the state. Plentiful grazing lands and relatively moderate winters contributed to the large numbers that now inhabit Arizona's forestlands. Elk travel in small herds and can often be seen dining along Route 87, north of Payson - sometimes at dusk, traffic will be forced to stop when a herd crosses the highway. An up-close sighting of a large antlered buck is a humbling experience.

Scorpions

Long, curvy-tailed arachnids, nobody likes a scorpion. Every species is poisonous and ill-tempered. Like the black widow, females often eat the male after mating. And if momma scorpion is hungry, she'll often eat her young as well. Scorpions have existed for more than 450 million years. Needless

to say, they're more than adaptable, they're indestructible. Remaining hidden most of the time, they
can exist a year without food. Their water supply
comes from the fluids of the insects that comprise
their meager diets.

Solpugida

The nocturnal habits of this spider account for the
lack of sightings. The solpugida compensates for its
poor vision with a pair of gooey appendages that
are used to capture prey. Because of its speed, it's
commonly referred to as a windscorpion. Once a
victim is captured, the solpudiga's remarkably powerful jaw makes escape impossible. This nighttime
feeder contributes to the environment by control-
ling the population growth of a bunch of nasty buggers. Way to go, solpugida!

Sonoran Beavers

Regarded by some as impish pests, beavers are
do-gooders nonetheless. Dams erected by them create meadows and with the meadows, new forestlands. Their construction skills are legendary.
Their efforts keep silt from washing away and
reduce erosion. This enrichment of the land equates
to more abundant wildlife.

Natural born builders, they're vanguards of recy-
cling. They'll use anything to build their dams and
homes. Beavers build with one purpose - safety -
for home, hearth and kits. They create dams which
in turn create ponds which in turn create water
sources which allow beavers to build safe havens
amid water, creating protective moats. Whew - no

wonder they're so busy. And busy they are, building for themselves and doing more than any other species to improve the ecosystem. And they're so dam cute.

Sonoran Desert Tortoise

A wild desert tortoise may live for more than a hundred years. Slow and steady definitely pays off for these denizens of the desert. By hibernating during the long hot months these antediluvian animals beat the summer heat. The fruit of the prickly pear cactus is their favorite food but they're also fond of grass and flowers. Although their hatchlings are easy prey for many of the lizards, animals and birds of the desert, the existence of the Sonoran Desert Tortoise is more seriously threatened by development of their environment and by off-road recreation.

Spadefoot Toads

Spadefoot toads are an odd species of desert amphibians who spend most of their adult lives below ground, emerging only to mate and sometimes to eat. Talk about making the most of calories, these toads can exist for a year on a couple of nights worth of dining - living proof of the adage, it's not how much but rather what you eat. Termites are the insects of choice, their high fat content providing an abundant energy source for the toads. Their mating habits are just as unusual. Spadefoot toads become amorous during the summer monsoons, often traveling great distances to locate a standing pool of water, the preferred mating locale. Males sing a song of love guaranteed to attract females. After a hug and a couple of laps in the pond, the egg making process is complete. Although thousands are conceived, only a few survive but when they do, they can live twenty years or more.

Spotted Skunks

One of four species found in the mountains of southeast Arizona, the spotted skunk can become quite emboldened at nightfall. Curious buggers, they've been known to invade campsites, sometimes rifling through campers' backpacks. Human or animal, no one messes with a skunk. These little "stinkers" are fearless fellows with a strong scents of power.

Tarantulas

They might look scary but these cocoa brown hirsute arachnids are gentle, fragile giants. And you'd have to go out of your way to be bitten by one. Slow moving, they rarely travel far from their furrows. Surviving on a diet of grasshoppers and crickets, females generally live 25 years, about double that of their male counterparts.

Turkey Vulture

With a wingspan of more than five feet, the turkey vulture weighs in at about four pounds and is one of the largest raptors in the world. A protected species, they often get the worst "rap." Although seemingly awkward on the ground, in flight, they're "Nature's Concordes," achieving speeds of up to 34MPH, and flying with a graceful beauty that is mesmerizing to behold. They locate prey with their excellent sense of smell and 20/20 vision. Devoted parents, either sex will remain with the chicks, refusing to flee even when threatened by humans. Chicks are fed carrion and take their first flight after a couple of months. Many times mating vultures remain together with their grown offspring, creating family units.

Whitetail Deer

Less common than mule deer, they make their home in the pinyon-juniper area just below the Mogollon Rim. Not only can you tell a whitetail by its white tail but when they scamper, they're easily distinguishable from their cousins. While mule deer bound up and down, whitetails leap, exposing the white undersides of their tails.

The term, "in velvet" refers to that period of time before the bucks begin to rub the velvet from their antlers, readying themselves for simulated battles intended to prove their manliness before mating season. But like their mule deer cousins, when the stag party is over, they regroup into single sex groups. The males shed their antlers in March and begin the growing process anew.

White-Throated Wood Rats

These adorable rodents find safe refuge by digging holes at the base of cholla and prickly pear cactus. Bat-eared, you'll often see them perched on their hind legs, squirrel-like, before darting away to the safety of their burrows. They're also called pack rats because they'll collect anything they can carry - from buttons and twigs to bits of glass and paper.

NATIVE FLORA OF ARIZONA

From dense forests to arid deserts, a potpourri of flora blankets the great state of Arizona, awaiting your discovery. A sampling of the state's wildflowers and plants follows.

Acacia

A popular desert tree, acacia are similar to tourists-they thrive in and soak up as much sunshine as possible. Acacia trees are identifiable by their feather-like leaves and bouquets of small, yet showy, yellow or white flowers. In addition to the leaves and flowers, long, sharp thorns are usually present.

Ajo Lily

Resembling an Easter Lily, this tall-stemmed, creamy white flower thrives in the sandy areas of western Arizona.

Apricot Mallow/Globe Mallow

Several species of globe mallow are common in the Sonoran Desert. Growing to heights of 1-5 feet, most have scalloped leaves and peachy-pink flowers. Globe mallows are sometimes called "sore-eye poppies" because they can cause an allergic reaction in some people.

Barrel Cactus

A large, cylindrical plant, the barrel cactus is often mistaken for a young saguaro. During the flowering season, brightly colored buds cover the crown. The cactus also produces large yellow fruits, a delicacy for birds and animals.

Brittlebush

Dome-shaped, this winter-flowering bush has silvery leaves and grows to 2-3 feet in height. The brilliant yellow of brittlebush sprouts like sunshine from the often rocky desert terrain. Flower stems rise several inches above the brittle leaf-covered branches. Interestingly, this shrub exudes a gum which was chewed by desert Indians and also burned as incense by priests.

Century Plant

Otherwise known as the agave, this unique plant prospers in the arid areas of southern United States. Most commonly identified by its thick, sword-like leaves, the century plant experiences a sudden one to two month growth spurt. Within this short time, the stem can reach heights of up to 20 feet before blooming aromatic, yellow flowers. Contrary to its name, the century only takes about 25 years to bloom. But once the flowers blossom, the century's existence comes to a bittersweet end - this plant dies after just one bloom.

Chia

Often referred to as desert sage, this 3-foot high plant has small balls of tiny blue flowers along the stems. Although the chia is in the mint family, it emits a skunky scent. Southwestern Indians added powdered chia seeds to water to make a nutritious drink.

Cholla

Typically a low-growing, needle-rich cactus, the cholla's orchid-like blooms come in a range of rainbow-hued colors.

Staghorn: The skeleton branches are cylindrical and pointed and resemble a deer's antlers, hence the name. Deep reddish-lavender flowers bloom near the ends of the branches.

Teddy Bear: Each spine is encased in a sheath that looks like white tissue. The broken pieces which litter the ground may take root or die. In any case though, the stickers remain sharp. Flowers are green or yellow and the petals are often streaked with lavender.

Creosote Bush

One of the most abundantly widespread and successful arid land plants, its endurance and longevity can be attributed to its unusual method of securing its water supply. Old roots release a toxic substance which kills other plant seedlings who infringe upon its moisture potential.

Flowering year round, the yellow blooms are most profuse in April and May. This plant, which ranges from 2-8 feet tall is characterized by dark green leaves and blackish stems. After a rain, it emits a resinous odor. In Mexico, the plant is believed to possess medicinal value.

Desert Marigold

This wildflower blooms throughout the year, but March to October are its glory months. The bright yellow flowers sit atop long solitary stems and brighten the desert landscape in every direction.

Fiddleneck

Measuring 8-18 inches tall, the plant is identified by its curling head stems which resemble the scroll of a violin. Small yellow flowers decorate the stalk, while the leaves are long with bristly hairs. The plant provides a valuable food source to birds.

Fleabane

Blooming from late winter to early spring, the blossoms can vary in size from a dime to a quarter. White petals with yellow centers, they're related to the sunflower but look more like wild daisies. There's an ancient belief that the odor of some species repels fleas.

Fremont Pincushion

Showers bring flowers is true for this wildflower. Within each head, the white flowers vary in size, big on the outside, small in the center.

Heronbill

Measuring 3-12 inches tall, the heronbill has small, hidden flowers which bloom pink-violet in February and March. The seeds of this wildflower plant themselves by untwisting their moist corkscrew-like fruits, and literally screwing themselves into the soil.

Joshua Tree

Contrary to popular belief, the elegant Joshua tree is not a California exclusive. The area where the Sonoran and Mohave deserts meet in northwestern Arizona is home to a magnificent display of this unusual desert plant. In fact, this is the only place in the world where you'll witness Joshua trees and saguaro cactus growing side by side. With upstretched arms reaching heights of 25 feet and a possible lifespan of 500 years, the "praying plant" is a sight you won't soon forget and one that will be around for many generations to come.

Lupine

This 2-foot tall wildflower is part of the pea family. When ripe, the pod explodes and flings seed into the air. The seeds germinate easily, needing just half an inch of rain. The blooming period of this fragrant, violet-purple wildflower is January to May. You'll often see it mixed among other colorful flowers.

Mesquite Tree

The mesquite, like many desert trees, grows best in washes where the soil is very deep and underground water is reachable. In their continuing quest for water, the roots of the mesquite often work their way down as far as 100 feet. In order to germinate, the seed pods of the mesquite have to pass through the digestive tracts of any number of browsing animals. It is only then that they'll take root and sprout.

Mexican Goldpoppy

A subspecies of the California poppy, it blooms in the spring with four petals which are colored bright gold to orange. Flowers open only during sunny hours, and contain a profusion of blooms.

Ocotillo

This spidery plant is characterized by long, woody, thorny, unbranched stems which extend upward from 10 to 20 feet. In the springtime, the tips of the stems explode with scarlet red flowers which resemble wrapped and shredded crepe paper.

Organ Pipe Cactus

The uniqueness of this cactus is best captured in a 516-square mile area of the Sonoran Desert where the cactus thrives best - Organ Pipe Cactus National Monument. Besides Mexico, the monument is the only place you'll catch a first-hand look at this cactus species. With a cluster of trunks resembling 18 to 20 foot organ pipes, it's easy to see where the name originated.

Paloverde

Arizona's state tree, every spring the flowers of this tree paint the desert in brilliant mounds of yellow. Although the foliage resembles long, slender needles, it's actually leaves. The tree grows in abundance throughout the Sonoran Desert. Native Americans grind the dried seeds into flour for cooking. The immature seeds can be eaten raw, like green peas.

Pincushion Cactus

This small cactus looks like an egg covered with fine white spines and black needles resembling fish-hooks. You'll find this cactus tucked among rocks or hiding under chollas. A late spring bloomer, its flowers are pink or lavender.

Prickly Pear

Living only about twenty years, this plant is easily identified by its flat joint pads. There are many varieties but most have yellow blossoms. Young ears often break off a dying plant and take root as new growth. The pear-shaped fruits are red and juicy and are used to make scrumptious jelly and candy.

Saguaro

The saguaro is the largest and longest-living cactus in the United States. During the average life span of 150-200 years, a saguaro can grow up to fifty feet and weigh almost 10 tons. When the plant is about 75 years old, arms sprout at every conceivable angle from the main trunk. The saguaro's surface is fluted, thereby creating its own shade. The fluting allows the cactus to expand as it takes in water, and contracts when the water runs dry. Its pipe-like inner structure stores great quantities of water and can withstand many years of drought. Regardless of the amount of rain, every year clusters of white flowers bloom atop its crown. The waxy-looking flowers open at night and are a source of food for bats, moths and a variety of insects. The fruit of the saguaro is harvested and consumed by the Papago Indians.

Scorpionweed

Named for the curling habit of the blossoming flower heads which resemble a scorpion's tail in a striking position, the purple-violet blooms last from February to June. This 4-16 inch plant emits an offensive odor when crushed.

Strawberry Hedgehog

This cactus was named for the sweet, fleshy fruit that ripens in the summer. Most have needle-like yellow spines, pointing downward. The flowers run the gamut from magenta to pale pink, and every shade in between.

Yucca

This perennial plant comes in many shapes and sizes. But for the most part, the yucca are distinguishable by their long, sword-like leaves which bloom waxy, ivory-white flowers. The species most commonly found throughout Arizona is known as the Joshua Tree.

ARIZONA'S GHOST TOWNS & MINING CAMPS

Ghost towns and mining camps can provide interesting adventures for you and Fido. There are some precautions you should take to ensure a safe trip.

- Leash your dog. Use extreme caution when walking. Open and collapsing mine shafts can be deadly. Remain on traveled paths and trails. Check with local residents regarding weather and road conditions.

- Use care when exploring old buildings. Their foundations may be weathered and weakened.

- The treasure is the town, not the artifacts. Please take only pictures.

- Do a vehicle check to be certain your vehicle is road worthy and able to handle rough terrain. Ghost and mining towns are in remote areas. Carry sufficient water, food, a first-aid kit and other necessary supplies.

- Tell someone your planned itinerary. And stick with it. Make contact upon your return. Unforeseen dangers exist in ghost towns.

- Beware of weed-covered mineshafts.

- Explore in daylight, never at night.

The following ghost towns are detailed because they offer dog-friendly lodging. For a complete listing of ghost and mining towns throughout the state, contact the Arizona Office of Tourism, 2702 N. 3rd Street, Ste. 4015, Phoenix, AZ 85004, (602) 542-8687.

Bisbee

Established in 1875, this quaint town possesses an Old World charm. The climate is lovely year-round with summer temperatures averaging 84°, winter temperatures in the mid-sixties. Bisbee has managed to survive despite several fires and mine closings. Today it is a thriving, albeit small, art community.

By 1877, miners and prospectors began staking claims and Bisbee quickly emerged as a lucrative mining town. Phelps Dodge began digging for ore and built many of the structures that still stand today.

Annual events:

- April: Attracts cyclists for the La Vuelta de Bisbee. You and the pupster can watch these pedal pushers during four grueling days of steep competition.

- May: Heralds hardy runners who test their endurance in the Mule Mountain Marathon.

- July: Boasts Arizona's oldest July 4th Celebration and Parade.

- August: Bring thee to Bisbee and partake of the nationally recognized Poetry Festival.

- October: Town abounds with rockhounds attending the Bisbee Mineral Show.

- November: Features the Festival of Lights.

Weekend travelers can sometimes catch an old western melodrama or a showcase of local artwork. And any time of the year, check out the directory section of this book for outdoor adventures, or just mosey about Bisbee admiring the town's interesting structures. Take sometime to smell the roses in your wanderings, they seem to grow everywhere. For additional information, contact the Bisbee Chamber of Commerce, 7 Main Street, P. O. Box Drawer BA, Bisbee, AZ 85603, (520) 432-5421.

Goldfield

Leash up Laddie and get ready to explore this fascinating mining town. Depending on the size of the group visiting, tours of one of the old mines may be open to the pooch. The mine is interesting and offers insight into mining history and equipment. Mostly a ghost town today, Goldfield bloomed from the 1890s until the mine closings in 1915.

Directions: Located 5 miles from Apache Junction on State 88 For additional information contact, Mine Tours (520) 983-0333. Fees: $3.50 adults/ $1.50 kids/goldpanning $3 additional.

Oatman

Oatman offers visitors a chance to learn about the wilder west of the past. Weekends are riddled with staged gunfights, and wild burros beg for biscuits in the streets. Named after a family of slain settlers, Oatman maintains a hard-to-find flavor of the old southwest. The people that continue to reside in Oatman adhere to a "never say die" motto. Their determination and old-fashioned grit has kept Oatman alive through many adverse situations, including the closing of the gold mines in the 1940s and the rerouting of Route 66 in the 1950s.

Special events:

- September: Labor Day Weekend: Uh-oh Fido, it's a biscuit throwing contest. Sorry, burro biscuits only.

- Weekends: Depending on the weather, you and fur-face might be able to stomp your paws to some authentic country/western music.

Directions: Located 16 miles southeast of Bullhead City off State Route 95.

Jerome

Rich in historical sites and scenery, Jerome was declared a National Historic Landmark in 1976. Although the mines closed in the 1950s, the persistent efforts of a handful of residents brought new life to Jerome. Instead of becoming a forgotten ghost town, Jerome has become a thriving art community.

Pack your Kodak and plenty of film. Not only will you be treated to some breathtaking views of Sedona, the Mogollon Rim and the towering San Francisco Peaks, but Jerome itself is quaint and picturesque. Many of the structures have been left untouched from the early mining days and others have been restored. Victorian architecture reigns supreme, adding to the charming ambiance. Built and rebuilt after numerous fires, Jerome seems to be perched precariously on the slopes of Cleopatra Hill, overlooking the bounteous Verde Valley. Proudly referred to as Arizona's largest ghost town, Jerome offers year-round pleasure for you and your pooch.

<u>Annual events:</u>

- February: Don't be surprised if Rover holds his nose high in the air and begins to drool. He's probably sniffing out the Jerome Chili Cookoff.

- August: Dalmatians will be delighted to attend the Fireman's Picnic.

- December: If there's a twinkle in the pupster's eye, it could be from the Christmas Lighting Ceremony, or perhaps he's hoping to attend Jerome's town-wide Christmas party.

Directions: Located on scenic byway 89A between Prescott and Flagstaff. For additional information, contact the Jerome Chamber of Commerce, P. O. Drawer K, Jerome, AZ 86331, (520) 634-9621.

Tombstone

Coined "the town too tough to die," Tombstone is alive with legends like Wyatt Earp, Doc Holliday and the Gunfight at the O.K. Corral. Boot Hill and Allen Street offer visitors a genuine taste of the Old West. Although the lucrative mining and the tawdry reputation lasted only a few short years in the late 1800s, the town remains vibrant with those memories. Shoot-outs are commonplace most Sundays. So leash up the pooch, buy yourself a Stetson and then strut on out to Tombstone territory.

Annual events:

- March: Territorial Days capture our western heritage.

- May: Cinco de Mayo is a colorful celebration. Wyatt Earp Days immortalize the famous sheriff and gunfighter.

- June: Father's Day Parade prances through town.

- August: Vigilante Days recall the law of the west.

- September: Rendezvous of the Gunfighters is history with a bang.

- October: Helldorado Days are filled with parades, dances, and more shoot-em-ups.

- November: Clown around on Emmet Kelley, Jr. Days.

Directions: From Tucson, take I-10 east to 80 and head south. For additional information, contact the Visitor Information Center, Box 268, Tombstone, AZ 85638, (520) 457-3929.

ARIZONA INDIAN RESERVATIONS

Take your bow wow to an annual pow wow

Despite 25,000 years of natural hardships, encroachment of the white man and tribal rivalry, the Indian population remains strong in Arizona. Today, there are twenty Indian Reservations encompassing over 19 million acres and housing approximately a quarter million people from fourteen different tribes.

The following Indian Reservations attract many visitors, Arizonans and tourists alike. Pooches are welcome at all but two.

In February, 1859, Congress created what is now known as the Gila River Reservation, the first in Arizona. Initially established to isolate and remove the Indians from their land and "Americanize" them, the government was not entirely successful in its efforts. The people of the Indian Nations possessed an inner strength and determination to survive despite the hardships they were forced to endure.

The United States government eventually recognized all Indian Reservations as sovereign nations. In essence, each is like a foreign country, responsible for enacting and enforcing its own laws. Tribal Councils pass legislation, determine policies, levy taxes, control land use, and in every way, govern their own people.

Although you don't need a visa or a passport, when you visit any Indian Reservation, you are entering a world where the language, culture and customs are different. As in a foreign land, you are bound to obey the laws of the land. It is incumbent upon you to respect their land and property as you would respect your own.

Ten things you should know before visiting an Indian Reservation

1. Dogs must be kept on a leash.
2. Take nothing but memories, leave nothing but footprints.
3. Photographs and sketching of Native American Indians are not allowed without permission. A fee is often expected and video cameras are prohibited on most Indian Reservations.
4. Never enter a home without an invitation.
5. Excessive and loud talk is considered impolite.
6. A firm handshake is considered overbearing, a light touch is preferred.
7. Consumption and transportation of alcoholic beverages are prohibited.
8. Do not leave established roadways or trails without consent from the tribal office.
9. Seat belts are mandatory, as are helmets for motorcyclists and passengers.
10. Fishing, hunting, camping and trespassing permits are required for all visitors. They can be purchased at Tribal Headquarters.

AK-CHIN RESERVATION

Translated, Ak-Chin means "where water spreads." Today, while the old meaning holds true, another meaning has evolved - a method of irrigation in which plants are grown in depressions created by the strong force of the water. This system of irrigation is the main key to success for the Tribe.

This 22,000+ acre Reservation is home to nearly 600 Tohono O'Odham and Pima Indians. Skilled farmers, they strive to protect and harvest the land and preserve it for future generations. Through Ak-Chin farms and a water settlement agreement with the U.S. government, the Ak-Chin have achieved a level of independence unsurpassed by any other Indian Tribe. Basketweaving is a popular pastime, a time when the Ak-Chin reminisce about the past, discuss the present and sculpt the future.

Location: In Maricopa, thirty miles south of Phoenix, twelve miles northwest of Casa Grande.

Special events:

• October: St. Francis Church Feast

For additional information, contact the Ak-Chin Him-Dak Indian Community, P. O. Box 897, Maricopa, AZ 85239, (602) 568-9480 or (602) 568-9487.

COLORADO RIVER INDIAN RESERVATION

This large Reservation is flanked by the Colorado River and provides ninety miles of shoreline. A multi-faceted community, it is composed of 3,000 members from four individual tribal groups - Mojave, Chemehuevi, Hopi and Navajo. Distinctly different in language, culture and custom, each tribe contributes a singular quality to the Reservation.

The Mojave are best known for their beadwork and pottery, while the basketry of the Chemehuevi is highly regarded. The intricate Kachina Dolls of the Hopi are collected around the world. The wool rugs and silver of the Navajo are recognized works of art.

With land in both Arizona and California, the Reservation encompasses over 278,000 acres. The climate and fertile river bottomlands make agriculture one of the Reservation's most profitable industries. Crops include cotton, grain, alfalfa, wheat, lettuce and melons. The Colorado River also provides incredible fishing opportunities for trout, bass, catfish and crappie. Fishing permits are required and may be purchased from the Tribal Administration Office in Parker.

Location: In Parker and Poston in Arizona, Blythe and Earl in California.

Special events:
- March: La Paz County Fair.
- July: Fourth of July Celebration.
- October: National Indian Days Celebration.
- December: Christmas Water Parade; All Indian Rodeo.

For additional information, contact the Colorado River Indian Reservation, Route 1, Box 23-B, Parker, AZ 85344, (520) 669-9211.

FORT McDOWELL YAVAPAI RESERVATION

Originally a U.S. military outpost, Fort McDowell has been the Fort McDowell Indian Reservation since 1923. It is a sovereign nation for members of the Yavapai, Apache and Mojave Tribes. A successful farming community has been achieved on the 24,000+ acre Reservation. The core of this enterprise is the jojoba bean. In addition, the basketry of the tribes has also proven successful.

Location: In Fountain Hills, approximately 15 miles northeast of Phoenix.

Special events:

Its proximity to the Phoenix Metropolitan area makes the land of this Reservation a mecca for anyone wanting to frolic riverside and escape the summer heat. Recreation includes fishing, rafting and tubing along the Verde River.

For additional information, contact the Fort McDowell Yavapai Reservation, P. O. Box 17779, Fountain Hills, AZ 85268, (602) 837-5121.

FORT MOJAVE INDIAN RESERVATION

In 1910, Fort Mojave Indian Reservation was recognized as a sovereign nation. Since that time the Mojave have created a thriving, self-sufficient community within their 33,000-acre Reservation. Because of the seventeen miles of river which flow throughout their land, the Mojave are often referred to as the Pipa Aha Macave - The People By The River. The Mojave believe that the river, along with its flora and fauna, was created by their spirit mentor, Mutavilya. The crafts of the Mojave include basketry and beadwork.

Location: Bordering Arizona, California and Nevada.

Special events:
- Each year the Fort Mojave Indians sponsor a Pow Wow which is open to the public and their pooches.

For additional information, contact the Fort Mojave Indian Reservation, 500 Merriman Ave., Needles, CA 92363, (619) 326-4591.

FORT YUMA INDIAN RESERVATION

In the 1850s, Fort Yuma was a thriving U.S. military post and a valuable gateway to California. The land is now owned by the Quechan Tribe. More than 2,300 Quechan are committed to preserving the historic aspects of the land as well as securing prosperous enterprises for future generations. The rich, fertile soil of this region of the Colorado River has helped the Quechan establish a successful farming community. This Tribe is also recognized for its elegant beadwork.

Location: In the Yuma area, a portion of the Reservation is also in California.

Special events:

• March: Annual Pow Wow.

For additional information, contact the Fort Yuma Reservation, Quechan Tribal Council, Box 11352, Yuma, AZ 85364, (619) 572-0213.

KAIBAB-PAIUTE INDIAN RESERVATION

Kaibab refers to the area in which the Reservation is located - the Kaibab Plateau and the Kaibab National Forest. Paiute is a divisional name for those tribes found in southwestern Utah, southwestern Nevada and northwestern Arizona.

Found in the remote reaches of northern Arizona, the Kaibab-Paiute Indian Reservation is a large 120,000-acre community. A small Tribe consisting of approximately 250, the Kaibab-Paiute take particular pleasure in their serene and isolated surroundings. In winter, heavy snowfall blankets the landscape presenting a picture of breathtaking beauty. Summer in this high elevation region is cool and sublime. Although their present economy is centered around tourism and livestock, they are beginning to expand into various agricultural enterprises. The Tribe is noted for its coiled, shallow baskets known as "Wedding Baskets."

Location: On Highway 389, 14 miles west of Fredonia.

Special events:

• October: Heritage Day Pow Wow.

For additional information, contact the Kaibab-Paiute Indian Reservation, Tribal Affairs Building, HC 65, Box 2, Fredonia, AZ 86022, (520) 643-7245.

NAVAJO NATION RESERVATION

The Navajo beginnings can be traced back to Lake Athapascan in northwestern Canada. It is believed that the Navajo belong to the same linguistic group as the Apache. With over 16 million acres, the Navajo Nation is the largest Indian Reservation in Arizona, larger in size than the state of West Virginia. Their land also continues into part of New Mexico, Utah and Colorado.

More than 210,000 Navajos populate this incredibly diverse land. Elevation varies from 4,500 feet to 10,388 feet and includes every imaginable terrain - from deserts to towering mountain peaks. The land is also rich in natural resources of oil, gas, coal and uranium.

A spiritual people, the Navajo believe that their faith in the Great Spirit will ensure the everlasting continuance of an Indian Nation. They regard the high mountain peaks of their land (Mt. Blanca, Mt. Taylor, the San Francisco Peaks and Mt. Hesperus) as sacred dwellings of the spirits. Frequent pilgrimages, offering homage and prayer to the spirits, are made by the medicine men of the tribe. The beautiful rugs and elaborate turquoise jewelry of the Navajo are highly prized crafts.

In addition to the fifteen national monuments, tribal parks and historic sites contained within the boundaries of Navajoland, it is home to Four Corners, the only place in the U.S. where you can plant your hands and feet in Arizona, New Mexico, Utah and Colorado at the same time. Fishing, camping, hiking and houseboating are just some of the activities that await you on the Reservation.

Location: In northeast Arizona, the Reservation continues into New Mexico, Utah and Colorado.

Special events:

- September: Navajo Nation Fair. A five-day extravaganza, this is the world's largest American Indian Fair, attracting more than 100,000 visitors from across the country.

- October: Northern Navajo Fair in Shiprock, New Mexico.

FYI: The Navajo Reservation is the only area in Arizona to observe daylight savings time.

For additional information, contact the Navajo Nation Reservation, Tourism Department, P. O. Box 663, Window Rock, AZ 86515, (520) 871-6436.

PASCUA-YAQUI RESERVATION

Although Mexico is the birthplace of the Pascua-Yaqui Indians, Arizona is now their home. The newest Reservation in Arizona, more than a thousand tribal members live on nearly 900 acres. The Tribe's thriving economy consists of a landscape nursery, charcoal packing center and prosperous bingo centers. The crafts of the Tribe include Deer Dance

Statues and cultural paintings which are executed by children.

Location: Fifteen miles southwest of Tucson.

Special events:

- Lenten Ceremonies are held on each of the seven Fridays preceding Easter. Open to the public, cameras and videocameras are banned.

For additional information, contact the Pascua-Yaqui Reservation, Pascua-Yaqui Tribal Council, 7474 S. Camino de Oeste, Tucson, AZ 85746, (520) 883-2838.

SALT RIVER RESERVATION

This 49,000+ acre Reservation was established on the Salt River in 1879. Today it is a thriving community and home to over 4,100 Pima and Maricopa Indians. Farming, cattle and horse raising fuel the economy. Crafts include pottery and basketry.

Location: In Scottsdale, fifteen miles northeast of Phoenix off Highway 87 and Ft. McDowell Road.

Special events:

- Although the fairs at the Reservation do not permit dogs, the Salt River Recreation Area welcomes visitors with their pooches. Fishing, tubing, camping and picnicking opportunities abound.

For additional information, contact the Salt River Reservation, Salt River Pima-Maricopa Tribal Council, Route 1, Box 216, Scottsdale, AZ 85256, (602) 874-8056.

SAN CARLOS RESERVATION

From desert highlands to mountain meadows, dense forests to sun-splashed lakes, this 1,850,000-acre Reservation encompasses a beautiful array of nature. Since its establishment in 1871, the San Carlos Reservation has held the title of the largest Apache Reservation in Arizona, and is the only Reservation that mines peridot stones. In addition to peridot, the harvesting of the jojoba nut is a prosperous enterprise. The waters of San Carlos Lake beckon and challenge all anglers to bring their rods and reel in a fish or two. The Tribe is noted for basketry, beadwork and peridot jewelry.

Location: East of Globe in San Carlos, AZ.

Special events:

• November: Annual Pow Wow.

For additional information contact the San Carlos Reservation, San Carlos Apache Tribal Council, P.O. Box O, San Carlos, AZ 85550, (520) 475-2361.

TOHONO O'ODHAM RESERVATION

1916 is a year forever etched in the minds of the Papago Indians. It marks the creation of the 2,700,000-acre Reservation in Sells, AZ. Formerly the Papago Indian Reservation it is known as the Main Reservation, the largest of four Papago Reservations in Arizona. The Reservation is home to over 9,000 tribe members who take pride in and celebrate their Spanish ancestry in their daily lives, annual festivals, fairs and religious ceremonies. Spanish is the tribe's official language for prayers and songs. This Reservation also holds the world-wide honor of being the first totally electric Indian village.

With over 90,000 acres of grazable land, it's no wonder that cattle raising is the stronghold of the Tribe's economy. The Papago also rely on the income generated from the leasing of copper mines. But these Indians are best known for their successful basketweaving enterprise. Each year the Papago produce thousands of intricately woven baskets. These highly prized, beautiful baskets come in a myriad of countless shapes and sizes. You're bound to find one that pleases you.

Location: An hour west of Tucson on State Highway 86 in Sells, AZ.

Special events:

• The Papago Tribal Fair and Rodeo is held each fall.

For additional information, contact the Tohono O'Odham Reservation, P.O. Box 837, Sells, AZ 85634, (520) 383-2281.

TONTO-APACHE RESERVATION

Established in October, 1972, this Reservation is one of the State's newest and, at eighty-five acres, one of the smallest. But the land it encompasses more than makes up for the size. Located just beneath the Mogollon Rim, the terrain and climate are perfect for outdoor enthusiasts. Tribal members are noted for their beautiful beadwork and basketry.

Location: In Payson on Highway 87.

Special events:

• July: Fourth of July Festivities.

For additional information, contact the Tonto-Apache Reservation, Tonto-Apache Reservation #30, Payson, AZ 85541, (520) 474-5000.

YAVAPAI-PRESCOTT RESERVATION

Yavapai means "People of the Sun." The Yavapai are part of the Yuman Tribe. Over one hundred Yavapai make their home on the 1,400-acre Reservation. The Yavapai have developed various successful enterprises on their land. They are also well regarded for their basketry.

Location: Located in the mile-high town of Prescott.

Special events:

• Annual Pow Wow.

For additional information, contact the Yavapai-Prescott Reservation, Yavapai-Prescott Tribal Council, 530 E. Merritt, Prescott, AZ 86301, (520) 445-8790.

The following Indian Reservations are dog-friendly but require that pooches be leashed.

CAMP VERDE RESERVATION
Located in Camp Verde, AZ.

COCOPAH RESERVATION
Located south of Yuma in Somerton, AZ.

FORT APACHE RESERVATION/
WHITE MOUNTAIN APACHE TRIBE
Located south of Show Low in Whiteriver, AZ.

GILA RIVER RESERVATION
Located south of Phoenix in Sacaton, AZ.

HUALAPAI RESERVATION
Located northeast of Kingman in Peach Springs, AZ.

The following Indian Reservations do not allow dogs.

HAVASUPAI INDIAN RESERVATION
Located in Supai, AZ.

HOPI INDIAN RESERVATION

This Reservation does not encourage visitors. The Hopi are a very private people who revere their land which is filled with archaeological sites.

EVERYTHING YOU WANT TO KNOW ABOUT PET CARE AND WHO TO ASK

Whether you've always had dogs or you're starting out with your first, the following organizations and hotlines can provide information on the care, feeding and protection of your loyal companions.

Pet behavior information

Tree House Animal Foundation: If you are concerned with canine aggression, nipping, biting, housebreaking or other behavioral problems, the Tree House Animal Foundation will try to help. But don't wait until the last minute. Call for advice early on and your animal's problems will be easier to correct. Consultation is free, except for applicable long distance charges. Call (312) 784-5488, 9AM to 5PM CST, seven days a week.

Dial-Pet: Health and care topics for pets including dogs, cats, horses, small animals, exotics and fish. Call (312) 342-5738 any time. (You must have a touch-tone phone to use the service.) Basically, it's a hotline sponsored by the Chicago Veterinary Medical Association. Vets who belong to the organization write and then record 5-7 minutes messages on subjects ranging from ear problems to training tips. There's no charge except applicable long distance charges. Or, if you prefer, write for a list of topics to: DIAL-PET, Chicago Veterinary Medical Association, 161 S. Lincolnway, North Aurora, IL 60542.

Animal Behavior Helpline: This organization is sponsored by the San Francisco Society for the Prevention of Cruelty to Animals. It will assist you in solving canine behavioral problems. Staffed by volunteers, you may reach a recorded message. However, calls are returned within 48 hours by volunteers trained in animal behavior. Problems such as chewing, digging and barking are cited as the most common reason dog owners call. Housebreaking tips, how to deal with aggression and other topics are covered. Callers are first asked to speak about the problem and describe what steps have been taken to correct inappropriate behavior. After evaluating the information, specific advice is given to callers. The consultation is free, except for applicable long distance charges or collect call charges when a counselor returns your call. Messages can be left any time. Call (415) 554-3075.

Poison Control Center: There are two telephone numbers for this organization. The 800 number is an emergency line for both veterinarians and pet owners for emergency poisoning information. Calls are taken by the veterinarian-staffed National Animal Poison Control Center at the University of Illinois. When calling the 800 number, there is a charge of $30 per case. Every call made to the 800 number is followed up by the NAPCC. Calls to the 900 line pay $20 for the first 5 minutes and $2.95 for every minute thereafter with a minimum charge of $20 and a maximum of $30. The 900 number is for non-emergency questions and there is no follow up.

When calling the NAPCC, be prepared to provide your name and address and the name of the suspected poison (be specific). If the product is manufactured by a company that is a member of the Animal Product Safety Service - the company may pay the charge.

In all other cases, you pay for the consultation. You must also provide the animal species, breed, sex, and weight. You will be asked to describe symptoms as well as unusual behavior. This detailed information is critical - it can mean the difference between life or death for your dog.

For emergencies only, call (800) 548-2423. Major credit cards are accepted. For non-emergency questions, call (900) 680-0000. The Poison Control Center offers poison control information by veterinarians 24 hours a day, 7 days a week.

Poinsettias and other toxic plants... pretty but deadly

During the Christmas holidays, the risk of poisoning and injury is greater for your dog. If eaten, poinsettias and holly berries for example, can be fatal. Although there are conflicting reports on the effects of mistletoe, play it safe and keep your dogs away from this plant. Be alert - swallowed tree ornaments, like ribbon and tinsel can cause choking and/or intestinal problems.

Christmas wiring is another potential problem . Your dog can be electrocuted by chewing on it. And don't forget about the dangers of poultry bones. The same goes for aluminum foil including those disposable pans so popular at holiday time.

Keep your trash inaccessible. And remember that the holidays are a source of excitement and stress to both people and animals. Maintain your dog's feeding and walking schedules and provide plenty of TLC and playtime. Then everyone, including your pooch, will find the holidays more enjoyable.

FYI...
common plants that are toxic to dogs:*

Amaryllis (bulbs)
Appleseeds (cyanide)
Azalea
Boxwood
Caladium
Cherry Pits (cyanide)
Climbing Lilly
Daffodil (bulb)
Delphinium
Dumb Cane
English Ivy
Foxglove
Holly
Hydrangea
Japanese Yew
Jerusalem Cherry
Laburnum
Laurel
Marigold
Mistletoe (berries)
Mushrooms
Nightshade
Peach
Poinsettia
Privet
Rhubarb
Stinging Nettie
Tobacco
Walnuts
Yew

Andromeda
Arrowglass
Bittersweet
Buttercup
Castor Bean
Chokecherry
Crown of Thorns
Daphne
Dieffenbachia
Elephant Ear
Elderberry
Hemlock
Hyacinth (bulbs)
Iris (bulb)
Jasmine (berries)
Jimsonweed
Larkspur
Locoweed
Marijuana
Monkshood
Narcissus (bulb)
Oleander
Philodendron
Poison Ivy
Rhododendron
Snow on the Mountain
Toadstool
Tulip (bulb)
Wisteria

NOTE: This is only a partial list.

PET LOSS SUPPORT HELPLINES

Chicago Veterinary Medical Association:

If you are experiencing the loss of a beloved pet, there is help provided by the Chicago Veterinary Medical Association. Call and leave a voice mail message. A counselor will return your call. Veterinarians staff the hotline and are trained to help owners accept the loss of a pet. Written materials are sent on request. When needed, referrals to professional grief counselors are also provided. Consultation and call are free except for applicable long distance charges. Call (708) 603-3884, any time. Calls are returned from 7PM to 9PM, Monday through Friday.

University of California at Davis:

Another valuable hotline, calls are staffed and answered by veterinary students. Whether you're grieving for a pet who has already died or in anticipation of a sick or elderly pet dying, the Pet Loss Hotline will help you deal with your grief. Parents may also call to learn how to explain the loss of a pet to a child. Consultation is free except for applicable long distance charges. Return calls are *COLLECT*. Messages can be left any time. The Hotline is staffed 6:30PM to 9:30PM EST, Monday through Friday during the school year. Call (916) 752-4200.

University of Florida at Gainesville College:

Their hotline is staffed by veterinary students as well as other volunteers who provide grief counseling for pet owners. Owners leave a message on a voice mail system and calls are returned by a counselor (at no charge) between 7PM and 9PM EST. Counselors are trained to help grieving owners and will provide written materials upon request. Call (904) 392-4700, Ext. 4080, any time. Consultation is free, except for applicable long distance charges.

College of Veterinary Medicine at Michigan:

Provides a Pet Loss Support Hotline staffed by veterinary students trained in crisis intervention. Volunteers help owners cope with their loss. Calls are followed up with pet loss related materials as well as information about the pet loss support group. Consultation and call are free except for applicable long distance charges. Return calls are *COLLECT*. Call (517) 483-2692, any time. Hotline is staffed on Tuesday, Wednesday and Thursday, from 6:30PM to 9:30PM EST.

Pet nutrition information — ALPO, HILLS, IAMS

These three organizations are manufacturers of products to the animal market. Each has a Pet Nutrition Hotline offering information on their own products as well as pet health and other pet-related questions. Free written materials are also available on such topics as canine obesity, pet loss, training, feeding guidelines and puppy-proofing a house. All consultations and printed materials are free.

ALPO: (800) 366-6033. 9AM to 5PM EST, Monday through Friday.

HILLS: (800) 445-5777. 8AM to 6PM CST, Monday through Friday.

IAMS: (800) 525-4267. 8AM to 8PM EST, Monday through Saturday. This hotline is also available to international calls, with translation in 140 languages.

ANIMAL ETHICS ORGANIZATIONS

American Humane Association:

63 Inverness Drive East, Englewood, CO 80112; (303) 792-9900 or toll-free at (800) 227-4645.

This national, non-profit animal welfare organization has been dedicated to the prevention of cruelty, neglect, and exploitation of animals since it's founding in 1877. Key programs include: improving the care and welfare of pet animals, developing training and resources for animal shelters and humane societies across the country, strengthening animal cruelty laws and enforcement, being a national coordinator of emergency animal relief for natural disasters and legislative advocacy for pets, wildlife and lab animals. $15/year includes updates and quarterly magazine.

American Society For Prevention of Cruelty to Animals:

424 E. 92nd St., New York, NY 10128; (212) 876-7711; 9AM to 5PM EST, Monday through Friday.

An organization that places emphasis on prevention of cruelty to animals.

Humane Society of the United States:

2100 L St., NW, Washington, DC 20037; (202) 452-1100.

Non-profit animal welfare organization involved in numerous animal welfare issues.

National Animal Interest Alliance:

P. O. Box 66579, Portland, OR 97290; (503) 761-1139.

A national animal welfare umbrella organization that provides factual information on issues that may be unknown or confusing to the public. $25/year includes "The Alliance Alert" newsletter.

National Anti-Vivisection Society:

53 West Jackson Boulevard, Chicago, IL 60604; (800) 888-NAVS.

Non-profit, charitable animal welfare organization devoted to stopping the use of animals in biomedical research. $25/year (discounts for students and seniors) includes updates and a quarterly publications, plus special publications, such as "Personal Care for People Who Care," a guide to over 750 companies that are cruelty-free.

People for the Ethical Treatment of Animals (PETA):

P. O. Box 42516, Washington, DC 20015; (301) 770-7444.

Non-profit, animal rights organization that works through undercover investigations and research, and grass-roots activist and public education campaigns, to teach people about the cruelties involved in beef production, the fur trade, laboratory experiments, and various animal entertainment acts. $15/year includes "Guide to Compassionate Living," the quarterly magazine "PETA News," action alerts and updates.

FIDO FACTS

The following assortment of facts, tidbits and data will increase your knowledge of our canine companions.

- Gain the confidence of a worried dog by avoiding direct eye contact or by turning away, exposing your back or side to the dog.

- When dogs first meet, it's uncommon for them to approach each other head on. Most will approach in curving lines. They'll walk beyond each other's noses sniffing at rear ends while standing side by side.

- Dog ownership is a common bond and the basis of impromptu conversations as well as lasting friendships.

- Chemical salt makes sidewalks less slippery but can be harmful to your dog's footpads. Wash you dog's paws after walks to remove salt. Don't let him lick the salt either. It's poisonous.

- Vets warn that removing tar with over-the-counter petroleum products can be highly toxic.

- Although a dog's vision is better than humans in the dark, bright red and green are the easiest colors for them to see.

- Puppies are born blind. Their eyes open and they begin to see at 10 to 14 days.

- The best time to separate a pup from his mother is seven to ten weeks after birth.

- It's a sign of submission when a dog's ears are held back close to his head.

- Hot pavement can damage your dog's sensitive footpads. In the summer months, walk your pooch in the morning or evening or on grassy areas and other cool surfaces.

- Never leave your dog unattended in the car during the warm weather months or extremely cold ones.

- Always walk your dog on a leash on hotel/motel grounds.

- Want to register your puppy, or locate a breeder in your area? The American Kennel Club has a new customer service line at (919) 233-9767. Their interactive voice processing telephone system is open twenty-four hours a day, seven days a week. Information is available on dog and litter registrations. You can also use the number to order registration materials, certified pedigrees, books and videos. If you want to speak with a customer service rep, call during business hours.

- Stroke a dog instead of patting it. Stroking is soothing. Patting can make some dogs nervous.

- If your dog is lonely for you when he's left alone, try leaving your voice on a tape and let it play during your absence.

- When a dog licks you with a straight tongue, he's saying "I Love You."

- Don't do anything on the road with your dog that you wouldn't do at home.

- Never put your dog in the bed of a pickup truck as a means of transportation.

- Black dogs and dark colored ones are more susceptible to the heat.

- When traveling, take a spray bottle of water with you. A squirt in your dog's mouth will temporarily relieve his thirst.

- Changing your dog's water supply too quickly can cause stomach upset. Take along a container of water from home and replenish with local water, providing a gradual change.

- One in five dogs suffers from some form of allergy. Sneezing and watery eyes could be an allergic reaction caused by pollen or smoke.

- Inflamed skin can indicate a sensitivity to grass or chemicals used in carpet cleaning.

- Patches of hair loss, itching and redness are common signs of fleas, particularly during warm months.

- Normal temperature for dogs: 100° to 102°.

- No matter how much your dog begs, do not overfeed him.

- Spay or neuter your dog to prevent health problems and illnesses that plague the intact animal. Contrary to popular belief, spaying or neutering your canine will not result in weight gain. Only food and lack of exercise can do that.

- Spend ample quality time with your canine every day. Satisfy his need for social contact.

- Obedience train your dog, it's good for his mental well being and yours too.
- Always provide cool fresh drinking water for your dog.
- If you have an outdoor pooch, make sure he has easy access to shade and plenty of water.
- If your pooch lives indoors, make certain he has access to cool moving air and ample fresh water.
- In the summertime, avoid exercising your dog during the hottest parts of the day.
- Never tie your dog or let him run free while he's wearing a choke collar. Choke collars can easily hook on something and strangle him.
- The Chinese Shar-Pei and the Chow have blue-black tongues instead of pink ones.
- The smallest breed of dog is the Chihuahua.
- Poodles, Bedlington Terriers, Bichon Frises, Schnauzers and Soft-Coated Wheaten Terriers don't shed.
- Terriers and toy breeds usually bark the most.
- The Basenji is often called the barkless dog.
- Golden Labs and Retrievers are fast learners, making them easy to train.
- Climate counts when deciding on a breed. Collies and Pugs will be unhappy in hot, humid climates. But the Italian Greyhound and Chihuahua originated in hot climes, the heat won't bother them, but winter will. They'll need insulation in the form of dog apparel to protect them from the cold. And as you might think, heavy-coated dogs like the Saint Bernard, Siberian Husky and the Newfy thrive in cooler weather.

- Apartment dwellers, consider the Dachshund and Cairn Terrier. Both can be content in small quarters.

- Fido's fitness counts towards insuring a longer, healthier life. In this arena, you're the one in control. The most common cause of ill health in canines is obesity. Approximately 60% of all adult dogs are overweight or will become overweight due to lack of physical activity and overfeeding. Much like humans, the medical consequences of obesity include liver, heart and orthopedic problems. As little as a few extra pounds on a small dog can lead to health-related complications.

- Is your pooch pudgy? Place both thumbs on your dog's backbone and then run your fingers along his rib cage. If the bony part of each rib cannot be easily felt, your dog may be overweight. Another quickie test - stand directly over your dog while he's standing. If you can't see a clearly defined waist behind his rib cage, he's probably too portly.

- It's easier than you might think to help your dog lose those extra pounds. Begin by eliminating unnecessary table scraps. Cut back a small amount on the kibble or canned dog food you normally feed your pooch, if he's accustomed to two full cups each day, reduce that amount to 1 3/4 cups instead. If you normally give your pooch biscuits every day, cut the amount in half. And don't feel guilty. Stick with the program and you'll eventually see a reduction in weight. Slow and steady is the best approach. And don't let yourself imagine that your dog is being deprived of anything. Even when he looks at you with a woebegone expression, remember you're doing him a favor by helping him reduce and you're adding years of good health to his life.

- Exercise. Not enough can be said about the benefits. Establish a daily exercise routine. Awaken twenty minutes earlier every morning and take a brisk mile walk. Instead of immediately watching TV after dinner, walk off some calories. Your pooch's overall good health, as well as your own, will be vastly enhanced.

- Lewis and Clark traveled with a 150-pound Newfoundland named "Seamen". This pooch was a respected member of the expedition, and his antics were included in the extensive diaries of these famous explorers.

- The infamous Red Baron owned a Great Dane named Moritz who lived on the military base with the pilot. The Red Baron fondly referred to Moritz as his "little lapdog."

- Frederick the Great owned an estimated 30 Greyhounds. His love of these animals led him to coin the saying: "The more I see of men, the more I love my dogs."

- The English have a saying: The virtues of a dog are its own, its vices those of its master.

- Lord Byron, in his eulogy to his dog Boatswain, wrote, "One who possessed beauty without vanity, strength without insolence, courage without ferocity, and all the virtues of man without his vices."

- "Be Kind To Animals Week" (May 7-13) was established in 1915. Recognized by Congress, this is the oldest week of its kind in the nation.

- The "Always Faithful" Memorial, which honors Dogs of War, was unveiled on June 20, 1994. It now stands on the US Naval Base in Orote Point, Guam.

- During WWII, the Doberman was an official member of the US Marine Corps combat force.

- The domestic dog dates back more than 50,000 years.

- Ghandi once said, "The greatness of a nation and its moral progress can be judged by the way its animals are treated."

- England's Dickin Medal is specifically awarded to dogs for bravery and outstanding behavior in wartime.

- Napoleon's wife, Josephine, had a Pug named Fortune. She relied on the animal to carry secret messages under his collar to Napoleon while she was imprisoned at Les Carnes.

- Former First Lady Barbara Bush: "An old dog that has served you long and well is like an old painting. The patina of age softens and beautifies, and like a master's work, can never be replaced by exactly the same thing, ever again."

- Dogs and Halloween don't mix. Even the mellowest of pooches can become frightened and overexcited by all the commotion. Save the candy collecting and chocolate for the kids, and leave the dog at home.

- Most outdoor dogs suffer from unnoticed parasites like fleas.

- In winter, the water in an outdoor dog dish can freeze within an hour.

- In summer, dogs consume large quantities of water. Bowls need frequent refilling.

PET POEMS, PROCLAMATIONS, PRAYERS...& HOMEMADE DOG BISCUITS!

Ode to Travel with Pets

We're all set to roam

Going far from home

With doggies in tow

Off shall we go

To wander and gadabout

Since travel we're mad about

With Rosie and Max by my side

We'll all go for a ride

As we travel for miles

And bring about smiles

Rosie will grin

Max will chime in

Driving into the sunset

Odometers all set

But enough of these word rhymes

Let's roll with the good times!

— Eileen Barish, November 1994

Alone Again

I wish someone would tell me what it is
   That I've done wrong.
Why I have to stay chained up and
   Left alone so long.
They seemed so glad to have me
   When I came here as a pup.
There were so many things we'd do
   While I was growing up.
They couldn't wait to train me as a
   Companion and a friend.
And told me how they'd never fear
   Being left alone again.
The children said they'd feed me and
   Brush me every day.
They'd play with me and walk me
   If only I could stay.
But now the family "Hasn't time,"
   They often say I shed.
They do not even want me in the house
   Not even to be fed.
The children never walk me.
   They always say "Not now!"
I wish that I could please them.
   Won't someone tell me how?
All I had, you see, was love.
   I wish they would explain
Why they said they wanted me
   Then left me on a chain?

                  — Anonymous

A Dogs Bill of Rights

I have the right to give and receive
  unconditional love.
I have the right to a life that is beyond
  mere survival.
I have the right to be trained so I do not become
  the prisoner of my own misbehavior.
I have the right to adequate food and
  medical care.
I have the right to fresh air and green grass.
I have the right to socialize with people
  and dogs outside my family.
I have the right to have my needs
  and wants respected.
I have the right to a special time with
  my people .
I have the right to only be bred
  responsibly if at all.
I have the right to be foolish and silly, and
  to make my person laugh.
I have the right to earn my person's trust
  and be trusted in return.
I have the right to be forgiven.
I have the right to die with dignity.
I have the right to be remembered well.

Rainbow Bridge

There is a bridge connecting Heaven and Earth. It is called the Rainbow Bridge because of its many colors. Just this side of the Rainbow Bridge there is a land of meadows, hills and valleys with lush green grass.

When a beloved pet dies, the pet goes to this place. There is always food and water and warm spring weather. The old and frail animals are young again. Those who are maimed are made whole again. They play all day with each other.

There is only one thing missing. They are not with their special person who loved them on Earth. So each day they run and play until the day comes when one suddenly stops playing and looks up! The nose twitches! The ears are up! The eyes are staring! And this one suddenly runs from the group!

You have been seen, and when you and your special friend meet, you take him or her in your arms and embrace. Your face is kissed again and again, and you look once more into the eyes of your trusting pet.

Then you cross Rainbow Bridge together, never again to be separated.

Anonymous

A Dog's Prayer

Treat me kindly, my beloved master, for no heart in all the world is more grateful for kindness, than the loving heart of mine.

Do not break my spirit with a stick, for though I should lick your hand between the blows, your patience and understanding will more quickly teach me the things you would have me do.

Speak to me often, for your voice is the world's sweetest music as you must know by the fierce wagging of my tail when your footstep falls up on my waiting ear.

When it is cold and wet, please take me inside...for I am now a domesticated animal, no longer used to bitter elements...and I ask no greater glory than the privilege of sitting at your feet beside the hearth...though had you no home, I would rather follow you through ice and snow, than rest upon the softest pillow in the warmest home in all the land...for you are my God...and I am your devoted worshipper.

Keep my pan filled with fresh water, for although I should not reproach you were it dry, I cannot tell you when I suffer thirst. Feed me clean food, that I may stay well, to romp and play and do your bidding, to walk by your side, and stand ready willing and able to protect you with my life, should your life be in danger.

And beloved master, should the Great Master see fit to deprive me of my health or sight, do not turn away from me. Rather hold me gently in your arms, as skilled hands grant me the merciful boon of eternal rest...and I will leave you knowing with the last breath I draw, my fate was ever safest in your hands.

HOMEMADE DOG BISCUITS
(Makes about 8 dozen biscuits)

3 1/2 cups all-purpose flour
2 cups whole wheat flour
1 cup rye flour
1 cup cornmeal
2 cups cracked wheat bulgur
1/2 cup nonfat dry milk
4 tsp. salt
1 package dry yeast
2 cups chicken stock or other liquid
1 egg and 1 tbsp. milk (to brush on top)

Combine all the dry ingredients except the yeast. In a separate bowl, dissolve the yeast in 1/4 cup warm water. To this, add the chicken stock. (You can use bouillon, pan drippings or water from cooking vegetables.) Add the liquid to the dry ingredients. Knead mixture for about 3 minutes. Dough will be quite stiff. If too stiff, add extra liquid or an egg. Preheat oven to 300 degrees. Roll the dough out on a floured board to 1/4" thickness, then immediately cut into shapes with cookie cutters. Place on an ungreased cookie sheet and brush with a wash of egg and milk. Place in oven. After 45 minutes, turn off the heat and leave biscuits overnight in the oven to get bone hard.

General Information & Visitor Information Bureaus

GENERAL INFORMATION

Observed state holidays

Below is a list of holidays observed by the state of Arizona. New Year's Day, July 4 and Christmas are observed on the actual date of the holiday. If a holiday falls on a Saturday, it is celebrated the preceding Friday. If it falls on a Sunday, it is celebrated the following Monday.

New Year's Day*
Martin Luther King's
  Birthday
Labor Day*
Columbus Day*
Thanksgiving*
Christmas Day*

Memorial Day*
Independence Day*
Lincoln's Birthday*
President's Day*
Veterans Day*
Easter*
Cinco de Mayo

National holidays - banks and government agencies are closed.

Arizona's state and national parks

Arizona is home to twenty-four state parks, affording numerous recreational activities such as hiking, camping, fishing, boating and picnicking. Two more state parks are scheduled to open in 1996. For more information contact: Arizona State Parks, 1300 W. Washington, Phoenix, AZ 85007; (602) 542-4174.

With a total of seventeen, Arizona encompasses more national parks and monuments than any other state. For more information contact: National Parks & Monuments, 202 E. Earll Dr., #115, Phoenix, AZ 85012; (602) 640-5250.

National Forests

Arizona contains six national forests, covering over 11 million acres. For information on the individual forests, contact: United States Forest Service-Southwestern Region, Federal Building, 517 Gold Avenue, SW, Albuquerque, NM 87102; (505) 842-3292.

Outdoor recreational activities

Water Recreation
- Lake Havasu Visitors and Convention Bureau, 1930 Mesquite Ave., Ste 3, Lake Havasu City, AZ 86403; (800) 242-8278 or (520) 453-3444.
- Lake Mead National Recreation Area, 601 Nevada Highway, Boulder City, NV 89005; (702) 293-8920.
- Lake Powell, ARA Leisure Services, 2233 W. Dunlap, Ste. 400, Phoenix, AZ 85021; (800) 528-6154 or (602) 331-5200.

Fishing and Hunting
- Arizona Game & Fish Department, 2222 W. Greenway Road, Phoenix, AZ 85023; (602) 942-3000.
- The Arizona Game & Fish Department Hotline: (602) 789-3701.
- For fishing updates call (602) 271-5656, then code 3474 (FISH).

Skiing
- Arizona Snowbowl, P.O. Box 40, Flagstaff, AZ 86002; (520) 779-1951.
- Mt. Lemmon Ski Valley, P.O. Box 612, Mt. Lemmon, AZ 85619; (520) 576-1400.
- Sunrise Ski Area, P.O. Box 217, McNary, AZ 85930; (520) 735-7669.

Road safety tips:

- Don't drink and drive - a blood alcohol level of .10 percent or higher is considered legally intoxicated.

- A blood alcohol test is mandatory for anyone arrested for driving while under the influence. Refusal may result in a 6-month suspension of license.

- Open alcohol containers in a moving vehicle are illegal.

- 18 is the minimum driving age; 16 with parental consent.

- Seatbelts are the law for the driver and front-seat passenger.

- Child safety seats are mandatory for children ages 4 years and under or who weigh under 40 lbs.

- Helmets are the law for all motorcyclists and passengers under the age of 18.

- Radar detectors are legal.

For information on road conditions, contact:

Arizona Department of Public Safety:
Phoenix Area- (602) 279-2000, then press ROAD.
Tucson Area- (520) 292-1000, then press ROAD.
Highway Patrol- (602) 223-2000.
Statewide (emergency only)- (800) 525-5555.

Notes

VISITOR INFORMATION BUREAUS & CHAMBER'S OF COMMERCE

AJO CHAMBER OF COMMERCE
321 Taladro, Ajo, AZ 85321,
(520) 387-7742.

ALPINE CHAMBER OF COMMERCE
P.O. Box 410, Alpine, AZ 85920,
(520) 339-4330.

APACHE JUNCTION CHAMBER OF COMMERCE
P.O. Box 1747, Apache Junction, AZ 85217,
(602) 982-3141, Fax: (602) 982-3234.

ARIZONA/MEXICO CHAMBER OF COMMERCE
5946 W. Osborn, Phoenix, AZ 85033,
(602) 247-6571.

ARIZONA OFFICE OF TOURISM
1100 W. Washington Street, Phoenix, AZ 85007,
(602) 542-8687, Fax: (602) 542-4813.

ARIZONA CITY CHAMBER OF COMMERCE
13640 S. Sunland Gin Rd., #105,
Arizona City, AZ 85223,
(520) 466-5141.

ASH FORK CHAMBER OF COMMERCE
P.O. Box 494, Ash Fork, AZ 86320,
(520) 637-2442, Fax: (520) 637-2442.

AVONDALE- SEE TRI-CITY WEST CHAMBER OF COMMERCE.

BENSON/SAN PEDRO VALLEY CHAMBER OF COMMERCE
P.O. Box 2255, Benson, AZ 85602,
(520) 586-2842, Fax: (520) 586-3375.

BISBEE CHAMBER OF COMMERCE
P.O. Drawer BA, Bisbee, AZ 85603,
(520) 432-5421, Fax: (520) 432-2597.

BLACK CANYON CITY CHAMBER OF COMMERCE
P.O. Box 1919, Black Canyon City, AZ 85324,
(520) 374-9797, Fax: (520) 374-9225.

BOUSE CHAMBER OF COMMERCE
P.O. Box 696, Bouse, AZ 85325,
(520) 851-2391.

BOWIE CHAMBER OF COMMERCE
P.O. BOX 287, Bowie, AZ 85605,
(520) 847-2448.

BUCKEYE CHAMBER OF COMMERCE
P.O. Box 717, Buckeye, AZ 85326,
(520) 386-2727, Fax: (520) 386-7527.

BULLHEAD CITY CHAMBER OF COMMERCE
1251 Highway 95, Bullhead City, AZ 86429,
(520) 754-4121, Fax: (520) 754-5514.

CAMP VERDE CHAMBER OF COMMERCE
P.O. Box 1665, Camp Verde, AZ 86322,
(520) 567-9294.

CAREFREE/CAVE CREEK CHAMBER OF COMMERCE
P.O. Box 734, Carefree, AZ 85377,
(602) 488-3381.

CASA GRANDE CHAMBER OF COMMERCE
575 N. Marshall, Casa Grande, AZ 85222,
(520) 836-2125 or (800) 836-8169, Fax: (520) 836-6233.

CHANDLER CHAMBER OF COMMERCE
218 N. Arizona Ave., Chandler, AZ 85224,
(602) 963-4571 or (800) 836-8169, Fax: (602) 963-0188.

CHINO VALLEY CHAMBER OF COMMERCE
P.O. Box 419, Chino Valley, AZ 86323,
(520) 636-2493.

CHLORIDE CHAMBER OF COMMERCE
P.O. Box 268, Chloride, AZ 86431,
(520) 565-2204.

CLARKDALE CHAMBER OF COMMERCE
P.O. Box 308, Clarkdale, AZ 86324,
(520) 634-9591, Fax: (520) 634-0407.

CLIFTON CHAMBER OF COMMERCE
P.O. Box 1237, Clifton, AZ 85533,
(520) 865-3313.

CONGRESS CHAMBER OF COMMERCE
P.O. Box 206, Congress, AZ 85332.

COLORADO CITY CHAMBER OF COMMERCE
P.O. Box 70, Colorado City, AZ 86021,
(520) 875-2646.

COOLIDGE CHAMBER OF COMMERCE
P.O. Box 943, Coolidge, AZ 85228,
(520) 723-3009.

COTTONWOOD/VERDE VALLEY CHAMBER OF COMMERCE
1010 S. Main Street, Cottonwood, AZ 86326,
(520) 634-7593.

DOLAN SPRINGS CHAMBER OF COMMERCE
P.O. Box 274, Dolan Springs, AZ 86441,
(520) 767-3530.

DOUGLAS CHAMBER OF COMMERCE
1125 Pan American Avenue, Douglas, AZ 85607,
(520) 364-2477, Fax: (520) 364-6535.

DUNCAN CHAMBER OF COMMERCE
P.O. Box 814, Duncan, AZ 85534.

EHRENBERG CHAMBER OF COMMERCE
P.O. Box 800, Ehrenberg, AZ 85334,
(520) 923-9601, Fax: (520) 923-9602.

ELFRIEDA- SEE SULPHER SPRINGS VALLEY
CHAMBER OF COMMERCE

ELOY CHAMBER OF COMMERCE
P.O. Box 788, Eloy, AZ 85231,
(520) 466-3411.

FLAGSTAFF CHAMBER OF COMMERCE
101 W. Route 66, Flagstaff, AZ 86001,
(520) 774-4505 or (800) 842-7293, Fax: (520) 779-1209.

FLAGSTAFF CONVENTION & VISITORS BUREAU
211 W. Aspen Avenue, Flagstaff, AZ 86001,
(520) 779-7611, Fax: (520) 556-1305.

FLORENCE CHAMBER OF COMMERCE
P.O. Box 929, Florence, AZ 85232,
(520) 868-9433 or (800) 437-9433.

FOUNTAIN HILLS CHAMBER OF COMMERCE
P.O. Box 17598, Fountain Hills, AZ 85269,
(602) 837-1654, Fax: (602) 837-3077.

FREDONIA CHAMBER OF COMMERCE
P.O. Box 547, Fredonia, AZ 86022,
(520) 643-7241, Fax: (520) 643-7685.

GILA BEND CHAMBER OF COMMERCE
P.O. Box A, Gila Bend, AZ 85337,
(520) 683-2002, Fax: (520) 256-7856.

GILBERT CHAMBER OF COMMERCE
P.O. Box 527, Gilbert, AZ 85299,
(602) 892-0056, Fax: (602) 250-1521.

GLENDALE CHAMBER OF COMMERCE
P.O. Box 249, Glendale, AZ 85311,
(602) 937-4754 or (800) IDSUNNY,
Fax: (602) 937-3333.

GLOBE/MIAMI CHAMBER OF COMMERCE
P.O. Box 2539, Globe, AZ 85502,
(520) 425-4495 or (800) 448-8983, Fax: (520) 425-3410.

GOODYEAR- SEE TRI-CITY WEST CHAMBER OF COMMERCE

GOLDEN VALLEY CHAMBER OF COMMERCE
P.O. Box 10300, Kingman, AZ 86401,
(520) 565-3311.

GRAHAM- SEE SAFFORD/GRAHAM CHAMBER OF COMMERCE

GRAND CANYON CHAMBER OF COMMERCE
P.O. Box 3007, Grand Canyon, AZ 86023,
(520) 638-2901.

GREENLEE COUNTY CHAMBER OF COMMERCE
P.O. Box 1237, Clifton, AZ 85533,
(520) 865-3313.

GREEN VALLEY CHAMBER OF COMMERCE
P.O. Box 566, Green Valley, AZ 85622,
(520) 625-7575 or (800) 858-5872.

GUADALUPE CHAMBER OF COMMERCE
c/o Town of Guadalupe, 9050 S. Avenida del Yaqui,
Guadalupe, AZ 85283,
(520) 730-3080, Fax: (520) 730-3096.

HAYDEN TOWN HALL
P.O. Box B, Hayden, AZ 85235,
(520) 356-7801, Fax: (520) 356-6334.

HEBER/OVERGAARD CHAMBER OF COMMERCE
P.O. Box 550, Heber, AZ 85928,
(520) 535-4406, Fax: (520) 535-5762.

HISPANIC CHAMBER OF COMMERCE
2400 N. Central Avenue, #303, Phoenix, AZ 85004,
(602) 252-1101 or (800) 742-8269, Fax: (602) 252-6110.

HOLBROOK/PETRIFIED CHAMBER OF COMMERCE
100 E. Arizona St., Holbrook, AZ 86025,
(520) 524-6558 or (800) 524-2459, Fax: (520) 524-1719.

JEROME CHAMBER OF COMMERCE
P.O. Drawer K, Jerome, AZ 86331,
(520) 634-2900 or (520) 634-5716.

JOSEPH CITY CHAMBER OF COMMERCE
P.O. Box 36, Joseph City, AZ 86032,
(520) 288-3281 or (520) 288-3605.

KEARNY/COPPER BASIN CHAMBER OF COMMERCE
P.O. Box 206, Kearny, AZ 85237,
(520) 363-7607, Fax: (520) 363-7527.

KINGMAN CHAMBER OF COMMERCE
P.O. Box 1150, Kingman, AZ 86402,
(520) 753-6106, Fax: (520) 753-1049.

LAKE HAVASU CITY VISITOR & CONVENTION BUREAU
1930 Mesquite Ave., #3,
Lake Havasu City, AZ 86403,
(520) 453-3444 or (800) 242-8278, Fax: (520) 680-0010.

LAKESIDE- SEE PINETOP/LAKESIDE CHAMBER OF COMMERCE

MARANA AVRA VALLEY CHAMBER OF COMMERCE
13660 N. Sandario Rd., Marana, AZ 85653-8939,
(520) 682-4314, Fax: (520) 682-2303.

MARICOPA COUNTY PARKS & RECREATION
3475 W. Durango, Phoenix, AZ 85009,
(602) 506-2930.

MAYER CHAMBER OF COMMERCE
P.O. Box 248, Mayer, AZ 86333,
(520) 632-4031, Fax: (520) 632-7445.

McMULLEN VALLEY CHAMBER OF COMMERCE
P.O. Box 477, Salome, AZ 85348,
(520) 859-3846.

MESA CONVENTION & VISITORS BUREAU
120 N. Center St., Mesa, AZ 85201,
(602) 969-1307 or (800) 283-MESA,
Fax: (602) 827-0727.

MOHAVE COUNTY PARKS & RECREATION
P.O. Box 390, Kingman, AZ 86402,
(520) 757-0915.

MOHAVE VALLEY CHAMBER OF COMMERCE
P.O. Box 9101, Ft. Mohave, AZ 86427,
(520) 768-2777, Fax: (520) 768-3371.

MIAMI- SEE GLOBE/MIAMI CHAMBER OF COMMERCE

MT. LEMMON TOURISM COMMITTEE
12781 N. Sabino Canyon Park Rd., Mt. Lemmon, AZ 85619,
(520) 576-1542 or (800) 652-1542.

NATIVE AMERICAN TOURISM CENTER
4130 N. Goldwater Blvd., Scottsdale, AZ 85251,
(602) 945-0771, Fax: (602) 945-0264.

NAVAJO COUNTY PARKS & RECREATION
P.O. Box 668, Holbrook, AZ 86025,
(520) 524-6161, ext 344.

NAVAJO NATION TOURISM OFFICE
P.O. Box 663, Window Rock, AZ 85615,
(520) 871-6659, Fax: (520) 871-7381.

NOGALES/SANTA CRUZ CHAMBER OF COMMERCE
Kino Park, Nogales, AZ 85621,
(520) 287-3685, Fax: (520) 287-3688.

NORTHWEST VALLEY CHAMBER OF COMMERCE
P.O. Box 1519, Sun City, AZ 85372-1519,
(602) 583-0692, Fax: (602) 583-0694.

OATMAN/GOLDROAD CHAMBER OF COMMERCE
P.O. Box 64, Oatman, AZ 86433,
(520) 768-7353.

ORACLE- SEE SAN MANUEL / MAMMOTH / ORACLE
CHAMBER OF COMMERCE

ORO VALLEY CHAMBER OF COMMERCE
490 W. McGee Rd., Tucson, AZ 85704,
(520) 297-2191, Fax: (520) 797-1825.

OVERGAARD- SEE HEBER/OVERGAARD
CHAMBER OF COMMERCE

PAGE/LAKE POWELL CHAMBER OF COMMERCE
P.O. Box 727, Page, AZ 86040,
(520) 645-2741, Fax: (520) 645-3181.

PARADISE VALLEY CHAMBER OF COMMERCE
3135 E. Cactus Rd., Phoenix, AZ 85032-7155,
(602) 482-3344, Fax: (602) 482-2261.

PARKER AREA CHAMBER OF COMMERCE
P.O. Box 627, Parker, AZ 85344,
(520) 669-2174, Fax: (520) 669-6304.

PATAGONIA COMMUNITY ASSOCIATION
P.O. Box 241, Patagonia, AZ 85624.

PAYSON CHAMBER OF COMMERCE
P.O. Box 1380, Payson, AZ 85547,
(520) 474-4515 or (800) 6- PAYSON,
Fax: (520) 474-8812.

PEARCE/SUNSITES CHAMBER OF COMMERCE
P.O. Box 308, Pearce, AZ 85625, (520) 826-3535.

PEORIA CHAMBER OF COMMERCE
P.O. Box 70, Peoria, AZ 85380,
(602) 979-3601, Fax: (602) 486-4729.

PHOENIX & VALLEY OF THE SUN CONVENTION
& VISITORS BUREAU
400 E. Van Buren, #600, Phoenix, AZ 85004,
(602) 254-6500, Fax: (602) 253-4415.

PHOENIX CHAMBER OF COMMERCE
201 N. Central Ave., #2700, Phoenix, AZ 85073.
(602) 254-5521, Fax: (602) 495-8913.

PHOENIX CITY PARKS & RECREATION
2333 N. Central Avenue, Phoenix, AZ 85004,
(602) 262-6861.

PIMA CHAMBER OF COMMERCE
P.O. Box 489, Pima, AZ 85543,
(520) 485-2288.

PIMA COUNTY PARKS & RECREATION
1204 W. Silver Lake Road, Tucson, AZ 85713,
(520) 740-2690.

PINAL COUNTY (WEST) CHAMBER OF COMMERCE
Rt. 3, Box 722, Maricopa, AZ 85239,
(520) 568-2262.

PINAL COUNTY VISITOR AND INFORMATION CENTER
P.O. Box 967, Florence, AZ 85232,
(520) 868-4331.

PINE/STRAWBERRY CHAMBER OF COMMERCE
P.O. Box 196, Pine, AZ 85544,
(520) 476-3547.

PINETOP/LAKESIDE CHAMBER OF COMMERCE
592 W. White Mountain Blvd., Lakeside, AZ 85935,
(520) 367-4290, Fax: (520) 368-8528.

PRESCOTT CHAMBER OF COMMERCE
P.O. Box 1147, Prescott, AZ 86302,
(520) 445-2000 or (800) 266-7534, Fax: (520) 445-0068.

PRESCOTT VALLEY CHAMBER OF COMMERCE
P.O. Box 25357, Prescott Valley, AZ 86312,
(520) 772-8857, Fax. (520) 772-4267.

QUARTZSITE CHAMBER OF COMMERCE
P.O. Box 85, Quartzsite, AZ 85346,
(520) 927-5600 or (800) 815-2694.

QUEEN CREEK CHAMBER OF COMMERCE
P.O. Box 720, Queen Creek, AZ 85242,
(520) 987-0406.

ST. JOHNS REGIONAL CHAMBER OF COMMERCE
P.O. Box 178, St. Johns, AZ 85936,
(520) 337-2000.

SAN LUIS, TOWN OF
P.O. Box S, San Luis, AZ 85349,
(520) 627-2027, Fax: (520) 627-3879.

SAN MANUEL/MAMMOTH/ORACLE CHAMBER OF COMMERCE
P.O. Box 1886, Oracle, AZ 85623,
(520) 896-9322, Fax: (520) 385-4846.

SAFFORD/GRAHAM COUNTY CHAMBER OF COMMERCE
1111 Thatcher Blvd., Safford, AZ 85546,
(520) 428-2511, Fax: (520) 428-0744.

SALOME- SEE McMULLEN VALLEY CHAMBER OF COMMERCE

SCOTTSDALE CHAMBER OF COMMERCE
7343 Scottsdale Mall, Scottsdale, AZ 85251-4498,
(602) 945-8481 or (800) 782-1117, Fax: (602) 947-4523.

SEDONA/OAK CREEK CANYON CHAMBER OF COMMERCE
P.O. Box 478, Sedona, AZ 86336,
(520) 282-7722 or (800) 288-7336, Fax: (520) 204-1064.

SELIGMAN CHAMBER OF COMMERCE
P.O. Box 65, Seligman, AZ 86337,
(520) 422-3352.

SHOW LOW CHAMBER OF COMMERCE
P.O. Box 1083, Show Low, AZ 85901,
(520) 537-2326, Fax: (520) 537-2326.

SIERRA VISTA CHAMBER OF COMMERCE
77 S. Calle Portal, #A140, Sierra Vista, AZ 85635,
(520) 458-6940 or (800) 288-3861, Fax: (520) 452-0878.

SNOWFLAKE/TAYLOR CHAMBER OF COMMERCE
P.O. Box 776, Snowflake, AZ 85937, (520) 536-4331.

SOMERTON, CITY OF
City Manager, P.O. Box 638, Somerton, AZ 85350, (520) 627-8866.

SONOITA/ELGIN CHAMBER OF COMMERCE
P.O. Box 264, Sonoita, AZ 85637,
(520) 455-5613, Fax: (520) 455-5613.

SOUTH MOUNTAIN CHAMBER OF COMMERCE
P.O. Box 8172, Phoenix, AZ 85066-8172,
(602) 268-0068.

SPRINGERVILLE/EAGAR/ROUND VALLEY
CHAMBER OF COMMERCE
P.O. Box 31, Springerville, AZ 85938,
(520) 333-2123, Fax: (520) 333-5690.

STRAWBERRY- SEE PINE/STRAWBERRY
CHAMBER OF COMMERCE

SULPHER SPRINGS VALLEY CHAMBER OF COMMERCE
P.O. Box 614, Elfrieda, AZ 85610.

SUN CITY- SEE NORTHWEST VALLEY CHAMBER OF COMMERCE

SUNLAND VISITOR CENTER
P.O. Box 300, Arizona City, AZ 85223 or
3640 N. Toltec, Eloy, AZ 85231,(520) 466-3007.

SUPERIOR CHAMBER OF COMMERCE
151 Main Street, Superior, AZ 85273,
(520) 689-2441.

TAYLOR- SEE SNOWFLAKE/TAYLOR CHAMBER OF COMMERCE

TEMPE CHAMBER OF COMMERCE
60 E. 5th St., #3, Tempe, AZ 85281,
(602) 967-7891, Fax: (602) 966-5365.

TEMPE CONVENTION & VISITORS BUREAU
51 W. 3rd St., #105, Tempe, AZ 85281,
(602) 894-8158 or (800) 283-6734, Fax: (602) 968-8004.

TOLLESON CHAMBER OF COMMERCE
9555 W. Van Buren, Tolleson, AZ 85353,
(602) 936-5070.

TOMBSTONE CHAMBER OF COMMERCE & VISITOR CENTER
P.O. Box 917, Tombstone, AZ 85638,
(520) 457-9317 or (800) 457-3423, Fax: (520) 457-3929.

TUBAC CHAMBER OF COMMERCE
P.O. Box 1866, Tubac, AZ 85646,
(520) 398-9797.

TUCSON CITY PARKS & RECREATION
900 S. Randolph Way, Tucson, AZ 85716, (520) 791-4873.

TUCSON (METROPOLITAN) CHAMBER OF COMMERCE
P.O. Box 991, Tucson, AZ 85702,
(520) 792-1212, Fax: (520) 882-5704.

TUCSON (METROPOLITAN) CONVENTION & VISITORS BUREAU
130 S. Scott Avenue, Tucson, AZ 85701,
(520) 624-1817 or (800) 638-8350, Fax: (520) 884-7804.

THATCHER, TOWN OF
P.O. Box 670, Thatcher, AZ 85552.

TRI-CITY WEST CHAMBER OF COMMERCE
501 W. Van Buren, #K, Avondale, AZ 85323,
(602) 932-2260.

WELTON CHAMBER OF COMMERCE
P.O. Box 455, Welton, AZ 85356, (520) 785-9651.

WICKENBURG CHAMBER OF COMMERCE
P.O. Drawer CC, Wickenburg, AZ 85358,
(520) 684-5479 or (800) 942-5242, Fax: (520) 684-5470.

WILLCOX CHAMBER OF COMMERCE
1500 North Circle 1 Road, Willcox, AZ 85643,
(520) 384-2272 or (800) 200-2272, Fax: (520) 384-0293.

WILLIAMS/FOREST SERVICE VISITOR CENTER
P.O. Box 235, Williams, AZ 86046,
(520) 635-4061, Fax: (520) 635-1417.

WINSLOW CHAMBER OF COMMERCE
P.O. Box 460, Winslow, AZ 86047,
(520) 289-2434, Fax: (520) 289-5660.

YARNELL/PEEPLES VALLEY CHAMBER OF COMMERCE
P.O. Box 275, Yarnell, AZ 85362,
(520) 427-6588, Fax: (520) 427-6443.

YAVAPAI COUNTY PARKS
918 Prosser Lane, Prescott, AZ 86301,(520) 771-3324.

YOUNGTOWN- SEE NORTHWEST VALLEY
CHAMBER OF COMMERCE

YUMA CVB & CHAMBER OF COMMERCE
P.O. Box 10831, Yuma, AZ 85366-8831,
(520) 783-0071, Fax: (520) 343-0038.

INDIAN RESERVATIONS

AK-CHIN HIM-DAK INDIAN COMMUNITY
P.O. Box 897, Maricopa, AZ 85239,
(602) 568-9480 or (602) 568-9487.

CAMP VERDE RESERVATION
Yavapai-Apache Indian Community,
P.O. Box 1188, Camp Verde, AZ 86322,
(520) 567-3649.

COCOPAH RESERVATION
Cocopah Tribal Council,
Bin "G", Somerton, AZ 85350,
(520) 627-2102.

COLORADO RIVER INDIAN RESERVATION
Route 1, Box 23-B, Parker, AZ 85344,
(520) 669-9211.

FORT APACHE RESERVATION
White Mountain Apache Tribe Office of Tourism,
Box 700, Whiteriver, AZ 85941,
(520) 338-1230.

FORT McDOWELL YAVAPAI RESERVATION
P.O. Box 17779, Fountain Hills, AZ 85268,
(602) 837-5121.

FORT MOJAVE INDIAN RESERVATION
500 Merriman Avenue, Needles, CA 92363,
(619) 326-4591.

FORT YUMA RESERVATION
Quechan Tribal Council,
Box 11352, Yuma, AZ 85364,
(619) 572-0213.

GILA RIVER RESERVATION
Gila River Indian Community,
P.O. Box 97, Sacaton, AZ 85247,
(520) 562-3311.

HAVASUPAI RESERVATION
Havasupai Tribal Council,
Box 10, Supai, AZ 86435, (520) 448-2961.

HOPI RESERVATION
Hopi Tribal Council,
Box 123, Kyakotsmovi, AZ 85039, (520) 738-2441.

HUALAPAI RESERVATION
Hualapai Tribal Council,
Box 179, Peach Springs, AZ 86434, (520) 769-2216.

KAIBAB-PAIUTE INDIAN RESERVATION
Tribal Affairs Building,
HC 65, Box 2, Fredonia, AZ 86022, (520) 643-7245.

NAVAJO NATION RESERVATION
Tourism Department,
P.O. Box 663, Window Rock, AZ 86515, (520) 871-6436.

PASCUA-YAQUI RESERVATION
Pascua-Yaqui Tribal Council,
7474 S. Camino de Oeste, Tucson, AZ 85746, (520) 883-2838.

SALT RIVER RESERVATION
Salt River Pima-Maricopa Tribal Council,
Route 1, Box 216, Scottsdale, AZ 85256, (602) 874-8056.

SAN CARLOS RESERVATION
San Carlos Apache Tribal Council,
P.O. Box O, San Carlos, AZ 85550, (520) 475-2361.

TOHONO O'ODHAM RESERVATION
(formerly the PAPAGO INDIAN RESERVATION)
P.O. Box 837, Sells, AZ 85634, (520) 383-2221.

TONTO APACHE RESERVATION
Tonto Apache Reservation #30, Payson, AZ 85541,
(520) 474-5000.

YAVAPAI-PRESCOTT RESERVATION
Yavapai-Prescott Tribal Council,
530 E. Merritt, Prescott, AZ 86301, (520) 445-8790.

NATIONAL FORESTS, PARKS AND MONUMENTS

APACHE-SITGREAVES NATIONAL FOREST
P.O. Box 640, Springerville, AZ 85938,
(520) 333-4301.

COCONINO NATIONAL FOREST
2323 E. Greenlaw Lane, Flagstaff, AZ 86004,
(520) 527-3600.

CORONADO NATIONAL FOREST
Federal Building, 300 W. Congress, 6th Fl.,
Tucson, AZ 85701, (520) 670-4552.

GLEN CANYON NATIONAL RECREATION AREA
P.O. Box 1507, Page, AZ 86040,
(520) 645-8200.

GRAND CANYON NATIONAL PARK
P.O. Box 129, Grand Canyon, AZ 86023,
(520) 638-7888.

KAIBAB NATIONAL FOREST
800 S. Sixth Street, Williams, AZ 86046,
(520) 635-2681.

LAKE MEAD NATIONAL RECREATION AREA
601 Nevada Highway, Boulder City, NV 89005,
(702) 293-8920.

NATIONAL PARKS- SOUTHERN ARIZONA GROUP OFFICE
202 E. Earll Dr., #115, Phoenix, AZ 85012,
(602) 640-5250.

PETRIFIED FOREST NATIONAL PARK
P.O. Box 2217, Petrified Forest, AZ 86028,
(520) 524-6228.

PRESCOTT NATIONAL FOREST
344 S. Cortez Street, Prescott, AZ 86303,
(520) 771-4700.

TONTO NATIONAL FOREST
2324 E. McDowell Road, Phoenix, AZ 85006,
(602) 225-5200.

TONTO NATIONAL MONUMENT
HC02- Box 4602, Roosevelt, AZ 85545,
(520) 467-2241.

STATE, COUNTY & CITY PARKS

ARIZONA STATE PARKS
800 W. Washington, #415, Phoenix, AZ 85007, (602) 542-4174.

ALAMO LAKE STATE PARK
P.O. Box 38, Wenden, AZ 85357, (520) 669-2088.

BOYCE THOMPSON SOUTHWESTERN ARBORETUM
37615 E. Highway 60, Superior, AZ 85273, (520) 689-2723.

BUCKSKIN MOUNTAIN STATE PARK
54751 Highway 95, Parker, AZ 85344, (520) 667-3231.

CATALINA STATE PARK
P.O. Box 36986, Tucson, AZ 85740, (520) 628-5798.

DEAD HORSE RANCH STATE PARK
P.O. Box 144, Cottonwood, AZ 86326, (520) 634-5283.

FORT VERDE STATE HISTORIC PARK
P.O. Box 397, Camp Verde, AZ 86322, (520) 567-3275.

HOMOLOVI RUINS STATE PARK
HCR 63, Box 5, Winslow, AZ 86047, (520) 289-4106.

JEROME STATE HISTORIC PARK
Box D, Jerome, AZ 86331, (520) 634-5381.

LAKE HAVASU STATE PARK (CATTAIL COVE)
P.O. Box 1990, Lake Havasu City, AZ 86405, (520) 855-1223.

LOST DUTCHMAN STATE PARK
6109 N. Apache Trail, Apache Junction, AZ 85219, (520) 982-4485.

LYMAN LAKE STATE PARK
P.O. Box 1428, St. Johns, AZ 85936, (520) 337-4441.

MARICOPA COUNTY PARKS & RECREATION
3475 W. Durango, Phoenix, AZ 85009, (602) 506-2930.

MOHAVE COUNTY PARKS & RECREATION
P.O. Box 390, Kingman, AZ 86402, (520) 757-0915.

NAVAJO COUNTY PARKS & RECREATION
P.O. Box 668, Holbrook, AZ 86025, (520) 524-6161, ext. 344.

PATAGONIA LAKE STATE PARK
P.O. Box 274, Patagonia, AZ 85624, (520) 287-6965.

PHOENIX CITY PARKS & RECREATION
2333 N. Central Ave., Phoenix, AZ 85004, (602) 262-6861.

PICACHO PEAK STATE PARK
P.O. Box 275, Picacho, AZ 85241, (520) 466-3183.

PIMA COUNTY PARKS & RECREATION
1204 W. Silver Lake Road, Tucson, AZ 85713, (520) 740-2690.

ROPER LAKE STATE PARK
101 E. Roper Lake Rd, Safford, AZ 85546, (520) 428-6760.

SLIDE ROCK STATE PARK
P.O. Box 10358, Sedona, AZ 86339, (520) 282-3034.

TONTO NATURAL BRIDGE STATE PARK
P.O. Box 1245, Payson, AZ 85547, (520) 476-4202.

TUCSON CITY PARKS & RECREATION
900 S. Randolph Way, Tucson, AZ 85716, (520) 791-4873.

YAVAPAI COUNTY PARKS
918 Prosser Lane, Prescott, AZ 86301, (520) 771-3324.

SAN CARLOS APACHE GAME & FISH AGENCY
P.O. Box 97, San Carlos, AZ 85550, (520) 475-2343 or 475-2653.

WHITE MOUNTAIN APACHE GAME & FISH AGENCY
P.O. Box 220, Whiteriver, AZ 85941, (520) 369-0938.

City Park Districts

CITY OF FLAGSTAFF PARKS AND RECREATION
(520) 779-7690

GLENDALE RECREATION DEPARTMENT
(602) 930-2820

CITY OF PEORIA PARKS
(602) 412-7137

PHOENIX CENTRAL DISTRICT
(602) 262-6412

PHOENIX CENTRAL DISTRICT-EAST
(602) 256-3220

PHOENIX CENTRAL DISTRICT-WEST
(602) 262-4539

PHOENIX NORTHEAST DISTRICT
(602) 262-6696

PHOENIX NORTHWEST DISTRICT
(602) 262-6575

PHOENIX SOUTH DISTRICT
(602) 262-6111

CITY OF PRESCOTT PARKS AND RECREATION
(520) 445-5880

SCOTTSDALE COMMUNITY SERVICES
(602) 994-2408

TEMPE CITY PARKS
(602) 350-5200

FOREST RANGER DISTRICTS

APACHE-SITGREAVES NATIONAL FOREST
ALPINE RANGER DISTRICT
P.O. Box 469, Alpine, AZ 85920, (520) 339-4384.

CLIFTON RANGER DISTRICT
HC Box 733, Duncan, AZ 85534,
(520) 687-1301.

CHEVELON RANGER DISTRICT
HC 62, Box 600, Winslow, AZ 86047,
(520) 289-2471.

HEBER RANGER DISTRICT
P.O. Box 968, Overgaard, AZ 85933,
(520) 535-4481.

LAKESIDE RANGER DISTRICT
RR 3, Box B-50, Pinetop-Lakeside, AZ 85929,
(520) 368-5111.

SPRINGERVILLE RANGER DISTRICT
P.O. Box 760, Springerville, AZ 85938,
(520) 333-4372.

COCONINO NATIONAL FOREST
BEAVER CREEK RANGER DISTRICT
HC 64, Box 240, Rimrock, AZ 86335,
(520) 567-4501.

BLUE RIDGE RANGER DISTRICT
HC 31, Box 300, Happy Jack, AZ 86024,
(520) 477-2255.

LONG VALLEY RANGER DISTRICT
HC 31, P.O. Box 68, Happy Jack, AZ 86024,
(520) 354-2216.

MORMON LAKE RANGER DISTRICT
4825 S. Lake Mary Road, Flagstaff, AZ 86001,
(520) 774-1147.

PEAKS RANGER DISTRICT
5075 N. Highway 89, Flagstaff, AZ 86004,
(520) 526-0866.

SEDONA RANGER DISTRICT
P.O. Box 300, Sedona, AZ 86336-0300,
(520) 282-4119.

CORONADO NATIONAL FOREST

DOUGLAS RANGER DISTRICT
RR 1, Box 228-R, Douglas, AZ 85607,
(520) 364-3468.

NOGALES RANGER DISTRICT
2251 N. Grand Avenue, Nogales, AZ 85621,
(520) 281-2296.

SAFFORD RANGER DISTRICT
P.O. Box 709, Safford, AZ 85548-0709,
(520) 428-4150.

SANTA CATALINA RANGER DISTRICT
5700 N. Sabino Canyon Road, Tucson, AZ 85715,
(520) 749-8700.

SIERRA VISTA RANGER DISTRICT
5990 S. Highway 92, Hereford, AZ 85615,
(520) 378-0311.

KAIBAB NATIONAL FOREST

CHALENDER RANGER DISTRICT
501 W. Bill Williams Avenue, Williams, AZ 86046,
(520) 635-2676.

KAIBAB PLATEAU VISITOR CENTER
P.O. Box 248, Fredonia, AZ 86022,
(520) 643-7298 (May 1st- Sept 30th).

NORTH KAIBAB RANGER DISTRICT
P.O. Box 248, Fredonia, AZ 86022,
(520) 643-7395.

TUSAYAN RANGER DISTRICT
P.O. Box 3088, Tusayan, AZ 86023, (520) 638-2443.

USDA FOREST SERVICE/ CITY OF WILLIAMS VISITOR CENTER
200 W. Railroad Avenue, Williams, AZ 86046,
(520) 635-4707 or 635-4061.

WILLIAMS RANGER DISTRICT
Rt 1, Box 142, Williams, AZ 86046, (520) 635-2633.

PRESCOTT NATIONAL FOREST

BRADSHAW RANGER DISTRICT
2230 E. Highway 69, Prescott, AZ 86301-5657,
(520) 445-7253.

CHINO VALLEY RANGER DISTRICT
P.O. Box 485, Chino Valley, AZ 86323-0485,
(520) 636-2302.

VERDE RANGER DISTRICT
P.O. Box 670, Camp Verde, AZ 86322-0670,
(520) 567-4121.

TONTO NATIONAL FOREST

CAVE CREEK RANGER DISTRICT
P.O. Box 5068, Carefree, AZ 85377, (602) 488-3441.

GLOBE RANGER DISTRICT
Rt 1, Box 33, Globe, AZ 88501, (520) 425-7189.

MESA RANGER DISTRICT
P.O. Box 5800, Mesa, AZ 85211-5800, (602) 379-6446.

PAYSON RANGER DISTRICT
1009 E. Highway 260, Payson, AZ 85541,
(520) 474-7900.

PLEASANT VALLEY RANGER DISTRICT
P.O. Box 450, Young, AZ 85554, (520) 462-3311.

TONTO BASIN RANGER DISTRICT
P.O. Box 649, Highway 88, Roosevelt, AZ 85545,
(520) 467-2236.

National Forest Hiking Trail Locator

APACHE- SITGREAVES NATIONAL FOREST

COCONINO NATIONAL FOREST

TONTO NATIONAL FOREST

Toll-Free
800 Numbers

Hotel/Motel
Toll-Free 800 Numbers

Auberges Wandlyn Inns
800-561-0000

Best Western Intl Inc
800-528-1234

Budget Host
800-283-4678

Budgetel Inn
800-428-3438

Choice Hotels
800-424-6423

Comfort Inn
800-221-2222

Courtyard by Marriott
800-321-2211

Crown Sterling Suites
800-433-4600

Days Inn
800-329-7466

Doubletree Hotels
800-222-8733

Downtowner Inns
800-251-1962

Drury Inn
800-325-8300

Econo Lodge
800-424-4777

Economy Inns of America
800-826-0778

Embassy Suites
800-362-2779

Exel Inns of America
800-356-8013

Fairfield Inn by Marriott
800-228-2800

Fairmont Hotels
800-527-4727

Forte Grand Hotels
800-225-5843

Four Seasons Hotels
800-332-3442

Friendship Inn
800-424-4777

Guest Quarters
800-424-2900

Hampton Inn
800-426-7866

Harley Hotels
800-321-2323

Hawthorn Suites
800-527-1133

Heartland Inns
800-334-3277

Helmsley Hotels
800-221-4982

Hilton Hotels Corp
800-445-8667

Holiday Inns
800-465-4329

Howard Johnson Hotels
800-446-4656

Hyatt Hotels
800-233-1234

IMA Hotels
800-341-8000

Inter-Continental Hotels
800-327-0200

Knights Inn
800-843-5644

L-K Motels Inc
800-282-5711

La Quinta Motor Inns
800-531-5900

Lees Inn
800-733-5337

Lexington Hotel Suites
800-537-8483

Loews Hotels
800-235-6397

Marriott Hotels
800-228-9290

Master Hosts Inns
800-251-1962

Meridien
800-543-4300

Motel 6
800-440-6000

Omni Hotels
800-843-6664

Park Inns Intl
800-437-7275

Princess Hotels
800-227-5650

Quality Inns
800-221-2222

Radisson Hotel Corp.
800-333-3333

Ramada Inns
800-272-6232

Red Carpet/Scottish Inns
800-251-1962

Red Lion-Thunderbird
800-733-5466

Red Roof Inns
800-843-7663

Residence Inn by Marriott
800-331-3131

Ritz-Carlton
800-241-3333

Rodeway Inns Intl
800-424-4777

Sandman Inns
800-726-3626

Sheraton Hotels & Inns
800-325-3535

Shilo Inns
800-222-2244

Sleep Inns
800-221-2222

Sonesta Hotels
800-766-3782

Stouffer/Renaissance
800-468-3571

Super 8 Motels
800-800-8000

**Susse Chalet
Motor Lodges/Inns**
800-258-1980

**Travelodge Intl/
Viscount Hotels**
800-578-7878

Vagabond Hotels Inc
800-522-1555
800-468-2251 (Canada)

Westin Hotels
800-228-3000

Woodfin Suites
800-237-8811

Wyndham Hotels
800-996-3426

CAR RENTAL
Toll-Free 800 Numbers

Advantage Rent-A-Car
800-777-5500

Agency Rent-A-Car
800-321-1972

Airways Rent-A-Car
800-937-3748
800-669-1588 (CT)
800-952-9200 (O'Hare)

Alamo Rent-A-Car
800-327-9633

Allstate Rent-A-Car
800-634-6186

American Intl Rent-A-Car
800-527-0202

Autoglobe Intl Car Rentals
800-858-1515

Avis-Reservations Center
800-331-1212

Aztec Rent-A-Car
800-231-0400

Brooks Rent-A-Car
800-634-6721

Budget Rent-A-Car
800-527-0700

Dollar Rent-A-Car
800-421-6868

Enterprise Rent-A-Car
800-325-8007

Fairway Rent-A-Car
800-634-3476

General Rent-A-Car
800-327-7607

Hertz Corporation
800-654-3131
800-654-3001 (Canada)

Inter American Car Rental
800-327-1278

National Car Rental
800-227-7368

Payless Rent-A-Car Inc
800-237-2804

**Rent Rite Reservation
Network**
800-554-7483

Rent-A-Vette
800-372-1981 (except NV)

Rent-A-Wreck
800-535-1391

Sears Rent-A-Car
800-527-0770

Showcase Rental Car
800-421-6808

Thrifty Rent-A-Car
800-367-2277

Tilden (National Car)
800-227-7368

U-Haul Intl RV Rentals
800-468-4285

**U-Save Auto Rental
of America**
800-272-8728

USA Rent-A-Car System Inc
800-872-2277

Ugly Duckling Rent-A-Car
800-843-3825

Value Rent-A-Car
800-327-2501

Viva Van & Car Rentals
800-926-6926

STATE DEPARTMENTS OF TOURISM
Toll-Free 800 Numbers

Alabama
800-252-2262

Alaska
800-426-0082

Arizona
800-842-8257

Arkansas
800-628-8725

California
800-862-2543

Colorado
303-592-5510
800-433-2656

Connecticut
800-282-6863

Delaware
800-441-8846

Dist. of Columbia
202-789-7000

Florida
800-868-7476

Georgia
800-847-4842

Hawaii
808-923-1811

Idaho
800-635-7820

Illinois
800-233-0121

Indiana
800-289-6646

Iowa
800-345-4692

Kansas
913-296-2009 (in Kansas)
800-252-6727 (outside Kansas)

Kentucky
800-225-8747

Louisiana
800-334-8626

Maine
800-533-9595

Maryland
800-543-1036

Massachusetts
800-447-6277

Michigan
800-543-2937

Minnesota
800-657-3700

Mississippi
800-927-6378

Missouri
800-877-1234

Montana
800-541-1447 (outside Montana)
406-444-2654 (in Montana)

Nebraska
800-228-4307(outside Nebraska)
800-742-7595 (in Nebraska)

Nevada
800-638-2328

New Hampshire
603-271-2343

New Jersey
800-537-7397

New Mexico
800-545-2040

New York
800-225-5692

North Carolina
800-847-4862

North Dakota
800-437-2077
800-537-8879 (in Canada)

Ohio
800-282-5393

Oklahoma
800-652-6552 (outside Oklahoma)
405-521-2409 (in Oklahoma)

Oregon
800-547-7852

Pennsylvania
800-847-4872

Rhode Island
800-556-2484

South Carolina
803-734-0235

South Dakota
800-732-5682 (in S. Dakota)
800-843-1930 (outside S. Dakota)

Tennessee
615-741-2158

Texas
800-888-8839

Utah
801-538-1030

Vermont
802-828-3236

Virginia
800-847-4882

Washington
800-544-1800

West Virginia
800-225-5982

Wisconsin
800-432-8747 (outside Wisconsin)
800-372-2737 (in Wisconsin)

Wyoming
800-225-5996

INDEX

City Names Are In ALL CAPITAL LETTERS

City Names Are In ALL CAPITAL LETTERS

City Names Are In ALL CAPITAL LETTERS

City Names Are In ALL CAPITAL LETTERS

City Names Are In ALL CAPITAL LETTERS

City Names Are In ALL CAPITAL LETTERS

Mormon Trail Hike............................. 248
Morse Canyon Trail to Johnson
    Saddle Hike...................................... 385
MOUNT LEMMON............................. 189
Mount Lemmon Drive, The................ 189
Mountain View Nature Trail Hike..... 239
Mountain View Park........................... 295
Mrytle Park... 155
Mud Spring to Sycamore
    Trail Hike.. 285
MUNDS PARK..................................... 190
Murphy Park....................................... 209
Murphy Ranch Trail Hike................... 396
Nankoweap Trail Hike........................ 165
National Trail Hike (aka Sun
    Circle Trail).................................... 248
Native Plant Trail Hike......................... 75
Nature Area... 295
Nelson Trail Hike................................ 110
Nelson Trail to Pine Mountain
    Trail Hike.. 111
Nelson Trail to Willow Springs
    Trail Hike.. 111
New World Park................................... 152
NOGALES... 190
North Canyon Trail Hike..................... 165
North Mingus Trail Hike..................... 102
North Mountain Recreation Area...... 235
North Mountain Summit Trail
    Hike.. 235, 239
North Wilson Mountain
    Trail Hike.. 311
Northsight Park................................... 295
O'Neil Park.. 152
Old Spanish Trail Hike........................ 371
Old Town Springs Park....................... 129
Oldham Trail Hike............................... 130
Olive Park.. 209

One Mile River Trail Hike................... 179
Optimist Park...................................... 354
ORACLE... 193
Osborn Park.. 295
OVERGAARD....................................... 194
Overland Road Historic
    Trail Hike.. 392
Oversite Canyon Trail Hike................ 325
Pack Saddle Historic Trail Hike.......... 157
PAGE.. 194
Painted Desert Trail Hike................... 400
Paiute Park.. 295
Palmer Park... 354
Papago Park (Phoenix)....................... 236
Papago Park (Scottsdale) 296
Papago Park (Tempe).......................... 354
Papago Park Trail System Hike.......... 355
PARKER.. 196
Parker Creek Trail Hike...................... 186
Parsons Trail Hike.............................. 103
Pasadena Park..................................... 155
Paseo Racquet Center......................... 155
Pass Mountain Trail Hike................... 185
PATAGONIA... 198
Patagonia Lake State Park.................. 199
Patriots Square Park........................... 236
PAYSON... 200
Pemberton Trail Loop Hike................ 140
Pendley Homestead Trail Hike........... 311
Penny Howe Barrier Free Trail....236, 239
PEORIA.. 208
Peralta Trail Hike................................. 77
Perl Charles Memorial Trail
    Hike.. 237, 239
Petersen Park...................................... 355
Petrified Forest National Park
    Trails... 162
Petroglyph Trail Hike......................... 328

City Names Are In ALL CAPITAL LETTERS

City Names Are In ALL CAPITAL LETTERS

City Names Are In ALL CAPITAL LETTERS

City Names Are In ALL CAPITAL LETTERS

Get The Book 100 Million Pet Owners Want!

EILEEN'S DIRECTORY OF PET-FRIENDLY LODGING

VACATIONING WITH YOUR PET!

OVER 20,000 LISTINGS OF HOTELS, MOTELS, INNS, RANCHES AND B&B'S THAT WELCOME GUESTS WITH PETS!

Locate Lodging In Your Price Range At Popular Vacation Destinations In The U.S. & Canada!

VACATION WITH YOUR PET!

Over 20,000 Listings of Hotels, Motels, Inns, Ranches and B&B's That Welcome Guests with Pets!

United States & Canada • 688 Pages • Illustrated

Toll-Free Numbers Of:
Car Rental Agencies,
Hotels/Motels,
State Tourism Offices

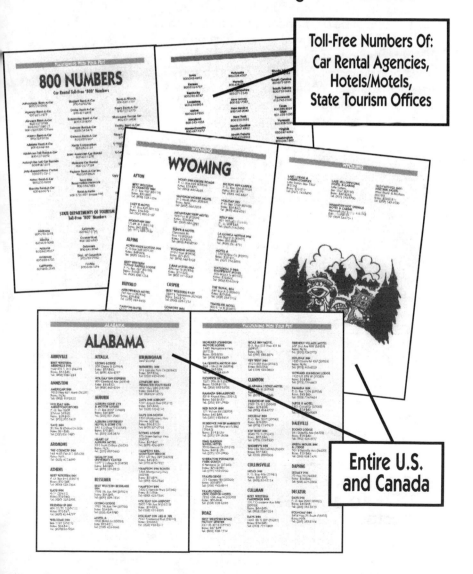

Entire U.S.
and Canada

WINNER OF MAXWELL AWARD FOR BEST REFERENCE BOOK

Vacationing With Your Pet! is the definitive travel directory for pet owners who wish to travel with their pets. In addition to more than 20,000 Hotels, Motels, B&B's, Ranches and Inns in the U.S. and Canada that welcome vacationers with pets, this directory contains over 100 pages of training tips, travel tips and handy reference sources. Written and compiled by Eileen Barish, noted authority on pet travel, the book is illustrated and easy to use.

1ST PLACE · DOG WRITERS ASSOCIATION OF AMERICA · PRESS · BEST REFERENCE BOOK

VACATION WITH YOUR PET!

with Eileen's Directory of Over 20,000 Pet-Friendly Lodgings

NORTH AMERICAN EDITION

VACATIONING WITH YOUR PET!
EILEEN'S DIRECTORY OF PET-FRIENDLY LODGING
UNITED STATES & CANADA
Eileen Barish
Over 20,000 Listings of Hotels, Motels, Inns, Ranches and B&B's that Welcome Guests with Pets

1ST PLACE BEST REFERENCE BOOK

illustrated by gregg myers

Order NOW!

VISA MasterCard

$19.95
plus $3.95 S&H

ORDER TOLL-FREE: 24 HRS. EVERY DAY!
1-800-638-3637

or Send Check, Cash or Money Order To:
PET-FRIENDLY PUBLICATIONS
P.O. BOX 8459,
Scottsdale, Arizona 85252

Name_____

Address_____

City_____

State_____ Zip_____

Bring Your Pet Along When You Vacation or Travel!

From rustic to ritzy...here's the most comprehensive directory of how and where to find quality lodging that welcomes you and your pet.

Imagine staying at the Plaza Hotel in New York City, or the Beverly Hilton in exclusive Beverly Hills? Those and thousands more can be found in this directory. No more kennels or pet caretakers. It's easy. It's fun. You'll have a safer vacation and you'll save money. No matter where you're vacationing or traveling you can take your pet with you.

Pets, They're Your Best Friends

"I began traveling with my two Golden Retrievers, Rosie and Maxwell, when they were only twelve weeks old. Now they're more than just pets... they're my traveling companions. Sharing my wanderlust with Rosie and Max has enhanced my world."

From sea to sea, city streets to alpine lakes and pine forests, you can find quality lodging for you and your pet with this directory.

Over 20,000 Listings of Hotels, Motels, Inns Ranches and B&B's That Welcome Guests with Pets!

EILEEN'S DIRECTORY OF DOG-FRIENDLY LODGING & OUTDOOR ADVENTURES IN CALIFORNIA

DOIN' CALIFORNIA WITH YOUR POOCH!

Where To Stay...What To Do...How To Do It!

From Adeanto to Yucca Valley, the most comprehensive guide to California's dog-friendly hotels, resorts, beaches, forests and outdoor adventures.

$19.95
plus $3.95 S&H

- 1,500 Places To Stay
- 200 Pages of Travel/Pet Tips
- 1,000 Outdoor Adventures including 500 Day Hikes

ORDER TOLL-FREE: **1-800-638-3637**

Fill out the coupon below and mail it to:

DOIN' CALIFORNIA WITH YOUR POOCH!
PET-FRIENDLY PUBLICATIONS • P.O. BOX 8459
SCOTTSDALE, AZ 85252

PLEASE SEND ME _____ COPIES OF DOIN' CALIFORNIA WITH YOUR POOCH!

NAME _____

ADDRESS _____ APT#/STE#_____

CITY_____ STATE _____ ZIP_____

NUMBER OF BOOKS @ $ _____ = $ _____ _____

   SHIPPING & HANDING CHARGES   = $ _____

TOTAL AMOUNT OF ORDER (INCLUDING SHIPPING & HANDLING) = $_____

   ENCLOSED IS MY CHECK OR MONEY ORDER   _____

   PLEASE BILL MY (CHECK ONE)   MASTERCARD _____ VISA _____

CREDIT CARD #_____ EXP. DATE _____

SIGNATURE _____

ORDER EXTRA COPIES

OF

Doin' Arizona With Your Pooch! is the perfect gift. Additional copies can be purchased directly from the publisher at the following prices:

1 to 3 copies: **$19.95 each**
plus $3.95 shipping and handling per order.

4 to 8 copies: **$16 each (20% discount)**
plus $7.95 shipping and handling per order.

9 copies or more: **Call publisher at**
1 (800) 638-3637
for volume discount pricing.

**Fill out the coupon below
and mail it to:**

DOIN' ARIZONA WITH YOUR POOCH!
**PET-FRIENDLY PUBLICATIONS • P.O. BOX 8459
SCOTTSDALE, AZ 85252**

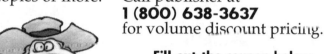

PLEASE SEND ME _____ **COPIES OF DOIN' ARIZONA WITH YOUR POOCH!**

NAME _____

ADDRESS _____ **APT#/STE#** _____

CITY _____ **STATE** _____ **ZIP** _____

NUMBER OF BOOKS @ $ _____ = $ _____ _____

SHIPPING & HANDING CHARGES = $ _____

TOTAL AMOUNT OF ORDER (INCLUDING SHIPPING & HANDLING) = $ _____

ENCLOSED IS MY CHECK OR MONEY ORDER _____

PLEASE BILL MY (CHECK ONE) **MASTERCARD** ____ **VISA** ____

CREDIT CARD # _____ **EXP. DATE** _____

SIGNATURE _____

"HEY EILEEN!
HERE'S DOG-FRIENDLY LODGING OR ACTIVITIES THAT YOU MISSED!"

When compiling this directory, every effort was made to be inclusive and provide the name of every accommodation that allows pets. If we missed any and you would like to see them in the next edition of *Doin' Arizona With Your Pooch!* please furnish the names, addresses and phone numbers as well as the average rate per night's lodging.

If you have any comments or suggestions, pass them along as well. It's our desire to keep an open line of communication with our readers and provide them with the most informative pet-friendly directory. The special tips and hints that you share with us may be included in the next edition.

Your input is welcome and we appreciate the time you've taken to keep us current on vacationing and traveling with pets.
Continued happy trails to you and your pet.

Send your suggestions, comments or additions to:

Eileen Barish
Pet-Friendly Publications
P.O. Box 8459
Scottsdale, Arizona 85252

Notes

Notes

_____

_____

_____

_____

_____

_____

_____

_____

_____

_____

_____

_____

Notes

_____

_____

_____

_____

_____

_____

_____

_____

_____

_____

_____

_____

Notes

Notes

_____

_____

_____

_____

_____

_____

_____

_____

_____

_____

_____

Notes

_____

_____

_____

_____

_____

_____

_____

_____

_____

_____

_____

Notes